NAPLES, FROM ROMAN TOWN
TO CITY-STATE

The research was conducted with the aid of a grant in 1985 from the Consiglio Nazionale delle Ricerche.

To

Germana Laura Arthur *née* Rasini

and

Elizabeth Germana Arthur

NAPLES, FROM ROMAN TOWN TO CITY-STATE:

An Archaeological Perspective

Paul Arthur

ARCHAEOLOGICAL MONOGRAPHS OF THE
BRITISH SCHOOL AT ROME
No. 12

Published by The British School at Rome, London
in association with the Dipartimento di Beni
Culturali, Università degli Studi di Lecce

2002

© The British School at Rome, *at* The British Academy
10 Carlton House Terrace, London SW1Y 5AH

Registered charity no. 314176

ISBN 0 904152 38 3

Cover illustration: The bell-tower of the Pietrasanta (church of Santa Maria Maggiore) and a Neapolitan coin
(© Copyright The British Museum; reproduced courtesy of The British Museum)

Typeset by Gina Coulthard
Printed by Stephen Austin and Sons Ltd, Hertford, Great Britain
Cover design by Gina Coulthard

CONTENTS

LIST OF FIGURES

PREFACE AND ACKNOWLEDGEMENTS

The history of the Mediterranean would probably have been profoundly different had not Naples and Campania maintained a certain pre-eminence throughout late antiquity and the Dark Ages. It was thus able to participate in the commercial revolution of the Middle Ages, alongside towns such as Genoa and Venice, and it became the centre respectively of Angevin, Arragonese and eventually Bourbon power in Italy, falling short of becoming the country's capital. Naples remained autonomous for some 400 years during the second half of the first millennium, when other states, and even empires, rose and fell. Though certain general developmental trends are clearly evinced through historical source material, the scarcity of material evidence has not permitted scholars to focus more clearly on the dynamics of early medieval Naples and its gradual rise to what was to be, by the later Middle Ages, virtually a world power. Indeed, in 1978, the historian Vera von Falkenhausen was able to write that, 'unfortunately, for the medieval towns of southern Italy there are no usable excavation reports to conduct research on urban land *intra muros*, [and] it has been necessary to turn, above all, to the written sources' (von Falkenhausen 1978a: 150). When she wrote, there was in fact little such evidence for the whole of the peninsula, and only with the growth of urban archaeology in the 1980s could a genuinely fresh debate on early medieval urbanism in northern Italy take place.[1] Now the time is ripe for southern Italy to contribute to the 'urban' debate, with recent work not only on abandoned sites such as Ordona (Mertens 1995) in northern Apulia, but also at many of the major modern cities and towns such as Bari (Andreassi and Radina 1988), Otranto (Michaelides and Wilkinson 1992; D'Andria and Whitehouse 1992), Salerno (Peduto *et al.* 1989), Benevento (Rotili 1986) and Naples.

In the case of Naples, the lack of archaeology prior to the 1980s was caused by a relative immobility in urban development after the Renaissance and Baroque reorganizations, save for the episode of the *Risanamento* at the end of the nineteenth century that led to much destruction and little recording (Russo 1960). Over the 1980s, a series of events, first and foremost of which was the violent earthquake of 23 November 1980, permitted the examination of a number of areas within and around the ancient town walls. The decade thus saw the excavation of eighteen sites, leading to the creation of a new database of information for the history of the town (Fig. 0:1). This intense activity led to two conferences, held in 1983 and 1986, and a major exhibition, held in 1985.[2] Extraordinary government legislation for job creation, passed in 1986, also permitted the funding of Project EUBEA. In three years and with the employment of over 220 young people, it led to the creation of a computerized archive of archaeological material for Naples and the Phlegrean Fields, including much post-excavation work on some of the excavations.[3]

---

[1] On urban archaeology in the 1980s see Francovich 1987: 15. On the 'north Italian debate' see Balzaretti 1991; Ward-Perkins 1997; Brogiolo and Gelichi 1998.

[2] For the conferences see Muscettola and Gastaldi 1984, and the review of the conference by Brogiolo and Manacorda (1983), and *Neapolis* (1988). The exhibition is represented by a catalogue: Pozzi 1985.

[3] Summary results of the 1980s excavations with bibliographies are provided in Appendix I. The Project EUBEA archive is held by the Soprintendenza Archeologica delle Province di Napoli e Caserta in the Museo Archeologico Nazionale. It was my good fortune to be able to run the project as scientific director, with a committee composed of Profs Paolo Amalfitano, Giuseppe Camodeca, Andrea Carandini, Georges Vallet and myself. The project was managed by a firm called Pinacos (a Bull Italia and Sipe Optimation consortium) and a managing director, Dr Elio Papasergio.

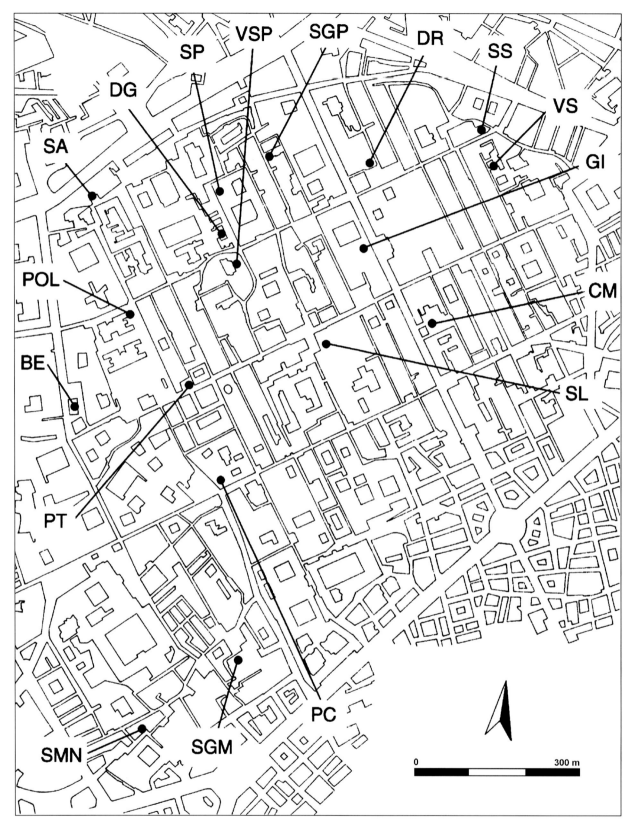

Fig. 0:1. The location of excavated sites in Naples. See Appendix I for a key to the site abbreviations.

The archaeological samples recovered in those years were a minute fraction of what exists, though they represent more than had hitherto been recovered. The scale of urban excavation has now declined, and the time is ripe to stand back and attempt to assess the new data in the light of previously acquired knowledge.[4] Though the stimulus for this work is the new material evidence, the rich documentary evidence is brought into play to construct the picture.

Other reasons for writing this book, if they are needed, include the absence of any recent synthesis, and none in English, despite the indubitable importance of Naples. In addition, it is hoped that this work might contribute to the city taking its due place in the history of Byzantium and of early medieval Europe, and further developing a public conscience towards the physical remains of its past.

With this premise, I hope to examine how the complex system represented by Naples fared through the late Roman and early medieval phase of European economic involution. It will be maintained that geographical conditions of the area and traditional links with the East guaranteed a quality of cultural development through the second half of the first millennium AD that facilitated the rise of Naples to the position of a major mediterranean power, a position that it was to retain up until the unification of Italy. This will be demonstrated by showing how it maintained the characteristics of an urban settlement throughout the so-called Dark Ages and how this put it in a position to participate in the regeneration of mediterranean trade and the economy.

The need to demonstrate that Naples was a city stems from criticisms that this was possibly not the case (Galasso 1965: 68; Whitehouse 1986; 1988; 1989). Gregory of Tours (*Hist.* III. 19), I think, would have had little doubt about calling Naples a *civitas*, particularly if he could be amazed that Dijon did not qualify. Although even in his case the problem is largely one of definitions. In Italy, however, given that 116 Roman towns or cities out of a total of 372 have now vanished, one might be curious as to what the remaining 256 were really like during late antiquity and the Middle Ages.

The last decade has seen great changes in scholarly conceptions of change in the mediterranean basin over the second half of the first millennium AD. Henri Pirenne's (1939) view of a Roman world disappearing beneath the tidal wave of Islam has given way to a vision of gradual economic decline and political fragmentation, many seeds of which were sown by the Roman Imperial system. Italy, from being a productive agricultural unit based on, and administered through, a system of agro-towns politically dependent on Rome, slipped back into being a land of independent states, hankering to this or to that central power according to the lord of the day. Within this context, some old Roman towns and cities were abandoned, being no longer necessary to sustain the world-system that had been Rome. Others may have become minor centres dependent on ecclesiastical or military power, whilst yet others continued to serve a complex of functions and thus provide conditions, though not necessarily of 'Roman type', that still permit us to use the words 'town' and 'city' in defining them. Indeed, one of the major problems is just that of typifying the various surviving settlements that, at least according to Finley, could be classed as a single definable type in classical times (Finley 1981: 22–3). Consideration of the problem of the late antique and early medieval city is now coming of age, as is shown by the recent flood of literature.[5]

Thus, given authoritative reservations and the fact that it may seem surprising to some scholars that the early medieval economy could support complex urban structures, if I decide to call Naples an early medieval city, the burden of proof is put fairly and squarely on my shoulders.

First of all, it may be noted that there is no mutual agreement amongst scholars as to the definition of a city or town when applied to extinct cultures. Richard Hodges has discussed this point (1982: 20–5), and I take the lead from his *Dark Age Economics*, subtitled *The Origins of Towns and Trade, AD 600–1000*. He concluded that:

> an urban community is a settlement of some size and population which is markedly larger than communities concerned with subsistence alone; the majority of its inhabitants, moreover, are not engaged in full-time agrarian pursuits. Such a community should include the presence of more than one institution, so that a monastery or palace can only be termed urban if it is the focus of more people than merely monks or ministers and royalty.

---

[4] For an assessment of the archaeology of Naples in the 1980s see Arthur 1991b; 1995.

[5] Recent studies, with references, are collected by Rich 1992. See also Carver 1993; Brogiolo and Gelichi 1998.

This seems a fair definition, though does not provide the specific elements needed to identify an urban community through historical or archaeological evidence, or both. A solution may be found by resorting to a bundle of accepted criteria within which individual elements may be represented and sustained by one or more concrete objects or data-sets.

Hodges (1982: 20–5) did, in fact, present such criteria, originally advanced by Gordon Childe (1950) and by Martin Biddle (1976: 100). Working upon their views, I would suggest that the following seven points should be satisfied by a settlement in order for it to be defined as urban.

1. The settlement must be a *central place*, possessing a dependent territory, and thus it should also be a node in an economic network.
2. *Administration* of the settlement should be autonomous or semi-autonomous.
3. This is likely to lead to the creation of *public works*.
4. The *economic base* should be *diversified* in so far as, though agriculture may play a leading part in the sustenance of the urban structure, a *surplus* is fundamental in stimulating manufacturing activities and an interregional exchange system, upon which wealth and power may be based.
5. It thus follows that the town should possess a substantial proportion of *non-agricultural adult labour* (say greater than one-third), excluding subsidiary domestic labour or household activity.
6. Administration, a diversified economic base and diversified labour should, in turn, lead to the development of a *social hierarchy*.
7. Finally, these conditions should bring about a concentrated and quantitatively *substantial population*, or citizen body, with an absence of generalized kinship ties, though these will, of course, exist in certain sectors of society.

As we shall see, Naples seems to satisfy the criteria that have been advanced above for the identification of a medieval town or city.[6] Though I shall develop my argument using archaeological and textual data, I want to stress the lacunosity of the various types of evidence for the construction of real temporal sequences, whether they be historical or archaeological. The latter may soon be rectified through the archaeological research that continues in the town. None the less, given the mass of evidence, and despite the ups and downs of its political and economic history, I doubt that Naples ever evaded the required conditions to confer upon it urban status. My intention is to try to explain why this was so.

ACKNOWLEDGEMENTS

New knowledge of Naples has come out of the ground by the hands of numerous students and graduates in archaeology, many of whom, over the years, have put up with my demands both during excavation and during the processing of finds and data in Naples. They have acted as a constant stimulus and, I believe, have learnt something about that strange creature that is British archaeology in the process. Of these, special thanks must go to Vittoria Carsana, Giuliana Miraglia, Marialaura Raimondi and Gianluca Soricelli, colleagues in Project EUBEA and digging companions who, more than most, have grasped and debated my particular views.

However, none of this would have been possible without the constant friendship, faith and encouragement provided by Enrica Pozzi, Archaeological Superintendent of Naples in the 1980s.

Various other friends and colleagues have taken me further in my understanding of the city's archaeology, in particular Giuseppe Vecchio, once Archaeological Inspector of Naples. Umberto Albarella and Anthony King have taught me much about Neapolitan fauna and the environment, whilst Clementina Panella has constantly put my

---

[6] They closely fit the four points advanced by Hammond (1974: 5–6) as defining criteria for a city: 1. 'numbers should be sufficient as to permit a variety of occupations'. He suggested that numbers might reach below 5,000, though were rarely larger than 40,000, with an average of around 10,000; 2. 'a community whose members live in close proximity under a single government and in a unified complex of buildings, often but not necessarily surrounded by a wall'. In classical cities, however, citizenship was often extended to country residents; 3. 'a community in which a considerable number of the population pursue their main activities within the city, in non-agricultural occupations'; 4. 'a community which extends at least its influence, and often its control, well outside the area necessary to maintain its own self-sufficiency. This influence or control may be religious, military, commercial, political or intellectual'.

knowledge of ancient amphorae as economic indic-
ators to the test. Other ideas, information and
advice have come from Trevor Anderson,
Vincenzo Albertini, Gioia Bertelli, Domenico
Camardo, the late Gianfranco Caniggia, Gabriele
Capone, Margherita Cecchelli, Giovanni De
Pasquale, Giancarlo Ferulano, Girgi Fiorentino,
Bruno Genito, Piero Gianfrotta, Antonio Guarino,
John Hayes, Hubert Houben, Silvana Iodice,
Libero Mangieri, Federico Marrazzi, Ulrico
Panutti, Catello Pasinetti, Paolo Peduto, Antonio
Rigillo, Lucia Travaini, Giovanna Ventrone
Vassallo, David Whitehouse and John Wilkes.
Brunella Bruno provided fundamental help in
finishing the chapter on the church.

I also wish to thank Francesco D'Andria, who
provided necessary pressure to get the volume
finished, despite increasing university commit-
ments and my attention having turned to Apulia
and the East.

Most of the artwork that illustrates this volume
is by Sally Cann and Michele Varchetta. Mario
Alberti produced the lovely reconstruction in Fig.
3:6, whilst Giancarlo De Pascalis permitted use of
the illustrations of the catacombs of San Gennaro.
Giuseppe Gravili has kindly prepared the illustrations in electronic format, and Antonella Lippo of
my departmental library provided much-needed
assistance in checking references.

Before seeing the light of day, Chris Wickham,
Richard Reece, Patricia Skinner and two referees
have read the text, rightly taking me to task over
various matters and making many useful
comments. Had I taken heed of all their advice and
views, shortcomings would have been fewer. I
should also like to thank Gill Clark and Gina
Coulthard who, in the final stages, did a splendid
job of editing.

The Consiglio Nazionale delle Ricerche (CNR)
generously provided financing towards the
research in 1985.

I dedicate this work to my mother Germana,
who passed away before seeing its completion, and
to my daughter Elizabeth, who I hope will forgive
me for not having dedicated more time to her.

February 2002

1

FROM TOWN TO CITY-STATE

Some 4,000 years ago there was a large and beautiful south-facing bay, rimmed to the north and west by an almost continuous series of recently formed volcanic hills and craters. To the east, low-lying land presented a series of marshes reaching out towards the slopes of the enormous crater of Mount Vesuvius. Woods, gashed by a series of run-off and spring channels, may have stretched down towards the water's edge. A number of clearings was probably inhabited by small population groups of the initial Bronze Age, known as the Gaudo culture. It has left testimony of its presence in two tombs carved out of the volcanic tuff hill of Materdei (Marzochella 1985). Other prehistoric peoples, frequenting the land between Materdei and the sea, discarded flints and pottery in the area later to be occupied by *Neapolis*.[1]

This is about as far as the evidence goes to illustrate human exploitation in Naples before the arrival of the Greek settlers. However, it is probable that future excavations will demonstrate that increasing exploitation of the land took place right through the second and first millennia BC.[2]

The land of Naples is rather unstable on account of its active vulcanism, made infamous through the eruption of Mount Vesuvius that destroyed both *Pompeii* and *Herculaneum* in AD 79. A less violent one in AD 472, according to the historian Procopius, projected ashes as far as Byzantium.[3] Yet another eruption was described by a cleric, Gregory, on his return to Rome from the second ecumenical council of Nicea, held in AD 787. Vesuvius burned for six days until a procession to the mountain led by Bishop-Duke Stephen II was able to placate its fury (Sauget 1968).[4] The more

recent eruption of Monte Nuovo, Pozzuoli, in 1538, led to a substantial contraction of lake Lucrino, itself a crater, where the Roman fleet once moored. The fumaroles, or gas vents, still provide eloquent testimony as to why the ancients so readily attached infernal legends to the area.

Earthquakes are also frequent, as is the related phenomenon of bradyseism, the slow rise and fall of the earth's crust, which seriously effects some coastal areas. Indeed, the abandonment of most of *Puteoli* in late antiquity might be attributed to bradyseism (see below, pp. 10–11). It was certainly the cause of a more recent exodus of the population in 1982–1984, which has led to the creation of a new town at Monte Ruscello.[5]

Most of the basic rock of the area is the yellow volcanic tuff (*tufo giallo napoletano*). In classical and later times, this was the principal building stone, available both beneath and around the city. An even softer surface rock often provided the widely exported *pulvis puteolanus*, or pozzolana, made famous in Roman times as a basic ingredient of hydraulic mortar. Excavations in the heart of Naples have revealed a thin deposit of very soft degraded rock lying above the more compact, though still rather soft, volcanic tuff. The former requires very careful excavation, as it can easily be mistaken for anthropically redeposited material. These soft pyroclastic deposits are prone to atmospheric erosion. As a result, periods of climatic deterioration lead to profuse erosion and redeposition of surface rock. Such volcanic terrain undoubtedly contributed to the formation of the sunken roads, or *cupe*, typical of Campania, and it was a *cupa* that hemmed in and led to the defeat of

---

[1] Late bronze or iron age pottery fragments and a flint waste flake have been recovered from excavations at Via Carminiello ai Mannesi, whilst another flint was unearthed at Vico della Serpe. To the north of the antique city, various ceramic fragments have come from excavations beneath the monastery of Santa Maria Antesaecula.

[2] Despite the numerous excavations conducted in Naples, no buried pre-classical soils have been identified yet.

[3] Proc. *Bell. Goth*. VI. iv. 26; also Marcell, *Chron.*, *MGH AA* XI. 90; Cass. *Var.* IV. 50; *Paschale Campanum, MGH AA* IX. 265, 330. In general, see Colucci Pescatori 1986, on the chronology of this and other near-contemporary events.

[4] An eruption in AD 685 is mentioned in *Lib. Pont.* I (*vita Benedicti*).

[5] For the general problems of bradyseism in the area see Luongo 1987.

a Neapolitan cavalry force outside the town during the Hannibalic Wars (Frederiksen 1984: 239). However, given the particularly fortunate mineral composition of the pyroclastic deposits, erosion probably had little effect on the land's agricultural potential, as infertile and uncultivable rocks were practically never laid bare.

Thus, despite the negative effects of an area of active volcanism, the resulting mineral composition of the soils, together with the climate, is such that throughout historic times agricultural fertility was ensured and productivity has been consistently higher than that of the majority of other mediterranean lands (see, for example, Ruocco 1970). A large area, centred on the bay of Naples though stretching from the river Garigliano to the north to the river Sele to the south, is one of the few areas of southern Italy regarded as having a particularly rich agricultural regime. Permitted by the environment and geographical position, this was guaranteed by a large and dependable market, varying from the minimum, but considerable, demands of Naples to the larger demands of other parts of Italy and other mediterranean lands. Whether the present agricultural complexity derives from forms of organization developed between medieval and Renaissance times, as has been suggested, or was partly ensured by a continuity of land-use since Roman times, is a matter to be explored (Gambi 1989: 19, fig. 1).

THE CLASSICAL LEGACY

The Greeks who had settled *Cumae* around 725 BC chose the volcanic crest of Pizzofalcone as the site for the foundation of *Partenope* (*Palaeopolis*) by 650 BC, as part of their design to control the gulf (Càssola 1986).[6] This admirable cliff-site, traditionally occupied by Rhodian seafarers in the ninth century BC, rises abruptly to some 50 m above sea level and overlooks both the sea and the small island of *Megaris* (present-day Castel dell'Ovo), now linked to the mainland by a causeway. Early occupation of the area is demonstrated by the discovery of a cemetery with artefacts dating from the seventh to the third centuries BC, with a hiatus from the second half of the sixth to the end of the fourth centuries (De Caro 1985). In archaic times, settlers may well have cultivated the site later occupied by *Neapolis* and may have erected a rural sanctuary on its

highest point at Sant'Aniello a Caponapoli (Greco 1986: 188–9). Pre-colonial occupation is demonstrated by the discovery of a well, sited to the immediate west of Via L. Armanni, in the centre of Naples, containing late sixth-century BC pottery (Appendix I: site 17).

The city-state of *Neapolis* was probably founded by Greeks from *Cumae*, following a decisive victory over the Etruscans in 474 BC. Its territory in both Greek and Roman times did not extend over more than about 17 km^2, smaller than the territory of many other Campanian towns, such as Capua (89 km^2) or even *Nola* (29 km^2).[7] It was surrounded by often hostile, autochthonous cultural groups, perhaps explaining the enormous expenditure on the urban defences described below. Contacts with other Greek colonies were maintained primarily by sea.

The Greek and Roman walled settlement of *Neapolis* stood on a tuff platform, with a high point of 65 m above sea level in its northwestern corner (Sant'Aniello a Caponapoli), sloping southwards to 15–20 m from where a rock-face dropped sharply to the sandy beach (Fig. 1:1). The various positions of the ancient coastline are a matter of debate, which may be exemplified by the maps published by Bartolomeo Capasso and Mario Napoli (Fig. 1:2). Boreholes for the construction of a building sited between Via Marina and the Faculty of Letters of the University of Naples (Porta di Massa) have revealed a stratigraphy of sandy sediments. This suggests that at this point the coastline lay at least 250 m inland from the present built-up water's edge, unless the sediments represent the infill of a cove.

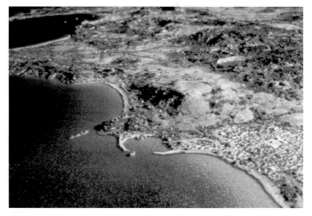

Fig. 1:1. Naples under the Empire (Project EUBEA: reconstruction by Marco Travaglini).

---

[6] On the foundation of *Neapolis* see also Ravida 1995.
[7] On the size of Campanian town territories see Lepore 1969: 146, 148.

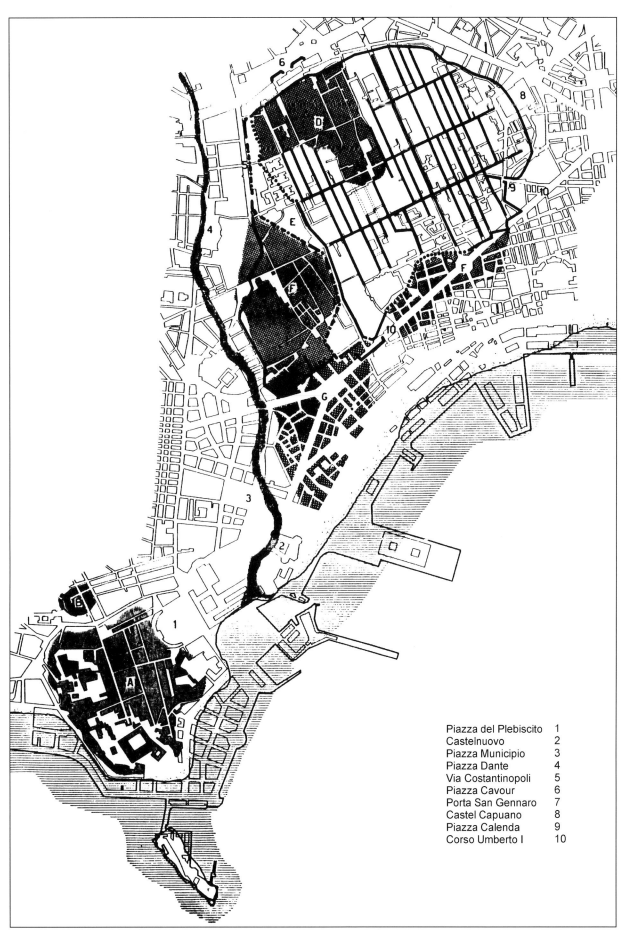

Piazza del Plebiscito   1
Castelnuovo   2
Piazza Municipio   3
Piazza Dante   4
Via Costantinopoli   5
Piazza Cavour   6
Porta San Gennaro   7
Castel Capuano   8
Piazza Calenda   9
Corso Umberto I   10

Fig. 1:2. Naples according to Mario Napoli (1967).

The platform upon which the town developed seems to have been separated from the surrounding land by a series of natural features. Marshes spread to the east of the city, past the ancient river Sebethus, in an area known as Le Paludi since medieval times, when flax for linen may have been soaked and water-mills are attested (Schipa 1892: 591; Capasso 1895: 196–9). Backing the coastal dunes, they stretched inland as far north as Poggio-reale, where the ground begins to rise towards Capodichino (Frederiksen 1984: 19).[8] To the immediate north of the city the platform was truncated by a gully running along the line of Via Foria and Piazza Cavour, later adapted as a defensive ditch (*fossatum*) (Andreucci Ricciardi 1991: 17). Here, the ancient ground surface seems to lie some 20 m below the present level. Water running down from the hills of the Vomero was collected along a line formed by Via Santa Maria di Costantinopoli/Via Pessina, Piazza Dante, where the ancient surface may have lain 16 m below the present level, and Via Sant'Anna dei Lombardi, Via Monteoliveto and Via Medina.[9] This formed a fairly large watercourse that drained into a bay in the area of Piazza Municipio, probably adapted in classical times as a harbour and explaining the later siting of the Angevin castle. Excavations in the piazza show marine sediments stratified beneath structures that appear to date to around the sixteenth century.[10]

Little survives of the initial colony, apart from the walls and the Hippodamean street-grid. The remains of the walls indicate a primary construction during the first half of the fifth century BC, and a major alteration during the fourth century (Fig. 1:3). The two phases appear to be distinguished by the use of two qualities of volcanic tuff, the earlier being more granular, perhaps derived from the quarrying of surface material. The walls were formed of two parallel structures united by cross-walls and having rubble-filled *emplekta*. A quarry, found over 19 m beneath the cemetery of Santa Maria del Pianto, was used for the extraction of the tuff blocks of the fourth-century BC circuit (Pozzi 1990: 268). It originally ran for *c.* 3.8 km,

Fig. 1:3. The Greek walls of Neapolis *at Piazza Cavour (photo: author).*

enclosing an area of about 72 to 81 ha. Re-entrant gates may have existed on the crest of Sant'Aniello a Caponapoli and at Via Mezzocannone.[11] Other gates were at San Pietro a Majella, Piazza San Domenico Maggiore, Forcella (*porta Furcillensis*), Castel Capuano, perhaps at Via Santa Sofia and at Porta San Gennaro. *Propugnacula*, or defensive outworks, are surmised in Piazza Cavour and Corso Umberto.[12]

The street-grid is one of the best surviving examples in Italy.[13] It consists of three *plateiai*, or main roads (the later *decumani*), running southwest to northeast and parallel to the sea front, though the existence of a fourth one towards the sea wall is not to be excluded. The *summa plateia* is now Via

---

[8] A map of Naples by the Duca di Noja, dated 1775, shows the land immediately to the south of the territory of the *casale*, or village, San Pietro a Patierno and the church of Santa Maria del Pianto marked as 'Le paludi'.

[9] These depths are indicated by Ferrajoli 1961. The publication of excavations conducted at Piazza Dante in the 1990s should help to define the topography of this area.

[10] I should like to thank Bruno Genito for this information. Large-scale excavations have been conducted recently (1999–2000).

[11] I should like to thank Dr G. Vecchio for this suggestion.

[12] For the gates see Greco 1985b: 136; *propugnacula*: Napoli 1959: 33–4.

[13] Greco (1986) provided a well-balanced appraisal of the evidence and the outstanding problems. See Johannowsky 1961: 9, for stratigraphical evidence.

Sapienza, Via Pisanelli, Via Anticaglie, Via Santi Apostoli and Via Santa Sofia. The *media plateia* is traced by Via San Pietro a Maiella and Via dei Tribunali. The *imma plateia* is followed by Via Benedetto Croce, Via San Biagio ai Librai and Via Vicaria Vecchia. They were crossed at right angles and at regular intervals by a series of *stenopoi* (the later *cardines* or *vici*). Though the exact number of these minor roads is not known, between twenty and 23 have been counted. Three have been verified archaeologically, at San Lorenzo Maggiore, beneath the cathedral and at Via Carminiello ai Mannesi, whilst further surfaces have been recorded at Via Atri and Via Paladino. Only that at San Lorenzo has an undoubted Greek or Hellenistic origin. At Carminiello ai Mannesi the road does not seem to have been in existence prior to Roman Imperial times, and even then was not surfaced with the traditional lava road blocks that survive beneath San Lorenzo and the cathedral. The *plateiai* exist to this day, though their widths have changed. They are now *c.* 6 m wide, whilst the *stenopoi* vary from 3 to 3.5 m. The building plots, or insulae, enclosed by the street-grid measure 185 m, and are about 35 m wide.[14]

The *stenopoi* have, in part, disappeared with time. None of them is now quite straight. It will be seen how the narrowing of street widths, partial disappearance of the *stenopoi* and the irregularity of road layouts may be explained by the dynamics of medieval Naples.

The highest area of the town, towards Sant'Aniello a Caponapoli, has been interpreted as an acropolis occupied by religious sanctuaries. Deposits of terracotta objects, principally female heads, busts and seated figures, found in 1933 beneath the convent of San Gaudioso, and dated between the fourth and third centuries BC, suggest the presence of a sanctuary dedicated to Demeter (Borriello and De Simone 1985). The toponym *regio marmorata* existed in medieval times, and has been explained as referring to the concentration in the area of marble-faced buildings (Greco 1985b: 138).

Tradition and inconclusive discoveries have led local antiquaries to hypothesize the existence of public buildings that may have had a Greek or Hellenistic origin. A temple dedicated to Jupiter, for instance, is said to have stood beneath the site

of the cathedral, temples dedicated to Hercules beneath the church of San Giovanni Maggiore and at Forcella, and temples of Mercury and Aesculapius at other points within the city (Capasso 1905).

Most of the Greek objects known from *Neapolis* come from cemeteries, distributed at various points outside its walls.[15] How many of the burials represent inhabitants of the *polis* or of the *chora*, or surrounding territory, we do not know. The fact that most of the tombs were excavated many years ago, without accurate documentation, denies fine analysis.

This, in sum, is the material documentation for Greek *Neapolis*. If one were to judge human activity on the archaeological evidence alone, despite the excavation of over twenty sites within the walls, the resulting picture would be that of a large area delimited by massive defences enclosing a system of roads or boundaries and a sanctuary on the acropolis or high point of Sant'Aniello. Indeed, evidence of early domestic activity is all but absent, suggesting three possibilities:

1. that pre-Republican settlement has been almost totally destroyed and its traces removed, although this is unlikely, as residual Greek material in later contexts is virtually absent;
2. that archaeologists have not yet excavated in the 'right' places, and that Greek settlement may thus have been concentrated in one or more areas, for example towards the acropolis or the sea;
3. that there was no substantial settlement within the walls themselves, which served to delimit the administrative area, a cult/market area and refuge site as well as to protect the harbour.

An interesting fact, perhaps in support of the third hypothesis, is that *Partenope* and not *Neapolis* was the effective centre of resistance against the Roman forces in 327–326 BC, at the outbreak of the Second Samnite War. This suggests that the lower settlement could not be defended satisfactorily by the available manpower. Indeed, it is said that some 6,000 soldiers occupied the upper site.[16] Calculations based on the number of possible Greek houses within the reconstructed insulae suggest that *Neapolis* itself may have held as many as 7,000 to 8,000 inhabitants, though this

[14] On the whole problem of the measurements see Greco 1985b: 137–8.
[15] The cemeteries are treated in various papers in the volume edited by Pozzi 1985.
[16] On the event see Frederiksen 1984: 208–10. Hardly any excavation has been done at Pizzofalcone, though material from a cemetery has been published by De Caro (1985).

is a maximum figure (Greco 1986: 215–16). Whatever the case, the political and economic importance of Greek and Hellenistic *Neapolis* cannot be denied (Lepore 1952; Mele 1985). The emission of coinage is an indicator of the political and economic importance of *Neapolis* right from its very foundation. It terminated around the year 241 BC, at the close of the First Punic War (Rutter 1979).

Roman conquest of the area following the Second Punic War clipped the wings of Neapolitan autonomy. *Puteoli* was made a Roman colony in 194 BC, and rapidly developed into one of the most important emporia in the Mediterranean. It lay only 11 km from Naples, and was sited upon what appears to have been an ephemeral Greek settlement known as *Dikearchea*. By 126 BC, when it had been termed *Delos Minor*, it had become quite visibly more important than Naples (Dubois 1907; Frederiksen 1984: 319–58).

However, the notion of Naples's vitality cannot be dismissed outright. We might perhaps take Campana A black glaze pottery as a clue to economic expansion during the late Republic, as it probably reflects the routes and markets for wine produced for export on the bay of Naples.[17] Kiln wasters have been found along Corso Umberto, perhaps an 'industrial' area close to port facilities (Accorona *et al.* 1985). The pottery first appeared in the second half of the third century BC. By the later second century it had become the single most exported class of table-ware in the mediterranean basin and would seem to have held an important place in the pottery market until the late Republic. With the general change-over in the Roman world from black- to red-gloss table-ware during the course of the first century BC, Campana A was substituted by a red-slipped ware that continued to be made and exported in significant quantities until the mid-first century AD (Soricelli 1987).

Though evidence of wine exportation dates back to the third century BC, mass production was a result of the reorganization of agricultural holdings following the Second Punic War (Tchernia 1986: 202–3). Some of the new-found wealth found its way into Naples, where various estate owners possessed urban properties. There is abundant archaeological evidence for new slave-based villa estates, and textual and epigraphic evidence for urban properties and proprietors. They included L. Licinius Lucullus, Servilia, the mother of M. Iunius Brutus, probably L. Iulius Caesar, uncle of the dictator, and L. Domitius Ahenobarbus (D'Arms 1970: appendix).

In 90 BC Naples was elected to the status of *municipium*. It was from about that time, perhaps because of stable conditions following the Social Wars, that a number of houses, or *domus*, was erected. Development under the Empire is signalled by further building activity. Taken with the evidence for wine and pottery exportation, it rather contradicts the somewhat drastic view of some scholars of the decline following the town's submission to Sulla, and the confiscation of its fleet and the island of Ischia after it had supported the cause of Caius Marius.[18] Though patently still less important than *Puteoli*, building development seems to have been more lavish than at other neighbouring coastal towns, especially under the early Empire. Much domestic architecture seems to date to the last century of the Republic, and examples of socially well-placed houses have been recognized in various excavations around the central *plateia*.[19]

Major early Imperial public buildings include the gymnasium, or *Caesareum*, built under Augustus around AD 2, the temple of the Dioscuri, and later the theatre, the *theatrum tectum/odeion* and the *macellum*, or covered market, at San Lorenzo. In the theatre complex were held the quinquennial *Sebasta*, dramatic and musical contests, once presided over by Claudius, and in which Nero may have taken part.[20] Both an amphitheatre and a stadium were sited in the eastern part of the settlement, although they have not been located.

The temple of the Dioscuri and the *macellum* are all that survive of the Roman forum. It is likely that it was sited in the area of the Greek *agora*, and the terrace of the *macellum* lies above a large wall of squared tuff blocks that may have acted as a terrace wall to the earlier square. The precise form of the forum is a matter of conjecture, though it extended some way in front of the temple and probably gave access to the area of the two theatres, to the north, by way of a colonnaded square. The existence of an open space between the theatres and the temple is suggested by the

---

[17] The most recent analyses are by Morel (1985).

[18] Most recently Lepore 1985. Compare the initial, though guarded, criticisms by Baldassare (1986: 223–4).

[19] Under the cathedral, at the site of Carminiello ai Mannesi, under the monastery of the Girolomini, under the historical archives of the Banco di Napoli and beneath the church of Santa Maria Maggiore.

[20] Suet. *Claud.* II. 2; Cass. Dio LX. vi. 1–2; Suet. *Nero* XX. 2; Tac. *Ann.* XV. xxxiv. 1–2; see D'Arms 1970: 94.

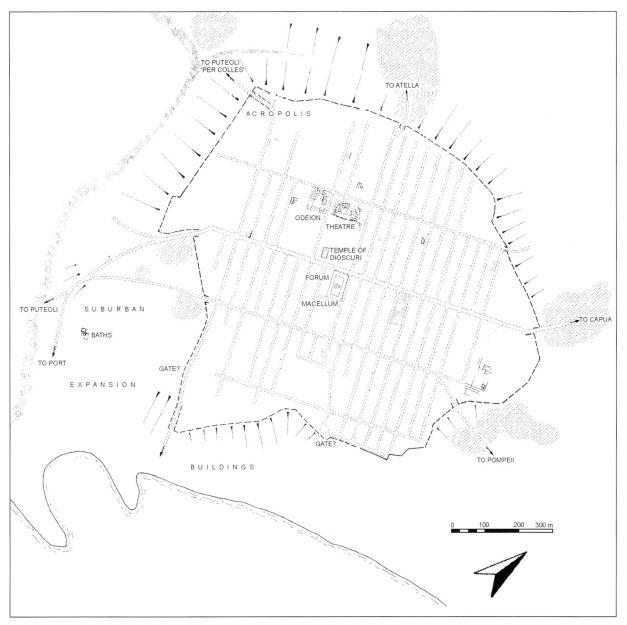

Fig. 1:4. Naples in the second century AD *(drawn by Sally Cann).*

haphazard development of later building in the area, contrasting with the more regular development in the rest of the city, which was conditioned by pre-existing architecture.[21]

Another important construction was the Augustan aqueduct of the Serino (*aqua Augusta*), which tapped water from a spring rising at Aquaro (*fons Augusteus*) in the Sabato valley, about 10 km southeast of Avellino. It was the longest in Italy, running for some 96 km, and supplied *Nola, Atella, Acerrae, Pompeii*, the Phlegrean Fields and Naples, where a tract on brick-faced concrete arches still survives as the Ponti Rossi (red bridges) (Beloch 1989: 86–8; Johannowsky 1985). In the centre of

Naples it fed an incredible network of channels and cisterns. Often lying over 30 m beneath present ground level, it was reached by numerous wells. Only one of these, lying at the corner of Via San Biagio ai Librai and Vico Figurari, may be closely dated as, instead of being cut solely through the volcanic tuff, it is reinforced with *opus reticulatum*. Pliny referred to the system when he singled out Naples as a city relatively protected from earthquakes, as the buildings were suspended above a network of caves and galleries (*NH* II. 197; Celano and Chiarini 1858–1859; Guidoboni 1989). It was used until the new municipal aqueduct was laid out at the beginning of the last century, and reused

---

[21] For the *curte commune* see *MND* II. 1. 356–7.

during the Second World War for air-raid shelters.[22] Thus many of the cisterns, wells and channels have been recut over the centuries, creating difficulties in precise dating. It is conceivable that the Roman water system replaced an earlier one of Hellenistic date, which lies around 10 m below the present ground level, perhaps connected to the 'Greek' cistern beneath San Lorenzo (Melisurgo 1889).[23]

It has been estimated that the surviving remains can hold approximately 4.5 million cubic metres of water. Despite recutting, it is clear from this that the Roman system could have held far more water than was practically needed. At Constantinople, three open-air cisterns, containing not quite a million cubic metres of water, were built during the fifth century, so as to guarantee supply to its inhabitants (Mango 1986: 122). The case of Naples can be explained if we regard the construction of the aqueduct and cisterns not only as expedient in guaranteeing the populace with an abundant and ready supply of water, but also in providing quarries for the principal building material, the yellow volcanic tuff, of which the town was built. It is no coincidence that both the aqueduct of the Serino and the principal urban building projects date to the early Empire.

By the early Empire, much of the space within the walls was probably occupied, as the suburbs were being developed (Fig. 1:4). A large bathing-complex was built towards the end of the first or beginning of the second century at Santa Chiara, probably connected to the Augustan aqueduct, in an area that earlier had been used as a cemetery (Vecchio 1985a). Another small bath-building, probably attached to a private dwelling, was built around the same time at nearby Santa Maria Nova (see below, Appendix I).

Probably also in early Imperial times the main roads were paved with dark grey Vesuvian lava blocks. The principal thoroughfare to *Puteoli* and the Phlegrean Fields (Via Antiniana) originally crossed the hill of the Vomero. Under Augustus communication systems were renovated by cutting a number of impressive tunnels through the hills of Naples and the Phlegrean Fields, perhaps largely the work of L. Cocceius Auctus, architect of Augustus and Agrippa. Cut through the hill of Posillipo is the *crypta Neapolitana*, running for 705 m, linking *Puteoli* and *Neapolis*, avoiding the longer and more tiring route *per colles* (Amalfitano 1990: 38–41). It was an important piece of engineering, though muddy and dusty according to

Fig. 1:5. The Augustan tunnel or crypta Neapolitana *at Fuorigrotta, in an anonymous print of the later eighteenth or early nineteenth century (courtesy of Guido Di Lorenzo — Associazione Cultural Oltre l'Averno).*

[22] Many parts are now blocked by rubbish that has been dumped down the wells over the last century. Apparently various galleries have been used, most recently by the Camorra, as hideaways and shooting-ranges. I owe most of the information on the system to Enzo Albertini, who has mapped much of it. See Esposito 1992.

[23] For the 'Greek' cistern, abutting a wall dated to the early fourth century BC, see De Simone 1985: 190.

Seneca (*Ep*. LVII. 1–2) (Fig. 1:5). Before reaching the tunnel, the new road to *Puteoli* crossed the low-lying area of Piazza Plebiscito to Piazza dei Martiri and Via Carlo Poerio, and then continued, coasting the beach just above the Riviera di Chiaia, which is largely reclaimed land.[24] A milestone testifies to restoration of this road as late as Constantinian times (Johannowsky 1985: 337). The so called 'Grotta di Seiano', 800 m long, linked the settlement around the villa of Vedius Pollio, at Posillipo, with the plain of Coroglio and *Puteoli*.

Alongside the numerous Republican villas and farms, examples of which have been excavated recently at Marianella and Ponticelli, impressive maritime villas developed along the coast.[25] The most famous are those of Lucullus, probably on the island of *Megaris*, and the estate of P. Vedius Pollio at Posillipo, which passed into Imperial hands on his death in 15 BC.[26] *Vici* or satellite settlements are virtually unknown, save the complex at Fuorigrotta with its public baths, which some identify with a site called *Marcianum* (Napoli 1967: 469).[27]

Very little evidence exists to clarify the conditions of *Neapolis* during mid-Imperial times. Lepore has interpreted this negatively, as a sign of the crisis of the Empire (1985: 122). Though, along with the rest of Italy, Naples gradually suffered the economic emancipation of the provinces, she was none the less able to profit from the urban development inherited from Julio-Claudian times and from her position in one of the most fertile tracts of Italy en route to Rome. The relative lack of archaeological contexts dating to the second century is more a sign of efficient urban management than of malaise. The abundant late Republican and early Imperial contexts relate to the massive building programmes that were to give *Neapolis* its Roman imprint. The abundant late antique and early medieval contexts relate to abandonment of urban spaces and decline in social services. The absence of mid-Imperial contexts is thus probably to be viewed not only as evidence for an absence of large building programmes, but also as an indication of functioning services that kept the town clean. Indeed, the only substantial group of mid-second-century archaeological strata comes from excavations at Santa Patrizia, where dumps of urban waste and rubble were used to fill a platform for the construction of a large, possibly public, brick-faced concrete building (Appendix I: site 7).

A little construction or renovation took place around the forum during the mid-Empire. A wall in *opus listatum*, dated to the third century, was erected on the eastern side of the *stenopos* alongside the *macellum* at San Lorenzo. Marble fragments of the same century were found in excavations (De Simone 1985: 186–7). Work was also carried out on the port facilities immediately to the south of the town, reached by a road dropping from the *imma plateia*, roughly on the line of the present-day Via Mezzocannone. Building works in 1961 uncovered part of a mole and two inscriptions close to the church of San Pietro Martire. The earliest indicated that the mole was constructed under Antoninus Pius, at a cost of 300,000 sestertii. The other records that, due to inundation, it was rebuilt in AD 202 under Septimius Severus and Caracalla (Sogliano 1892: 479–81; Napoli 1967: 414).

On the religious side, like many other Roman towns, the emergence of the cult of Mithras is attested during the Empire. At least one *mithraeum* existed in the city centre, sited in a subterranean service-area of the insula at Carminiello ai Mannesi. Another *mithraeum* is attested through a bas-relief also found in this part of Naples, whilst a third was inserted into the *crypta Neapolitana* (Beloch 1989: 102; Lacerenza and Morisco 1994).

It may have been under Marcus Aurelius that the town was elevated to *Colonia Aurelia Augusta Antoniniana Felix Neapolis*, developing away from the Greek *polis* on Italian soil to a town of more typical Roman order. Indeed, through the third and fourth centuries Greek gradually gave way to Latin as the institutional language. By Constantinian times, an *ordo Neapolitanorum* is attested in place of the antique *demarchia*, members of which are known into the Tetrarchy (Beloch 1989: 58–60). This change may have taken place with Diocletian's reforms, when the consular province of Campania was instituted, and a governor based at Capua. There is also evidence of Constantinian interest in Naples. The restoration of the forum and aqueduct in 323/324 is a rare example of Constantinian patronage in small towns, and may be an early indication of the growing importance of the city under the late Empire (*Lib. Pont*. I. 186 (*vita Sylvestri*); *AE* 1939: no. 151; Ward-Perkins 1984: 30). Two statues erected by the town to honour Helena, mother of Constantine, may be an appreci-

---

[24] Soprintendenza archives N 8/30 (6.2.1954); Sgobbo 1926.
[25] On the villas of Marianella and Ponticelli see De Stefano and Carsana 1987: 61–9.
[26] For the role-call of wealthy and influential gentry with property around the bay of Naples see D'Arms 1970.
[27] For the site see Laforgia 1981.

ation of his patronage (*CIL* X: 1483–4). Above all, the emperor built the church of the Saviour or Holy Apostles and provided it with a rich endowment, thus laying the foundations for the growth of the local church (*Lib. Pont.* I. 186).[28]

Later, between 379 and 382, the *ordo* dedicated a statue to Anicius Auchenius Bassus, senator, *proconsul Campaniae* and patron of the city (*AE* 1892: no. 143; Sogliano 1892: 165–7; Miranda 1985). His is one of the figures representing the new post-Diocletianic regime that had put an end to effective municipal self-government in favour of government agents. In the role of *patroni*, they were to enforce the collection of taxes and supplies necessary to ensure state security in the difficult times of the late Empire.

At the turn of the fourth century the bay of Naples was still of great strategic importance. The imperial fleet was housed at *Misenum* and the great aqueduct of the Serino had been restored in 324, and again in 399 (*Cod. Theod.* XV. 2, 8; *AE* 1939: no. 151). Naples itself was still the frivolous scene of *delectatio* for the Roman élite, as were Bacoli and Baia, even though the gradual search for alternative sites had began much earlier, perhaps by Flavian times (D'Arms 1981: 90–6). Symmachus, none the less, owned a property outside the city and adjacent to an estate of his friend, Virius Nichomachus Flavianus, consul in 394 and *praefectus praetorio per Italiam* from 389 (D'Arms 1970: 226–9). Both were engaged in renovating them. Caecina Decius Albinus, *praefectus urbi* of 402, was a neighbour (D'Arms 1970: 226–9).

LATE ANTIQUITY

The first major factor that was to secure the city's fortunes through early medieval times was the dramatic decline of Campania's leading commercial city, *Puteoli*, through the fifth century. Campania, like Rome, suffered the crises of later antiquity, and by the latter half of the century *Puteoli* seems to have been virtually abandoned and the imperial fleet had been pulled out of neighbouring *Misenum*.[29] The fact that bishops of *Puteoli* are attested into the later sixth century is no

basis from which to argue continuity in urban life and organization after the fifth (*CIL* X: 3299; *Lib. Pont.* I. *Ep.* 9 (*vita Pelagii*)). However, there is sufficient reason to believe that the town was still of prime importance to Rome a century earlier. From the time of Constantine, and during most of the fourth century, it had been one of the few centres privileged with the assignation of the *annona*, at first of 150,000 *modii* of grain, enough for some 2,500 or 3,600 people.[30] Late antique dedications to provincial governors and benefactors are also known, dating up to 409, the year before the invasion by Alaric's Visigoths (*CIL* X: 1702; *PLRE* II: Paulinus 16). It still appeared to be a cosmopolitan settlement in the fourth century, embracing people from various parts of the Empire and with a resident Hebrew community.[31] Epigraphic material of this date is extraordinarily rich and contrasts with a virtual absence of later documents (Camodeca 1981). Indicative of the declining significance of *Puteoli* during the fifth century is the transportation of the body of Ianuarius, bishop of *Beneventum* and later patron saint of Naples, from the town, where he was martyred, to the Neapolitan catacombs that bear his name, between 413 and 431. Thus it might not be too rash to suggest that fear of the Visigoths, and, even more so, the Vandals, which had led to a reconstruction of the antique walls of Naples, contributed to the demise of the unwalled city.[32] So important were walls by the sixth century that Cassiodorus was in doubt whether to call *Scolacium* in Calabria a *civitas ruralis* or a *villa urbana*, as it lacked them (Cass. *Var.* XII. xv. 5).[33]

Amongst the reasons for the town's submission to *Neapolis* are not only the absence of a city wall, but also coastal bradyseism. Martin Frederiksen drew attention to an important apocryphal text, the *Acts of Saint Peter and Saint Paul*, dating perhaps a little earlier than 890, that makes clear that the sea had long submerged part of the town (Frederiksen 1977; 1984: pl. XIV). Frederiksen was not able to find any evidence to suggest when the event might have happened, save that it was presumably later than 530, when Cassiodorus was still able to praise the glories of the gulf (Cass.

---

[28] See below, Chapter 4. Geometric mosaics found beneath the cathedral may belong to a late Roman *domus* (Di Stefano 1974). The excavations beneath the cathedral have never been published adequately and records do not exist in the Soprintendenza.

[29] For the evidence bearing on this see below, Chapter 5.

[30] For the complex story see Cracco Ruggini (1969), who also summarized other views.

[31] For example, *CIL* X. 3303, for a Jewish lady; *CIL* X. 3309, for a citizen of Constantinople.

[32] On fear of the Visigoths and the relative security of Sicily, which had become a haven for both Melania and Nichomachus Flavianus Iunior, see Wilson 1990: 330. The rewalling of Naples through fear of the Vandals is discussed in Chapter 3.

[33] See La Rocca (1992: 164–5) on the significance of the walls.

Var. IX. 6).[34] Recent underwater excavations of a nymphaeum at Punta Epitaffio, at nearby Baia, demonstrate that the building, though having lost its primary functions towards the beginning of the fourth century, was robbed of marbles and lead pipes, and was later used for burials, possibly in the first half of the sixth century. Piero Gianfrotta believed that bradyseism was already affecting the site between the fourth and the sixth centuries (Gianfrotta 1987: 107–9).[35] Afterwards, the building seems to have sunk definitively beneath the water and now lies at -7.30 m.[36] *Puteoli* was never totally abandoned, though settlement largely retreated to the lofty promontory of Rione Terra, where it later developed as a *castrum*.

Even *Neapolis* seems to have suffered a population decline and thus cannot be seen simply as a sponge in the absorption of the inhabitants of *Puteoli* and the surrounding countryside. However, continuing investment in the city helps to argue its importance through late Roman times. Archaeology suggests the continuing agricultural well-being of its hinterland (see below, Chapter 5). Why this is so, is hard to tell. Campania was apparently a land of substantial *agri deserti* (abandoned land) at the end of the fourth century, estimated to have been in the region of 133,000 ha (528,000 *iugera*), enough to cause sufficient concern in government to grant tax-relief (*Cod. Theod.* XI. xxviii. 2).[37] However, we do not know which areas of Campania were affected, nor is there any general agreement as to what *agri deserti* really were. They may have been fiscally deserted lands, as the law stated that they 'must be removed from the tax lists', without necessarily signifying the abandonment of farmed land. It has been surmised that the law concerned solely marginal, mediocre or otherwise unproductive land. Whilst the *agri deserti* may have lain anywhere in the larger imperial province of Campania, it could have been the fiscal exemptions that guaranteed a continuing economic stability to those who attempted to farm them. Further and very substantial tax-relief, amounting to eight-ninths of the total sum, was granted in 418 following devastation during the Visigothic invasion.

Campania was held to be a granary of Rome during the fourth century, according to the *Expositio totius mundi*, and Symmachus praised the region's fertility (*Exp. tot. mund.* LIII; Symm. *Ep.* I. vii. 1). I feel sure that this continued to be the case until the Lombards conquered much of the area at the end of the sixth century. But despite the current interpretation of the *agri deserti*, the evidence for a decline in the number of rural settlements through the late Empire also suggests a certain decline in the proportion of land cultivated (see below, Chapter 5).[38]

The curtailment of the supply of African grain and oil to Rome, largely as tax in kind, with the Vandal invasion of the Maghreb in 429, probably set a premium on the agricultural produce from remaining parts of the Empire. Despite some trade with Vandal Africa, Sicily and other parts of southern Italy seem to have regained a certain importance in supplying the capital with agricultural revenues, and this might be shown archaeologically by the appearance of new amphora types, albeit probably for wine, in Campania, Calabria and eastern Sicily.[39] It is likely that these amphorae represent the tip of a commercial iceberg within the peninsula that also included grain from Sicily and pork from Lucania.

None the less, Naples continued to import foodstuffs from the provinces down to the end of the Empire and beyond, in such quantity as to suggest either that it remained a viable market-place or that it was buttressed through state intervention. Evidence for economic buttressing in the later sixth and seventh centuries is discussed in Chapter 7. There may have been earlier occurrences of the practice, as the area suffered seriously as a result of the volcanic eruptions of the late fifth and early sixth centuries, as well as the protracted affair of the Gothic War, both of which required government intervention.

Archaeological evidence, instead, appears to give some indication of the scale of damage that needed to be attended to, probably because of the eruption of 472. Building trenches at Ponticelli have revealed burials and plough-soil stratified

---

[34] Frederiksen (1984: 45) asserted that the event took place in the eighth or ninth century, partly contradicting his more cautious earlier view (1977).

[35] See also Zevi and Andreae 1982; and now De Caro 1999.

[36] The moles at *Misenum* have sunk at least 6.50 m below sea level, whilst part of the villa of Vedius Pollio at Posillipo lies at least 4.20 m below sea level. See Gianfrotta 1988.

[37] On the current views of *agri deserti*, contra Jones (1964: 812–23), see Lepelley 1967: 142–4; Whittaker 1976; Vera 1986a: 261–2; Lewit 1991: 71–6.

[38] This is despite the methodological observations of Lewit 1991: chapter 2.

[39] The new Calabrian and Sicilian amphora type (Keay LII) is discussed in Arthur 1989c. For the fifth- and early sixth-century Campanian type see below, Chapter 6.

beneath more than 1 m of volcanic ash, whilst over 2 m of ash have been identified at Cimitile.[40] Various other sites seem to have been badly damaged or destroyed, as witnessed at the town of *Abellinum* (Colucci Pescatori 1986), lying some 30 km from Mount Vesuvius, and at villas at Sant'Anastasia, near *Pompeii* (Parma and Gifuni 1987; Pagano 1991; Conticello De' Spagnolis 1995; Soricelli 1997).[41] The fact that this was also a period of widespread economic recession, indicated by the substantial abandonment of numerous villas and farms in Italy, suggests the immense difficulty that owners of land damaged by volcanic eruptions would have had with reconstruction. Perhaps in the minds of many it was just not worth the effort.

Thus, despite the general political and economic ebbs and flows of the fourth and fifth centuries, Naples seems not to have been as badly hit as many other southern Italian towns. Crises were staved off or dealt with by state and church, whose vested interests lay in the unique strategic position of the city, economically and militarily, both as regards Campania itself and as a stepping-stone between Rome and the East. Indeed, the data suggest that it continued to retain great importance to successive states, from that of the late Roman Empire in the west, through the Ostrogothic regime, to that of the New Rome at Constantinople.

THE GOTHIC WAR AND BYZANTINE NAPLES

The long period from the end of the Roman Empire in the west in 476, through both the Byzantine and the later independent administration of Naples, witnessed a number of major historical events that were to re-shape the political geography of Europe and the Mediterranean. During the course of the fifth century the migration of peoples of Germanic and Scandinavian origin into the Mediterranean broke the political unity of the Roman Empire. Vandals settled in north Africa and Visigoths occupied southern France and most of the Iberian peninsula. In 488 the Ostrogoths moved from the Balkans to Italy. With the blessing of the eastern Emperors Zeno and Anastasius, they created a kingdom that, though closely adhering to Roman administrative practices and paying lip-service to Byzantium, was finally dismantled through the direct intervention of Justinian's generals. The so-called Gothic War, which lasted some twenty years from 535 to 552/554, left the Italian peninsula greatly weakened. From 568, fourteen years after the end of the war and only three years after the death of Justinian, the Lombards swept down the peninsula as far as *Beneventum* and established a new kingdom that was to fracture finally what remained of Italian unity (Fig. 1:6).

More momentous to the history of the Mediterranean was the birth and spread of Islam. From the 630s the Arabs were to conquer the Near East and north Africa, crossing the straits of Gibraltar in 711, only to be stopped at Poitiers by a growing Carolingian power in 732. Their domination of sea trade and their piracy were to last virtually unchallenged until the rise of the Italian maritime states around the turn of the millennium. South Italian urban autonomy was, however, not to last the Norman invasion of the eleventh century, and it is this event that often has been blamed for the dichotomy that was to develop between the north and the south.

Throughout this whole period, the eastern Roman government was to survive as an increasingly marginal state centred on western Asia Minor and the Aegean, with evermore marginal outposts on the Black Sea, along the Dalmatian coast and in Italy. At the same time, Naples passed from being one of many Roman towns to a privileged Byzantine city and then an independent duchy, prior to witnessing the demise of Byzantine power in Italy and the establishment of a new state under the Normans.

The civic government of most of the old Roman towns around Naples, including *Puteoli*, had collapsed totally during the course of the fifth or early part of the sixth century. The imperial fleet had left *Misenum* and, by the time of the Gothic War, it was only *Cumae* and Naples, and no longer the once great *Puteoli*, that were able to assume a significant strategic role. Already by the beginning of the sixth century Cassiodorus informed us, on the appointment of a count of Naples, that his joint civil and military authority extended a certain distance along the coast (Cass. *Var*. VI. 23). A letter to the 'honoratis possessoribus et curialibus civitatis Neapolitanae' leaves no doubt that the local *ordo* was now under the new count's direct control (Cass. *Var*. VI. 24).

---

[40] The deposits at Cimitile appear to overlie remains of an early Roman villa. It would be interesting to assess the damage to the ecclesiastical complex, discussed in Chapter 4. Information supplied by G. Vecchio.

[41] Another such site with fifth-century pottery was excavated by Ernesto De Carolis at Via Lepanto, near *Herculaneum*.

Fig. 1:6. Italy around AD 600 (drawn by Sally Cann).

Towards the end of the century, Pope Gregory wrote of a *iudex Campaniae*, a certain Scholasticus (Greg. *Ep*. III. 1). It is also through the correspondence of the pope, frequently with Naples's *maior populi*, that we find the revenues from the island of Procida (*Prochyta*) being paid in to the municipal treasury (Cassandro 1969: 25–6). Thus local public spending still took place at the close of the sixth century. Town elders, also mentioned in his letters, may in some way have corresponded to a *curia* or town council that would appear to have

survived through the Dark Ages. Yet when the institution is again mentioned, in documents of the ninth and tenth centuries, it appears as a college of notaries (Brown 1984: 18–19).[42] Its surviving strength may have been dealt a severe, if not definitive, blow with the appointment of Basilius as duke of Naples under Constans II in 661/662, and indeed the nominal *curia* seems evermore to have played a passive role in the city's affairs. In 821, the *cives* were apparently still strong enough to be able to overthrow Duke Stephen III (*Gesta Ep*.

---

[42] Also found at Amalfi: Schmidt 1957: 122–4.

Neap. c. 53). By all accounts, Naples seems to have been rather exceptional. Recent studies suggest that aristocratic interest or power in the old Roman towns after *c.* 400 was confined mainly to northern and central Italy, closer to the seats of government (see Barnish 1988: 133–4). Unlike most old southern Italian towns, inscriptions and sources for Naples still show an active involvement of *illustres* in local politics as late as 598, when senatorial families were able to override the interests of the local bishop (Richards 1980: 166–8; Barnish 1988: 133–4, 151). He had attempted to secure control of the city's gates and aqueduct, though to the evident disapproval of Pope Gregory (Richards 1980: 165–8). This suggests continuity in traditional links between Rome and central Campania, quite evident in the fifth century when various high Roman officials owned properties around the city. In the first half of the seventh century, we are told of a *vir magnificus*, Stephen, of Greek origin, who gave land in and around Gubbio to the church of Ravenna (Tjader 1955: 334–42, nos. 18–19; cited by Bavant 1989: 511). How compact a group these Neapolitan *illustres* were is hard to tell, though evidence from other parts of the Empire does suggest that they possessed their own personal courts and *clientes*. Though influence of individual families in both local and central government was not new, their increasingly autonomous action does point to a breakdown of the centralized power base characteristic of earlier times. Thus the needs of towns and the general public were ever less voiced to the central government through the instrument of municipal councils, and it was up to individual patrons to ensure protection for their client-groups. Against this backcloth it is easier to understand the rise in prestige and power both of local bishops and of the later ducal families of Naples and other Campanian city-states, as well as the incessant internal social conflicts characteristic of this era. Above all, it starts to become clear how and why Naples took its flight from an often distant and apparently uncaring Byzantium around the middle of the eighth century.

The process of militarization, however, seems to have had its roots as far back as the mid-fifth century. The first step, apparently taken during the reign of Valentinian III, was to refortify the city against the Vandals in the 440s, though this is unlikely to have led to the deployment of any permanent military contingent (see below, Chapter 3). Indeed, the same emperor, hard-pressed for permanent troops, stated that citizens of the Empire were obliged to defend their towns and restored their right to bear arms (Val. III *Nov.* V, IX). A permanent guard, however, must have been present during the stay of the Emperor Romulus Augustulus at the *Lucullanum*, probably sited on the small island of Castel dell'Ovo, just off the coast of Naples, who had been overthrown and put into comfortable exile there by the Herul Odoacer in 476 (Anon. *Val.* 37–8).[43]

Not long after, the city was armed by the Ostrogoths, following their invasion of Italy in 488. There is no apparent archaeological evidence for Ostrogothic presence in Naples, nor in Campania for that matter.[44] However, it is clear from Procopius that they established a strong garrison, perhaps the only one in southern peninsular Italy, composed of over 800 men (Proc. *Bell. Goth.* V. x. 37). The city was placed under the dual military and civil command of a *comes civitatis*, such as we find controlling the contemporary garrison at Syracuse in Sicily (Cass. *Var.* VI. 22–4).[45] Indeed, so fortified had Naples become that, in 535, during the Gothic War, it offered the only serious resistance to the advance of Justinianic forces up the peninsula.

In late antiquity, the population seems to have become evermore heterogeneous, reflecting the city's role as mediterranean entrepôt, though perhaps making for a rather unstable political unity.[46] Whilst a philo-Byzantine notable, Stephanus, and a Syrian merchant, Antiochus, tried to convince the populace to open the gates to Belisarius, two teachers, Pastor and Asclepiodotus, supported by the Hebrew community, rallied around the Goths to defend the walls. The status of Antiochus accords well with the apparent interest of eastern merchants in Justinian's reconquest of the West. Despite what archaeological evidence for trade might have us believe, there must have been a certain difficulty, even if only financial, in the east–west movement of goods under the Gothic and Vandal regimes in Italy and north Africa

---

[43] For the *Lucullanum* see below, Chapter 3.

[44] Even the so-called Ostrogothic bracelet from the area of the Massico, in northern Campania, seems more likely to be a product of a 'Roman' workshop, rather than an indicator of Ostrogothic presence (Vickers 1972; Ciampoltrini 1987).

[45] On Sicily see Wilson 1990: 336.

[46] On the ethnic composition of Naples see below, Chapter 2.

(Lewis 1951: 25).[47] When, twenty days later, Naples finally capitulated to Belisarius, the Byzantine troops, and the Hun contingent in particular, massacred the inhabitants (Proc. *Bell. Goth.* V. viii–x; Llewellyn 1975: 36–8). Belisarius left the city in the hands of a garrison composed of Romans and Isaurians under the command of Conon and Paulus. It presumably included naval forces, as the recapture of the city by Totila in 543 involved two maritime battles.

Naples lasted some ten years in the hands of the Goths and, in 552, was retaken by the imperial troops under the command of Narses after Teia's Ostrogothic forces were conclusively vanquished in the battle of Monti Lattari. Subsequently a garrison was installed and presumably continued to exist until the moment of the city's effective independence about 100 years later, though it appears to have been inadequate until the election of a duke in 598 (von Falkenhausen 1992: 16). A garrison also held the *castrum* at *Cumae* from the first half of the sixth century (Proc. *Bell. Goth.* V. xiv. 2). Other Campanian towns may have hosted small garrisons or have relied upon local militia. Narses himself retired to Naples after his campaigns, though he died in Rome in 568, ironically the year in which the greater part of Italy was once again lost to barbarian hordes.

The weakened Byzantine forces were not able to halt the Lombard invasion into northern Italy, nor to contain the Lombards through their recruitment as *foederati* (Guillou and Bulgarella 1988: 279–81). When the Lombards swept into Campania in 570, they encountered a strongly fortified territory around Naples, whilst much of the inland territory seems to have offered relatively little resistance.[48] Indeed, archaeology suggests that many of the inland settlements were already in severe economic decline by this time. Only *Beneventum* may still have been of some substance, having perhaps been refortified not long before; though it may have held a fifth column of Lombards, originally serving the Byzantine garrison (Rotili 1986).[49] The monastery of Monte Cassino, half-way between Rome and Naples, was sacked and abandoned around the year 580. At the

close of the following year, Naples was attacked for the first time. Shortly afterwards, during the early years of the reign of Emperor Maurice (582–602), a supreme command was established at Ravenna, effectively initiating the exarchate. *Nuceria*, controlling the Sarno valley and the principal route into southern Campania, fell to the first Lombard attack in 593. Capua probably fell the year after, when the clergy fled to Naples (Greg. *Ep.* V. 14, 27). Lombard occupation of most of what is now the province of Caserta, right down to the coast, as well as the effective abandonment of Formia in 590, practically cut off all secure land routes between Naples, Rome and Ravenna. This undoubtedly led to a further strengthening of strategic Byzantine ports such as Anzio, Terracina, Gaeta, Naples, Amalfi and Salerno (to cite those along the central Tyrrhenian coast), upon which much of Byzantium's residual power in Italy by then depended (Schmiedt 1978a). Around Naples, it seems that *Misenum* and *Puteoli* were fortified. The contested Lombard–Byzantine frontier towns of *Nola* and *Atella* also must have been garrisoned (see below, Chapter 5).[50]

All this activity can only have strengthened Naples's position as a leading Byzantine stronghold. Until the time of Gregory the Great, local bishops had often attended to military affairs. The intervention of the Church in both civil and military affairs is a characteristic of much of the period under consideration. The secular authorities did not always view this as an infringement of prerogatives. There were often close ties between the various institutions, later reinforced by blood relationships such that at times duke and bishop were embodied in one man, and individual competencies frequently were blurred.

It has been noted already that, in 598, the local ecclesiastical authorities had attempted to usurp responsibility over the gates and aqueduct of Naples, when Maurentius was *magister militum*. This might suggest that Byzantine military presence in the city was so weak that the local bishop sensed insecurity and attempted personally to make repair. Indeed, in 592 Gregory had urged the Emperor Maurice and the exarch to send a duke

[47] If nothing else, a lucrative system of state supply may have been damaged. For the abundant archaeological evidence for trade in this period see below, Chapter 6.

[48] It is a mute point as to whether *Beneventum* was part of Campania or of Samnium at this time. See Thomsen 1947: 251–2.

[49] See Bognetti 1967: 457. Whether or not *Beneventum* was actually a Byzantine duchy, founded prior to the Lombard 'invasion', is impossible to say. For the confused period and the differing views of scholars see the good synthesis by Fonseca (1990). I should like to thank Chris Wickham for his view of the matter.

[50] The areas around Rome and the Byzantine duchy of Perugia were similarly strengthened by the fortification of a whole series of small towns (Llewellyn 1975: 112).

(*dux*) or military governor to Naples. This may have resulted in the appointment of Maurentius, who appears to have been a landowner in Sicily and a member of the Roman senatorial aristocracy, with a brother in the pope's monastery on the Caelian hill in Rome (von Falkenhausen 1992: 16). In the meantime, Gregory felt obliged to confer exceptional powers of *custodia civitatis* on a tribune, Constantinus (Greg. *Ep.* II. 34, 45). That it was amongst the functions of the *magister militum* to give shipping licences (*licentia navigandi*), as he had been requested to do for the son of the *vir magnificus Domitius*, is surely also an indication of the increasing military role of the sea (Greg. *Ep.* IX. 160). During the Gothic War, the port already housed part of the Byzantine flotilla. The strength of the fleet seems to have survived well into the ninth century, if not later, as its intervention proved decisive against the Arabs at the battle of Ostia in 849 (*Lib. Pont.* II. 118 (*Leo IV*); John the Deacon, *Gesta Ep. Neap.* 433). It was by then, however, quite clearly under the direct command of the duke and not of any Byzantine official.

The first attested duke of Naples was Guduin, in 603, though a certain Gudeliscus had already been instated as *dux Campaniae* by 600 (Greg. *Ep.* IX. 17).[51] If the order is correct, it may be suggested that the change in titles from *magister militum* to *dux Campaniae* and then to *dux Neapolim*, at the beginning of the seventh century, reflects both an increase in power of the military commander and a belated realization that Byzantine territory in Campania had now become effectively an enclave centred on Naples. It has been argued alternatively that Gregory's prompting for the appointment of a duke was due to the fact that the seat was vacant, whilst the role in effect had already been created during the Byzantine administrative reorganization of Italy under the Emperors Tiberius II (578–582) and Maurice (582–602) (Luzzati Laganà 1982).

Very little is known about the high command until Basilius was nominated duke in 661/662. During a brief moment of instability, caused by the assassination of the exarch, a certain John of Conza (*Compsa*), perhaps a count, took power in Naples in 616–617, proclaiming himself emperor. He was rapidly brought to justice by the new exarch (Paul.

Diac. *Hist. Lang.* IV. 34; *Lib. Pont.* I. 319; Cassandro 1969: 36).[52] A certain Anatolius seems to have governed the city during the pontificate of Honorius I (625–638).[53] Basilius himself was perhaps nominated by the exarch, though his position was confirmed directly by the Emperor Constans II during his visit to Naples in 663, as one of a series of reforms (von Falkenhausen 1992: 17–18). Indeed, at the same time, a mint was established, perhaps because of increasing difficulties in wage supply, and the local garrison was probably strengthened. There were certainly enough men stationed in the city to join forces with Istrian troops when the need arose to defeat the murderers of the emperor in Syracuse in 668. Later, the economic base that ensured the upkeep of the Neapolitan militia was created through assignment of land plots that no longer depended on any great centralized system of taxation, accountancy and payment (Wickham 1988b: 108).

INDEPENDENCE

By the mid-seventh century civic power in the city had passed squarely to the duke and his armed forces. Later on, political power was, on occasion, also strengthened by the joining in one man of the two titles of duke and bishop, as under Athanasius II at the end of the ninth century. The duke controlled his territory through *praefecti* or tribunes and *comites* (counts), the latter apparently serving above all as military commanders of the *castra* and their lands.[54] At *Puteoli* a *palatium comitis* is attested, whilst, in 840, Sergius I was able to pass from being count of *Cumae* to duke of Naples (see below, Chapter 5).

Prior to Neapolitan autonomy, nominations to high posts seem to have been made by the exarch in Ravenna, though 'court' titles continued to be granted by Constantinople well into the later eighth century. In 721, Theodore was both duke of Naples and *hypatos*. Later, the assignation of Byzantine titles was rare. Duke Gregory was nominated imperial *patrikios* for his participation in the campaign against the Arabs near the river Garigliano in 915. In 973 Duke Marinus bore the title of *anthypatos patrikios* (von Falkenhausen

---

[51] For Guduin see Greg. *Ep.* XIV. 10, for Gudeliscus, *Ep.* X. 5. See also Jones 1964: 313. It is interesting to note that neither of these two dukes appear from their names to be from Roman or Greek families, and it has been suggested that they were Lombard (Brown 1984: 72–3).

[52] There is some uncertainty as to whether the *kastron Kampsa* mentioned by George of Cyprus for 549 is to be identified with modern Conza. See Zanini 1998: 253, n. 127, 275, n. 207.

[53] On Anatolius see Brown 1984: 54, n. 31.

[54] See Cassandro's (1969: 200, 202) examination of titles under the duchy.

1978a: 37). The great power delegated to the dukes by Constantinople stimulated the growth of a new provincial aristocracy. In Asia Minor, this led to the rise of an evermore powerful landed military class that could claim a great deal of autonomy from the central administration and build up enough wealth and influence to be able to seize power, as under Alexius Comnenus (Ostrogorsky 1968: 317–18; Harvey 1989: 3). In Naples, a similar process eventually led to separatism.

A certain measure of western autonomy may be seen from the time of the Lombard invasions, for the simple reason that the East could spare little military aid and finance with more pressing problems to resolve in the Balkan peninsula. This negligence in respect to western possessions undoubtedly helped the energetic Pope Gregory the Great (590–604) to reach the pinnacle of political power, even though he was a loyal supporter of a united Roman Empire. It may be said that Naples at this time, though formally dependent on Constantinople, was substantially dependent on Rome, a fact clearly evinced from Gregory's correspondence. This is despite the fact that Emperor Maurice established the exarchates of both Ravenna and Carthage, investing the exarchs with joint civil and military authority over their respective territories. The creation of the two exarchates appears to have been stimulated, respectively, by the Lombard invasion of Italy and the Berber incursions in north Africa, as well as the difficulty of the central administration in coping with such far-flung possessions.[55] The Persian invasions of Syria and Palestine during the early seventh century, by keeping Byzantium occupied, did little to foster close links between the East and West, which were only temporarily repaired with the policy of Emperor Constans II. Though harsh towards Rome and the papacy, which were in open disagreement with the imperial monothelite heresy, he seems to have been lenient in his fiscal policy towards the Byzantine possessions in southern Italy and Sicily, where he had entertained the idea of establishing his capital.[56]

The precise occasion of Naples's move to autonomy is a matter of dispute and, indeed, it was probably a somewhat gradual process. However, a moment may be searched for when the city went its own political way. Capasso placed undue emphasis on the nomination of

Basilius as duke in 661/662 (*MND* I: 30–1). This is quite obviously too early, as the duke was no more than a high official in the Byzantine public service and the city may be seen to continue following eastern polity for some time afterwards. Cassandro, and more recently Luzzati Laganà and Russo Mailler, have seen autonomy as an event of the ninth century (Casssandro 1969; Luzzati Laganà 1982; Russo Mailler 1988: 356). Indeed, it was only in the ninth century that the eastern capital eventually accepted Naples's autonomy, though in this there was far more form than substance. *De facto*, the city probably broke away from the East under Duke Stephen II, not long after the fall of Ravenna to Aistulf in 751 (Brown 1984: 140–2, 161–2).

In the early eighth century Naples was still a formal Byzantine territorial possession. Between 723 and 724 Pope Gregory II refused to support a tax census with which the eastern government, under Leo III Isauricus, would probably have further despoiled the Church and Roman territories. An unsuccessful attempt on the pope's life, followed by retaliation with the assassination of the Exarch Paul, led the emperor to send a new exarch, Eutichius, with the express mission of eliminating the pope. Eutichius landed in Naples, obviously considered a secure haven, though his mission was to fail. Later, in 732, the emperor was able to effectively seize papal possessions by transferring the provinces of Sicily, Calabria, Terra d'Otranto, Greece and Dalmatia to the jurisdiction of the eastern patriarch. Much of what may have remained nominally dependent on Saint Peter's, outside of the territory of Rome, in fact seems to have been fiscally dependent on Byzantium.[57]

With the fall of Ravenna, Naples's government was made to depend upon the *strategos* resident at Syracuse in Sicily, as is witnessed by a deed of location drawn up in Naples in 763 in favour of Duke Stephen II (755–766) (von Falkenhausen 1992: 21). Indeed, Stephen had initially acted in accord with the policy of the eastern government, even over the thorny problem of iconoclasm, despite a measure of local opposition. However, also in 763, he acknowledged the ecclesiastical supremacy of the iconodulist pope, and effective independence may have begun with this act. Such a volte-face seems to be marked by the substitution of the imperial effigy on coin types with that of the

[55] On the exarchate of Ravenna see Diehl 1888, which is fundamental; Brown 1984: 48–53; Guillou and Bulgarella 1988: 19–24.
[56] On monotheletism and its effect on east–west relationships see Haldon 1990: 297–317.
[57] Much of this has been discussed recently by Marazzi (1991).

patron saint Ianuarius or the monogram ST. This may have helped smooth his irregular election to the episcopate following the death of Bishop Paul in 768, as his nomination was promptly confirmed by the pope, thus further distancing the city from the Byzantine patriarch and the state (von Falkenhausen 1978a: 11). It is doubtful if Stephen's political stance would have been considered acceptable to the eastern Empire until at least 775, with the accession of Emperor Leo IV. It is likewise doubtful that the iconclast party in Naples had much say in the matter (Gay 1904: 17–18). Furthermore, if the coin type depicting Saint Ianuarius was, in any way, official tender, it is doubtful whether the Byzantine government would have accepted it without the reigning emperor's effigy. Further indication of Naples's autonomy seems to be given by the fact that the contemporary archbishops' seals bore Latin, and not Greek, legends, though ducal seals remained Greek (Laurent 1962: 5.1, nos. 918–19). The fact that the system of dating all official documents remained firmly based on the years of the reigning Byzantine emperor was probably dictated more by tradition and convenience than anything else (Garzya 1976: 8).

The reasons for a fairly rapid assertion of autonomy may be seen as a defensive measure during a period of rapid change in the political set up of the Italian peninsula. With the fall of Byzantine Ravenna in 751, the balance of power in Italy started to shift from Byzantium to the expanding Carolingian state. As northern Italy was under pressure from the Franks, the duchy of Benevento grasped the opportunity to assert a greater measure of independence. In 757, Desiderius, king of the Lombards, attacked Duke Liutprand of Benevento, who had been scheming with Pipin, king of the Franks. Liutprand fled to Byzantine Otranto, where he was accorded refuge. To ensure that Liutprand could not attempt a comeback, Desiderius met the representative of Emperor Constantine V in Naples in 758, to obtain the assistance of the Sicilian fleet in capturing Liutprand, in return for which Otranto was to remain a Byzantine possession (Corsi and Fonseca 1989). Clearly Naples still felt Byzantine at this early date.

By 774, the Lombard kingdom had fallen to Charlemagne, who was crowned king at Pavia. Benevento, under Arechis II (758–787), thus became the capital of the sole remaining Lombard state in Italy, with territorial possessions that included most of Apulia and a good part of Calabria. Arechis, having assumed the title of *princeps* as a clear declaration of pretensions against Frankish supremacy, proved to be a most

powerful and effective monarch, of whom both Naples and Pope Hadrian I were justifiably wary. He extended the urban defences of Benevento, perhaps partly to host Lombard refugees who had fled from the papal and Byzantine territories to the north, and erected a *palatium* and the palatine church of Santa Sofia as regal symbols, modestly imitating the seat of the Byzantine emperors. Benevento even assumed Byzantine forms of national dress and grooming, doing away with the typical Lombard beards, perhaps in an attempt to appear more acceptable, if not legitimate, to the eyes of the eastern Empire, from which protection could be sought (*Codex Carolinus* LXXXIII. 617.5–31). Under his reign the erstwhile Neapolitan *castrum* and port of Salerno was revitalized so as to function as Benevento's outlet to the sea. This emphasized Benevento's desire to be part of a revived mediterranean network and, indeed, laid the foundations for Salerno's subsequent growth as an autonomous trading power. None the less, though relations between Benevento and Naples were forever strained, attempts were made to lessen the strain from time to time, as is indicated by a revealing treaty, signed between Arechis and Duke Gregory II around 786, regarding valuable agricultural land that was effectively held in common.

During this entire period, beginning with the Arab sieges of Constantinople in 674–678 and 717–718, the presence of the Empire in the East cannot have been greatly felt by western possessions, and particularly by such small territories as Naples, which was encircled by hostile and aggressive powers. In Brown's words, 'consciousness of belonging to the empire waned', and few people in Naples actually would have seen Ravenna, let alone Byzantium (Brown 1984: 163). It should come as no suprise that the city often turned not to Byzantium but to the papal state or the Carolingians for matters of security.

A significant aspect of Neapolitan autonomy from the eastern government was the unabashed creation of an hereditary 'monarchy' under Stephen II, who came to power in 755. His dynasty lasted 77 years, whilst that initiated by Duke Sergius in 840 lasted some 300 years, virtually to the end of the duchy (Skinner 1995: 48, 85, fig. 2.4). Under Byzantium the title of *dux* had been regarded as that of an office of military command, originally on active campaign, and was not hereditary, unlike lesser offices, which were likely to be seen as burdens (Diehl 1888: 141–56; Hartmann 1889: 56–7; Brown 1984: 53–6).

Naples's political autonomy was also expressed by a number of events that took place during the first half of the ninth century. In 812, on the occasion of a Muslim assault on Sicily, the city refused to supply a contingent to the eastern Byzantine fleet deployed in counter-attacks, despite the fact that in the same year the Neapolitan island of Ischia was also sacked (Cilento 1989: 101). In 836, the city requested Muslim aid against the Lombards and perhaps, in 842/843, furnished help to Sicilian Muslims in capturing Byzantine Messina. This stance may have been germane to developing commercial ties with the Muslim world. However, when Emperor Basil I (867–886) strove to reconquer southern Italy in the latter half of the 870s, Naples bowed to eastern power. The action, meant to establish the theme of *Langouvardia* as a bulwark against the Muslims in Sicily and their Bulgar allies in the Balkan Peninsula, originally had been requested by Pope John VIII, after appeals for help to the Carolingians had come to no avail. Indeed, for very brief moments, as in 885–886, Naples rejoined the sphere of Byzantium (Toynbee 1973: 277–8). The reigning Duke and Bishop Athanasius II struck coins in the name of Emperor Basil, something that had not happened since Emperor Leo III, over 100 years earlier. The first mention of the new theme comes in 892, the year after the capture of Benevento, when Emperor Basil's general, Symbatikios, was given the title *stratigos Macedonie, Tracie, Cephalonie atque Langibardie*. It was intended to comprise Lombard territory rejoined to the Empire though, according to the *De administrando imperio*, written by Constantine Porphyrogenitus between 948 and 952, it included the then independent duchies of Naples, Gaeta and Amalfi. Naples's political opportunism, however, was checked but briefly by the immediate and uncomfortable presence of eastern Byzantine troops on Italian soil after a period of 200 years.

Indeed, after the Neapolitan attack on Byzantine *Sipontum* in 949, the *strategos* of Calabria and *Langouvardia*, Marianos Argiros, with an eastern expeditionary force, had to block the port of Naples in 956 to bring the city once again under nominal Byzantine suzerainty (Fig. 1:7) (von Falkenhausen 1978a: 39).[58] On the evidence of a Greek text, the action conducted by the forces of Constantine Porphyrogenitus was

Fig. 1:7. Duke John III (928–969), on the throne during the brief period of the Byzantine reconquest of Naples (Cod. 4, f. 196v., Cava dei Tirreni).

provoked by the city's politics of strategic compromise with the Saracens and its consequent distancing from Byzantine foreign policy. This may be so, and the aborted Saracen siege of Naples in 958 might be viewed as a reaction. A Byzantine sea-force armed with 'Greek fire' had apparently been sent to the aid of Naples, though did not see any action as, in the meantime, the city had been able to buy off the Arabs with the cathedral treasure, later recovered (Cassandro 1969: 162–4). Both attempts at Byzantine reconquest were none the less ephemeral, and Naples continued to forge its own way in history (Fig. 1:8).

---

[58] See also the cautionary attitude of Cassandro (1969: 165).

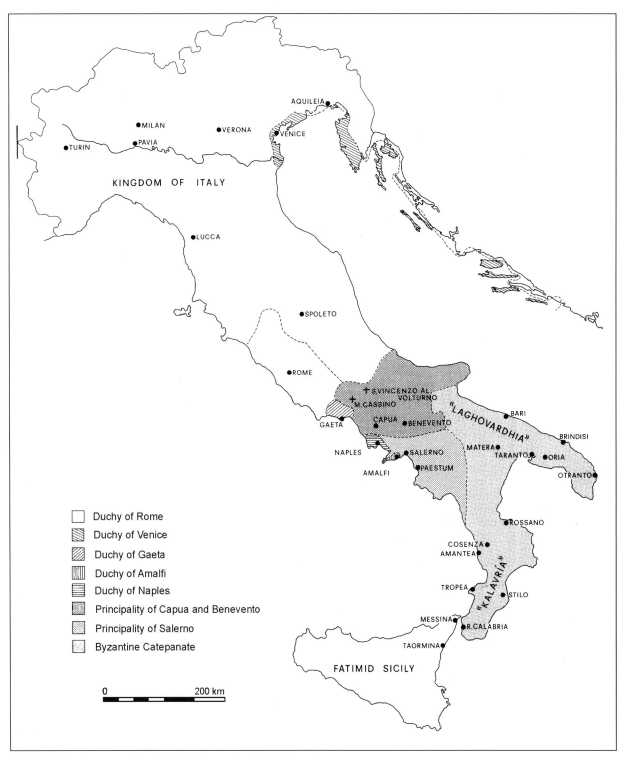

Fig. 1:8. Italy around AD 1000 (drawn by Sally Cann).

Thus, effective independence is probably to be assigned to the mid-eighth century, after almost a century of neglect by the eastern authorities, occupied in staving off the Arab menace.[59] Autonomous rule, which had lasted quite singularly for some 500 years, ended only with the arrival of the Normans in 1140. It is often said that the present character of both the city and its inhabitants was conditioned by the subjection to foreign powers of the second millennium; but, as will be made clearer in the following pages, sure foundations for the future were laid by the independent duchy.

[59] I find it hard to accept Toynbee's view (1973: 277) of increasing independence being datable as late as the reign of Empress Eirene (797–802), even if the East was reluctant to admit to the state of affairs that had come about.

2

SOCIAL TRANSFORMATION

POPULATION

One of the major debates about the mediterranean 'dark ages' concerns the question of populations. As early medieval contexts are rare compared to earlier centuries, the question has been raised of whether or not the population generally declined in number with respect to Roman times, or if people simply changed their settlement pattern so drastically as to leave us with the impression of depopulation in both town and country. Needless to say, the available evidence, both textual and archaeological, is not satisfactory, and it has been possible to argue either way according to one's own particular historical perspective (Moreland 1993). Although my own view is that the weight of the evidence demonstrates a decline, it is also now irrefutable that settlement distribution changed drastically over the second half of the first millennium. By the end of the millennium, when the mist began to rise, Italy is characterized by a plethora of village communities unlike anything that had been seen before.

The material evidence for population in Naples is to some extent similar to that for some other Italian towns. Whilst some were clearly abandoned, major late Roman towns continued to be occupied, witnessing some form of continuity throughout the early Middle Ages. Naples is one of the latter, and is to be ranked at the top end of the settlement scale, alongside such sites as Rome, Milan and Syracuse, as this study will demonstrate. Indeed, I am not so sure that Naples's population did decline significantly during late antiquity, and, moreover, its political and economic sphere of influence actually increased when compared to

classical times. That is not to say that overall population figures in the bay of Naples did not regress. Indeed, there is clear evidence of substantial shrinkage for the satellite towns of *Cumae*, *Misenum*, *Puteoli* and *Nola*, with no signs of corresponding growth in the countryside (see below, Chapter 4). However, both documentary and material evidence confirm substantial settlement continuity in the city.

The development of open spaces within the town walls, used as orchards or rubbish dumps, and the evidence for the abandonment of suburban areas, such as Santa Maria la Nova or the baths at Santa Chiara, may be used to argue population decline. At the same time, intramural living patterns changed. Large Roman *domus*, such as those known from *Pompeii*, were broken down into smaller domestic units. However, the quantity of rubbish produced in Naples during late antique and early medieval times, and regularly encountered in excavations, suggests that the surviving populace was by no means small. Indeed, the quantity of pottery from excavated sites is much larger than that of Roman times, though much of this must be accounted for by the fact that from the fifth to the eighth centuries urban rubbish was often deposited within the shells of abandoned buildings within the walls, instead of being discarded outside the walls.

It is hard to escape the conclusion that population decline set in from the time of the late Empire, though Naples may have been less affected than other areas. The Gothic War, which dragged on for twenty years, together with the devastating plague that broke out in 541, was perhaps the last straw, leading to desertion of many Roman towns and their decline to little more than village status.[1]

---

[1] It is very hard to judge the effects that a plague may have had on a population, and much will depend upon the nature of the population itself and its means for recovery. In some cases this could be fast, as has been suggested for Wharram Percy, where total recovery of the village could have taken place within twenty years of the Black Death (Hurst 1984: 102). Whilst I might agree with Whittow (1996: 66–8) in playing down its effects in the sixth-century Near East, perhaps largely because of a buoyant economy and demographic recovery rate, I am less convinced as regards Italy. For probable plague victims from Venosa see Macchiarelli and Salvadei 1989.

Procopius could remark that 'Italy has become everywhere more destitute of men than Libya' (*Anecdota* XVIII. 13). The causes of the demographic crisis are complex. Apart from wars and plagues, we may consider higher infant mortality, lowering of the average life-span, poorer nutrition and monastic celibacy, and we know little regarding fertility at the time.[2]

The problem of relative changes in population figures in Naples may be addressed by establishing average floor area *per capita* figures, albeit with all the limitations that this method possesses. Naroll calculated the population of prehistoric settlements as being in the order of one tenth of the floor area in square metres (Naroll 1962).[3] Our own calculations begin with the examination of the walled settlement of Naples. Emanuele Greco has suggested that the Greek *polis* was planned around a maximum of 7,000 to 8,000 inhabitants within the walled area, which was about 72 ha by the fourth century BC (Greco 1986: 215–16). This yields an average of around 100 people per hectare, or an average living area of 100 m² per person. On the basis of Naroll's equation, Naples could have held as many as 72,000 people. However, from this it is necessary to remove areas occupied by roads, squares, public buildings and other places such as *atria*, gardens and orchards. In Roman times this may have been as high as 50%, which would leave a total living area of 36 ha and a maximum population figure of 36,000, though this seems quite large.[4] The only clear figure relevant to early medieval population is the total of 126 priests and deacons of the city mentioned by Pope Gregory (*Reg.* XI. 22). Even if we imagine a low ratio of one priest to 100 members of the rest of the population, we would obtain a total of 12,600 inhabitants for the city and its immediate hinterland at a date not long before what was probably the lowpoint in its population.

Arnaldo Venditti indicated the middle of the eighth century as the beginning of a demographic revival, though various later writers would shift this moment later, to the tenth century (Venditti 1967: 468; and, for example, Wickham 1994: 745). I do not believe that sufficient evidence yet exists to be able to pinpoint a precise moment in which the demographic revival started. If, however, economic revival may be used as an indicator, then we may note that the eighth century witnessed the lowest point in ecclesiastical construction in Naples, and that afterwards building expanded once again.[5]

I would venture that Naples's population fluctuated between 10,000 and 20,000 during the course of the second half of the first millennium. These figures might also seem appropriate when compared to estimates for the city's later growth. Jules Beloch, on the basis of an Angevin document, estimated a population for Naples of between 25,000 and 30,000 around 1278, when Naples had started to expand beyond its walls (Beloch 1937). Cesare De Seta agreed on 30,000 to 36,000 by the fourteenth century (De Seta 1981: 63). In 1547 Naples had a population of 212,103, or a tenth of the total for southern Italy, which would suggest an increase in births, coupled with immigration. The sixteenth-century figures are the first to seem well-founded and add weight to relatively high figures in earlier times. On these figures it has been calculated that there was an average of 150–200 people per hectare before the Black Death in the fourteenth century (Russell 1985: 198–9).

Of course, these calculations provide very crude estimates indeed. Rome's population is frequently cited as being around 1,000,000 at the time of Augustus and 500,000 under the reign of Diocletian. Krautheimer would have it dropping to 30,000 to 40,000 by the seventh to eighth centuries.[6] If we see Naples as possessing a smaller population than Rome, which is hard to dispute, then a 10,000 to 20,000 estimate, perhaps closer to the bottom end of the scale, may not be far off the mark.

---

[2] The standard work on Roman population decline is Boak 1955, though it should be read in conjunction with its review by Finley (1958). On the poverty of peasants and mortality see Jones 1964: 1044.

[3] It is worth noting a possible correspondence between his calculations and the fact that the average floor space of early medieval houses in Salerno was of 50 m² which, if divided by the average family of five, would give us his order of 10 m² per person. The average family of five is calculated with reference to several tax census figures available for later medieval and post-medieval Campania, which give both numbers of hearths (*fuochi*) and numbers of inhabitants in various areas.

[4] Camodeca (1981: 75) suggested between 15,000 to 18,000 and 21,000 to 25,000 inhabitants for fourth-century *Puteoli*, when the number may have been on the wane when compared to late Republican/early Imperial times.

[5] This pattern appears similar to Rome (Delogu 1988). If conditions were once more stable, if not developing, then population would presumably have increased.

[6] On the late Roman city see Barnish 1987: 162–4; Février 1993: 45. On early medieval Rome see Krautheimer 1980: 291–2; Hodges (1993a: 356–7) ventured 5,000, which seems incredibly low.

The drop in population figures through late Roman and early medieval times might have released almost three-quarters of the inhabited space to alternative functions, such as intramural agriculture, which, as we shall see, was a fairly common feature of the early medieval city.

We may also question what proportion of the population actually lived within the walls. The meagre evidence available indicates that there was no substantial suburban settlement after the Empire, and that people living outside Naples tended to group together in *castra*, or in the various villages attested in the sources from the ninth century onwards (see below, Chapter 5). Beloch has estimated some 4,000,000 people in Italy around 700, with the south possessing no more than 750,000 to 800,000 (Beloch 1937). In accepting these figures, Galasso suggested that they may be broken down into some 150,000 to 160,000 families which, divided into the present area of 70,000 km^2 for southern Italy, would give a mean average of two families per km^2 (calculated on families of five) (Galasso 1982: 16–18).[7] When the nucleated settlements are taken into account to absorb their due quota, the rural density figure would drop even more. It may also be suggested that in the seventh century very few people cared to live scattered in the open country, or, if they did, they are proving quite elusive archaeologically. The surviving 'urban' nuclei, providing relative security, were agro-towns *par excellence*, which becomes immediately clear on reading Erchempert's tale of the sack of Capua in 884, when the entire populace, including the aristocracy, had left the walls to harvest the vineyards (Erchempert, *MGH, Historia Langobardorum Beneventanorum*: chapter 56). This, in turn, may be corroborative evidence for low population figures, incapable of sustaining a significant non-agrarian social group.

In sum, although there is not enough evidence to warrant much more than an inspired guess at actual figures, the various calculations all tend to indicate that Naples possessed a fairly substantial population and that the countryside was relatively depopulated. Why should this be so?

From the late Empire onwards, immigrants and refugees apparently arrived in Naples at various times, at least temporarily augmenting the population. The Vandal invasion of *Africa Proconsularis* and *Byzacena* in 429 drove to flight such distinguished personages as Quodvultdeus, bishop of Carthage, who had settled in Naples, and probably represents the tip of a small yet significant iceberg (Jones 1964: 1059–60; see also below, Chapter 4). Other immigrations, from the Byzantine East, followed the iconoclast movement of the eighth century. Local demographic shifts also took place. According to Landulph Sagax, writing in the tenth–eleventh centuries, during the Gothic War Belisarius's sack of the city led to the need to repopulate it, bringing in people from the surrounding territory: *Cumae, Puteoli, Liburia, Chiaia, Sola, Piscinola, Trocchia, Somma, Surrentum, Stabiae, Nola* and elsewhere (Landulfi Sagacis, *Historia Romana* XVIII. 14 (Crivellucci 1913); Schipa 1931: 3; von Falkenhausen 1992: 10).[8] By Lombard times, many of these settlements had become virtually depopulated. Indeed, in 592 the sees of *Cumae* and *Misenum* were united, perhaps because of depopulation, whilst other settlements disappear from the records (Jones 1964: 312).

What evidence we have also indicates that early medieval Naples possessed an extremely varied citizen-body, composed of natives, Greeks of all sorts, northern European peoples (including Goths and Lombards), African refugees and sufficient Jews for there to have been a synagogue.[9] Naples, ever since her foundation in the early fifth century BC, had been an unusual city in Italy, maintaining Greek administrative rights and a stable eastern population. Much of this mixture was also due to the town's role in mediterranean trade and its proximity to the cosmopolitan port of *Puteoli*, though, undoubtedly, the later movements of the 'migration period' helped further variegate the ethnic composition of the citizen-body.

The Vandal invasion of north Africa may have led to an influx of Mauretanian Jews, such as those attested in the fifth-century funerary inscriptions found at Corso Malta, to the northeast of the city (Serrao 1989: with bibliography), where clearly was a Jewish cemetery. It yielded a funerary inscription attesting to a certain Benjamin, head of the Hebrew community (Serrao 1989: 105–6;

---

[7] Lizier (1907: 71) also proposed a figure of ten inhabitants per km^2. Lower figures have been estimated globally for sixth-century England (two inhabitants per km^2), Germany (2.2) and Gaul (5.5) (Duby 1975: 16).

[8] There is doubt as to the truth of this source (Cuozzo and Martin 1995: 9).

[9] Much work is still to be done on the composition of the Neapolitan populace. See, however, Cracco Ruggini 1964; Palmieri 1981; 1982.

Miranda 1995: 117–18). In 536, during the Gothic War, the Jews were called upon to guarantee that Naples would not be short of victuals, presumably in their capacity as merchants (Proc. *Bell. Goth.* V. viii. 41). By 984 there was at least one synagogue (R. 243) and possibly three Jewish quarters in the town, suggesting that they formed a fairly substantial part of the populace. Their penetration of the hinterland is documented less well, though a Mirina presbytera is attested by a funerary inscription of the later fourth or fifth century from excavations at Nocera (Conticello De' Spagnolis 1993).

It is likewise difficult to judge the importance of the Greek component of the citizen-body. Some immigration is recorded. The iconoclast movement led to the arrival of monks, amongst whom might be counted Constans, patron saint of Capri. Other monks seem to have fled Calabria and Lucania on account of the Arab raids on southern Italy in the later tenth century, augmenting the populations of Greek monasteries such as San Sergio e Bacco (Luzzati Laganà 1982: 751–2).

However, apart from the influx of Greeks during early medieval times, evidence shows continuity in Greek cultural patterns from very early times. Though many official Roman inscriptions were in Greek, Latin became increasingly common under the Empire. Graffiti in the catacombs of San Gennaro are mainly in Latin, and this was the language of Church liturgy. There is some evidence that when Naples depended upon Byzantium, Greek was used. Of the few monumental inscriptions, the two eighth-century examples published by Capasso are in Greek, including the funerary epitaph of Theodore (719–730), duke prior to Neapolitan autonomy. Later inscriptions are usually in Latin, although sometimes employing Greek characters. Members of the leading families were often bilingual and, in over 200 tenth-century documents examined, a third were written in Latin with Greek characters (*MND* II: 215; Mazzoleni 1973; von Falkenhausen 1978b: 88–90; Luzzati Laganà 1982).

A fairly consistent group of Armenians must also have been present by the ninth century, when their national saint, Gregory the Armenian, was included in the town calendar, together with their martyrs Hripsimé and Gayiané. By 921, an important monastery bore Gregory's name. The influx of Armenians could date to early Byzantine times. They were present in the army of the exarch at Ravenna as a *numerus Armeniorum* by the end of the sixth century, whilst others accompanied Constans II on his visit to Italy, including his assassin and usurper Mzezh or Mezezius.[10] Alongside Armenians, we may count a minority group of Bulgars, attested by 1003 (D'Amico 1935: 45–6). Furthermore, at least one resident Syrian *naukleros* is also known in Naples by 536, though doubtless he was not the only Syrian in the city (Proc. *Bell. Goth.* V. viii. 21).

Lombards also seem to have been integrated into Neapolitan society. However, the reverse, an influx of Neapolitans into Lombard territory, does not appear to have been of great significance. Political motivations aside, Naples, as in more recent times, may have been viewed as a powerful and wealthy metropolis to many dwellers of the Campanian hinterlands and acted as a magnet. Onomastic studies suggest that Lombard presence, from Benevento, Capua, Caserta and Salerno, was a constant in Neapolitan territory, and there is absolutely no evidence to indicate profound anti-Lombard sentiments within Neapolitan society. Quite the reverse is true. Families, or at least names, of 'Byzantine' and Lombard origin quite freely intermixed.[11] Doubtless it was integration that helped to produce essentially similar material cultures in Lombard, Byzantine and formerly erstwhile Byzantine territories. This is particularly indicated by ceramics throughout much of Italy, which cannot easily be affixed cultural or ethnic labels after the initial moment of the Lombard invasions (Arthur and Patterson 1994). Typical Lombard stamped pottery is absent in southern Italy, and has a short life span even in the north of the peninsula, dating to the first generation of invaders. Indeed, 'Lombard' pottery at Benevento is similar to 'Byzantine' pottery produced in Neapolitan territory, both deriving from a Roman tradition, suggesting a common artisanal background and milieu.[12] In fact, the greater proportion of the labour force in Lombard territory was probably composed of the pre-invasion population, until such a time as social integration had taken place between the local peoples and the new

[10] For the calendar, see Mallardo 1974; Fonseca 1987: 216–17. Narses and the exarch Shak (624–644) were also of Armenian origin.
[11] On *Liburia* see below, Chapter 5. Wickham (1981) has warned against too strong a division between Neapolitans and Lombards in analyses of the area. On this see Palmieri 1981: 42–4; and Cassandro 1940, on integration in the countryside.
[12] On Beneventan pottery see Lupia 1998. On the whole question see also Arthur and Patterson 1994.

families. Only then could 'nationalistic' sentiments develop to divide the population of the Lombard south from that of Byzantine areas, whatever the various ethnic origins may have been.

The presence of an Arab community, dating to at least the second half of the eleventh century, is attested by three tombstones. Two of these were discovered in 1903, in Via del Vasto, immediately to the northeast of Castel Capuano, and seem to have been *in situ* (Nallino 1941; Scerrato 1967: 150–1, 153, 156–7). They suggest that the community may have been located in the eastern part of the city, perhaps just outside the walls in the area now known as the Duchesca, interestingly now also a centre for Muslim immigrants. There is no clear evidence as to when the first Arabs settled in Naples, though this is likely to have been from the ninth century at least, when the city began to enter into commercial relationships with the Maghreb. Some Aghlabids were certainly admitted to Neapolitan territory in the 880s by Athanasius II, though probably more for strategic than commercial reasons, and they were soon expunged. By the early ninth century Arabs would appear to have established themselves in the nearby territory of Salerno, according to the charters (Kreutz 1991: 52).

With such an ethnically assorted citizen-body, with diverse interests and allegiances, it is by no means surprising that the city could entertain vacillating political and economic positions after her break away from Byzantium. National sentiment could more easily be identified with a feeling of *neapolitanitas* rather than one of *romanitas* towards the eastern Empire; however, individual group sentiments were probably even stronger, most notably amongst the Jewish and Arab communities.[13]

Modern Naples seems very much to be an agglomeration of individual communities, as though various villages have been welded together, and is marked by parochialism. This is reinforced paradoxically by both the Camorra and the Church. An individual is, indeed, 'protected' within his community, as though part of an extended family. How much this may be traced back through time is difficult to say, and it is doubtful that archaeology will be able to furnish a reply. None the less, it is possible that institutions such as the Graeco-Roman *fratrie* or the medieval *seggi* or *sedili*, or

indeed the churches themselves, helped to foster parochial sentiments in the past. The Jewish communities and other immigrant units appear to have been fairly cohesive, whilst the habit of extended families concentrating in specific areas or selected streets, and also as specific traders or artisans, is known for later medieval times and may have earlier origins. Old street- and place-names like Vico dei Panettieri or gli Orefici indicate the concentration of bakeries and goldsmiths respectively. At least in these cases, specific artefact distributions of bread ovens and crucibles may, in time, provide information as to the chronology and organization of activities within the walls.

SOCIAL STATUS

Amongst the criteria indicated for the definition of a town, particular significance has been attached to the condition that a significant proportion of adult labour be employed in non-agricultural sectors. In other words, the surplus produced by part of the community was large enough to maintain a substantial permanent workforce employed in the production of services and consumer goods.[14] It is clearly impossible to play with figures, though an idea of the significance of the subsidiary workforce perhaps may be gained through an analysis of the quantity and complexity of the non-agrarian professions recorded in the sources (see below, Chapter 6). Roman traditions in class structure, the need for local authorities that responded to central government, property value differentiation, as well as the conditions that permitted continuity of labour in non-agricultural sectors, including commerce, all helped to maintain a relatively articulated class structure within the territory of Naples.

Von Falkenhausen has examined the class structure of southern Italy. According to her, it was based on two separate traditions, Byzantine and Lombard (von Falkenhausen 1978a: 154–7). The Latin documents indicate division into *maiores*, *mediani* and *minores*. Their existence in Naples seems clearly stated in a document of Duke Sergius IV (*MND* II: 2, 157). On the basis of Italian texts, they would appear to reflect military capacity based on wealth. As late as 1021 the will of a certain Sergius of Amalfi, Neapolitan citizen, leaves all military gear and horses (*omnes armas et loricas et caballos cum illorum paraturiis*) to his

---

[13] Today's Neapolitan generally regards himself as first and foremost belonging to Naples. The state, identified politically in Rome and economically in Milan, has assumed the connotation of an external and oppressive force.

[14] It may be noted that, if there was a surplus, it was not through any natural process, but because it was required of society.

sons, so that they might fulfil their military obliga-
tions, presumably in accordance with the family's
social standing (Cassandro 1969: 154). The
maiores et potentes possessed horses and full
military gear, the *mediani* horses and light
armaments, whilst the *minores* (or *cunctus
populus*) had bows and arrows. The *maiores* also
included the bishop, whilst the *mediani* included
the greater part of the clergy.

The higher end of the social scale in Naples was
composed of both soldiers and clergy, the dukes,
bishops, their families and relations, as well as
large landowners, and it can be shown that these
families were frequently interlinked (for example,
Skinner 1994). Their power would seem to have
been based predominantly on landed wealth and
not on any direct involvement in trade, though the
use of middlemen might well obscure links
between wealth and commerce. This would
confirm a ruling-class mentality similar to the
Byzantine model. It may also help to explain why
Naples did not achieve the same sort of patently
obvious commercial success as Amalfi, Venice or
Genova, where power passed fairly and squarely
into the hands of local merchant venturers, with
little use of outside middlemen. It will be argued
that Naples made much use of Amalfitans and
other maritime traders, as in the last few centuries
she has made use of seafaring families from Torre
del Greco and Ischia.

Social dominance and élite status in the city
were symbolized perhaps first and foremost by
wealth display, in particular that of 'courtly'
ceremony, which had been passed down from late
antiquity. Use of the martial accoutrements of
warfare and hunting in status display seems to have
been of lesser importance, despite their use
amongst barbarian groups and in later medieval
times. This may perhaps reinforce the notion of
Naples's relatively non-aggressive polity in early
medieval times. Unlike other leading powers of
the day, élite status was also reinforced by a display
of culture.

Not only the clergy and monks, but also the lay
administration, appear to have been exceedingly
well-educated for the time, seemingly keeping
alive Naples's role as a centre of Greek culture.
Much was obviously mediated by the Church and
its schools, and a renowned monastic scriptorium
had already been established by the sixth century

(see below, Chapter 4). Athanasius II, both duke
and bishop, towards the end of the ninth century
commissioned the *Vita Athanasii*, a biography of
his uncle, Athanasius I, and personally translated
the *Passio Arethae*, or martyrdom of Saint Arethas.
He also encouraged John the Deacon to complete
the history of the bishops of Naples, from the time
of Stephen I down to his own reign. Another work
of John was the translation of the *Vita* of Saint
Nicholas, bishop of Mira, whose remains were
removed from Asia Minor to Bari in 1087. Paul the
Subdeacon, a further member of Athanasius's
group, sent his works to Charles the Bald, king of
the Franks, so testifying to the international repute
of Athanasius's literary circle (Gigante 1982: 618–
19).[15]

A century later, Duke John III possessed a
library so large that, it was said, the number of
books could not be counted. The archdeacon, Leo,
was probably commissioned by him and his wife,
Theodora, to copy further works, including Livy
and a history of Alexander the Great, whilst on a
political mission at Constantinople in 947 (Cary
1956; Frugoni 1969).[16] The Sergian dynasty,
which came to rule from the middle of the ninth
century, seems to have been effectively bilingual.
Duke Sergius I, his son the *magister militum*
Gregory and Bishop Stephen III could all read and
write both Greek and Latin (von Falkenhausen
1978a: 38–9; Fuiano 1986; also Garzya 1976: 11).
All this book production was a costly affair, and
perhaps a fair indicator of emerging capital by the
ninth century (for example, Mango 1980: 238).
Literary prowess was also displayed on various
funerary epitaphs. Towards the end of the ninth
century, Naples was one of the few significant
centres of Greek cultural and literary diffusion in
the West (Rabbow 1922: 60; cited by Gigante
1982: 618).

The movement of literary works also illustrates
how social standing and élite relationships were
reinforced by gift-exchange. The process seems
also to have involved the movement of costly
jewellery amongst the ruling classes, whilst the
production of gold objects seems to have been
controlled directly by the duke (see below, Chapter
6). Other items, such as silks, spices and perhaps
certain wines, also formed part of these mechan-
isms, and thus lay out of the realm of the ordinary
merchants' fare.

---

[15] On this Paul and his writings see Vuolo 1987.

[16] On the mission see also Cassandro 1969: 165–6. Bertelli (1978: 123) suggested that John's library in Naples followed the
model of John the Grammatician's library in Constantinople.

Though merchants were not considered highly within the Byzantine social structure, they played an important role in Naples's survival as an urban community, and a number of them became quite wealthy. The Jews, especially, seem to have done well out of commerce, often aided by their rather ambiguous political status.[17] They formed substantial communities in the early medieval city and are attested throughout Christendom and in leading Islamic centres. Yet it was not until after the first millennium that merchants became socially accepted by the upper class. Some had eventually paid their way to the top through their wealth, as has now been demonstrated so clearly for Gaeta (Skinner 1995).

It is particularly in the area of status and wealth display that archaeology may eventually play a leading role, and, in this context, cemetery evidence is badly needed. All that we possess for Naples so far, aside from scattered burials and a couple of unpublished cemeteries discussed below, are the burials in catacombs or the occasional church sepulchre. The catacombs are notably devoid of grave-goods, though *arcosolia*, painted or decorated with mosaics, were reserved for leading members of the clergy. Sepulchres in churches were again simple, though sometimes accompanied by elaborate epitaphs in the case of leading figures such as dukes or bishops, notable amongst which is that of the early ninth-century Duke Bonus at Santa Restituta. Their remains were often interred in reused Roman sarcophagi, such as those of the late fourth-century Bishop Maximus, placed beneath an altar with the inscription MAXIMVS.EPISCOPVS.QVI.ET.CONFESSOR in the cathedral, or the example that housed the spoils of Duke Theodore (Mallardo 1959; de Franciscis 1977). The practice continued well into later medieval times, implying a ready supply of Roman sarcophagi (Bridges and Ward-Perkins 1956).

HEALTH AND DIET

Information on the health and diet of the inhabitants of Naples is slowly beginning to emerge. Evidence for food consumption is based principally on animal bones, palaeobotanical remains and commercial amphorae from excavations within the city, as well as a number of documents, all of which

is discussed in Chapter 6. I shall not dwell on diet here, save to say that Naples was probably better-stocked than most other parts of southern Italy.[18] The importance of the settlement and its citizen-body was such that the Byzantine government and, later, the Church attempted to provide at least subsistence level supplies to the town. In 600 Gregory the Great complained to John, praetorian prefect of Italy, when the government suspended what seems to have been a regular subsidy (*annonae et consuetudines*) to the local *diaconia*, the ecclesiastical body in charge of seeing to the welfare of the urban poor (Greg. *Ep.* X. 8; Jones 1964: 898–9). Gregory probably won his case as, during the second half of the seventh century, *diaconiae* are again attested as distributing food, principally grain and wine, though perhaps also meat, and it is to this that some of the archaeological evidence may relate (*Gesta Ep.* 418).

The breakdown of Roman public services, however unsatisfactory they may seem when compared to contemporary western standards, must have negatively affected public health in early medieval times, both from the physical and the psychological points of view. Archaeology has not yet been brought to bear with great effect on these problems, though this is a far from redundant line of enquiry.[19]

That sanitary conditions in late Roman and early medieval Naples were bad, and almost certainly more so than in Republican and early Imperial times, seems to be demonstrated by the frequent discovery of substantial waste deposits within the walls dating from the late fourth century AD onwards.[20] Apart from standard domestic rubbish, dead dogs, cats and, on occasion, even amputated human limbs seem to have been thrown in to rubbish pits, to putrefy and contribute to the development of an undesirable and far from healthy fauna. Human faecal remains were probably more carefully disposed of on account of their value in the fertilization of agricultural land, whether within or without the walls; a practice attested in Naples as late as the beginning of the twentieth century, and certainly current in early medieval times (De Azevedo 1974: 675).[21] There is no evidence that pottery chamber-pots appeared much before the sixteenth century, and the first private toilets mentioned date to 924 in Naples (R.

---

[17] See Proc. *Bell. Goth.* V. viii. 41, for their role in supplying Naples during the Gothic War.
[18] On early medieval health and diet in southern Italy in general see Skinner 1997.
[19] See, for example, Addyman (1989) discussing York.
[20] For sanitary conditions in Roman towns see the important paper by Scobie (1986).
[21] The term *stercorare* is attested in Neapolitan medieval documents.

60: *monimen*) and to 1188 in Salerno (Amarotta 1989: 242 — *camera necessariorum*). It must have been even more difficult to manage the excrement from the various animals that roamed the town, and this was a sure way of spreading disease, though even the fertilization of plants with infected manure was a very real health risk (Rudolfs 1951).[22] The collection and reuse of animal dung, together with kitchen waste such as remains of cauliflowers, broccoli, artichokes, cabbages, lettuce and garlic, in fertilizing Naples's extramural orchards, is described well by Wolfgang Goethe during his trip to Italy (Goethe 1973: 237). I doubt that this activity did not also take place regularly in early medieval times, with the significant difference that a fair percentage of the filth could have been recycled within the walls.

Conditions cannot have been better, and may have been worse, than pre-industrial Naples. A study published in the year of the unification (that is 1861) describes Via Toledo, one of the city's principal streets leading to the Royal Palace, as badly paved (when it *was* paved), and littered with piles of rubbish, dung and pottery. We are informed that food fried in rancid oil provoked bad smells. Mules carrying waste dirtied the street, which resembled a swamp impregnated with domestic liquids, whilst various animals fed off the waste (Turchi 1861: 8–10). Private lavatories were hand-cleansed at all hours, whilst the small drains became clogged constantly (Turchi 1861: 14, 33). Though the study lamented the lack of public services, there was no real awareness by most inhabitants of the real risks of such conditions to society, still very much echoed by the unclean practices in parts of modern-day Naples, despite improved municipal control.

Rubbish in early medieval Naples was disposed of in many ways. That deposited within the shells of abandoned buildings represents the main source of archaeological evidence for all sorts of material conditions. Waste, principally organic, was also spread over cultivated plots, both within and outside the town walls. A large amount must also have been dumped at specific sites just outside the gates, such as in the depression (*fossatum*?) to the west of the walls close to Piazza Bellini (Capasso 1895: 23). Whatever the case, much waste clearly lay about the town, providing ideal culture grounds for all sorts of microfauna, and feeding grounds for larger animals, from rats to dogs and even pigs.

There is little anthropological evidence for public health or life expectancy in Naples or her surrounding territory (see below, Appendix I, *s.v.* Via Botteghelle, Ponticelli). However, skeletal samples are not absent, and an analysis of the burials in the catacombs would be highly instructive. An analysis of 24 tombstones gives an average life expectancy of 36.8 years (Ambrasi 1980: 222–4; Serrao 1989; *MND* II: 2). The people recorded on the inscriptions are from middle- and upper-class society. Thus their ages cannot be translated into general life expectancy figures for the population as a whole, nor can the resulting figure be considered more than a very general indication because of the small size of the sample and the fact that it covers the long period from the fourth or fifth to the ninth centuries. Indeed, if the same calculation is performed only on the fourteen fourth- or fifth-century inscriptions, the resulting life expectancy figure is of 32.6 years. None the less, the results give an idea of how long privileged members of society might have lived after having survived the critical first few years of life, whilst poorer members of society presumably died when younger. Indeed, as anthropological analyses for Byzantine Greece have yielded an average life expectancy figure of 33.75, it may well be that our figure lies not far off the mark (Angel 1947). Instead, what is interesting is that the females recorded in Naples have a higher life expectancy than males, that is 39.3 as against 34.0. This is in contrast to other data available for pre-industrial societies in Europe (for example, Brothwell 1972: 83).

With the available material, we can only try to shed light on pathology through indirect evidence. Leaving aside high infant mortality, the scourge of the Middle Ages was the plague. Though severe episodes were not unknown in Roman times, a number of outbreaks occurred between the great plagues of 542 and 767 (*Gesta Ep.* 421; Paul Diac. *Hist. Lang.* II. 4; Schipa 1892: 369). No further outbreaks are then recorded until the infamous Black Death of 1348–1350.

The black rat (*Rattus rattus*) aided the spread of plague. The earliest examples come from late second-century BC *Pompeii*. By the late Empire, if not before, there was a well-established population in Naples (King 1994: 387–8). The animal has also been identified at the mid-fifth-century basilica of San Costanzo, on the island of Capri (Albarella

---

[22] I have found dog faeces, with high calcium contents, at *Pompeii*, though they were not common, despite the scale of the excavations: Arthur 1986b, for the site.

1992: 54–5).[23] All this raises two points. The first is that sanitary conditions in general cannot have been particularly good and, as in modern Naples, there must have been a considerable amount of waste available upon which the animals could thrive. Indeed, some mammal bones from butchered meat recovered in fifth- and sixth-century contexts at the site of Carminiello ai Mannesi display rat gnawing marks (King 1994: 388). The second point is that some of the numerous plagues that are attested through Imperial times, and the devastating outbreaks that have been used to argue population decline in early medieval times, may have been bubonic, as opposed to pulmonary or septicaemic.[24] Paul the Deacon, writing two centuries later, described the symptoms of the plague of 570 thus: 'glands as large as nuts or dates began to appear in the groins of the men and in other very delicate parts of the body, followed by an intolerable feverish blaze, such that in three days the man died', recalling the symptoms of bubonic plague, right down to the buboes (*Hist. Lang.* II. 4). The accuracy of the description might also be judged by the fact that modern medicine also gives three days, in severe cases, for the appearance of delirious hallucinations, vomiting, diarrhoea, pulmonary and circulatory disturbances, rapidly followed by coma and death through syncope.

Plague is often endemic amongst rodents, especially amongst black rats, and transmission of the bacteria *Pasteurela pestis* is provoked by the bites of the flea *Xenopsylla cheopis*.[25] Prior to the discovery of drugs, the only real, though largely ineffectual, way of combating the disease was through isolation of victims and surgery on the buboes, apart from attempting to destroy both rat and flea populations. Whilst there is little archaeological evidence for plague in early medieval Naples, such a disease probably struck the seven children, hastily buried together and partly covered with quicklime, in a disused Roman fountain at the site of Carminiello ai Mannesi (Arthur 1994).

Other diseases will also have had their effects, though they are not yet quantifiable. In particular, malaria, endemic in parts of Italy in the past, has been called into play as a factor in the decline of the Roman Empire (Braudel 1975: 65–6). Certainly areas around Naples, such as Baia or Ponticelli, were dangerous in more recent times, and the *mazzonari* of the Volturno flood-plain were constantly affected by the disease. Work on other diseases such as leprosy, which, according to Grmek, became endemic in medieval times, has yet to be carried out, once again drawing attention to the necessity of analysing anthropological remains (Grmek 1985: 296–9).[26]

[23] For Pompeii see Arthur 1986b.
[24] There are various medical texts discussing plagues. I have used the manual by Penso (1974).
[25] Not, incidentally, the 'human flea', *Pulex irritans*.
[26] The earliest church for lepers that I know of in Naples is Sant'Antonio Abate, founded outside the walls in 1370.

3

URBAN TRANSFORMATION

Amongst the most significant elements for understanding the status of Naples during the early Middle Ages is the transformation of urban functions. It is generally agreed that the role of the medieval town was substantially different to that of its Roman antecedent. Both, in their own ways, clearly reflected the essence of the culture systems of which they formed part. This chapter examines the data for both public and private contributions to the changing physical aspect of Naples, as this, in turn, should yield important evidence for the changing role of the city. It is clear that the public contribution to urban transformation, including that of the Church, which is examined later, was far more amenable to systematic development than the private contribution. However, it will be seen how the latter, which appears rather haphazard and spontaneous, followed a number of unwritten rules, clearly influenced by the dictates of a strong, though at times unstable, local government. The most vivid evidence of this lies in the near perfect survival of the street-grid planned by the Greeks.

The urban topography of Naples has fascinated scholars since the Renaissance, largely because of the survival of a rich collection of documents.[1] This study cannot do justice to all the evidence, which is worth a number of books in itself. The first major studies to synthesize the material were conducted by Bartolomeo Capasso around the turn of the last century (Capasso 1895; 1902; 1905).[2] More recent years have seen the appearance of the *Storia di Napoli* and a number of lesser works, cited in the bibliography. To this must now be added the archaeological evidence accumulated during the 1980s.

Building activity in Naples seems to have been fairly lively throughout the early Middle Ages with respect to most other surviving towns, in both ecclesiastical and vernacular building. Much architecture was of less durable construction than had been the norm in earlier times. Moreover, it is difficult to define early medieval building techniques, given the rarity of excavated examples and the apparent variety created by the use of *spolia*.[3] Columns, altars, threshold slabs and basalt road blocks are to be seen built into walls throughout the historic town centre, and their reuse almost certainly began in late antiquity.[4] Tiles and bricks were stripped from buildings to be re-employed in monuments like the bell-tower of the Pietrasanta (Figs 3:1, 3:2). The reuse of tile and brick dates from at least the fifth century, going by the material visible in the apse of San Giorgio Maggiore and in the construction of the church of San Costanzo, Capri, or by the stripping of the insula block of Carminiello ai Mannesi. The use of *spolia* for roofing is attested as late as the tenth century, alongside wooden slates (Arthur and Whitehouse 1983).[5] Some Roman buildings were still standing in one form or another into later medieval times, providing handy quarries. A fortress built by Emperor Frederick II in the thirteenth century made use of building material from aqueducts, temples and theatres (Greenhalgh 1989: 54). Both the temple of the Dioscuri and the theatre are still recognizable in a bas-relief of King Alfonso d'Aragona dating to the mid-fifteenth century (Bernabò Brea 1935; Russo 1960: fig. 193; Adamo Muscettola 1985), whilst the façade of the former survived into the late sixteenth century. At

---

[1] Mustilli (1952) provided an overview of the historiography, though mainly in the context of ancient topography.

[2] See also Schipa 1892; 1893; 1894; Beloch 1989.

[3] Even the traditional dated typologies of Roman building techniques should be used with caution. The fourth-century *opus reticulatum* recognized at Ostia stands as a lesson (van Dalen 1991).

[4] Many of these fragments are listed on the map of Naples published by Pozzi (1985). Generally on the use of *spolia*, see: Greenhalgh 1989: chapter 7; but see Ward-Perkins 1984, for a different approach. Most recently, on legislation in the late Empire and civic and political connotations, see Alchermes 1994, and some interesting observations in Carver 1993: chapter 4.

[5] Richard Hodges has told me that roof-tiles were produced at San Vincenzo al Volturno in the ninth century. See De Azevedo (1974: 655–6) for Rome, where lead, probably stripped from earlier buildings, was also used.

Fig. 3:1. The twelfth-century bell-tower of the Pietrasanta at Santa Maria Maggiore, built of spolia (photo: author).

Fig. 3:2. Reuse of classical fragments at the base of the twelfth-century bell-tower of the Pietrasanta at Santa Maria Maggiore (photo: author).

Carminiello ai Mannesi, first-century wall-paintings and stucco decoration survived on some walls as late as the seventh century, even if stripping of the building's fabric had begun earlier (Raimondi 1994).[6] Cassiodorus had strongly recommended the reuse of building materials for the embellishment of new constructions, instead of letting them lie in ruin (Cass. *Var.* III. 9).

Distinction may be made between the use of *spolia* for the sake of economy, and the symbolic or decorative reuse of ancient sculpted objects. The latter may have travelled long distances to their final destination (Settis 1978; Franciosi 1978 (for Campania)). An example is the basalt krater now standing in the cathedral. It was perhaps a late antique or early medieval gift to the Church, as was presumably the similar object found at San

Vincenzo al Volturno, or it may have arrived in Naples at an even later date.[7] Various classical inscriptions found in the city apparently came from the site of *Puteoli* (A. Parma, pers. comm.).

Not all material was reused. The building profession survived, supported by a need for new buildings, especially ecclesiastical ones. After the sixth century, it revolved increasingly around crafts that permitted the adaptation of pre-existing structures: replastering, demolition, creation of partition walls, re-roofing, and so on. In the fifth century, both curved (*imbrices*) and flat (*tegulae*) roof-tiles were still being produced, the latter sometimes bearing stamps such as SPES IN DEO or SPES DEI.[8] Kiln wasters of Roman type flanged tiles have been found in the later sixth- to seventh-century backfill of a well at San Martino Valle

---

[6] Such longevity in the survival of wall-paintings may have resulted in the occasional reference to *casae pictae* in medieval documents (for example, R. 687).

[7] I should like to thank Amanda Claridge for information on the San Vincenzo find. On the krater see also below, Chapter 4.

[8] SPES IN DEO appears at Vico Equense (*CIL* X: 8042.139); SPES DEI is attested on *tegulae* used in the tile graves at Ponticelli (De Stefano and Carsana 1987: 21). Some may even have been exported to Carthage during the fifth century, if they are not residual (Fulford and Peacock 1984: 246).

Caudina, near Benevento.[9] It may be suggested that limited quantities of tiles were still produced around Naples up to at least the mid-sixth century, so as to cover the requirements of the major basilica churches, the last of which was San Giovanni Maggiore, consecrated in 555 (see below, Chapter 4). Buildings of middle Byzantine times, such as the the baths at Santa Chiara (see below, p. 45) or the church of San Costanzo on Capri (see below, Chapter 4), may not have required tiles. It is not known whether they were roofed with simple domes, or whether they had tile-covered domes, as did other similar architectural forms in southern Italy and the Byzantine East. As use of tiles was essentially for impermeability, it could be argued that Campanian domes could do without them on account of the optimal qualities provided by the local impermeable mortars.[10] When the large-scale production of tiles recommenced is uncertain, though it is unlikely to have occurred much before the end of the millennium. Though both the words *tecule* and *tiguli* appear in surviving documents, roof-tiles are rare in medieval contexts excavated within the city.[11] Those that do appear, after the end of the millennium, are the convex imbrex type (Italian: *coppo*), common to much of Italy.

Buildings like San Giorgio Maggiore show that the accurate preparation of rectangular tuff bricks continued into the fifth century, when they were used interspersed with tile courses. Instead, the later sixth-century tuff blocks at Santa Patrizia are larger, far more slovenly cut, and tend to be squarish. Continued use of the yellow volcanic tuff (*tufo giallo napoletano*) for masonry is likely, given the eminently workable nature of the stone and its availability. Indeed, the fame of Campanian stonemasons or *magistri commacini*, in particular those from Cava dei Tirreni, spread far and wide in later medieval and Renaissance times.[12] The first specific mention of a stone quarry (*mons a pretis*) appears in a document of 979 (R. 220).

Much less is known about the continued use of mortar and pozzolana, for which the bay of Naples was famous in antiquity. The Roman *pulvis puteo-*

lanus, a hydraulic mortar characterized by the use of the volcanic pozzolana quarried especially in the hinterland of Pozzuoli, permitted buildings such as the large domed baths at Baia and the construction of underwater harbour works. In classical times it was widely exported, not only to Rome but also to north Africa (Williams 1984). It may be argued that there was a decline in the ability to prepare mortar and *opus caementicium* as a result of recession in the building trade. This would have led to the decrease of vaulted and domed architecture in early medieval Italy. Most surviving examples, such as the tenth- or eleventh-century Byzantine Cattolica at Stilo, make use of overlapping or concentrically laid and up-ended bricks or stones.

Wood seems to have been extensively employed, though only in part does this explain the absence of surviving medieval vernacular architecture. I believe that the use of wood was secondary to the use of stone, as in many parts of southern Italy.[13]

Early medieval wall-plaster was also simpler than its Roman predecessor. Not only was it significantly lighter in weight, with fewer ingredients, but examples from the catacombs of San Gennaro and the church of San Costanzo, consist of a single layer of fine plaster applied directly to wall surfaces, as opposed to a series of ever finer strata. This rendered it brittle and less resistant to wear.

What little continuity there might have been in the technology of brick production, of stone cutting, in the use of mortar and of other subsidiary crafts, is to be accredited largely to the Church, the single most affluent and demanding patron of late antique and early medieval architecture.

HARBOUR WORKS

The gulf of Naples provides some of the best harbours of the entire mediterranean basin. The Surrentine peninsula and Capri to the east, and the Phlegrean Fields and Ischia to the west, stretch out like the claws of a crab. The inner bay of the Phlegrean Fields, with lakes Lucrino and Averno, provided an ideal port, which developed enorm-

[9] The excavation, in località Varretele, was conducted in 1980 by Carlo Franciosi, to whom I am indebted for information.

[10] I owe this suggestion to Catello Pasinetti. Medieval Campanian domes appear to have used a lime mortar to which were added local volcanic *lapilli* (small pumice stones). The preparation is known as *battuto*, as masons literally pounded it into shape so as to compress the mortar and remove as many air vacuoles as possible.

[11] *Tecule*: R. 67, R. 619; *tiguli*: R. 45, R. 187, R. 238, R. 380. Perhaps the majority of roofs was flat and did not require tile. Just under 50% of the roofs illustrated in the late fifteenth-century *Tavola Strozzi* are flat (De Seta 1981: fig. 42), whilst many of the gabled and tiled roofs depicted appear to belong to churches.

[12] See Peduto (1982: 16–17), who interpreted the *commacini*, often understood as meaning 'coming from Como', as being 'cum macinis' (with mills), necessary for the preparation of their mortar.

[13] However, see below, p. 47 for statistics from Salerno, and for documentary evidence for timber houses. For surviving fifth- to sixth-century chestnut timbers in the catacombs of San Gennaro, see the note by Elio Corona in Fasola (1974: 221–3).

ously as entrepôt and military arsenal after the Second Punic War and the foundation of the colony of *Puteoli* in 194 BC.

With the decline of *Puteoli* during the fifth century, we may presume that Naples's own facilities, sited in an area known at the turn of the millennium as *iunctura civitatis*, grew rapidly in importance. Under Ostrogothic rule, port trade was controlled by the *comites* of the city, as at Syracuse. This is perhaps an indication of the transference of state-managed activity, originally linked to the *annona*, from *Puteoli*, which is attested as having a *procurator portus Puteolanorum* in the mid-fourth century (Houston 1980), to Naples, as well as signifying the new military importance of the site after the disappearance of the *classis misenensis* in the fifth century (Cass. *Var.* VI. 23–5; Jones 1964: 257).[14]

During the siege of Naples, in 536, Belisarius's ships were able to anchor in the harbour, beyond the range of any missiles which the Goths could launch from the town (Proc. *Bell. Goth.* V. viii. 5, VI. v. 1). Because of both the economic and strategic importance of the port, Narses took the trouble of protecting it through an extension of the city walls (see below, p. 35). It is further possible that Justinian's naval policy required Naples to overhaul ships, if not to build them (see Lewis and Runyan 1990: 19–22). This might have laid the foundations for the city's maritime prowess in later years and the need to develop a second port.

A document dating to 1018 records two ports, the larger *portus Vulpulum*, and the smaller *portus de Arcina*. We may suppose, from the toponym, that the latter was at some stage the military and state installation, with an arsenal close to the city walls and the important re-entrant gate that gave access to the ducal palace.[15] It was located to the northeast of the *portus Vulpulum*. By the time of Frederick II, in 1239, it seems to have diminished in size through silting, and so was not able to contain more than two galleys (Capasso 1895: 174–86). Because of its position, I suspect that this was the original port of the city, gradually supplanted towards the end of the millennium by the *portus Vulpulum*. This suggestion is supported by the discovery of inscriptions and of a Roman mole at the site (Napoli 1967: 414). Until then, the

larger port must have been little more than an ungoverned estuary. Indeed, corresponding to a fair area around and including the present Piazza Municipio, it seems to have received the abundant waters draining from the slopes to the immediate north and west of the city. A watercourse is traceable, approximately, between the parallel roads of Via Roma and Via Santa Maria di Costantinopoli, and then along the area now marked by Via Monteoliveto and Via Medina. If its strategic importance had only been realized in post-classical times, by 1279 it had become so significant as to warrant the positioning of the Angevin castle (Castel Nuovo) to its immediate west. Even the large basin suffered similar problems of infilling, through the redeposition of debris eroding from the hills, such that King Charles I was pressed to organize its drainage between 1301 and 1307 (De Seta 1981: 46). In the marvellously explicit engraving of Dupérac and Lafréry, dating to 1566, the large basin has virtually disappeared, the small basin is clearly shown as being used only for minor embarkations, whilst large galleys and other ships have to anchor alongside the large jetty known as 'il molo grande' (for example, Pane and Valerio 1988: 41, 44). Little is known about the process of sedimentation of either basin, though, unlike other antique towns, it seems to have taken enough time so as to have never compromised Naples's political and economic position. Indeed, the fortunate configuration of its port, located within a bay guarded by peninsulas and islands, was fundamental to its well-being during the later first millennium (Ahrweiler 1978: 272).

DEFENCES

Landwards, Naples was equally defensible. This was appreciated by the Greeks, who chose the site for the foundation of their colony, and by Procopius 1,000 years later: 'for the wall of Naples was inaccessible, on one side by reason of the sea, and on the other because of some difficult country, and those who planned to attack it could gain entrance at no point, not only because of its general situation, but also because the ground sloped steeply' (Proc. *Bell. Goth.* V. viii. 44).

[14] We do not know precisely when the naval activity at *Misenum* ceased. A prefect with joint military and civil responsibilities still existed there in the late fourth century (*CIL* X: 3344), whilst the aqueduct that fed the Phlegrean Fields was restored under Honorius in 399 (*Cod. Theod.* XV. 2, 8). In 324 it had been restored to serve the fleet (*AE*: 1939: 151). Sirago (1984: 110–12) had the fleet surviving into the fifth century, and whilst claiming that the Ostrogothic government did not have a fleet, went on to recount how Theoderic was able to assemble 1,000 *dromones* in a short space of time.

[15] See Schulz (1991: 431) on arsenals. Whether that of Venice was indeed earlier than that of Naples is, to my mind, not proved.

The rigid morphology of a roughly rectangular tuff platform, gouged on its sides by watercourses, is undoubtedly a further element that has permitted the preservation of the ancient town centre as a coherent unity (Rigillo 1985: 406–7). The favourable position, however, has required artificial strengthening on a number of occasions. The defences were of Greek origin, assignable to two principal phases, datable to the fifth and the fourth centuries BC (Greco 1986).[16] With the *pax romana*, little further work was felt to be necessary and, indeed, parts of the walls were dismantled or built over, as at Sant'Aniello a Caponapoli. The practice of building against the walls may have continued throughout medieval times and, indeed, at Byzantine Otranto aided the Normans in entering the city (von Falkenhausen 1978a: 151). An important security measure must have been that of providing open spaces with clear visibility outside the walls. Capasso thus explained the *campus Neapolis* to the east of the city, and the *campus oppidi lucullani* to its southwest, both devoid of trees (Capasso 1895: 199). When the walls were refurbished in late antiquity, it is likely that all externally abutting buildings were swept away.

The first known restoration of the Greek defensive circuit was under Valentinian III (425–450), around the same time that he ordered the *praefectus urbi* to repair the capital's defences (*CIL* C: 1485; Johannowsky 1960: 493).[17] Similar works along the coasts of Italy were under the charge of the *magister militum*, Sigisvult (Sid. Apoll. *Carm.* V. 388–424; Courtois 1955: 194–6; Christie and Rushworth 1988: 82). All this was a reaction to the threat of the Vandals, who had seized Carthage in 439. In the event, the construction was far-sighted. In 455 the Vandals raided Campania and sacked Capua and *Nola*, to be finally thwarted by the Emperor Majorian in 458.

Further works are attested under both Belisarius and Narses in the mid-sixth century. Seven new towers ('mirificas turres') are attributed to Belisarius by the *Vita Athanasii Episcopi*, whilst the documentary evidence suggests that Narses not only repaired the defences razed by Totila during the war, but enclosed the port of Naples within an extension, highlighting the ever increasing importance of the Neapolitan fleet (*MGH, SS. Rer. Lang. et Ital.* 439; *Acta Sanctorum Iulii* IV. 78; Proc. *Bell. Goth.* V. viii. 5). The extension is probably to be assigned to the mid-sixth century, and not to Valentinian and Theodosius as some have argued (Napoli 1969: 739–52; Christie and Rushworth 1988: 85, n. 47). It was, after all, during the Gothic War that Naples seems to have hosted a substantial number of refugees from the surrounding territories, augmenting the population. Furthermore, the negative bradyseism that affected *Puteoli* seems to have occurred after 530, and may have led part of the already diminished population to flee to Naples (see above, Chapter 1). In 536 the harbour still lay at some distance from the walls, whilst the *Vita Athanasii Episcopi* (*MGH, SS. Rer. Lang. et Ital.* 440) tells us that Narses later enclosed the port. The reconstructed extension (Fig. 3:3), whilst not including the port itself, effectively enclosed adjacent land. The new and quite sizeable area resulting from the proposed works provides a suitable context into which to set the decision to build the major church of San Giovanni Maggiore. Indeed, whilst the church was consecrated by Bishop Vincent (555–578), the idea of building it might have been born alongside the plan to enclose the southwestern harbour-side suburbs. It is worth noting that a document of 961 describes the church of San Nicola in this area as being 'intus castellione novum' (R. 111).[18] Does this refer to a new fort built at the start of the tenth century against the Arab menace, as Capasso would have (Capasso 1895: 136–7), or could the term have referred by tradition to the new defences erected during the sixth century?

The first mention of a fort in the suburbs dates to 536.[19] Whilst it is not certain where it was sited, it is possible that it lay by Santa Lucia, either on the rock of Pizzofalcone above or on the island of *Megaris* (Castel dell'Ovo) directly below (see below, pp. 69–71). Considering the financial shortages of the Imperial administration following the wars of reconquest, these mid-sixth-century works are further eloquent evidence for the fundamental role that Naples had assumed in eastern eyes (see Christie and Rushworth 1988: 81, n. 26).

---

[16] Of particular interest is also one of the original Greek tuff quarries, discovered below the modern cemetery of Santa Maria del Pianto, on the road to Capodichino (Pozzi 1990: 268).

[17] On Naples's defences, see also Pani Ermini 1994: 195–8. For Rome, see Val. III, *Nov.* V. 2–3.

[18] See Feniello (1991) for an interesting and erudite, though not totally convincing, reconstruction of the southern tract of wall in the tenth century. I find it hard to accept the coastline as proposed in his fig. 5, as the church of Sant'Aspreno would seem to end up in the sea!

[19] For Valentinianic fortification, see *CIL* X: 1485; Christie and Rushworth 1988. For Justinian, see Proc. *Bell. Goth.* V. viii. 5.

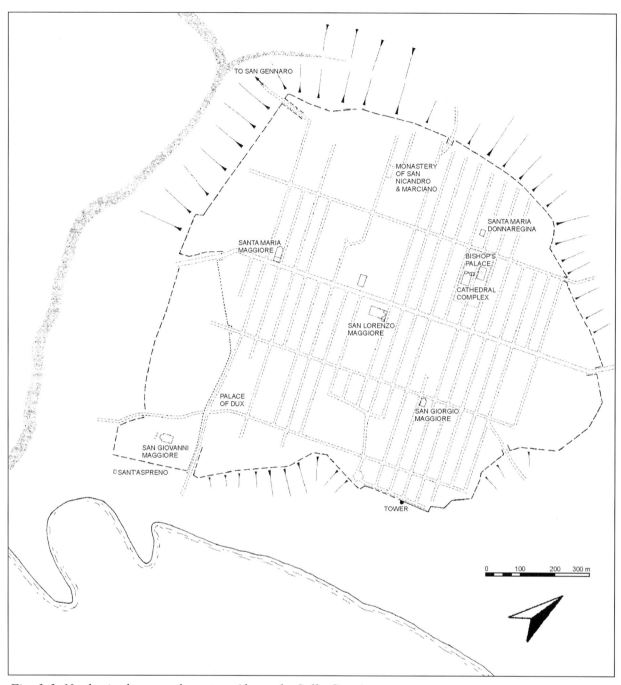

Fig. 3:3. Naples in the seventh century (drawn by Sally Cann).

Be that as it may, the Greek wall-circuit was about 3.8 km in length, whilst Falco of Benevento, writing around 1140, gave a length of 4.47 km (2.363 *passus*) (Feniello 1995: 37). Figure 3:3 presents a tentative reconstruction of the main features of Naples in the seventh century, where much doubt lies in the position of the wall-circuit in the southwestern and southern sectors. The southwestern sector is based on the assumption that the church of San Giovanni Maggiore lay within the walls, as well as on the hypothesis that the area of the later monastic complex of Santa Chiara lay outside (see, for example, Napoli 1969: 741).

Mario Napoli has argued that the works of Valentinian and Theodosius effectively extended the southwestern walls as far as the watercourse now represented by Via Sant'Anna dei Lombardi, Via Monteoliveto and Via Medina, shifting a city gate from Piazza San Domenico Maggiore to Piazza del Gesù (Napoli 1967: 455; Pelosi 1985). This would consequently have enclosed an important and large area of suburbs that had developed from the end of the Republic in the direction of the port at Piazza Municipio, represented archaeologically by the public baths at Santa Chiara and the *domus* at Santa Maria la Nova. There is, however, very little evidence to support this thesis, and indeed the area has yielded evidence for abandonment in late antique times. The only tract of wall that could possibly be associated with the Valentinianic adjustments, to sustain Naples's reconstruction, was located at Via del Cerriglio. All we know about it is that it was 3.0 m in thickness, with an inner facing of Roman road blocks (Capasso 1905: 101–2, 152, 202, n. 449). Clearly, this is not sufficient to confirm the thesis, as it could equally date to Narses or later. As opposed to Mario Napoli (1967: 455), I prefer to identify a wall line linking the area of San Giovanni Maggiore directly to the known Greek walls at Piazza Bellini, following the line of Via San Sebastiano and Via Santa Chiara, rather than hypothesizing an initial extension solely around the church. This would fit with the fact that a watercourse ran along Via San Sebastiano and Via Santa Chiara, which might, by the time of Procopius, have acted as a suitable *fossatum*, later to be backfilled. Recent excavations within the main cloister of the monastery of Santa Chiara have yielded a substantial infill that may support this view.[20]

Evidence for sixth-century works is limited. However, a characteristically Byzantine pentagonal prow-tower, associated with a long stretch of wall of Greek origin, was discovered on the seaward side of the town in 1958 (Fig. 3:4). The tower had been built of reused architectural fragments, tombstones and the like. Though it has been dated to the fifth century, evidence to support this view has never been presented. Similar towers are known from *Sergiopolis*, Resapha and Antioch, and date from the fifth to the sixth centuries, though, apparently, they did not come into regular use until the Arab-Byzantine wars of the seventh to tenth centuries (Pozzi 1985: 486–9, cat. nos. 185–6).[21] The closest local parallels are the pentagonal towers standing beside the Arco del Sacramento gate and at the Rocca dei Rettori at Benevento, which have been dated to the late sixth century, and likewise make much use of *spolia* (Peduto 1984b: 393, fig. 1; Rotili 1986).[22] One wonders if this was one of the seven towers ('mirificas turres') attributed to Belisarius, and if Naples's walls might also have presented a 'saw-like' façade towards the sea, recalling the walls of both Salona and Ankara

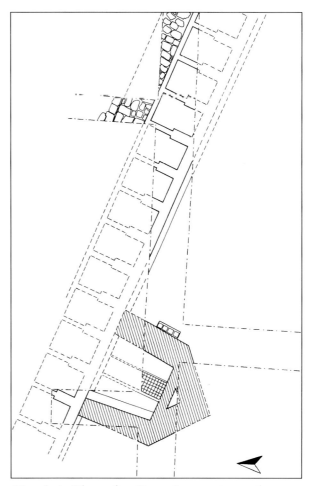

Fig. 3:4. Plan of a Byzantine pentagonal prow-tower, Naples (redrawn by Sally Cann from a plan in the archives of the Soprintendenza Archeologica delle Province di Napoli e Caserta, with kind permission).

(Dunn 1998). The sources also attest to a *fossatum* or ditch encircling the walls of Naples (Capasso 1895). It is not known when this was originally dug or where it ran, though it probably used pre-existing natural gullies. The natural configuration of the tuff bank suggests that a *fossatum* was unnecessary to the south and along much of the western and northwestern sides of the city, though natural gullies may have been revetted.[23] To the northeast it probably followed the line of the present Via Carbonara, which runs parallel to the line of the walls and recalls the *carbonarius publicus* attested there by 916 (R. 4; Capasso 1895: 12–13). It would have been breached by a gate at

---

[20] I should like to thank Vittoria Carsana for this information.

[21] For this type, see Foss and Winfield 1986: 30–1, fig. 30. The type was not encountered in the northwestern part of the Roman empire by von Petrikovits (1971).

[22] Seventh-century burials have been discovered during excavations abutting the exterior of the Rocca dei Rettori tower (*L'Italia meridionale* 1998).

[23] See Capasso (1895: 14, n. 3), where a large wall in squared drystone is described as running parallel to and on the outside of the city wall. It was revealed at 18 m below present ground level.

Castel Capuano, where the Normans were to erect a fort, perhaps on or near the site of an earlier attested *castrum vetus* (De Seta 1981: 36).

The southern sector of the walls, east of Via Mezzocannone, is based on Mario Napoli's reconstruction (Fig. 1:2), where a re-entrant is influenced by the escarpment still traceable along the line of Via Bartolomeo Capasso. I doubt that there was any significant suburban building in this area until later medieval times and, as Procopius implied (*Bell. Goth.* V. viii. 44 (AD 536)), the walls might have let on to the sea edge. Evidence from boreholes indicates that sedimentation and land reclamation have taken place in this area, which, apart from recent episodes, is difficult to date.

Further extension of the walls might have occurred during the tenth century, so as to encompass important suburbs in the eastern part of the city, where a *regio Portanovense* is attested (Bordone 1991: 528–9; Skinner 1994: 281).

The rigid conservation of the ancient street alignments indicates that the original city gates, presumably rebuilt at various stages, remained throughout medieval times. None has been excavated, though remains have apparently been identified under Castel Capuano at the end of Via dei Tribunali, and by Piazza Calenda, whilst another might have been sited further to the southwest to give access to the sea. Remains of the Greek wall-circuit indicate the existence of re-entrant gates by Sant'Aniello a Caponapoli and Via Mezzocannone, whilst another, on topographical grounds, might have existed close to Piazzetta Casanova. The actual Porta San Gennaro, just to the west of the highest part of Via Duomo, where it is crossed by Via Luigi Settembrini, appears to reflect the opening of a road that, through the valley of the Sanità, originally led to the extramural church and catacombs (Capasso 1895: 17). Other gates are assumed at the end of Via Santa Sofia and in Piazza San Domenico Maggiore. With the extension of the walls in the southwestern part of the city, it is to be imagined that further gates were erected.

Very little is known regarding fortified buildings within the walls or attached to them. It is suggested below that the duke's palace or praetorium was fortified. Furthermore, Capasso suggested that a fort had been erected within the walls, following the attested desertion and destruction of *castrum*

Lucullanum in 901, around the area of Santa Maria la Nova and Rua Catalana, on the southwestern side of the city. He would have the early medieval church of San Nicola 'de intus castellione novum' sited within this fort (Capasso 1895: 136–7; see also below, Chapter 4). I suggest above that this may date from early Byzantine times.

STREETS AND COMMUNICATIONS

The survival of ancient street layouts has often been seen as a clue towards the identification of towns that survived the upheavals of late Roman and early medieval times. At least 27 cases of tolerably well-preserved classical street-grids are known from peninsular Italy (Fig. 3:5).[24] Naples provides an excellent example, with the Greek street pattern, possibly laid out in the fifth or fourth century BC, largely surviving to the present day, and creating no end of chaos for traffic. Not only is it one of the few examples preserved south of Rome, but it is the best preserved in the whole of Italy. It includes three main roads (*plateiai*) and no less than 22 lesser perpendicular roads (*stenopoi*) (Napoli 1969: 759–60, which includes a revision of Capasso 1895).

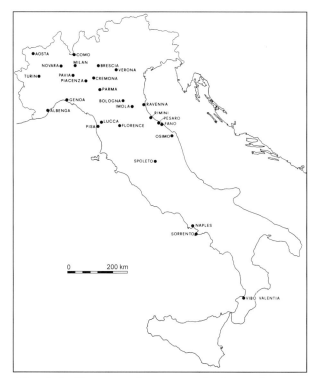

Fig. 3:5. Towns with preserved classical street-grids (drawn by Sally Cann).

---

[24] These are Albenga, Aosta, Bologna, Brescia, Como, Cremona, Fano, Florence, Genoa, Imola, Lucca, Milan, Novara, Osimo, Parma, Pavia, Pesaro, Piacenza, Pisa, Ravenna, Rimini, Sorrento, Spoleto, Turin, Verona, Vibo Valentia and Naples. For northern Italy see Ward-Perkins 1988.

Fig. 3:6. Reconstruction of the process of the rise in urban levels (drawn by Mario Alberti).

There is some evidence of a classical date for a fourth or lowest *plateia*, formed of the roads Vico San Marcellino, Via Bartolomeo Capasso and Via Arte della Lana, where a Roman ramp with reticulate masonry, providing access to the sea, has been found (Giampaola, Fratta and Scarpati 1996: 117).[25] It is parallel to the *imma plateia* and repeats the equidistance of the others. It is attested by the eighth century, when it may have served the monasteries of San Marcellino e Pietro and San Festo, and later that of San Severino e Sossio (Capasso 1895: 61). Sited on the edge of the ancient escarpment, though already within the Greek walls, it also signals the point at which the regular alignment of most of the *stenopoi* ceases.

The most recent hypothesis concerning the road system, presented by Emanuele Greco, suggested that the median *plateia* (Via dei Tribunali) was 13 m wide, by virtue of its importance; that both the upper and lower *plateiai* were 6 m wide; whilst the *stenopoi* measured 3 m in width (Greco 1986: 201–2; see also below, pp. 50–1). Confirmation of the lesser width of the *summa* and *imma plateiai* comes from the span of the flying buttresses constructed against the theatre at Via Anticaglie in Roman times. However, as Greco (1986: 200–2) himself admitted, excavation is required to check the measurements.

Of the various roads in Naples, only one or two *stenopoi* have been totally obstructed through the centuries. One of these, known as Vico Clusa in the early tenth century, has probably been identified at the site of Carminiello ai Mannesi as a thoroughfare blocked by extensive dumping of rubbish during the later fifth and early sixth centuries.

Other road surfaces, as well as spaces within the insulae, grew in height. This was the case of Vico Zuroli, bounding the eastern side of the insula of Carminiello ai Mannesi, where remains of the (semi-subterranean?) ground floor are now visible within a modern basement. Such a rise in levels is attested in early medieval contexts in other surviving Roman towns. A private building fronting a street at Via Dante, Verona, for instance, witnessed four successive floor and threshold levels during the early Middle Ages (Hudson 1985).[26] A general rise in levels may be explained by a number of factors, including the lack of a public system of waste disposal giving rise to accumulations in streets, the dumping of organic waste in gardens, the difficulty of repairing eroded floors of beaten earth, often replaced simply by adding a new floor level above the worn surface, and the consequent necessity to keep other levels in line with these rising surfaces (Fig. 3:6).

---

[25] The upper surface of the ramp bears a paving of bricks forming a herring-bone pattern, which the authors have claimed is of first-century date. I would venture that it is late medieval, as there are numerous parallels in Italy (for example, in Bologna (Di Carlo *et al.* 1985: 277), Genova (Mannoni 1983: 217, fig. 3), Savigliano (Micheletto 1994: 135)). The published photograph appears to show that the adjoining Roman masonry was cut to receive the surface, and the bricks, according to what Vittoria Carsana has told me, are of the same dimensions as those of the medieval surface found at Palazzo Giusso, Naples (Carsana 1996: fig. 2).

[26] For similar instances in Pescara, see Staffa 1991.

The persistence of the road pattern, none the less, implies the persistence of street frontages regulated by control of property boundaries. Indeed, as has been suggested for Pavia, it is likely that the continued presence of a strong centralized authority permitted maintenance of *viae publicae* (Bullough 1966: 98). Whilst on the one hand this ensured that the principal communication networks were kept free of obstacles so as to permit continued traffic flow, on the other it did not stop partial encroachment on to the carriageways by private and, later, public buildings. The result is that both medieval and modern roads are narrower than their classical counterparts. How much of this encroachment was illegal is hard to tell, though the process does indicate changes in the use of the urban structure that need to be examined.

Roman land transport was often based on wagons, so eloquently testified by the wheel-ruts that furrow the tough basalt road blocks at *Pompeii*. In early medieval times, with the collapse of large-scale long-distance commerce, degeneration of many old Roman roads and, presumably, the rise in costs of owning forms of wheeled transport, their use declined. This would have brought about a redundancy in the broad widths of classical streets which, at least as far as concerns main thoroughfares, should have permitted the passage of two vehicles in opposite directions. With the weight of the movement of goods shifted from the wagon to the packanimal, to the hand-cart or simply onto a man's shoulders, roads could be accordingly narrowed to the width that we now find common in Naples's *stenopoi*.[27] The irrelevance of large streets, save as processional ways, must have been evident to the medieval authorities, and some degree of encroachment thus explicitly or tacitly accepted. It is unlikely that the process happened in the seventh or eighth centuries, and it perhaps took place in the period of initial economic and demographic expansion from the ninth to the tenth centuries, and terminated essentially by Angevin times.[28]

The plan of Greek Naples represented such a fine attempt at implementing a functional urban layout that little of it has changed down to the present day. It largely overcame the uneven surface of the natural tuff platform through careful use of terracing, gradients, ramps and steps, and has been further modelled and smoothed over the ages. The gates and the street pattern tended to minimize movement both within the city and between it and the coast and surrounding countryside. The position of the *agora*/forum was practically central to the city, such that nobody within the walls lived more than 650 m away. Advantage seems to have been taken of the urban layout in late antique times. By the third quarter of the sixth century, the five major late antique basilical churches had been built. Their relative positioning within the city was such that nowhere was anybody living within the walls more than about 400 m away from a major church (see below, Fig. 4:17). In practical terms, a major church was available to all citizens at no more than about five minutes walking distance.

It was only towards the end of the millennium that urban expansion breached the walls and encouraged the development of new road systems radiating out from the core and breaking away from the strict Hippodamean scheme. Narrow winding streets (*strictulae*) dropping down the escarpment towards the coast and the port, sometimes quite steeply, can be traced (Di Stefano 1971: 180, for example). A surviving example is Via Santa Barbara, whilst another, known as 'strictula San Iohannis maioris' already in 1184, probably bounded by orchards since early medieval times, has been excavated recently (Carsana 1996). Little attempt was made in peripheral areas to extend the logic of the Hippodamean system, save around the later medieval monastic complex of Santa Chiara, which was already a key area of suburban expansion in Roman times.

PUBLIC BUILDINGS

The use of public buildings continued for some time after the collapse of the western Roman Empire, though functions often changed, the clearest example of which is the conversion of pagan temples to Christian churches. The most spectacular transformation is that of the church of San Paolo Maggiore, once the temple of the Dioscuri, illustrated in its classical form in a print of 1540 by Francesco d'Olanda (see below, Chapter 4).

---

[27] I have adapted the argument of Kennedy (1985: 26) and Bulliet (1975), who saw it as crucial in the change from classical *polis* to Islamic madina, though in the latter case there appears to have been little interest in maintaining street alignments.

[28] The principal works on roads in the city, aside from Capasso 1895, are Doria 1971, and Infusino 1987. Neither, however, has made much attempt at understanding their chronology or the dates at which they were given their names.

The amphitheatre was located somewhere in the eastern part of the city, in the *regio termensis*, perhaps to the south of Castel Capuano, just within the walls (Napoli 1967: 441–2). It is attested in the early eleventh century through a road of 'the amphitheatre' (State Archives, Fondo Monasteri Soppressi, fasc. no. 1391). It is quite surprising that no physical traces of what must have been a major monument are known to exist, as they do in many other towns from Lucca to Venafro. Indeed, cases are recorded of the reuse of the building type as early medieval fortresses, as at Capua or *Minturnae*, perhaps significantly on the edges of two Roman towns that were eventually abandoned, or more simply, as in various other examples in Italy, for the insertion of private dwellings (for example, Ward-Perkins 1984: 206, 211, for the case of Lucca). Perhaps its disappearance is to be explained by its location. Whilst it could have served as a fort for aggressors, it would have been too small to serve as a refuge for the substantial Neapolitan citizen-body. In a town that continued to thrive throughout the Middle Ages, it would most likely have served as a convenient quarry for building materials. The site of the stadium/ gymnasium, which survived into the fourth century, is also unknown, and a similar explanation for its disappearance may apply. It is referred to during the burial of Bishop Fortunatus, around 344, in a church 'foris urbem quasi ad stadia' (*MND* I: 163; *Gesta Ep.* 404; Capasso 1895: 206; Russo 1966: 157; Cilento 1969b: 721). In contrast, the Roman theatre and the *theatrum tectum* or *odeion*, both sited within the walls of Naples, are still standing, though they were converted into houses, as in Rome, Catania, Ivrea and elsewhere (Baldassare 1986; Arthur 1989b). The former is clearly identifiable within the modern urban layout, whilst the form of the latter has only recently been reconstructed (Fig. 3:7). It possessed the form of a small theatre enclosed within a rectangular outer wall that supported the roof, as at *Pompeii*, *Epidauros* and *Termessos*, and may have developed over the *bouleuterion*, as earlier monumental masonry is visible. In both cases it can be seen how durable ancient walls have conditioned the development of later architecture, with fairly recent additions following the radial layout of the antique substructures. The *theatrum tectum* was abandoned no later than the sixth century, when a burial, associated with a coin of Tiberius II (578–582), was inserted into the *scaena*. The presence of 'dark earth' deposits (see below, pp. 53–5) suggests that in early medieval times the building might have been

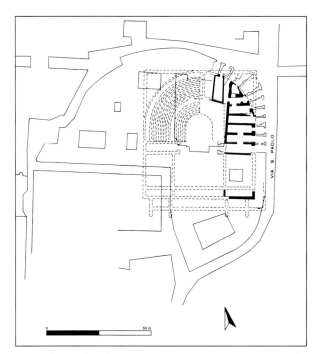

Fig. 3:7. The theatrum tectum *at Via San Paolo (after Arthur 1989b: fig. 2).*

converted into a series of private houses with associated orchards. Indeed, at least part of the area between the theatre/*theatrum tectum* and the forum, which seems to have been open public space in Roman times, may be that attested in medieval documents as a 'curtem communem' with its open spaces, sited close to the monastery of San Pellegrino and the *curtis* of Landulf (*MND* II: 1, 356). This would explain why modern property boundaries in this area are far more irregular than most others within the Greek town walls where development would have been conditioned by pre-existing Roman buildings.

Material evidence for new construction, outside the sphere of the Church, is slight, and we are obliged to make use almost exclusively of the textual sources. One of the most important public buildings was the duke's palace, upon which was based the administration of the duchy, lying in the area of the Monterone (*de Praetorio*), now beneath Naples University, on a site overlooking the sea (Capasso 1895: 193). Vera von Falkenhausen has implied that by this time the use of the term praetorium, also found at Reggio Calabria, indicates a fortified building, though there is some evidence that it remained a term implying the seat of the governor (von Falkenhausen 1978a: 151; see also Brühl 1977). Whether in Naples its use specifically distinguishes the residence from the *palatium* of the emperor in Constantinople, is not clear. Short of imagining that it can hardly have been less spectacular than the contemporary *palatium* of Salerno, where excavations have brought to light impressive fragments of Prince Arechis II's *cappella palatina* (Peduto *et al*. 1989; Di Muro 1998), we can only surmise as to its grandeur. It may have included a large portico, and seems to have housed the monastery of San Marcellino e Pietro, refounded by Theodonanda, widow of Duke Anthemius, in the second quarter of the ninth century (Capasso 1895: 192–3). For reasons of control, the mint seems to have been sited close by, in the area of San Marcellino, in the region of Portanova, where the toponym 'ad monetam' is attested from 763 (Capasso 1895: 108). The diaconicon of San Giovanni e Paolo was also in the area of the palace. It had been restored by Duke Theodore in 721, whilst the title of the church of San Iohannis in curte, nearby, presumably refers to the status of the area, if indeed it was not annexed to the palace (Capasso 1895: 105). Patricia Skinner (1995: 61, 83) has suggested that from about the tenth century much of the area between the *imma plateia* and the sea walls, close to the ports, might have formed part of the palace complex or, at least, have been owned by the dukes. This is based on the fact that no land transactions are recorded in the area and that analogous placing of ducal properties is evident at Gaeta and Amalfi.

PUBLIC SPACES

The Greek *agora* and the Roman forum lay central within the walls, developing around the *media plateia*. Little is known regarding its layout in Roman times, making it difficult to trace its development (Fig. 3:8). The only public building examined in the forum, excluding the temple of the Dioscuri, is the *macellum* supported by a cryptoporticus and lying beneath the later complex of San Lorenzo Maggiore. Various hypotheses have been made as to the layout of the area, the latest of which is the important study by Emanuele Greco (1985a). He interpreted the *stenopos* discovered to the immediate east of the *macellum* and its northern extension, Vico Giganti, as the easternmost limit of the public square. The actual Via San Gregorio Armeno is, instead, considered as not having an antique origin, whilst he saw Vico Purgatorio ad Arco/Vico Fico al Purgatorio as the westernmost limit. The limits posed by Vico Giganti to the east and Vico Purgatorio to the west respect the layout of the theatre complex by being tangential to its limits. By extension, Greco suggested that they also delimit a large square or piazza that extended

to the south of the theatres, probably as far as the *imma plateia* traced by Via San Biagio ai Librai. The piazza is visibly divided in two by Via dei Tribunali. The surviving temple of the Dioscuri gives us the original level of the northern half. It virtually corresponds to the present level of Via dei Tribunali, as well as to the level of the Roman *macellum*. The *stenopos* to the east of the *macellum* lies at a lower level, corresponding to the cryptoporticus, still visible on its eastern, southern and part of its western sides. On the basis of the evidence for split levels and a sixteenth-century text by Fabio Giordano stating that 'Hoc [forum] in urba nostra duplex', Greco has argued that the forum was divided into two halves, on different levels, by the *media plateia* (Greco 1985a).

Alternatives may be suggested. It is proposed that the effective division between the upper and lower piazze was not the *media plateia*. Apart from the lack of space available in front of the temple of the Dioscuri, surely the most important temple on the forum, and the resulting plunge of 5 m right on the edge of the street, an examination of the evidence for the western side of the cryptoporticus suggests an alternative solution. Indeed, whilst the southernmost structures identified along the western perimeter of the cryptoporticus are level with its floors, half-way along its western perimeter it would appear that there was also an outer upper level opening from the *macellum*. On this basis, it may be proposed that the upper piazza extended for over 50 m south of the *media plateia*. The result of this is that the upper public piazza occupied by the theatre complex, the temple of the Dioscuri and the *macellum* would have been far larger than the lower one. Such a division would help explain the position of Via Maffei, following the southernmost limit of the upper piazza, and the development of part of the monastic complex of San Gregorio Armeno, from the tenth century, below and to the immediate south. Perhaps the church of San Michele Arcangelo, attested as Sant'Arcangeli 'a foris sub muro publico' in 924, was also sited in the lower piazza, though its attribution to the *regio Portanovense*, apparently to the east, leaves some room for doubt (Capasso 1895: 98–9). Furthermore, it may be noted that excavations carried out by the Soprintendenza at San Gregorio Armeno in 1986, to the immediate west of the convent's cloister, revealed three rooms with mosaic pavements dating to the later first century BC or early first century AD. These floor levels are consistent with the level of the *media plateia*, and thus seem to provide a maximum width for the

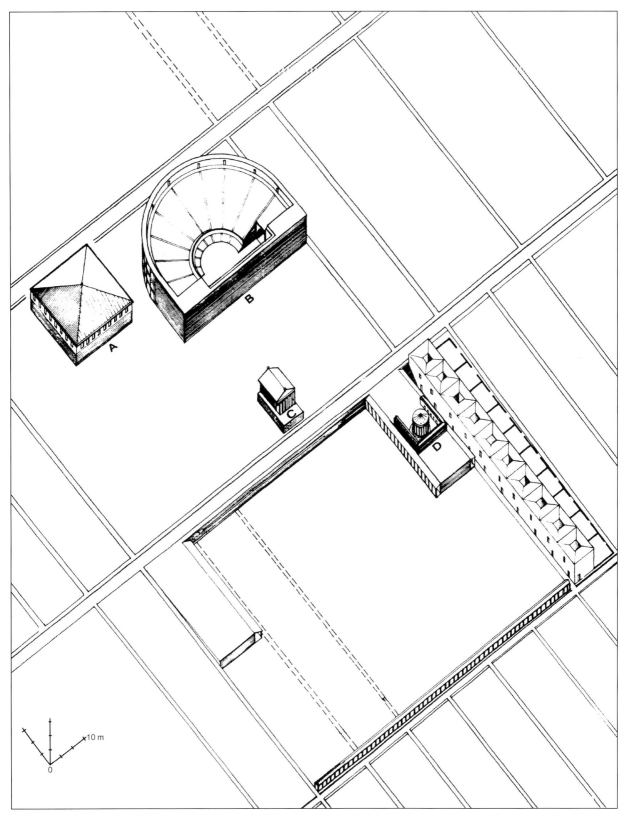

Fig. 3:8. The Roman forum (from Greco 1985a: fig. 38, with kind permission). A = theatrum tectum; B = theatre; C = temple of the Dioscuri, later San Paolo Maggiore; D = the macellum, *later area of San Lorenzo Maggiore.*

forum. Indeed, these finds separate the area of Emanuele Greco's public square into two east and west halves, lying almost in the middle of the two east and west limits, that is between the *stenopos* discovered to the immediate east of the *macellum* and Vico Purgatorio ad Arco/Vico Fico al Purgatorio.[29] Perhaps the forum duplex should thus be seen as a public area divided not into two north and south halves, but into two, east and west, halves, though only excavation can resolve the matter.

A passage by the Neapolitan Roman poet Statius informs us that colonnades enclosed part of the area (Stat. *Silv.* III. v. 89). Perhaps they linked the *media plateia* and the area to its immediate north, where reused columns are to be found. The *media plateia* (Via dei Tribunali) approaching the forum may have been organized as a processional way, delimited by two arches. An 'arcus antiquus qui vocatur cabredatus', demolished in the sixteenth century, seems to have been located at the junction of Via dei Tribunali with Via Atri and Via Nilo, whilst an 'arcum roticorum' may have lain at the point where Via dei Tribunali now meets Via Duomo (Capasso 1895: 47). Perhaps, to the eyes of a Byzantine citizen, the *media plateia* of Naples appeared as an oriental *embolos*, so common in the cities of Asia Minor and the Levant (Foss 1979: 65–6, n. 39).

Public building continued in the area of the forum into Ostrogothic times, as is attested by Procopius's anecdote (*Bell. Goth.* V. xxiv. 22–7) concerning a richly worked mosaic of Theoderic that, on the crumbling of the king's head, signalled the end of his life. This was said to have occurred in the year 526. It was perhaps in the second half of the same century that the forum effectively ceased to be the one and only centre of civic life in Naples, a further favoured area being the area around the cathedral. Pagan temples had already been abandoned by the end of the fourth century, and ecclesiastical building at first took place elsewhere. The *macellum* was out of use by the middle years of the sixth century, when the basilical church of San Lorenzo was erected over its northern half.[30] Town councils were evermore eroded through the course of the sixth century, so that, by the seventh, power was mainly in the hands of the duke and the ecclesiastical authorities, whose seats of government lay towards the upper part of Via Mezzocannone and the cathedral respectively. We may thus suppose the reconversion during this period of buildings such as the basilica and perhaps the *curia*, though the institution survived in the town, in quite altered form, into the seventh century and seemingly beyond (Brown 1984: 18–19). During the fifth century, the large colonnaded hall of the basilica at Ordona in Apulia was subdivided into a number of small rooms and even later turned into a cemetery, whilst that of Squillace in Calabria became a rubbish dump (Casteels 1976: 56–7). Indeed, archaeological evidence shows the fora of many Roman towns suffering gradual encroachment or changes of function, in some cases even as early as the fourth century.[31]

None the less, as late as 1540, the area is attested as 'platea Mercati Veteris', thus distinguishing it from the later market that developed by the sea from around 1270 (Diocesan Archive, Fondo Sante Visite, F. Carafa, 1540 f. 158; see Doria 1971: 301–2).

WATER SUPPLY

The Augustan aqueduct of Naples, restored under Constantine, continued in use until the Gothic War when, in 536, it was cut by Belisarius. Indeed, it became the Trojan Horse of the siege of Naples, being used by the Byzantine forces as a way into the city and an agent to its capitulation (Proc. *Bell. Goth.* V. x. 14–16). It was later restored. In 598, Pope Gregory ordered the bishop of Naples to return the charge of the city gates and the aqueduct to the secular authorities (Greg. *Ep.* IX. 76). Various documents dating from around the turn of the millennium refer to *putea*, which quite likely fed on the classical cisterns and the aqueduct, as in later times. If it were still functioning in early medieval times, the city would have suffered no problems with water supply, as it has been estimated that its urban cisterns contained some 4.5 million cubic metres of water (see above, Chapter 1). As water supply was also fundamental to the functioning of baths, and as there are various instances of baths recorded in early medieval Naples (Vitale 1985: 13–14), it may be concluded that for most of the time the aqueduct did continue to serve the city, even if its source lay in Lombard territory.

---

[29] I should like to thank Giuseppe Vecchio for the information on this unpublished excavation.
[30] It was probably built during the early years of John II's episcopate (533–555). See Venditti 1969: 812.
[31] Salona, Ephesus, Thasos, Cyrene and Thuburbo Maius were cited by Ellis (1988: 566).

Remains of one early medieval bath have now been recognized in Naples (Fig. 3:9). Two rooms of a bath-building are preserved in the later Franciscan monastery of Santa Chiara (Arthur 1999). The monastery was built in 1313, and an original hall of the complex is stratigraphically later than the remains of the bath. Excavations have shown that the area originally was occupied in part by Roman baths that, at the time of construction of Santa Chiara, had been abandoned (de Franciscis 1954). Of the medieval baths, the first room, with an exterior cross-vaulted roof, probably had a dome that was perhaps modified during the construction of Santa Chiara. The second room seems to preserve its original dome on pendentives, of slightly conical or ogival form, which recalls the more pronounced dome of the so-called *trullo* chapel at Olevano sul Tusciano, perhaps of tenth-century date (Venditti 1967: 388–90). A group of five pipes perforated its walls, just beneath the dome, at the juncture of each pendentive. The remains present analogies with some early Islamic baths, such as the early eighth-century Qusayr 'Amra baths in Jordan (Almagro *et al.* 1975). The discovery is rather exceptional, as Byzantine baths are rare after the sixth century.[32] Furthermore, they might well have been fed by a branch of the Augustan aqueduct located beneath Santa Chiara and, if so, would provide further evidence for the survival of the Roman water system throughout early medieval times. Documentary evidence suggests that there were various baths in Naples by the end of the millennium, and even nearby *Nuceria* had public baths by 955 (*CDC* I: 187). One rather interesting text details such a building erected at the monastery of San Marcellino e Pietro in 983 (Capasso 1895: 189–91).

There is no evidence in Naples for public latrines of Roman or later date, though they certainly must have existed. At Athens, public latrines continued to be maintained into the seventh century (Frantz 1988: 33–4). In the fourteenth century, Boccaccio described a cesspit in Naples, lying between two buildings in a narrow street, and precariously covered by planks upon which one sat (*Decameron* 3, 39–40). In early medieval times, much excrement must have gone to fertilize the intramural orchards, perhaps dumped directly out of windows. A charter of 1008 prohibited a certain

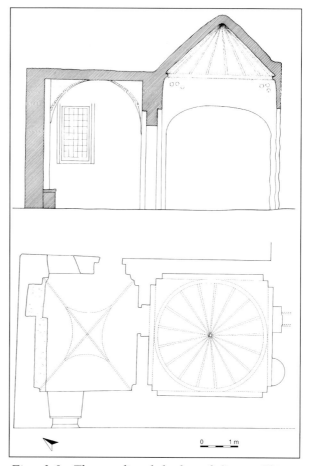

Fig. 3:9. The medieval baths of Santa Chiara (drawn by Michele Varchetta).

Stephen from dumping refuse out of a window onto a communal alley (R. 323). A few drains, however, continued to function, probably largely based on the original Roman network. A document of 935 mentions a *vicus publicus* 'per quem descendit aqua a fistula', presumably a pipeline of Roman date (R. 27), whilst excavations at Palazzo Corigliano have revealed a Hellenistic drain that might have remained in use until the fifteenth century (Gastaldi 1985: 28). It lay approximately on the line of the medieval *Lavinarius* or public conduit, which met the sea outside the walls, south of Via Mezzocannone (Capasso 1895: 186–7). However, at Carminiello ai Mannesi the street drain went out of use during the late fifth or sixth century, when it was frequented by rats (Arthur 1994: 68; King 1994: 387–8). A *clobaca pubblici* is also attested by the mid-tenth century, and some wealthy houses, at least, were able to make use of it (Vitale 1985: 12).

---

[32] See, for example, Kazhdan 1991: 271. Medieval baths have been excavated at the Crypta Balbi in Rome (Sagui 1990) and at Salerno (Peduto *et al.* 1989).

HOUSES AND GARDENS

Apart from the die-hard persistence of the ancient street pattern, itself indicative of settlement continuity, it is important to examine the architecture within the classical insulae. Studies around the Mediterranean show that the construction of houses of strict Roman plan does not seem to have survived the sixth century, though much reuse and adaptation took place (Ellis 1988). This was often the case in Naples. In the twelfth century, for instance, the monastery of San Teodoro e Sebastiano was known as *casapicta*, probably because it incorporated remains of a painted Roman building (Capasso 1895: 439; R. 687). Despite what must have been a rather heterogeneous architecture caused by reuse of parts of earlier buildings, certain recurrent characteristics in the development of medieval urban housing seem to be demonstrated by the sources, and may relate to the survival of ancient structures.

Gianfranco Caniggia, in a series of provocative studies, argued for a continuity in building plans from classical to later times through continuous reuse of outer walls and internal subdivisions (in particular, Caniggia 1984; 1985; 1989). Proof for his model will only come through excavation, though it is sufficiently interesting to be worth illustration, as it would create a decisive element against the vision of Naples as merely a series of 'hamlets' within a walled rural environment (Whitehouse 1988; Carandini 1993: 33). He defined a principal type of residential architecture surviving within the intramural area, despite the mutations of the centuries. It evolved from the Hellenistic and Roman *domus urbana*, amply illustrated by examples at *Pompeii*, where the primitive

domus is later divided into two distinct residential units, one developing from the atrium/tablinum plan and the other from the hortus/peristyle (Fig. 3:10). Thus his thesis would see an original antique *domus* forming the basis for two later, different sized, residential units for which he calculated mean averages of 15 m as regards street frontages, and 20 m and 12–15 m respectively as regards depth. These sizes depend upon development over an original *domus* that occupied the entire width of an insula, that is the space between two *stenopoi* or *cardines*, or roughly 30 m. Variations are obviously allowed for, including that of the development of a single residential unit over the entire area of an antique *domus*, and that of the aggregation of further space by partial occupation of the streets. This second case is well documented in Naples through the progressive addition and absorption of porticoes (discussed below). To this day, Caniggia's two residential unit forms preserve inner courts that, according to him, developed around the atria and peristyles. The missing link between the Roman atria and later medieval and Renaissance courts might be identified in the common *corte* or the diminutive *corticella*, so frequently mentioned in early medieval documents, which could have been a communal space, exploited by the surrounding properties, in which a well was often placed (De Azevedo 1974: 668, 672).[33] Thus, to his single residential unit developing around an atrium, we might add the probability of two or three distinct residential units developing around a single atrium, common court or 'trasenda communale', to which, furthermore, public access could be barred for reasons of security. Against this model, we might argue that external insula walls survived as property bound-

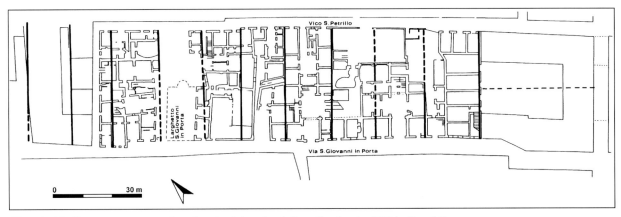

Fig. 3:10. Reconstruction of a classical insula (after Caniggia 1984: fig. 25).

---

[33] The wells often may have let on to old Roman cisterns beneath impluvia.

aries, whilst internal walls did not survive in so pedestrian a manner. Rather, in some cases, later subdivisions of internal spaces repeated a basic plan of pan-mediterranean court-dwellings, thus leading to pure coincidence between Roman and later house plans. Excavations at Palazzo Tabarelli, Trento, have brought to light a Roman *domus* of which one room along the street frontage was adapted and reused in early medieval times, whilst the interior walls of the insula were demolished so as to create open spaces, possibly for agriculture (Cavada and Ciurletti 1986). Whether Caniggia's rather mechanistic scheme functions might be shown through carefully placed key-hole excavations, though we should bear in mind that subdivision of spaces is well attested throughout the Roman world from late antiquity (Ellis 1988: 567–8).

Alongside the developments from the *domus*, one should also consider developments from Roman insulae or apartment blocks. These were characteristic of Rome and Ostia, but also present in Naples, at Carminiello ai Mannesi and possibly under both the cathedral and the Historical Archives of the Banco di Napoli. Axel Boethius drew attention to a type of house 'where the system of the insulae with *tabernae* is reduced to a narrow strip-house with only one or two *tabernae* and staircases towards the street', which became characteristic of medieval Rome (Boethius 1951–1953; 1960). Though it is, at present, difficult to cite buildings in Naples that seem to derive clearly from such a process (various *might* have), the rows of modern *bassi* or small, ground-floor, single or double room dwellings and shops, typical of poorer residential units in the centre of Naples, do seem to echo somewhat similar developments. Though some of these are clearly carved out of the ground floors of later medieval and Renaissance *palazzi*, others might have developed from earlier building types. This is clearly an area worthy of further study.

We possess a certain amount of information regarding early medieval building through Neapolitan documents, and a careful analysis has been conducted on those of nearby Salerno, though in both cases information dating earlier than the tenth century is scarce (Amarotta 1989: chapter 6). Already in 853, a wooden house is attested in the

nova civitas salernitana (*CDC* I: 43). There, the documents suggest that about 50% of domestic buildings during the tenth century were of wooden construction, dropping to some 2% of, presumably residual, buildings by 1266. It is possible that less wooden constructions existed in Naples, where solid, standing and adaptable Roman buildings might have been more frequent. There can have been no lack of material to be reused, and it is likely that structures, such as that discovered along the frontage of Via Dante in Verona (Hudson 1985: fig. 7), will one day come to light.[34] Wooden partition walls were, however, plentiful, and perhaps these subdivided old Roman room spaces (De Azevedo 1974: 48).[35] The use of *pisé* is not attested archaeologically, though this may be due to non-survival of the evidence. None the less, it is worth noting that at least one document cites the term *lutamentare*, which might refer to the construction or use of *pisé* (R. 664).[36]

The average surface area of dwelling plots in Salerno might have been in the order of just under 50 m^2 (though ranging from 10 to 152 m^2) (Amarotta 1989: 242), whilst those at Gaeta appear to have been around 36 m^2 (Skinner 1994: 286). We have no reason to believe that those in Naples, where direct evidence is lacking, were much different. An average family of five would yield a ratio of person/dwelling space in the order of 1:10 m^2, recalling calculations of average space requirements in peasant societies (Naroll 1962: 588).

Additional residential space could be had through vertical development of the *domus* units. Whilst some early medieval buildings possessed two storeys (the *casa solariata*), in later times, especially after the fifteenth century, the number of floors was increased so as to arrive at the average five floors that are visible today. Thus, two-storeyed houses in Salerno could have had an average surface area of almost 100 m^2, and slightly more if balconies were constructed, though living space would have remained the same if ground floors were used for byres, stables and other subsidiary activities. Going by the documents, by the tenth century the ground floors of Neapolitan houses seem often to have been devoted to agrarian activity, shops and stalls. Wells (*putea*), cisterns (*piscinae*), basins for ablutions (*canthari*) and rooms known as *cellae/cellarii* and *gryptae*

---

[34] See Capasso (1905) for a possible example.

[35] None have been identified yet, though the post-holes found cutting the pavements of Roman houses at Venosa may represent the practice (Salvatore 1991: 59–60).

[36] See Gelichi (1996: 74) for the apparent use of the term for *pisé* at Ravenna.

(possibly storerooms and cellars) are all attested (Capasso 1895: 194).[37] Many of these might have been classical survivals. Some ground-floor rooms opened onto back gardens or orchards (*cum curte*), which may be recognized in 'dark earth' deposits (see below, pp. 53–5). The *curte commune* was presumably a communal garden or space serving the various families whose houses surrounded it. Michelangelo Cagiano De Azevedo saw the *corte* or *corticella* as a communal space or courtyard, surrounded by properties, in which a well was placed (De Azevedo 1974: 668). This picture is intriguing in the light of the hypothesis of urban property development from the classical *domus* (see above, pp. 46–7), as one might imagine the *curte* growing out of the open spaces or atria and peristylia of Roman houses. If such was the case, the wells might have let onto the Roman cisterns frequently located beneath the atria. Some of the wealthier citizens of Naples were also able to afford comforts such as baths: in 984 we are told, for example, that the property of Giovanni Mandolo was 'conjuncta balneo domini Joannis' (Leone and Patroni Griffi 1984: 14).

True domestic activity was generally confined to the first floor, the solaria (*aheria*), organized with triclinia and cubicula (bedrooms). The triclinium was no longer that of the Roman *domus*. Archaeology has shown how in wealthy late antique buildings it took on the function of a formal audience chamber for selected guests and was no longer a straightforward dining-room (Ellis 1988: 571–2).[38] Though it is extremely improbable that dining-couches were ever sited in the early medieval triclinia of Naples, save perhaps in the case of the ruling classes, the term seems to have assumed the connotations of a reception room and living-room, indeed perhaps being multi-purpose. This may have been similar to the functions of the later Germanic *sala*, only once found used as a term in a tenth-century Neapolitan document. Vitale equated the term triclinium with the 'ala ubi manere videmur', the 'sala familiaria' and the 'saluciola' of the documents in the *Codex tradi-*

tionum Ecclesiae Ravennatis (Vitale 1985: 13; De Azevedo 1974: 660). Indeed, the *sala* may have gradually moved from the ground floor to the first floor during the phase of vertical expansion of domestic space.[39]

The *casa solariata* is the antecedent of the later medieval and Renaissance palazzo with its *piano nobile*, and I believe that it may find its origins in a blend of Germanic and Roman architecture of the late Roman northern provinces, typified by aisled villa forms. In later manor houses, it may be equated with an upper living-room, developed from the medieval hall (Thompson 1995). When and why the *dominus* moved his domestic activities as *caput familiae* to the upper floor is hard to say, though I have little doubt that the late Roman villa at San Giovanni di Ruoti (Small 1983), and possibly that at Quota San Francesco, Locri (Avetta, Marcelli and Sasso D'Elia 1991), are ultimately little more than a rural expression of the same building type. At Viterbo, *casae solariatae* are already attested in 789 (Bullough 1966: 107). First-floor living quarters in an urban environment were one remove from the stench and bustle of the streets. In the country they may have served to keep one's head above the crops, many of which reached almost as high as a single-storey building, whilst they certainly afforded greater visibility over distances. In both cases, they may have assured greater security, like the later towers and tower-houses, though they do not seem to have been at all common in southern Italy, perhaps reflecting greater centralized power. Some existed in Bari until they were demolished by Roger II in 1132.[40]

Intimately linked was the development of the *laubia*, origin of the later Italian *loggia*, which was especially characteristic of northern Italy (De Azevedo 1969). The emphasis of documents on *casae solariatae* suggests, none the less, that many houses were not *solariatae* and were, presumably, single-storeyed and probably lower down the social scale. The upper floor of high-status houses was apparently sometimes heated through a fixed structure, attested by the Greek-derived word

---

[37] In documents of Salerno and Amalfi the ground-floor or single-storeyed house is represented by the term *catodium*. *Putea* presumably refers to wells, though other meanings, such as irrigation systems, seem to have applied in certain areas (Guillou 1978). *Cantari* are now chamber-pots in Neapolitan dialect.

[38] This 'courtly' function must surely explain the representation of triclinia on late Roman silver, on the Sicilian villa mosaics (Piazza Armerina and Tellaro) and on the Virgil manuscript (Vergilius Romanus, folio 100; Painter 1988: 104). All this would provide a *terminus post quem* for the change in function.

[39] See Redi (1991: 303–4) for a discussion of the *sala* at Pisa.

[40] Andrews (1991: 83) stated: 'The tenor of the Constitutions of Melfi issued by the Emperor Frederick II in 1230 suggests that his Norman forbears had prohibited the construction of towers and unlicensed fortifications, both in these Constitutions, and in the earlier Assize of Capua. He argued that his castles were sufficient for the security of his realms without it being necessary for individuals to build their own defences'.

caminata (Italian: *camino*), perhaps a form of fireplace or room with a fireplace. At Venosa, rough hearths were inserted into the angles of rooms of old Roman buildings from as early as the fifth century (Salvatore 1991: 59). However, it seems not to have been until the fourteenth century, at least in northern Italy, that fireplaces with flues substituted for hearths in most vernacular architecture (Gadd and Ward-Perkins 1991: 124, n. 5). In Naples, much of this will ultimately have depended upon the opportunities and restrictions provided and imposed by surviving Roman architecture.

The only original early medieval domestic architecture yet revealed by excavation seems to be a small square building, surviving only at foundation level, with associated cesspit (?), at the site of Carminiello ai Mannesi (Arthur 1994: 64–5, 73–4). It was built over an infilled road or *stenopos*, nestling between two early Imperial insulae in decay. Two of its walls made use of standing Roman walls, whilst the foundations of the other two were built of crudely mortared rubble, probably gathered on the spot. The material discovered in the foundation trenches, including a fragment of forum ware, would seem to date it no earlier than the later eighth century.

Patricia Skinner has attempted a reconstruction of a unit of Neapolitan houses on the basis of a document of 970 (R. 181; Skinner 1994: 286–7) (Fig. 3:11). It lay in a residential area between two *stenopoi* (Vici Virginum and Bulgarum) above the *summa plateia*, and likely made use of pre-existing Roman walls. It is interesting as an example of early medieval, two-storeyed housing, illustrating the subdivision of the various functional areas, and it may be noted how the open space or courtyard was centred and not fronting the road, perhaps making use of a pre-existing atrium.

Towards the end of the millennium, expansion in the number and size of families necessitated further living space. Buildings along the street frontages of insulae occupied by gardens and orchards, could expand backwards, though in the first instance the proprietors, instead of sacrificing valuable agricultural land, probably found it more economic to expand either upwards or forwards over the public streets, architecture and technology permitting. As early as 1116, the wealthy family of the Inferi contemplated building upwards on a house already provided with three floors (R. 615;

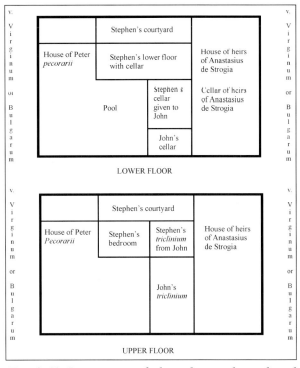

Fig. 3:11. Reconstructed plan of an early medieval house (after Skinner 1994: fig. 2).

Vitale 1985: 12). However, most proprietors would have had little choice but to build out over the streets, until an economical technology of construction permitted substantial vertical expansion. The requirement of space thus led primarily to an expansion in first-floor living space jutting over the streets as balconies, often sustained by ground-floor porticoes permitting public thoroughfare. Indeed, at Pavia *casa solariata* refers both to a two-storey house, where the principal room was probably on the upper floor, and also to part of a house, as in platform, gallery or balcony: a document of 970 referring to a 'solarium edifica[turum] super via publica' must surely refer to an extension of the first floor through the construction of a balcony built over a public thoroughfare (Bullough 1966). Early examples probably looked like the Roman Casa del Balcone Pensile at *Pompeii*, or the more impressive though less preserved examples at Ostia.[41] However, by stages, the supporting columns, pillars and arches were often blocked in, thus blocking public thoroughfares and effectively narrowing the width of streets. The scale of portico and balcony construction witnessed by the texts suggests that it was, at times, endorsed by the

---

[41] See Boethius (1960: chapter 4), who argued for continuity in the architectural type from Roman through medieval times. A history of porticoes also has been provided by Guidoni (1990), and the contributors to Bocchi (1990) have discussed the development of porticoes in general and especially in Bologna.

authorities, and, by later medieval and Renaissance times, the portico was rationalized so as to become a specific architectural form fronting palazzi and public buildings. They permitted activity whilst sheltered from inclement weather, either hot sun or rain, were ideal meeting places, and thus favoured commerce and political business.

Two late medieval examples survive along the southern side of Via dei Tribunali, to the west of Piazza San Gaetano, though they have been extensively remodelled (Fig. 3:12).[42] They front the Spinelli di Laurino palazzo and that of Philip d'Angiò, prince of Taranto. The first, between the piazza and the point immediately opposite Via San Paolo, fronting the palazzo of Philip d'Angiò, has eleven sub-rectangular piers. Five of them, numbering seven to eleven counting from the end nearest the piazza, visibly enclose reused columns and column bases on their inner sides. The other piers, built of the local grey volcanic *piperno* stone, are probably later. Each of the surviving column bases lies at exactly 0.73 m above the actual paving of the portico. This suggests that the present level of Via dei Tribunali is over 0.8 m lower than it was when the portico was first erected in medieval times, though perhaps not substantially lower than it was in classical times on the basis of evidence from the excavations conducted at the nearby site of the Pietrasanta. Analogies for the supposed rise in the street level in (early?) medieval times are found easily, whilst the later lowering is not yet easily paralleled, though could be part of a general rearrangement effected hand-in-hand with the construction of the palazzo at the end of the thirteenth century (see above, p. 39). Returning to the portico, there is little doubt that the original construction with reused columns was earlier than Philip's palazzo. The façade, which exhibits a reused Greek inscription, lies 5.3 m from the present street edge. The width of Via dei Tribunali in front of the palazzo of Philip d'Angiò is actually 6.75 m, which, when added to the width of the portico in its present state, would give an original street width of 12.05 m. If we accept 12 m for the original width of the *media plateia*, then almost half of the original carriageway would appear to have been invaded during medieval times on its southern side. If the columns represent an early medieval portico, subtracting the width (1.40 m) of

Fig. 3:12. Porticoes along Via dei Tribunali (photo: author).

the enlargement of the piers in Angevin times, then the early medieval portico may have invaded the original carriageway by some 3.90 m on its southern side. However, there is a difficulty here in that there also appears to have been a certain amount of encroachment on the northern side, testified further along the road by the clearly documented episode of the Pietrasanta, the arched belltower of Santa Maria Maggiore (Fig. 3:13). Thus, all told, the *media plateia* was probably wider than 12 m, perhaps 13 m as proposed by Emanuele Greco (1986: 201–2), if not closer to 16 m.[43]

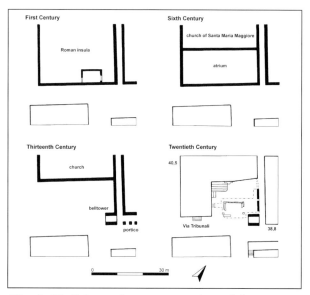

Fig. 3:13. Schematic reconstruction of the process of encroachment due to portico construction along Via dei Tribunali (drawn by author).

---

[42] I had first thought that a well-preserved example was to be seen at the corner of Vico Figurari and Via San Biagio ai Librai, though on closer examination it would seem that the columns there were used in the corners of an original façade to protect the building from attrition by turning vehicles.

[43] The measurements presented here were taken by the present author with Dante Di Cresce.

In the case of the Pietrasanta, the concept of providing public thoroughfare despite building encroachment of the streets is expressed by the east–west arched opening built into the base of the bell-tower, possibly dating to the twelfth century. This surely indicates the maintenance of a straight thoroughfare along the northern side of Via dei Tribunali, which has long since disappeared through the blocking in of the porticoes of neighbouring buildings. This is confirmed by the fact that existing properties show a raised floor level roughly coinciding with the original street frontage, corresponding to the inner (northern) side of the bell-tower's arched opening.

Balconies were also much more common than has been assumed, giving the streets the appearance of an area in which cantilevered buildings jostled for space (see Redi 1988). The underlying porticoes became so common that, by the thirteenth century, 29 of them had developed into *sedili* or meeting places for district councils by virtue of the fact that they had, in time, become traditional community gathering places (Capasso 1895: 191–2). In addition, they account for the fact that the medieval and modern roads are narrower than their original Greek and Roman counterparts, as later street frontages followed the façade created by the porticoes rather than the original façades of the porticoed buildings. Modern street frontages are somewhat irregular, indicating haphazard, as opposed to planned, expansion.

The unification of properties by monasteries or wealthier members of society probably also led to the appearance of *pontili*, imitating the two flying buttresses built against the Roman theatre along Via Anticaglie, during the early second century AD (Fig. 3:14). They linked buildings on opposite sides of a street by an arched bridge. I know of no evidence for early medieval examples, though surviving late medieval ones are to be seen along Via Anticaglie and Via San Gregorio Armeno.[44] Two similar bridges, crossing the parallel *stenopoi* Vico Fico al Purgatorio and Vico San Nicola a Nilo at their junctions with Via San Biagio ai Librai, create a continuous frontage along the latter, barely punctured by narrow arched lane entrances. The antiquity of the original construction at Vico San Nicola a Nilo seems almost to be emphasized by the heavy wear pattern present on a Roman inscription, inserted as *spolia* at the base of the wall so as to protect the corner at the

Fig. 3:14. The arched buttress of the theatre (photo: author).

junction of the lane and of Via San Biagio ai Librai from the iron-rimmed hubs of cart and carriage wheels, though again we possess no direct dating evidence (Capasso 1905: 162, n. 36; possibly *CIL* X: 1483).

A related architectural type is the *supporticus*, consisting of rooms supported by an arch that linked buildings on opposite sides of a road. Good examples survive at Vico Melofioccolo. A rather well-preserved example is to be seen at Via Diritto Portico in the town of Traetto, southern Lazio, where a series of arches along the road support horizontal beams and planked floors. Such bridges, *pontili* or *supportici*, will have saved venturing across what were probably far from amenable road surfaces.

We do not know when the actual invasion of public spaces commenced in Naples, though the process must already have been underway in late Roman towns, as it was prohibited by the *Codex Theodosianus* (XV. 1, 22, 39). Private building on

[44] Also attested in Lombard Benevento (Rotili 1990: 135–6).

public space has been found in excavations throughout the Mediterranean: however, unlike most other surviving towns, encroachment in Naples narrowed the streets but rarely altered their course.[45]

Many Roman buildings must have been reused, and evidence of such a practice is available at the site of Carminiello ai Mannesi (Fig. 3:15) (Arthur 1994). At least three rooms of the Roman insula were provided with doors fronting onto the partially infilled street, which had been smashed through the Roman brick-faced masonry sometime after the fifth century. Though not closely dated, they are likely to be more or less contemporary with the eighth-century(?) building discussed above, as they appear to form part of a general reorganization of the spaces in and around the decaying Roman edifice. They were not single-room dwellings, as other doors were smashed through interior walls (Fig. 3:16) to adjoining rooms. As they were originally sunken with respect to the Roman street, a backfill of rubbish helped raise their floor level to meet the street surface, though reducing their interior height of just under 5 m to under 3.50 m.

Other substantial Roman buildings were also converted in early medieval times. The amphitheatre, theatre and *odeion* are now hidden beneath houses, and were presumably inhabited after their original functions had lapsed. In the case of the *odeion*, this was not much later than the reign of Tiberius II (578–582), according to the coin found in the burial above the *scaena* (Arthur 1989b; see above, p. 41). Similar examples are be found throughout Italy, as theatres and amphitheatres had become expendable during late antiquity, partly because of maintenance costs and partly on account of spreading Christian attitudes against the activities held there (Ward-Perkins 1984: chapter 6).

Some of these architectural cadavers were inhabited by the urban poor, and it is probably to an old Roman structure that Procopius's tale of a poverty-striken woman living in 'a building which had entirely fallen into neglect' refers (Proc. *Bell. Goth.* V. x. 14–16). Conditions are unlikely to have improved over the next 150 years or so. Indeed, they may have got worse, as it is from the late fifth and early sixth centuries that archaeological evidence comes for the abandonment of buildings and conversion of spaces into rubbish dumps or cultivated intramural plots.

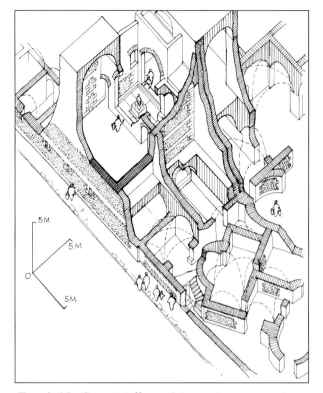

Fig. 3:15. Carminiello ai Mannesi — reconstruction by Sheila Gibson and Janet DeLaine (from Arthur 1994: fig. 1).

Thus, despite the building activity revealed by archaeology and the sources, a proportion of built-up areas within the walls either changed function through Roman and early medieval times or was abandoned. A clear example of functional alteration is given by the use of intramural areas for burial. Though certain changes in function seem to suggest an availability of space by the fifth or sixth century, perhaps resulting from a decline in population, true abandonment of certain areas within the city probably never took place. Thus, under the term abandonment, I have subsumed the concept of decayed buildings or areas that at least temporarily went into disuse. These may be recognized archaeologically by the identification of naturally formed silt deposits, collapsed masonry and waste accumulations. All three have been found, dating to various moments from the mid-fifth to the later seventh centuries, at Carminiello ai Mannesi. However, some buildings seem to have fallen into neglect already by the later fourth century. At the Girolomini site, a late Republican cistern, probably belonging to a *domus*, was sufficiently ruined for a large pit, filled with all sorts of rubbish, to have

---

[45] The clay and timber buildings over the forum at Luni (Ward-Perkins 1981), or the shops and houses invading the *Embolos* and the *Arcadiane* at Ephesus (Foss 1979: 97), provide explicit examples.

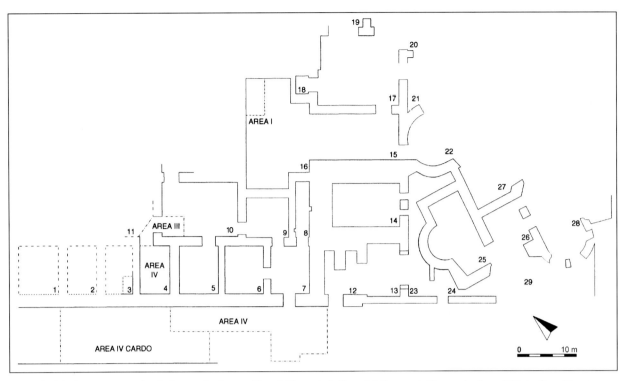

Fig. 3:16. Doors smashed through the walls of Carminiello ai Mannesi (from Arthur 1994: fig. 6).

been cut through part of its floor.[46] Dumps dating to the late fourth century were also revealed at Santa Patrizia, whilst waste accumulations of the fifth or sixth century were found in the building excavated at Santa Maria la Nova and in the baths discovered under the church of Donnaregina.

The ground-floor agricultural functions of the medieval house types described above are to be related to the increasing amount of agricultural land available within the town's walls from late antique times. Five sites excavated within the town have yielded accumulations of dark soil, up to 1.5 m in thickness, over demolished Roman buildings.[47] Given their resemblance to layers of 'dark earth' identified in Britain, dating from at least the third century at London (Vince 1990: 4; Courty, Goldberg and MacPhail 1991: 261–8), and the prevalent hypothesis that they represent accumulations of agricultural soil, detailed analysis is desirable.[48] Micromorphological studies of the London deposits led to their classification as debris of both substantial and insubstantial buildings (timber-framed and mud huts) with their 'dark homogenized fabric resulting from the mixing of domestic wastes, including graminae charcoal and airborne charcoal from fires, with decayed mud-

walled and mud-floored huts', occurring 'through rooting and faunal mixing, garden cultivation perhaps a later effect enhancing the biological activity' (Courty, Goldberg and Macphail 1989). I doubt that insubstantial building debris contributed to the Naples deposits as much as in London. Preliminary results from the accumulation at Via San Paolo, over the structure of the abandoned *odeion*, show that the slightly basic soil (average pH of 7.50) contained pottery, dating from about the sixth to the twelfth centuries, which was far more abraded and fragmented than the pottery from contemporary rubbish deposits at Santa Patrizia (Fig. 3:17). As the deposit had no visible internal stratigraphy, it was excavated in 0.1 m spits, and the most fragmented pottery was thus seen to be concentrated in the upper 0.3 m (Fig. 3:18). Furthermore, the general date range of artefacts became gradually older further down in the layer, with later medieval glazed pottery only towards the top. The absence of any soil profile suggests that the deposit was never left immobile long enough for one to develop. Flotation residues revealed abundant minutely fragmented pottery, bone and glass, often only 1–2 mm in size, of the sort we might expect to find in regularly turned agricultural

---

[46] Context US 52 (Arthur and Vecchio 1985: 421). The faunal remains and amphorae are examined in Chapter 6.

[47] The sites of Via San Paolo, Vico della Serpe, Santa Patrizia (Arthur 1995), Palazzo Giusso and San Marcellino (Carsana 1996).

[48] See also the general considerations of Yule (1990) and Watson (1998).

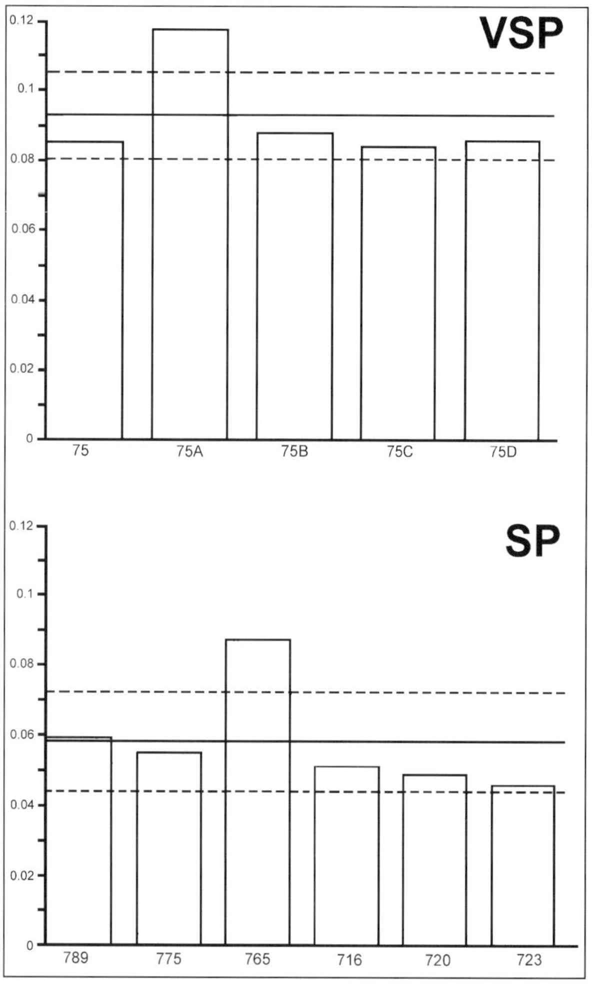

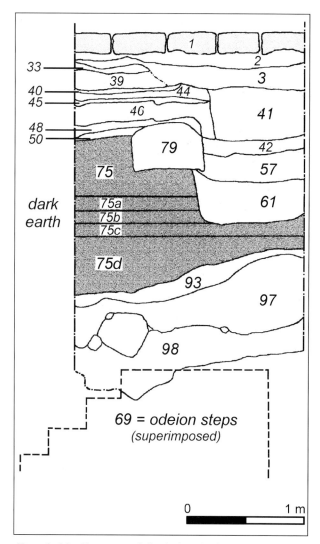

Fig. 3:17. The differing degrees of pottery fragmentation in various contexts at the excavations of Via San Paolo (VSP) and Santa Patrizia (SP) (from Arthur 1995: fig. 3).

Fig. 3:18. Section of dark earth deposits — Via San Paolo (drawn by Michele Varchetta).

soils or in areas subjected to incessant abrasion, such as street surfaces. The quantity of pottery, some 3 kg per cubic metre of soil, may indicate a certain amount of selection in the rubbish that was used to make up the soil deposit at Via San Paolo, and contrasts with the 10 kg of pottery per cubic metre registered for rubbish deposits, where we might expect to find larger proportions of non-biodegradable waste. At the Vico della Serpe excavations, analogous deposits were found overlying demolished late Roman structures along with a dump of smashed amphorae dating to the sixth century, whilst in the large cloister of the Girolomini they were found to overlie Roman floors. All this would seem to fit the suggestion that abandoned Roman buildings were razed and covered with imported agricultural soil so as to

enable cultivation within the town. The thick accumulations produce a wide range of artefacts, often abraded as a possible result of the continuous movement provided by hoeing, plant growth and the action of burrowing animals. Flotation of the soil has demonstrated the presence of carbonized and mineralized plums, nuts and cereals, though never in sufficient quantity to enable more than a guess about the eventual crop types cultivated within the walls, as many of these remains may have been introduced to the contexts through the process of rubbish disposal and fertilization.[49]

Archaeologically, 'dark earth' deposits are now being recognized in various Roman towns in Italy, particularly in the north at Alba, Aosta, Brescia (Brogiolo 1993), Verona (La Rocca 1992), Pescara (Staffa 1991) and elsewhere, suggesting that the

---

[49] The identification of plant remains was carried out by Jane Fitt and Marina Ciaraldi. See below, Chapter 6.

pattern in Naples is by no means unique.[50] Their concentration in the north of the peninsula is probably due partly to their successful identification by archaeologists and partly because of a greater survival of urban activity. In the south, possible examples of the phenomenon may be recognized in Sicily, both on the island of Ortigia at Syracuse (Voza 1982), which was to become the nucleus of the early medieval settlement, and at Marsala (Kennet, Sjöström and Valente 1989), and perhaps at Brindisi (Patitucci Uggeri 1976).

In late antiquity the *stenopos* by the *macellum* found beneath San Lorenzo Maggiore was totally filled with deposits of soil and waste (Fig. 3:19). As the site lies by the forum, and as the deposits effectively blocked all access to the substantial cryptoporticus underlying the *macellum*, which in Imperial times had served a variety of functions, including shops and possibly the town's *aerarium*, the reasons for the abandonment of the building and the street are of some importance. The excavator claimed that the infill was the result of an alluvial episode that took place during the fifth century, though the evidence, including the analyses and section drawings, has never been published (De Simone 1985: 191, 195, n. 27).[51] A large section of the fill fortunately still survives over the eastern part of the *stenopos*, to be excavated under controlled conditions in the future. Examination of the evidence reveals a sequence of dark soil layers that lie virtually horizontally and do not display any clear inclination or characteristics of silting or of water-borne material, which might be expected had it been washed downhill. Indeed, it may be questioned where above San Lorenzo did a suitable reservoir of soil lie in the fifth century, given that the area was substantially built up. The proposed chronology is also in doubt. Few of the finds have been published, but they include a lamp of the so-called Sicilian type, datable to the seventh or eighth century (De Simone 1985: 192, no. 30.10; see Garcea 1987; Ceci 1992). It may be that the *stenopos*, along with parts of the cryptoporticus, was purposefully back-filled between the fifth and eighth centuries, perhaps gradually, as at Carminiello ai Mannesi.

Unless Roman Naples possessed little housing development, which is extremely unlikely given the archaeological data and the evidence of the

urbanization of other Campanian towns such as *Pompeii*, *Herculaneum* and *Puteoli*, then it must have been during early medieval times that built-up areas gave way to open ground. By then, many orchards are mentioned in the documents (Cassandro 1969: 249, 392, n. 48).[52] This model reflects the results of urban excavations in northern towns such as Verona (La Rocca Hudson 1986a; 1986b) and Brescia (Brogiolo 1993).

It is suggested above that the existence of 'dark earth' deposits within the walls probably indicates a larger proportion of intramural agricultural land in the town when compared to Roman times, implying a greater ratio of the citizen-body directly involved in agriculture. This may be used to argue a ruralization of the town. Another possible indicator of ruralization, and certainly of altered productive forces, is the appearance of the *clibanus* in archaeological deposits dating from the fifth and sixth centuries. The *clibanus* is a ceramic bread oven (Fig. 3:20) sufficient for the preparation of a loaf (Cubberley, Lloyd and Roberts 1988; see also below, Chapter 6). It is still in use in present-day Dalmatia, where centralized bakeries do not exist or are insufficient to meet the demands of the rural society (Carlton 1988). In Roman *Pompeii* or Naples, where centralized bakeries existed, *clibani* do not seem to have been at all frequent, though they were produced in the *ager Falernus* and used

Fig. 3:19. The stenopos *beneath San Lorenzo Maggiore (photo: M. Iodice).*

---

[50] I owe the information on Aosta and Alba to Mariacristina Marchegiani.

[51] This unlikely thesis was picked up by Vecchio (1992: 91).

[52] It may be noted that no significant open areas dating to Roman times have yet been revealed through excavation, despite the examination of over eighteen sites.

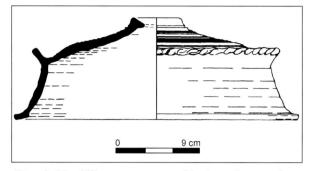

Fig. 3:20. Clibanus *or portable bread oven from* Matrice *(after Cubberley* et al. *1988: fig. 2).*

in such rural establishments as the villa of Matrice in Molise (Cubberley, Lloyd and Roberts 1988). Thus their appearance in late antique Naples, where they probably survived until the end of the tenth century, may indicate the breakdown of centralized commercial bread production and the assumption of the task by families or institutions such as monasteries and *diaconiae*.

Later medieval Naples was a city of monastic gardens and orchards, as shown by cartographic views produced by Renaissance and later artists. Those of Dupérac and Lafréry (1566), Bertelli (*c.* 1570), Braun and Hogenberg (1572) or Cartaro (1579) all show areas within the walls dedicated to gardens and orchards (Fig. 3:21).[53] Most of these are depicted within the insulae, rimmed by buildings fronting the streets. Various remnants still survive, hidden behind actual buildings or within monastic complexes, and in some areas significant portions of gardens and orchards existed until the nineteenth century (Coppola 1982).[54] It is thus hard to escape the conclusion that large areas inside the walls of the town were turned over to agriculture during the early Middle Ages. The pattern is not new. Even areas central to the Roman city of Milan, going by the toponym 'pasquario', seem to have been used as pasture in early medieval times (Bognetti 1959: 71) and the forum of Rome was depicted by artists as an Arcadian landscape as late as the eighteenth century. After the first millennium, increasing population and land prices gradually forced most families and institutions to relinquish their urban gardens and orchards in favour of extramural plots. Only a few wealthy

families and monastic groups were able to preserve open spaces within the walls, and by the twelfth century they had been breached by urban expansion around Piazza del Mercato towards the sea.[55]

CEMETERIES AND BURIALS

In late Roman times, organized burials seem to have taken place principally in cemeteries outside the walls, according to well-established custom and legislation. Though little is known of open-air cemeteries, two substantial catacomb complexes are preserved, those of San Gennaro and San Gaudioso, as well as smaller examples such as San Severo and Sant'Eufebio.[56]

The catacombs of San Gennaro, dedicated to Naples's patron saint, Ianuarius, and cut on two levels into the tuff hill of Capodimonte, after *c.* 400, were accessible through two arches opening out of the apse of a single-naved basilical church. They have numerous loculi and a few *arcosolia* reserved for dignitaries, and have many paintings and a few mosaics datable no later than the fifth century. Though the catacombs date from as early as the third century, the majority of burials is late Roman and, apart from Ianuarius himself, include those of such noted figures as Quodvultdeus, bishop of Carthage (ob. 454), possibly the third-century Bishop Agrippinus, and Bishop John I (ob. 432). Within the catacombs are the small fourth-century basilica of Agrippinus and a baptismal font erected by Bishop Paul II (763–768). Although the complex probably went out of use as a general burial ground by the time that Bishop John IV removed the remains of Ianuarius to the cathedral in the first half of the ninth century, it continued to be a site of pilgrimage, as is attested by paintings done under his successor Athanasius I.

The catacombs of San Gaudioso are named after the burial there of the bishop of *Abitinae* in north Africa, a further refugee from the Vandals. A sixth-century painting shows the martyrs Stephanus and Sossius. The nearby catacombs of San Severo, dedicated to the local fourth-century bishop buried there, have various fourth- and fifth-century frescoes also illustrating Severus, Saint Paul and Saint Protasius (Rassello 1985; Galante 1987).[57]

---

[53] The engravings may be consulted in Pane and Valerio 1988.

[54] Dalbono (1891: 124–6) referred to gardens in the marginal area around Santa Maria d'Agnone, close to the excavations of Vico della Serpe.

[55] For expansion outside the southern, coastal, walls, see Feniello 1991.

[56] Two sixth- or early seventh-century burials, one of a man in his early 20s and the other of an infant contained in an amphora, have been excavated at the bath-building of first-century date at Santa Maria la Nova, outside the walls (Appendix I).

[57] On the various catacombs, see the discussion of Fiaccadori (1993: 151–4).

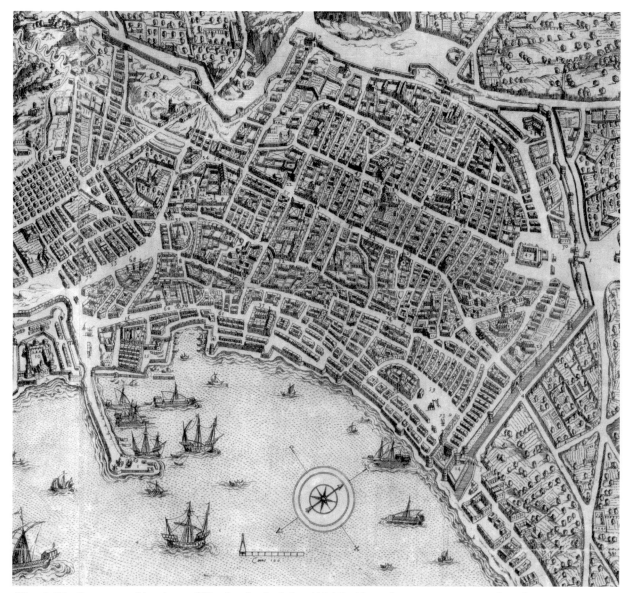

Fig. 3:21. Cartographic view of Naples by Lafréry (1566). Note the open spaces within the city.

Both bishops and dukes tended to find repose in the catacombs, the former particularly in a funerary basilica above the resting place of Saint Ianuarius (Fasola 1975; 1986).[58] Duke Theodore was instead interred within the city in 730–731, in the church of San Giovanni e Paolo that he founded close to the praetorium. His sarcophagus was removed in 1592 and may now be seen beneath his epitaph in the church of Donnaromita (de Franciscis 1977). The cathedral became a repository for translated burials during the ninth century, both because of Arab incursions, which led to insecurity in the integrity of extramural sepulchres, and because of the raid of Sico of Benevento on the catacombs of San Gennaro in 831. The spoils of the fourth-century Bishop Maximus, originally held in the catacombs of San Gaudioso, were removed from Monte Cassino to San Gennaro in 877, and later taken to the cathedral (Mallardo 1959). So were the spoils of Saint Restituta, probably removed from Ischia in 812. Those of Saint Sossius were removed from *Misenum* to the urban monastery in his name in 906. Though some important individuals continued to be buried in the catacombs, like Bishop Athanasius in the late ninth century, the acquisition of the mortal remains of powerful or holy individuals by urban churches served to underpin their significance in the eyes of the people (see below, Chapter 4).

---

[58] Excavations have been carried out at the catacombs recently, particularly by Nicola Ciavolino, though they remain substantially unpublished. Father Ciavolino showed me a collection of African red slip ware lamps and their local imitations from the catacombs.

Roman prescriptions against human burial within urban limits or *pomeria* are often quoted (Cic. *Leg.* II. xxiii; *Cod. Iust.* III. xliv. 12; *Cod. Theod.* IX. xvii. 6), and archaeology tends to show that they were adhered to. It is thus of some interest to find out when the practice came to an end. The earliest documented burial in an urban church is that of Candida, who died in 585, and was laid to rest at Sant'Andrea a Nilo (Ambrasi 1980: 225). Excavations have, however, revealed other early burials within the walls, though none are necessarily earlier than that of Candida. A single burial, dug into the steps of the *odeion* at Via San Paolo, which had a coin of Tiberius II (578–582), perhaps purposefully embedded in the mortar of the tile covering (a token gesture to pagan superstition?), is likely to date to the late sixth or seventh century. Four burials, two in tile-tombs and two in amphorae, were found in the courtyard of the ex-convent of Sant'Andrea delle Dame (De Petra 1892). Another amphora burial, dated to the late fifth or the beginning of the sixth century, was discovered in Via Pietro Colletta, close to Piazzetta Calenda and Via Santa Maria a Cancello, where further burials appear to date to the early seventh century (S. De Caro, pers. comm.). Burials in amphorae are unlikely to date after the seventh century, because of the increasing difficulty in obtaining such containers, whilst tile-tombs, often considered to be Roman, could date to the seventh century, if not later, as long as the tiles were available.[59] The cemetery at San Lorenzo Maggiore, where burials were inserted into the base of the *tholos* of the abandoned *macellum*, probably dates to the sixth century. Other burials were arranged in rows in the narthex of the basilica, whilst yet another was found in front of Santa Maria Maggiore. Various scattered or single burials, such as the children buried in a fountain at Carminiello ai Mannesi and partly covered with lime, are possibly plague victims of seventh- or eighth-century date. They probably represent spontaneous and totally unauthorized burial within the walls. The same may have been the case with the burial at Via San Paolo, whilst those at San Lorenzo were clearly associated with the church. At the site of the monastery of Santa Patrizia part of a cemetery of tenth- to eleventh-century date has been excavated. The five skeletons recovered were both male (four?) and female (one?), including that of a woman who had given birth.[60]

The phenomenon of dispersed burials is characteristic of many late antique urban centres. Even if some may have been plague victims, many were not, and, bearing in mind the existence of large burial grounds such as the catacombs of San Gennaro, dispersed burial needs some explaining. Could they have been organized by ecclesiastical authorities? I think not. Indeed, perhaps they represent members of society whose families could not afford to pay the price for regular interment commonly requested by church officials, though not always condoned by the Church.[61] Further burials will undoubtedly be brought to light, and careful excavation in the future should reveal more about the causes of death and the religious leanings of the deceased and their families, and explain phenomena such as the insertion of burials into earlier Roman mausolea, commonly found at Pozzuoli and elsewhere.[62]

[59] Some twenty tile-tombs dating to the end of the sixth or the seventh century were found in the centre of Lombard Piacenza, for example (Pagliani 1991: 33, 84).

[60] Unpublished report by P. Petrone.

[61] Perhaps others were die-hard pagans, whose burial could not be allowed to contaminate hallowed ground. Bishop Hypatius of Ephesus threatened excommunication of church officials who required payment for burial (Foss 1979: 44).

[62] For the sort of thinking that can produce results from the unspectacular burials of late Roman and early medieval date, see, for example, Randsborg 1991.

4

THE ROLE OF THE CHURCH

HISTORY AND THE PHYSICAL EVIDENCE

Given the position of the bay of Naples, on a main route from Rome to the East, it is not hard to imagine Christian communities there since Julio-Claudian times. Tradition associates their foundation with Saint Peter. During a visit to Naples in AD 42 he cured the ailing noblewoman Candida, who duly took up the Christian faith. She was instrumental to his encounter with Saint Aspren who, also cured by Peter, became the first bishop of the city. Tradition would also have him installing Celsus as bishop of *Puteoli*, and converting people to Christianity as far south as *Surrentum* (*Vita San Athanasii* and *Vita San Aspreni*).[1]

Apart from a record of bishops, whose validity is somewhat questionable, there is little evidence regarding the Church until the late Empire (see below, Appendix III). In 305, the Campanian Church was deprived of various leading figures, including Ianuarius, bishop of Benevento, through Rome's last-minute martyrdoms under Diocletian. That it was Ianuarius, martyred at *Puteoli*, who effectively became Naples's patron saint rather suggests that Naples had no particularly significant martyrs of its own. This might explain why various saints and martyrs, like Costantius, Giuliana and Restituta, were 'washed ashore', from time to time, during the early Middle Ages. Saints, it may be remembered, were prime agents of God, expected to intervene when life was difficult and the authorities turned a blind eye (Brown 1981: 5–9).

Throughout early medieval times Naples witnessed a steady collection of saints' bodies and bones from Campania and further afield, all helping to augment the city's prestige. The remains of local saints were gathered by the Neapolitan Church or the secular authorities from the declining or abandoned towns of *Puteoli*, *Liternum*, Ischia, *Misenum*, the *Lucullanum* and *Cumae*. Monastic refugees, who considered the city a safe haven, also brought remains from abroad. Amongst these we may include the body of Saint Severinus, from *Noricum*, and possibly remains of Saint Potitus, a martyr under Antoninus Pius, from Thrace (*Passio S. Potiti, BHL* II: 1006, nos. 6908–12; N. Del Re in *BiblSanct.* 1072–4).[2]

The city seems largely to have escaped the persecutions, perhaps because its cosmopolitan citizen-body acted as a buffer to certain forms of state intercession, and is singularly devoid of local martyrs. Furthermore, this lack of martyrs may explain why Naples possessed a particularly large number of bishop-saints. Ianuarius supplanted Agrippinus, a third-century bishop of the city around whose sepulchre the catacombs of San Gennaro had originally developed, as patron saint. His *vita* was perhaps not dramatic enough for the early faith.[3]

In 355/356, Bishop Maximus was ousted by Zosimus, supporter of the Arian heresy, and fled to the East. Zosimus was succeeded by Severus (*c.* 363–408/410), a contemporary of Paolinus of *Nola* and good friend of Bishop Ambrose of Milan, both acquaintances being guarantees for evaluating his pastoral activity. Economic well-being during his episcopate is indicated by the various churches that he erected in the city. He is particularly remembered through the catacombs sited in the old Hellenistic and Roman cemeterial valley of the Sanità.

---

[1] See also Capasso 1878: 118–19. Here Candida is the product of a legend that appears to have evolved through the duplication of a Candida who died in 585, and was commemorated by a metrical inscription now in the church of Sant'Andrea a Nilo (Ambrasi 1985: 26, fig. 1).

[2] The earliest reference to his cult is in the *calendarium marmoreum* of Naples, dated between 847 and 877. On the Neapolitan translations see Cilento 1969b: 686–9.

[3] On the legends of Campanian saints see Oldoni 1993: 302–18.

60 CHAPTER FOUR

The capture of Carthage by the Vandals in 438, and their persecutions, led many members of the African clergy to seek refuge in Italy. The bishops of both Carthage and *Abitinae*, Quodvultdeus and Gaudiosus, as well as Abbot Habetdeus, fled to Naples. It is believed that during his time in Campania, Quodvultdeus wrote the *Liber promissionum et praedictorum Dei*, as well as a series of sermons (Braun 1964). Various important relics were brought over from the Maghreb at the time, including those of Saint Stephen and of Saint Restituta, whose church at Carthage was converted by the Vandals to the Arian creed (Victor Vitensis *Historia persecutionis Africae* 1.15; Moorhead 1992: 8). Naples's role as a haven for refugees emphasizes the importance of the city during the fifth century. The welcome that the African bishops evidently expected is probably indirect evidence for the power of the local episcopate, which in many other cities of the West is attested as having assumed evermore civic responsibility alongside traditional pastoral duties (see, for example, Mochi Onori 1933).

Little is known of later periods. In the sixth century, which witnessed the turmoils of war, the Neapolitan Church may have passed from a stage of increased spending to one of financial difficulty. This is suggested by the construction of three major churches, followed by the instatement of the rector of the *patrimonium Sancti Petri* by the time of Gregory the Great, occasioned probably by concern over the safety of agricultural properties in the area with the Lombard invasions. Pope Gregory had given great impulse to the Neapolitan Church: however, with his death in 604, the Byzantine patriarchate was able to reaffirm its influence. Naples's subsequent ecclesiastical history was often a tug-of-war between Rome and Constantinople, until the all too vivid clash over iconoclasm (726–842), from which controversy, there is little doubt, the Latin Church came out stronger (Cilento 1969b: 650).

Today, ecclesiastical buildings represent the most tangible material evidence for the medieval urban transformation of Naples. The Church, in its various forms, seems to have been responsible for the largest proportion of building expenditure during late antiquity, thus confirming its very rapid development as a major power in the politics, administration and economy of the city.

However, little archaeological work has been carried out on the early history of the churches, and their chronology relies heavily on the written sources. Foundation dates for ecclesiastical constructions are few, though the fairly rich source material does, at least, provide us with *termini ante quem* for their presence (Fig. 4:1; Appendix II).

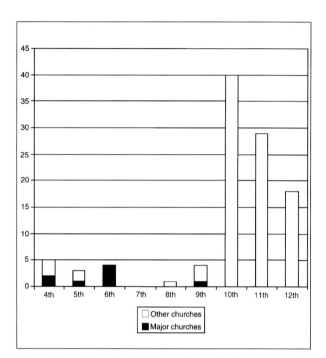

Fig. 4:1. Church building through late antiquity and the early Middle Ages (drawn by author).

Using the dates of earliest occurrence, the fourth to sixth centuries represent the first peak for newly constructed churches, monasteries and *diaconiae*. They witnessed the erection of all the major basilical buildings, save for San Paolo Maggiore.[4] The peak of new construction was followed by a slump, beginning in the later sixth century. Nothing is known about the seventh century, and only one building is attested for the first time in the eighth, and four in the ninth, though I find it very hard to believe that nothing was achieved by the early independent dukes. The tenth century appears as a veritable boom period in foundations, with the first documented reference to 40 church buildings, many of them probably private foundations. The numbers drop again in the eleventh and twelfth centuries, with 29 and eighteen buildings respectively.

[4] For the *diaconiae* see Ambrasi 1981. Both the church of Santa Maria Maggiore and that of San Giovanni Maggiore have been partly excavated in the past few years. The former has revealed traces of smashed apsidal mosaics, with both turquoise and gold-leaf tesserae, whilst excavations at the latter have brought to light a sixth-century *opus sectile* apse floor and traces of early medieval wall-paintings. None of the recent discoveries are published. Previous work was summarized by Venditti (1967).

Though much is rightly made of the slump in building works through early medieval times as an indicator of economic contraction, the major churches erected well into the middle of the sixth century may well have proved adequate in terms of servicing the Neapolitan congregation until the later first millennium, when the population seems again to have been on the increase. This pattern is similar to that of the middle Byzantine boom at Constantinople, though apparently lags behind Rome (Randsborg 1991: 102–5). However, the picture alters if monasteries (and monastic churches and *diaconiae*) are taken into consideration.[5] Initial signs of revival may then be dated as early as the second half of the eighth century, and continue into the early ninth. There is little evidence for construction throughout the rest of the century. If there was effectively an arrest in activity from the first half of the ninth century, this would agree with the hypothesis of a political and economic crisis interrupting revival and provoked by an intensification in the Arab raids on southern Italy. Recently, Paolo Delogu has illustrated the contraction in building activity in Lombard southern Italy that was to last until the 930s (Delogu 1992: 310–11). Various rural monasteries in southern Italy were raided and abandoned, including Monte Cassino and San Vincenzo. This had the counter-effect of driving refugee monks to more secure havens such as Naples, where alternative accommodation had to be found or constructed, such as the monastery of San Severino e Sossio and, perhaps, Santa Maria d'Agnone.

Few details exist concerning the accruement of church wealth in Naples, though already in the early fourth century, according to the *Liber Pontificalis*, Constantine appears to have endowed the new cathedral with about 10 lb of gold a year, agricultural land bringing in a revenue of 673 solidi and valuable church fittings (*Lib. Pont. Silvester* (Davis 1989: 25–6); Jones 1964: 90, 904). It seems particularly significant that, whilst a similar amount of gold was also given to the Capuan see, no such endowment is recorded for *Puteoli*, still a leading city at that date, thus presaging the overriding importance that Naples was to obtain during

the following century. Private benefactions must also have been substantial (Lepore 1952: 331). From an early date commerce may also have provided a reasonable income, if one may judge by the exemption from the *collatio lustralis*, a trade tax, granted by Constantine to clerics. However, by the mid-fifth century clerical trade seems not to have been favoured (Jones 1964: 907).[6]

Thus, with the breakdown of central government in the West, which had already showed signs of strain in the fourth century, but was all but nonexistent by Justinianic times, the Church gained increasing power, gradually assuming both civic responsibility and authority (Hammond 1974: 15). This process is nowhere made clearer than through the correspondence of Pope Gregory. He was concerned that Church money should be spent on ransoming Christians who had been taken captive by the Lombards. A letter of 596 urged the Campanian Rector Anthemius to liberate as many captives as possible (*Ep.* VI. 32; Richards 1980: 99–100). By the end of the century he had reason to complain of Bishop Paschasius of Naples, who not only spent too much of his time building ships, but lost 400 solidi through this activity (*Ep.* XIII. 29). Gregory's letter is particularly precious on two counts. In the first place it underlines the character of certain late Roman bishops. They often came from prominent families, usually of the landowning class, from whom members of the town councils were also picked. Given the excessive financial burdens that *curiales* were expected to sustain after the third-century recession, it is of little surprise to find that various people sought a bishopric. This was not always because of any compelling Christian spirit, but as both a means to avoid undue government pressure and to gain power and prestige. Indeed, the position offered such guarantees and possibilities of financial improvement that cases of bribery to obtain the post were not unknown and privative management of Church property was almost the order of the day.[7] Gregory's letter is, furthermore, a clear indication of the possible scale of ecclesiastical investment in commerce, despite the quite clear restrictions imposed by both Valen-

[5] See below, pp. 69–74, for monasteries and their associated churches.

[6] Though the income derived may not have lived up to the emperor's expectations, the impost was maintained into the fifth century, though apparently for the humblest grades.

[7] For the truly scandalous behaviour of various fifth-century bishops in Asia Minor, see Foss 1979: 14–15. Richards (1980: 201–2) recalled Natalis, archbishop of Salona, who delighted in lavish banquets and apparently distributed church plate amongst his relatives. Such custom was probably also frequent amongst the aristocracy, judging by both the importance attached to the possession of triclinia during the late empire and the relatively abundant finds of late Roman silver plate, often of a heterogeneous nature, suggesting mixed provenances (Lavin 1962; Painter 1988).

tinian III and by the *Concilium Arelatense*. Various monasteries also appear to have been particularly active in the exchange of produce from their *fundi*. Such produce was marketed locally through their own retailers and internationally through *negotiatores*, on ships that were often the property of the monasteries themselves (Cassandro 1969: 252–5).

Indirect evidence for trade by independent middlemen is provided by the regulation that apparently dismissed local monastic ships from paying the *portuaticum* on entering the ports of Naples, thus presupposing the existence of a significant quantity of lay ships: however, this dates to the early eleventh century (Cassandro 1969: 254). Monastic ships may have been exempted largely because they were not much used for explicit trade, but rather for guaranteeing the circulation of produce between monastic estates and communities within a closed economy. All these instances do nothing but confirm the increasing capital available to the Church throughout the course of the millennium. Though rendered financially solvent by the state and by the late Roman aristocracy, its opening to the most varied congregations very quickly ensured it a popular consensus and power base.

THE CATHEDRAL AND ECCLESIASTICAL BUILDING UP TO THE DUCHY OF NAPLES

The most striking material expression of Church wealth and power is the quantity and quality of construction that took place up to the mid-sixth century, when public and civil architecture was already stagnant. Indeed, it was most probably the Church that maintained high building standards and guaranteed a measure of architectural, technical and artistic continuity from Roman times, exemplified, first and foremost, by the cathedral complex (see, for example, Christie 1991: 354).

The history of the Neapolitan cathedral is intricate (Fig. 4:2).[8] Slipshod excavations carried out at the end of the 1960s and in the early 1970s have not resolved the layout or the sequence of construction, though they have revealed mosaic floors that may have belonged to rich Roman *domus* (Di Stefano 1974). The earliest identified ecclesiastical building is the Basilica del Salvatore (Saviour). It was perhaps originally dedicated to the Holy Apostles and Martyrs, and only later to Saint Restituta, on the arrival of her relics from Ischia, after an Arab raid of 812 (Cilento 1989:

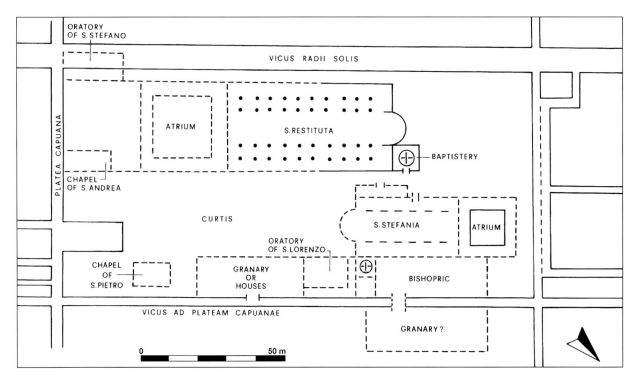

Fig. 4:2. Proposed reconstruction of the cathedral complex (after Ciavolino and Dovere 1991: fig. on p. 22; redrawn by Sally Cann).

---

[8] The evidence is now summarized in Desmulliez 1998.

101). Though dating from Constantinian times, under Pope Sylvester, it has been argued that the surviving basilica of Santa Restituta dates to the time of Constantius. In or shortly after 355, Constantius replaced Bishop Maximus with the Arian Bishop Zosimus, and he may have bestowed the church with various gifts to help support the new bishop (Jones 1964: 90; Davis 1989: xxvi). This complex was to be the nucleus of the present cathedral (Venditti 1969: 792). Santa Restituta is a basilical building with five aisles, reusing earlier Roman columns and capitals said to have come from a temple dedicated to Apollo. The statue of a horse, possibly the equestrian statue now represented by the splendid bronze *testa Carafa*, perhaps removed from the forum, was placed in the area, and apparently remained there during the early Middle Ages (see Cilento 1969b: 674; Pannuti 1988). It is possible that during the same period *spolia*, such as the fine Egyptian basalt krater with Bacchic masks of second-century date, now in the cathedral, and the two porphyry columns at its entrance porch, were recovered from earlier public buildings to embellish the developing Christian complex.[9] The annexed baptistery of San Giovanni in Fonte, probably dating to the early fifth century, during the episcopate of Severus, with modifications carried out under Bishop Soter (?465–492), still survives to show us the rich mural mosaics, quite on a par with those at Ravenna, and said to be 'the principal surviving monument of palaeochristian art in southern Italy' (Fig. 4:3) (Bologna 1993: 186; also Maier 1964; Pani Ermini 1978b: 210– 12). Further construction around this basilica included the episcopal palace, to which was added a refectory (*accubitum*) around the mid-fifth century by Bishop Vincent, and to which a polychrome mosaic floor appears to belong. At the turn of the century Bishop Stephen I constructed a second episcopal church, known as the *Stephania*, possibly at right angles to Santa Restituta and united by a rectangular atrium (Venditti 1967: 479).[10]

A second hypothesis sees the two churches lying parallel to each other (Fig. 4:2), separated by one of the *stenopoi* of the ancient Greek and Roman town. The largest and earliest church, that

Fig. 4:3. The baptistery of San Giovanni in Fonte (photo: L. Pedicini).

of Santa Restituta, would have faced south, and the other would have faced north. Each church would thus have had its own atrium (Ciavolino and Dovere 1991: 21, 22; also Sorrentino 1908). Whatever the case, it is the second cathedral that received most subsequent attention, with the addition of rich altars and ciboria.

All this activity was to add a new centre to the city that, in turn, conditioned future urban development as regards the distribution of society as reflected in the positioning of palazzi. Though not modifying the overall street pattern, the *stenopos* represented by the present Via Duomo clearly became a major thoroughfare. Indeed, the major basilica church of San Giorgio Maggiore was erected to one side of it, at the junction with the *imma plateia*.

A basilica of San Fortunato appears to have been built outside the walls, in the area of the Hellenistic and Roman cemetery of the Sanità, so as to accommodate the remains of the mid-fourth-century bishop-saint. Not much later, Bishop Severus (*c.* 363–408/410) built a cemeterial church and associated catacombs that bear his name close by. Little of the site has been excavated. What may be seen are two rooms, one with painted *arcosolia* and the other containing rectangular tombs cut into the floor. The fifth-century paintings of the first room bear representations of Saints Severus, Eutychetes, Ianuarius (?), Peter and Paul, and Protasius, as well as a golden jewel-

[9] The columns were placed in their present position around 1407, and the krater in 1618 (Galante 1872: 3, 31). Given the rarity of such pieces in primary contexts outside of Rome, it is possible that they were transported from the capital to Naples in late antiquity or later to embellish the cathedral.
[10] Twin cathedrals were frequent in late antiquity. Examples may be cited at Trier, Aquileia and many other sites. The bibliography is immense. See, for example, Krautheimer 1975.

Fig. 4:4. Fifth-century painting of a jewelled cross in the catacombs of San Severo (photo: V. Guida).

Fig. 4:5. The catacombs of San Gennaro (photo: P.C.A.S., reproduced courtesy of G. De Pasquale).

encrusted cross (Fig. 4:4).[11] Bishops Nostrianus, Gaudiosus and Maximus, the last of whom had died in exile, were buried nearby.

Severus is known as the builder of four further religious edifices, comprising San Giorgio Maggiore and the cemeterial church by the catacombs of San Gennaro, erected early in the fifth century, as well as the monasteries of San Potito and San Martino.[12] San Giorgio Maggiore, one of the large urban basilical churches, was probably dedicated to Saint George around the seventh or eighth century (Gesta Ep.; Krautheimer 1965: 208–9; Venditti 1967: 490–3; 1969: 778). Its earlier dedication is uncertain, though it once possessed apse mosaics that depicted Christ amongst the apostles. All that is preserved of the early structure is the open apse with deambulatory that opened towards the town's lower plateia. It is built in opus listatum, with two courses of reused tile alternating with a single course of rectangular yellow tuff blocks, similar to the Constantinian basilica at Capua (Pagano and Rougetet 1984: 1002).

Mention should also be made of the little-known catacombs of Sant'Eufebio, with a fifth-century painting. Bishop Ursus, successor to Severus, was buried there in the early part of the century (Fiaccadori 1993: 156).

The fifth century represented a period of great ecclesiastical building activity in Italy. The Church at Rome visibly put pressure on bishops to invest in such activity (Ward-Perkins 1984: 65–6). The sources assign the peak of such building in Naples to the late fifth and sixth centuries, with a severe

reduction in the seventh, a pattern characteristic of much of the Byzantine world, including Constantinople (Mango 1989: 53). Of the churches built in the course of the century, one must count the early fifth-century cemeterial church erected under Bishop Severus by the catacombs of San Gennaro (Saint Ianuarius).[13]

The catacombs (Fig. 4:5) grew up around the burial place of the third-century Bishop Agrippinus, in a Roman cemetery apparently of late second-century inception, though they were dedicated to Ianuarius, bishop of Benevento, martyred under Diocletian, and later patron saint of the city (Fig. 4:6). Their dedication must have occurred after the 'discovery' and transportation of his remains there from Marciano, near Puteoli, under Bishop John I, sometime in the years 413–432. The site had probably already been developing into a centre of pilgrimage by the early fifth century, when Bishop Severus built the basilical church. Indeed, it may be questioned whether Bishops Severus and John hastened to glorify the site with the new church and the spoils of the saint in competition with Bishop Paulinus's sanctuary at Cimitile, which was under development at the same time. In 492, Bishop Victor, who was also responsible for the foundation of the churches of Sant' Eufemia and Santo Stefano, added a portico and an oratory. In the mid-eighth century Bishop Paul II, exiled from the city on account of his stance during the iconoclast controversy, contributed a baptismal font. In the early eighth century Duke Caesarius II was buried there (Capasso 1879).

---

[11] On the catacombs of Severus and related remains see Galante 1987; Rassello 1985. Rassello (1985: 28–30) conjectured a representation of Bishop Ambrose of Milan, close friend of Severus.

[12] The question of Severus's churches has never been resolved satisfactorily. See, for example, Galante 1987: 77–8.

[13] On the catacombs in general see Achelis 1936; Fasola 1975. Liccardo 1995 is a useful pocket guide to the catacombs of Naples. A detailed publication of the catacombs of San Gennaro is urgently required, also presenting the wealth of objects recovered by the late Nicola Ciavolino. I should like to thank Giovanni De Pasquale for information concerning the site.

Prince Sico of Benevento raided Naples around 831, and the church and catacombs were sacked. The spoils of Ianuarius were taken and deposited in the Beneventan church of Santa Maria di Gerusalemme, whilst the funerary epitaph of Caesarius was removed to Salerno. Probably in the year 839, during the Lombard civil war that led to the division of Salerno from Benevento, Lothar I, an ally of Naples, obtained some relics of Ianuarius. He transferred them to the abbey of Reichnau, on lake Constance in Switzerland, where Abbot Witigow (985–997) built a chapel to house them (Houben 1987: 58–61).[14] The remaining bones were returned to Naples and eventually placed in the cathedral by Archbishop Alessandro Carafa in 1480. A physical examination of the remains that are contained in a vase in the cathedral, inscribed C[orpus]S.JANVARIJ BEN.EPI., has revealed the bones of an adult male of around 35 years of age, missing a tibia and other fragments (Ambrasi, 'Gennaro', in *BiblSanct*. 141; De Rosa 1964).

The catacomb cemetery, cut into the volcanic tuff, developed on two levels. The upper contains the bishops' crypt, with two surviving fifth-century portrait mosaics identifying the *arcosolia* of Bishops John I and Quodvultdeus. Wall-paintings in the western part of the catacombs suggest that they were used until the ninth century or later (Bertelli 1992: 137–9). At least until 1356, they were under the care of a Benedictine monastery founded by Bishop Athanasius I (Fasola 1975: 219, 223).

A fair amount of ecclesiastical building took place under the Ostrogoths. Apart from the afore-mentioned work on the baptistery of San Giovanni in Fonte, where the mosaics are all that survive to echo those of Ravenna, additions were made to San Gennaro and, in 533, the large basilica church of Santa Maria Maggiore was erected along the *media plateia* by Bishop Pomponius. Though the actual Baroque church reveals nothing of the original basilical building, excavations and documents have helped to define its nature. The site was originally occupied by a rich late Republican *domus*, which made way for early Imperial buildings. According to tradition, by the early sixth century the site had become a rubbish dump frequented by a demon in the form of a sow. To oust the demon, Pomponius erected the basilical church. It was probably not much smaller than the present church and, according to a sixteenth-century description, was brick-faced with three aisles divided by eighteen

Fig. 4:6. A fifth-century depiction of Saint Ianuarius in the catacombs of San Gennaro (photo: P.C.A.S., courtesy of G. De Pasquale).

columns (Diocesan Archives: *Sante Visite*, Annibale de Capua III, f. 219 (1580)). The excavations suggest that it was preceded by an atrium which fronted directly onto the *plateia* of Via dei Tribunali. On one side of the atrium was a wall in reticulate and tile masonry, dating to early Imperial times, which survived the construction of the Pietrasanta or bell-tower, added around the twelfth century (Alisio 1965: 48–9; see also above, p. 51). Excavation also revealed a floor of white marble around the original altar, whilst a number of glass paste tesserae, some turquoise or green in colour, others bearing gold foil, indicate that the apse was decorated with a rich polychrome mosaic. At least one burial, of uncertain date, was inserted in the area of the atrium. Amongst the prelates of the church was, it seems, a certain Gaudiosus, who became bishop of Salerno in the seventh century, and Athanasius, son of Duke Sergius I (Diocesan Archives: *Collegiata di Santa Maria Maggiore* 6, fasc. 1, no. 2).[15]

---

[14] On the movement of relics in general see Granier 1996.
[15] This is a copy of the papal bull of Sixtus V (15 March 1590). For evidence pertaining to the church, see De Crescenzo 1989.

In 535–555, following a fire, Bishop John II restored the *Stephania* (Venditti 1969: 792).[16] Not only this restoration, but also the construction of one of Naples's most important churches, San Lorenzo Maggiore, was conducted during the reign of Justinian. It lay by the forum and would appear to have been built by John (533–555) at the beginning of his episcopate (Fig. 4:7) (Parascandolo 1847: 90–1; Hirpinus 1961: 14; Venditti 1969: 812).[17] Excavations have revealed the three-aisled basilica with narthex and polychrome mosaics. It is the only early church within the walls of Naples that clearly possessed an annexed burial ground. Apart from burials within the church and regularly spaced beneath the exonarthex, six tombs may still be seen cut into the podium of the *tholos* of the abandoned Roman *macellum*, to the immediate south. These were excavated over 30 years ago and, though not closely datable, are probably considerably earlier than the arrival of the Franciscan friars in 1234, and might even date from the sixth century.[18]

Bishop Vincent (555–578), John's successor, appears to have erected the church of San Giovanni Maggiore in the early years of his episcopate, on a vantage point overlooking the road to the ports, now Via Mezzocannone (Venditti 1967; Borrelli 1967; Ambrasi 1980: 217–18). It was presumably enclosed within the fifth- or sixth-century extension to the Greek wall-circuit. Vincent placed his signature on the church with monograms carved on the *pulvini* of the columns flanking the triumphal arch. Margherita Cecchelli argued for an earlier date for its construction, during Gothic domination, suggesting that it was originally dedicated to the Arian creed, and that it was erected outside the city walls as a funerary church (Cecchelli 1989: 237). Though most of the original building has been destroyed, this grand church still presents the local characteristic, also present in San Giorgio Maggiore, of an apse opening onto an arched deambulatory. The arches, partly sustained by reused columns, also incorporated two magnificent Severan marble pilasters with inhabited floral friezes. Excavations have revealed part of the original apsidal floor in *opus sectile*, as well as scraps of painted plaster imitating marble, perhaps of ninth-century date, adhering to the inner face of a blocked arch on the southern side of the apse.

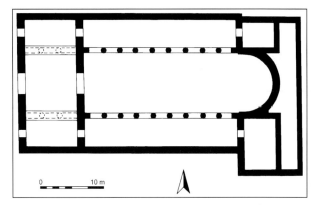

Fig. 4:7. Plan of San Lorenzo Maggiore (drawn by Sally Cann).

The famous ninth-century marble calendar of festivities probably graced this church, which was particularly dear to the ducal family in the later ninth and first half of the tenth centuries (Luzzati Laganà 1983). Bishop Vincent was also responsible for building within the episcopal palace annexed to the cathedral, where the sources attest to his construction of an *accubitum*. Traces of his work may be seen in a floor mosaic bearing the inscription VINC[ENTI]VS VOTVM SOLBIT (Farioli 1978: 159).

The late antique milieu of which Naples and much of central Campania formed part is reflected by some of the early ecclesiastical architecture: the Aegean-type impost blocks at San Giorgio Maggiore, the tripartite transepts paralleled at Milan and in north Africa, the north African style of Santa Restituta, and even more of Cimitile, as we shall see below (Krautheimer 1965: 209).[19] Yet again, the bay of Naples may be seen to lie along the road to Rome from Africa and the East.

ECCLESIASTICAL BUILDING UNDER THE INDEPENDENT DUCHY

Very little is known as regards the form and size of early medieval churches after the construction of the large palaeochristian basilicas. Indeed, little building took place for some time after the sixth century, though the construction in 680 of a new basilical church and *diaconia* of San Gennaro within the walls, removing his remains from the exposed suburban site at Capodimonte, is of note.

---

[16] Further work took place after another fire in 795.

[17] Laurentius, deacon and friend of Pope Sixtus II, martyred in AD 285, was one of the most popular post-apostolic saints, partly due to the works dedicated to him by Ambrose, Augustine and Prudentius.

[18] Restoration of the tombs by the Soprintendenza in 1990 yielded a sixth-century bronze coin.

[19] See now the general discussion by Bologna (1993).

Construction of churches in Naples seems to have recommenced by the second half of the eighth or early ninth century, though hardly on a grand scale, whilst there is more evidence regarding monasteries and monastic churches (see below, pp. 69–74). A baptismal font and painted altar were inserted into the catacombs of San Gennaro under Bishop Paul II (763–768) (Braun 1924: 225, pl. 38), who also built a triclinium, perhaps during his temporary exile to San Gennaro by Stephen II. A major project took place in the Roman forum, with the Christian conversion of the temple of the Dioscuri by Duke Anthemius between 801 and 816 (Fig. 4:8). This first church of the independent duchy was dedicated to Saint Paul (San Paolo Maggiore). None the less, it is possible that it was consecrated somewhat earlier, as it is rather difficult to imagine that the classical building, in such a central area, remained totally abandoned up to that date. The two Dioscuri, central to the tympanum, may have been removed at the moment of the temple's conversion, though their destruction is attributed to a miracle by Saint Peter.[20] The temple's original pronaos survived as the church façade into the late sixteenth century, as is illustrated by a relief carving. Externally it conserved the *cella* of the Roman temple, whilst the interior appears to have been quite richly painted (Capasso 1895: 109–10; Bernabò Brea 1935; Sole 1990).

The period of greatest Byzantine influence in church building is perhaps to be placed in the ninth to eleventh centuries, if it is believed that contacts between Naples and Byzantium remained strong. Some 40 churches are attested for the first time in the tenth century, though virtually nothing survives and the sources yield little information on architecture. There are no certain examples of typical Byzantine church forms, save for San Costanzo on Capri. Two possible exceptions are the church of Santa Maria Rotonda/*ad Presepem*, first attested in 1025, which formed part of a *diaconia*, and the church of San Demetrio. Santa Maria Rotonda's name derives from the fact that it was octagonal, with eight columns in the angles and covered by a vault (Capasso 1895: 93). Needless to say, the form could have been of eastern origin, of which one of the best examples in church architecture in Italy is San Vitale, Ravenna. However, parallels hark back to Roman architecture, such as the

Fig. 4:8. The surviving columns and podium of the temple of the Dioscuri, converted to the church of San Paolo around the early ninth century (photo: author).

mausoleum of Diocletian at Split. The church of San Demetrio, part of a monastic complex founded in 917, still survives. It has been heavily reworked in Baroque style, though is suspiciously Byzantine in form. It is tall and narrow, and consists essentially of a central dome supported by four large piers and four semicircular apses between the piers, one of which is pierced so as to form the entrance. With no great stretch of the imagination, the present form could have derived from a Byzantine cross-in-square or quincunx plan by eliminating the small corner bays and rounding off the angles of the arms of the cross.[21]

Thus, despite the use of eastern decorative elements, such as impost blocks and chancel screens, available evidence suggests that Neapolitan churches remained largely of traditional basilical form, with plans inspired primarily by late

[20] See the comments of Settis (1978: 101–3), who convincingly argued for a transference of cult from Castor and Pollux to Peter and Paul. Their torsos are now preserved in the Museo Nazionale in Naples (Adamo Muscettola 1985).

[21] It may be compared, amongst others, with some of the Macedonian churches (for example, Milijovic-Pepek 1986).

antique Italian and north African buildings. This must, at least in part, be due to patterns created by the survival of the major early basilical churches, as Byzantine influence is visible in the architecture of the Beneventan church of Sant'Ilario a Port'Aurea and probably in that of Santa Sofia, also at Benevento, erected under Prince Arechis II in 762 (Cavuoto 1964; Rotili 1990).

DIACONIAE

In 600 Pope Gregory complained to the praetorian prefect of Italy about the suspension of government subsidy made to a centre for poor relief (*diaconia*) in Naples (Greg. *Ep.* X. 8; Jones 1964: 899; Richards 1980: 88). This is the earliest reference to the existence of *diaconiae* in the city, and one of the last to the state distribution of food in the Empire. Hard times had, indeed, arrived. *Annonae populares* had been generally restricted to Rome and Constantinople, and it is not known when state distributions were first made in Naples. However, during the fourth century, neighbouring *Puteoli*, by way of its singular position, had received the *annona*. It is recorded as having been supplied to the Gothic garrison in Naples in the early sixth century, though this had nothing to do with the Church and cannot be used to argue the existence of public doles prior to the inception of the *diaconiae* (Jones 1964: 257).

The role of the *diaconiae* is fairly clear. They took over the late Roman distributions of the *annona* and the *panis gradilis*. A text of John the Deacon, referring to the establishment of the *diaconia* of San Gennaro in 680, informs us that the bishopric was responsible for the management of 210 *modii* of wheat (*triticum*) and 200 jars (*hornae*) of wine per year. *Diaconiae* provided by Bishop Agnellus in the later seventh century are attested as providing soap for washing twice a year, at Christmas and at Easter (*Gesta Ep. Neap.* 418). A letter of Pope Gregory also indicates that a new bishop was supposed to distribute 186 solidi to the poor and to 'professional' beggars (Greg. *Ep.* XI. 22; Durliat 1990: 557–8).[22] However, the institution may also be viewed as possessing a strong

political element, as the free distribution of prime necessities helped to reinforce the body of consensus for the ecclesiastical authorities and thus effectively reinforced the Church's power base, the *plebs*. Although it has been argued that the institution of the *diaconiae* was spread by monasticism, primarily from Egypt, it is clear that the Church developed it on Italian soil.[23]

By the end of the millennium, seven *diaconiae* are referred to in the sources. They were apparently the only examples existing to the south of Rome, save for one at Gaeta. Pope Gregory's reference to a *diaconia* may have been to Sant' Andrea *ad Nilum*, founded by his time. In the same spirit, however, Bishop Nostrianus had already constructed public baths around the mid-fifth century. Nothing is now visible of the *diaconia* of San Gennaro, which was founded by Bishop Agnellus along with its church and monastic cells. It may have been located just above the *imma plateia*, for the church of San Gennaro all'Olmo, now known as San Biagio Maggiore, though heavily reworked, seems to retain its original three aisles with reused Roman columns and capitals. In early medieval times it was also known as the church of San Nostriano, following the removal there of the saint's remains from the catacombs of San Gaudioso. Indeed, in 1583 a limestone urn bearing the inscription CORP.S.NOSRIANVS. EPC and containing human bones was discovered beneath the altar (Pane 1957: 18–20).[24] The possibility of the existence of a further *diaconia* in the seventh century is suggested by a document dating to the early eighth century that mentions the subdeacon Peter as *dispositor Monasterii sanctorum Theodori et Sebastiani*, the two monasteries united by Gregory the Great in 599 (*Reg. Neap. Archiv. Monum.* 1; Parascandolo 1847: 29).

In 721, Duke Theodore of Naples created the *diaconia* of San Giovanni e Paolo 'de praetorio', close to the ducal palace, whilst that of Santa Maria ad Cosmedin, now the church of Santa Maria di Portanova, had been founded in 700. In 937, San Giorgio *ad forum* or *ad mercatum* was presumably set by the Roman forum, and was followed shortly by the *diaconia* of San Pietro in 941. The latest

---

[22] Whilst I do not agree with Durliat that food procurement for the poor was not a direct preoccupation of the Neapolitan *diaconiae*, the liberal bestowal of coinage does suggest that a monetary economy was still functioning at this date.

[23] On the Neapolitan *diaconiae* see Tutini 1681; Ambrasi 1981; 1985. I mention, in passing, the discovery of half of a circular limestone bread-stamp, intended probably for Eucharistic bread but perhaps for loaves for the doles, which bears the design of two fishes surrounded by five loaves or 'rosette' (an Italian rosette-shaped bread form) found in excavations beneath the cathedral by Roberto Di Stefano. On such stamps see Galavaris 1970. On the spread of *diaconiae* from the East see Marrou 1940; Ambrasi 1981: 45.

[24] The inscription was incorrectly transcribed by Capasso in *MND* II: 2, 171.

attested example is Santa Maria Rotonda/*ad Presepem*, perhaps near Piazza San Domenico Maggiore, documented in 1021, though probably established earlier (see below, Appendix II).

Unfortunately, the precise location of many of the *diaconiae* is not known, nor has any archaeological evidence yet come to light. Ambrasi noted that they concentrated towards the centre of the town and that at least five of them seem to have been sited around the *imma plateia* (Ambrasi 1981: 48). It may be that much of the land between the *imma plateia* and the sea was inhabited by the needier classes that the *diaconiae* served.[25]

MONASTERIES AND CONVENTS

Monasteries were founded in and around Naples from the late fourth century, at times under the patronage of leading members of Neapolitan society. Indeed, the convent of Santa Maria was a testamentary foundation in the house of Rustica, despite her son's attempted challenge to her will. The monastery of San Sebastiano was in the house of the *vir clarissimus* Romanus. Both were founded during the pontificate of Gregory the Great. Petrus Marcellinus Felix Liberius, praetorian prefect of Italy, prefect of Gaul and general under Justinian, organized the foundation of the monastery of San Martino in 541 (Desmulliez 1986). However, the earliest monastery is allegedly that dedicated to San Martino e Potito, dating to the episcopate of Severus (*c.* 363–408/410), followed by the convent of San Gaudioso, perhaps founded by the bishop of *Abitinae* after his flight from Vandal north Africa. The dedication of a Neapolitan monastery to Potitus is intriguing, as he was an early martyr from *Sardica* in Thrace.[26] Given the chronology of its foundation, it may have gathered together holy men who had fled the Gothic invasion of Thrace. It had reached its peak at the time of the death of Valens and the Roman defeat at Adrianople, in 378, contemporary with the Neapolitan episcopate of Severus.

Many of the earliest monastic foundations lay on the margins of the city, respecting Theodosian prescriptions banning their presence within the walls (*Cod. Theod.* XVI. iii. 1, iii. 2). Later,

because of insecurity, and presumably aided by the liberation of space within Naples, they were shifted or founded inside. Sources attest to some 29 monasteries in Naples by the end of the duchy (Venditti 1969: 836). Many were Greek, including San Sergio e Bacco, San Teodoro e Sebastiano, Sant'Anastasio, San Demetrio, San Pantaleione, San Ciriaco e Iulicte and San Gregorio Armeno, and a number preserve documents in Greek (Capasso 1895; Luzzati Laganà 1982: 738–9).[27]

San Sergio e Bacco was probably founded during the sixth century, perhaps as a consequence of Byzantine success in the Gothic War, imitating the famous church at Constantinople built by Justinian prior to 536 and dedicated to the saints that supposedly saved his life. The monastery lay close to Santa Lucia and the *Lucullanum* (Capasso 1895: 153, 225). Sergius and Bacchus were fourth-century eastern martyrs and patron saints of the army. Tradition has it that they were officers of the *Schola Gentilium* martyred on the Syrian front of the Euphrates, presumably under Galerius (Jones 1964: 54). By the tenth century the monastery appears to have been patronized by the Isauri family, probably local nobility of eastern origin. If the family was indeed linked to the Isaurians present in Belisarius's army of reconquest, perhaps the Isaurian military élite founded the monastery (Luzzati Laganà 1982: n. 67; Skinner 1994: 290–1). Another important Greek monastery was San Teodoro e Sebastiano, also dedicated to soldier-martyrs. Apart from purely economic factors, the similarity in the saints' *vitae* and their significance may partly explain why the two monasteries were united by 920 (Skinner 1994: 283).

Not far from the city lay the island of *Megaris* (Castel dell'Ovo) and the *Lucullanum*, reputedly seat of the rich Republican villa of L. Licinius Lucullus (D'Arms 1970: 185–6). The late Roman and early medieval topography of the area was somewhat different to that of today, as the hill of Pizzofalcone, behind the island of *Megaris*, has been cut back over the centuries, or has collapsed, and much of the present seafront is reclaimed land. The island itself may have been larger and have shrunk on account of subsidence. Indeed, the 1775 map of the Duca di Noja illustrates ruins beneath

---

[25] There is also a singular absence of attested land transactions in this quarter, and Patricia Skinner has suggested that this might indicate that the area was ducal property (Skinner 1995: 281–2).

[26] See the ninth-century Passio San Potiti, *BHL* II. 1006, nos. 6908–12.

[27] The Norman invasion was decisive for the supremacy of the Roman Church. With the process of Latinization following the conquest, most of the Greek monasteries eventually converted to the Benedictine Rule, such as San Gregorio Armeno, Santa Patrizia, San Demetrio, Santa Maria ad Anglona and Donnaregina, whilst the dependency of Benedictine San Vincenzo al Volturno is attested as being Augustinian from 1259 (Venditti 1969: 836).

the sea. The most recent and convincing study of the area indicates that the Byzantine *castrum/ oppidum* was sited on the crest of Pizzofalcone (Capone 1991). It would appear that the seventh-century monastery of San Salvatore lay on the island below, whilst a monastery of San Pietro (*a castello*) and the oratory of Sant'Arcangelo, already attested in 591, lay in the *campus oppidi*, between the fort on Pizzofalcone and the flat land now occupied by the Palazzo Reale/Piazza Plebiscito and the Angevin castle. The sixth-century monastery of Santa Maria a Cappella (*Grattarense*) seems to have been sited beneath Pizzofalcone, whilst a church of San Venere appears to have been close to Santa Lucia.

Part of the island of *Megaris* and the adjoining mainland may have been imperial property from Augustan times. It was donated to the Church under Constantine, when the church of Santa Lucia was erected beneath the promontory in honour of the Syracusan virgin, martyred under Diocletian (Capone 1991: 10, 25). Romulus Augustulus was exiled on the island in 476. The area remained a focus of agreeable residence at least until 592, when the patrician Clementina lived near the *castrum* (Greg. *Ep.* III. 1, 2). The monastery of San Severino was probably founded during the reign of Pope Gelasius (492–496), when the noble widow Barbara donated land to the monks who had rescued the remains of Saint Severinus during their flight from *Noricum* in 488.[28] Several of these became abbots. In 600, one of them, Amandus, was elected bishop of *Sorrentum*. The most famed was Eugippus, also a refugee from *Noricum*. He became abbot, and died in 533, though not before establishing a Rule that might have been used by Saint Benedict at Monte Cassino, whose own Rule was probably composed after 535 (de Vogüé 1971). He also founded a scriptorium of world renown, patronized by the pope. There, he wrote the *Life of Saint Severinus* and prepared an anthology of the works of Saint Augustine, dedicated to Proba, daughter of Symmachus, cousin of Boethius and member of the great family of the Anicii (Llewellyn 1975: 11; von Falkenhausen 1992: 9). The family had interests in Naples, at least through Anicius Auchenius Bassus, patron of the city in the late fourth century. It is probable that the Anicii held

property in the area, as they did in Gaul, north Africa and Asia Minor.[29] The monk Dionysius the Small had worked in the scriptorium on his *Dionysia*, under the protection of Pope Gelasius. Fulgentius of *Ruspae* called on Eugippus to provide him with works whilst in Sardinia, exiled from the Vandal Africa of Thrasamund. In 560 a certain Facistus made a copy of the transcriptions of the letters of Augustine. A century later, in 668, codices were sent to the monastery of Lindisfarne in Northumberland (England), during the time of Saint Cuthbert. *The Lindisfarne Gospels* seem, in part, to derive from an Italian original (Kendrick 1956–1960; Cilento 1969a: 533–6). The monastery of Echternach (Trier) in Germany held an eighth-/ninth-century copy of a codex, reputed to have belonged to Saint Jerome, transcribed by Irish or Saxon monks, which finished up in the library of Eugippus (Fuiano 1986). Such was the fame of the monastery of San Severino that it was visited by Willibald of Wessex during his return from the Holy Land in 729 and continual requests were received from various parts of Italy for the saint's relics (von Falkenhausen 1992: 14, 31, n. 176).

The monastery seems to have closed down at the end of the ninth century, as the island upon which it lay was exposed to Arab raids (Fig. 4:9). The remains of Severinus, along with other goods of the monastery, were transferred to the new foundation of San Severino e Sossio, within the city walls, where the scriptorium probably produced the *Chronicon ducum et principum Beneventi, Salerni et Capuae et ducum Neapolis*, around the mid-tenth century (Capasso 1902: 22).

Meanwhile, by 937, the monastery of San Salvatore on the island appears to have been re-inhabited (Cassandro 1969: 21). The original monastery of Santa Patrizia is also attested as having been sited there in 835 (Altamura 1974: 113).

Though archaeological excavations have never been conducted on the island, remains have come to light in the past. In 1924–1925, a series of caves or monastic cells was found cut into the volcanic rock (Marini 1931: 49–51). Some of these were vaulted and had benches and niches. Skeletons were discovered in one or two loculi. Two of the caves had been used as chapels, as they contained

---

[28] Severinus died in *Noricum* in 482 and was buried there, in a church at Faviana (*Vita S. Sev.*; Alföldy 1974: 220–6; Lotter 1976; Ambrasi 1980: 206). Barbara was later sanctified and a chapel dedicated to her was constructed on the coast. The roles of Barbara, Rustica and possibly also of Clementina as patrons of the Church echo similar developments in Rome, where women of leading families achieved prominence after the Gothic sack 'through participation in Christian charity and church building associated with the cult of the saints' (Brown 1981: 46–7).

[29] Anicius Auchenius Bassus (*ILS* 8984); also *Beneventum* where he was born (*CIL* IX: 1568–9).

altars and were decorated with painted wall-plaster bearing the sign of the cross. A rectangular hall, possibly a monastic refectory, with twelve reused Roman columns, is still visible, encased within the Norman castle of Castel dell'Ovo.[30] A small seventh-century church dedicated to the Saviour, later rededicated to San Sebastiano, also existed on the site, whilst an oratory, built under Bishop Stephen II (768–800), is attested through a dedicatory inscription (*MND* II: 217–18).

The precise location of the *castrum* and monasteries is not known, though sources indicate that they were sited not only on the island of *Megaris*, which was larger than it is today, but also on the rock of Pizzofalcone and to the east, past modern Piazza Plebiscito, as far as the Angevin castle. The latter area was known as *campus oppidi* (Capasso 1895: 218). The site attracted other early monasteries. We have already referred to that of San Sergio e Bacco, whilst Capasso placed the sixth-century monastery, *Grattarense*, *Gazarense* or *Crateras*, along the coastal road leading to the *crypta Neapolitana* (*MND* I: 29; Capasso 1895: 239; Venditti 1969: 770; Doria 1971: 435). Offshore, to the east of the *campus oppidi*, lay another small island that, from 944, belonged to San Vincenzo al Volturno (Capasso 1895: 234).

The important monastery of *Niridano* was possibly sited on the island of Nisida. Its Abbot Hadrian, of African origin, was a close friend of both Pope Vitalian and of Emperor Constans II. In 671, having accompanied Archbishop Theodore of Tarsus to England, he succeeded Benedict Biscop as abbot of Saints Peter and Paul of Canterbury.[31]

Whilst Naples's church dedications to eastern saints are not particularly common, monastery dedications appear, instead, to testify to the immigration of eastern brethren. The political and religious policy of Duke Stephen must have furthered the process by providing a safe haven against the iconoclasts (*Vita Sancti Stephani Iunioris, monachi et martyris auctore Stephano diacono Ecclesiae Constantinopolitanae* CD 1117). The monastery of San Gregorio Armeno, one of the most renowned of the city, was founded in the lower part of the forum. It may have originated in a group of nuns who had fled from the iconoclast purges of the eighth century, bringing with them the corpse of the saint (Galante 1872: 200–4; Capasso 1895: 159–60). However, it is first attested in a document of 930, and in 1009 was amalgamated with San Pantaleone, founded under Duke Stephen II. Gregory was the first patriarch of Armenia, at Vagharshapat, dying as a hermit in 331. Pantaleimon was a martyr who had been decapitated under Diocletian. His blood is supposedly preserved at Ravello and, like that of Saint Ianuarius, is prone to liquefaction.[32] Both Gregory the Armenian and Pantaleimon were particularly venerated in the East. Excavations conducted in 1986 show that part of the present monastic complex lies above Roman buildings with mosaic floors, and that the chapel of the Madonna dell'Idria may have formed part of the original early medieval monastery.[33]

The Arab raids on southern Italy further encouraged the establishment of monasteries within the walls of Naples. The Greek monastery of Santa Maria ad Anglona (*ad Anglonum* or *de Agnone*) is traditionally held as having been founded in 833. The hypotheses surrounding its name, as deriving from a legend involving a snake or from the town of Agnone, near Chieti, are unlikely. What is more intriguing is the possibility of it having been founded subsequent to refugees fleeing the Arab occupation of the Byzantine site of Anglona, near Tursi in Basilicata in 826, seven years before the Neapolitan foundation. The church of Anglona was also dedicated to Saint Mary from Norman times, if not earlier, as remains of an early medieval church lie beneath the Romanesque building (Pedio 1993: 80).

Of the Latin monasteries, one of the most famous and powerful seems to have been the joint monastic foundation of San Severino e Sossio, dating to the beginning of the tenth century. In a moment of insecurity due to Arab incursions, Bishop Stephen III united within the walls of Naples the remains of Severinus of *Noricum*, transferred from the monastery of the *Lucullanum* in 901, and those of Sossius, fellow martyr of Ianuarius, transferred from *Misenum* in 906 (John

---

[30] See Gubitosi and Izzo 1968, for a trial trench dug around one of the columns in the hall. Also Dattilo 1956; Picone 1982.

[31] Fuiano (1986: 6–17) provided an interesting reconstruction of Hadrian's activities. On Hadrian and Canterbury see Colgrave and Mynors 1969: 332.

[32] Liquefaction of coagulated blood is a particularly Campanian miracle. The blood of Saint Ianuarius, which stains the stone where he was beheaded at the Solfatara, Pozzuoli, liquefies. So does the blood of Saint Patricia and of Saint John the Baptist, both held by the monastery of San Gregorio Armeno. There is no common accord as to how the process actually takes place, though its invention is perhaps to be credited to a later medieval Neapolitan alchemist.

[33] Giuseppe Vecchio kindly supplied this information.

Person	From	To	Date	Reason
Saint Potitus	Thrace	San Potito, Naples	Late fourth	Gothic invasion
Saint Ianuarius	*Puteoli*	Catacombs of San Gennaro	413–431	Decline of *Puteoli*
Saint Restituta	Carthage	Ischia	Fifth	Vandal invasion
Saint Giuliana	*Cumae*	San Ciriaco, Rome	Late fifth	Donation
Saint Severinus	*Noricum*	The *Lucullanum*	*c.* 488	Exodus from *Noricum*
Saint Proculus	*Puteoli*	San Sebastiano, Naples	*c.* 600	Decline of *Puteoli*
Saint Proculus	*Puteoli/Neapolis*	*Puteoli* cathedral (San Proculo)	*c.* 600	Decline of *Puteoli*
Saint Eutychetes	*Puteoli*	San Sebastiano, Naples	*c.* 600	Decline of *Puteoli*
Saint Acutius	*Puteoli*	San Sebastiano, Naples	*c.* 600	Decline of *Puteoli*
Saint Gregory	Armenia	San Gregorio Armeno	Eighth	Iconoclasm
Saint Acutius	San Sebastiano, Naples	Cathedral	768–800	Insecurity
Saint Eutychetes	San Sebastiano, Naples	Cathedral	768–800	Insecurity
Saint Fortunata	*Liternum*	San Gaudioso monastery	780–794	Decline of *Liternum*
Saint Restituta	Ischia	Cathedral	812	Arabs
Saint Ianuarius	Catacombs of San Gennaro	Benevento	831	Siege of Sico
Saint Gaudiosus	Catacombs of San Gaudioso	San Gennaro all'Olmo	842–849	Insecurity
Saint Nostrianus	Catacombs of San Gaudioso	San Gennaro all'Olmo	842–849	Insecurity
Saint Fortunatus	Naples *extra moenia*	Cathedral	842–849?	Insecurity
Saint Ephebus	Naples *extra moenia*	Cathedral	842–849?	Insecurity
Saint Maximus I	Catacombs of San Gaudioso	Monte Cassino		
Saint Proculus	*Puteoli?*	Reichnau	Prior to 871	Decline of *Puteoli*
Saint Eutychetes	*Puteoli?*	Reichnau	Prior to 871	Decline of *Puteoli*
Saint Acutius	*Puteoli?*	Reichnau	Prior to 871	Decline of *Puteoli*
Saint Athanasius	Monte Cassino	Catacombs of San Gennaro	877	
Saint Maximus I	Monte Cassino	Catacombs of San Gennaro	877	
Saint Maximus I	Catacombs of San Gennaro	Cathedral		Decline of catacombs
Saint Patricia	The *Lucullanum*	San Nicandro e Marciano	Late ninth?	Arabs
Saint Severinus	The *Lucullanum*	San Severino	902	Arabs
Saint Sossius	*Misenum*	San Severino e Sossio	904	Arabs
Saint Giuliana	*Cumae*	Donnaromita, Naples	1207	Decline of *Cumae*
Saint Maximus II	*Cumae*	Donnaromita, Naples	1207	Decline of *Cumae*
Saint Athanasius	Catacombs of San Gennaro	Cathedral	Thirteenth	Decline of catacombs

Fig. 4:9. The traditional, factual and hypothetical translation of the remains of saints to within the walls of Naples or elsewhere. Saint Maximus I = bishop of Naples; Saint Maximus II = bishop of Apamea.

the Deacon, *Translatio Sancti Sosii*, *MGH*; Gay 1917: 229; see below, Chapter 5). The importance attached to the monastery and to the relics of these saints is reflected by the site, not far from the ducal palace, on the bluff-edge of the city overlooking the sea. That a monastery already existed there is suggested by the fact that Vico San Severino was known as *vicus Monachorum* in the ninth century.[34]

Very little regarding any of these monasteries and convents is attested archaeologically. The only partially excavated site is that of the monastery of San Nicandro e Marciano, Campanian martyrs from *Atina* and *Venafrum* respectively. It became the convent of Santa Patrizia by the eleventh century, perhaps through the removal of her spoils from the monastery at

---

[34] The site appears to be that occupied by the State Archives. See Mazzoleni 1964.

Castel dell'Ovo during the late ninth century because of the Arab threat, though she died in the mid-seventh century.[35]

Patricia is alleged to have been niece of Emperor Constans II.[36] To avoid marriage, she fled from Constantinople to Naples, where she sojourned first at the *Lucullanum* and then at the monastery of San Nicandro e Marciano. Whilst on a visit to Rome, she learned of the assassination of her uncle at Syracuse and returned to Constantinople. From the capital she set forth for Jerusalem though, because of a storm, Divine Providence swept her ship to Naples. Tired and ailing, she died in a monastic cell at the monastery of San Salvatore on the island of the *Lucullanum*. During her funeral, oxen miraculously led her hearse to the monastery of San Nicandro e Marciano where she was duly buried. Her wet-nurse Aglaia founded a new monastery in her name, utilizing Patricia's funds and a donation by the duke of Naples in thanksgiving for the miracle of 'Saint Patricia's well'. This miracle runs as follows. As the monastery was placed high in the city it suffered a perennial water shortage. Aglaia, invoking Patricia, was instructed to excavate in the monastic garden, whereupon a spring of fresh and clear water gushed forth.

The monastery of San Nicandro e Marciano, which also housed a nail from the Holy Cross supposedly brought over by Patricia from Constantinople, became one of the most important monasteries of the city, well-documented in later times (Capasso 1895: 168–70). Located towards the upper end of present Via L. Armani, the site was excavated in 1983–1986.[37] A wall of a large brick-faced concrete building of second-century date was found reused as a side wall of a rectangular hall with three central piers (Fig. 4:10). The hall measures 7.5 m in width and probably just over 11.5 m in length, and at one end opens on to a small atrium. The three central piers and the end buttresses may suggest the presence of a second floor. Finds beneath the floors include African red slip ware of forms 105 and 109, which give a *terminus post quem* of the late sixth century for the initial construction (based on the chronology of

Hayes 1972), though later patching included a fragment of forum ware no earlier than the later eighth century. It is possible that the hall was a refectory. The ninth-century refectory of the monastery of San Vincenzo al Volturno has a central arcade, though it is over twice the size (Hodges 1985: 14). A similar building found at the *domusculta* of Santa Cornelia, north of Rome, dates to the eleventh century. Though slightly larger, it has been interpreted as a possible chapter-house with a dormitory on the second floor (Christie 1991: 65, room D).[38] The ground-plan of the construction at Santa Patrizia is also similar to the later pilgrims' hall of the 'Palatium' built by Abbot Thomas (1255–1264) at Cava dei Tirreni. This building not only has central columns to support cloister vaults, but also opens onto a small atrium or vestibule (Venditti 1967: 624–5, fig. 403).

The original church may have been built above the Roman brick-faced concrete building, as not only does the present church lie here, but early medieval burials were found just to its north. It would thus have been sited parallel to the hall.

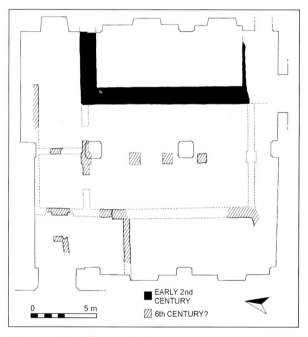

Fig. 4:10. Plan of the excavations at Santa Patrizia.

---

[35] Much use has been made of Farmer 1989 and of the *Bibliotheca Sanctorum* for general information on many of the saints and martyrs discussed here.

[36] Another tradition would have her as niece of Constantine the Great (for example, D'Engenio 1623: 178; Altamura 1974: 103), clearly impossible if this is to be reconciled with other events of her story.

[37] A preliminary report is given in Arthur 1984.

[38] The larger room A is interpreted as the refectory, though not enough of it was excavated to show that it did not also have central piers.

The building technique encountered in the hall and its associated rooms consists of small squared yellow tuff blocks, held together by a pozzolana mortar. The floor of the hall was of rough *opus signinum*, whilst the atrium revealed successive floor levels, raised together with the threshold of the door opening on to the hall (Fig. 4:11). Though there is no absolute proof that the building formed part of the monastery of San Nicandro e Marciano, documents demonstrate that the later convent of Santa Patrizia lay on the site.

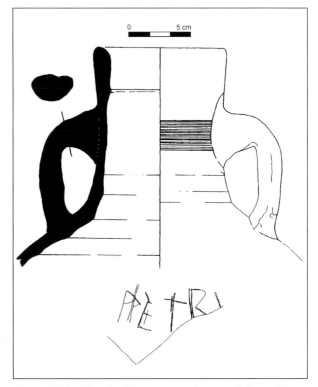

Fig. 4:12. North African amphora of form Keay LVA, with graffito PETRI, from Santa Patrizia.

is possible that the inscriptions were intended to mark vessels having a common destination in Naples. Indeed, this could be part of a picture of monastic self-sufficiency or *dirigisme*. Quite aside from the well-known examples of Monte Cassino and San Vincenzo al Volturno, even smaller monasteries tended to acquire scattered holdings in various places and environments, often through donations, which helped to satisfy the exigencies of diversified agricultural produce.

EXTRA-URBAN CHURCHES AND MONASTERIES

The little information regarding the early Church and monasteries outside the immediate hinterland of Naples comes mostly from textual sources. A network of episcopal sees is attested in Campania prior to the Lombard invasion, clearly based on the Roman administrative centres. Apart from Naples, we may list *Volturnum, Liternum, Vicus Feniculensis, Cumae, Misenum, Puteoli, Atella, Nola, Abella, Nuceria, Stabiae, Surrentum* and *Salernum* (Duchesne 1903; 1905; Calvino 1969; Fonseca 1987: chapter 1). The sole oddity would appear to be *Vicus Feniculensis*, a site still not identified, but

Fig. 4:11. Part of the early medieval monastery at Santa Patrizia, with roughly mortared paving including large Roman dolium and tile fragments (photo: author).

A particularly intriguing find is part of a Tunisian amphora bearing the graffito PETRI, incised prior to firing, datable to the mid- or later sixth century (Fig. 4:12). Another contemporary Tunisian amphora, bearing the same graffito, possibly by the same hand, was found off the coast at Stabia.[39] Who Peter was is not known, though it

[39] The vessel types are respectively LV and LVII of Keay's typology (1984). My dating of the types is based on evidence from the Naples's excavations. I should like to thank Claude Livadie for having brought the Stabia amphora to my attention.

perhaps lying somewhere between *Liternum* and *Volturnum*. Of these sees, *Volturnum*, *Liternum* and *Vicus Feniculensis* had disappeared by the time of Gregory the Great, if not earlier. Indeed, as should become evermore evident by the end of this study, the major disruption in the old Roman pattern of settlement and administration came with the Gothic War. In the case of some coastal sees, increase in marshland along the flat coast and around the river *Clanis* may be an additional factor that led to their abandonment. The see of Amalfi, in contrast, is not attested until Pope Gregory's time, though it may have been in existence earlier.

Until recently, local archaeology, having focused on classical remains, was responsible for having destroyed much important evidence relating to the early Church. Indeed, little excavation has been carried out on rural churches or cemeteries of late Roman or early medieval date within the territory of Byzantine Naples, and this must become a research priority if we want to assess the process of reorganization of rural settlement before the year 1000.[40]

One exception is the church of San Costanzo on the island of Capri (Arthur 1992).[41] Material from its foundation trenches dates its primary construction to the mid-fifth century. It was originally an apsed basilical church, with an interior space of *c.* 102 m², three naves, a lateral apse and a narthex (Fig. 4:13). The eight columns, without capitals, and the tile and brick masonry are all *spolia* and, indeed, the church was itself built upon a Roman building. It was later converted to its Byzantine inscribed-cross form, probably in the tenth century, when it became the centre of the bishopric of Capri and may have received its present dedication. Earlier it had depended upon the diocese of *Surrentum*, though when it had first been built it probably depended upon Naples.

Traces of another early church have been found at Santa Restituta, Ischia, through excavations beneath the present church by Father Pietro Monti (Monti 1980: 235–40). The original building, which is not closely dated, would appear, as at San Costanzo, to have made use of an early Imperial

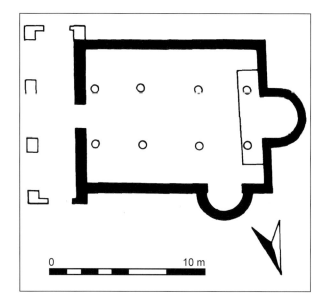

Fig. 4:13. Plan of San Costanzo, Capri (after Arthur 1992: fig. 23).

building or cistern in *opus reticulatum*. It was the centre of a late Roman cemetery with tile-tombs, amphora burials and *arcosolia*.[42] Of particular note are a burial with a hole for the pouring of libations and a splendid fourth-century sarcophagus of the Bethesda group that may, however, have been imported to the island at a later date. The church was dedicated to Saint Restituta, one of the martyrs of *Abitinae* in 304, whose spoils were probably brought over during the Vandal occupation of north Africa (*Passio SS. Dativi, Saturnini et aliorum*). The abundant pottery from the site indicates continuity of occupation from Roman times to the present day.[43]

On the mainland various churches are known, though few have been studied. Just to the south of *Liternum*, one dating to about the fifth century has been identified as dedicated to Saint Fortunata, a local martyr, whose body it was claimed was brought over from *Caesarea Marittima*, in Palestine, along with the corpses of her brothers, Carponius, Euachristus and Priscianus (Pagano 1989). Between 780 and 794, her remains were removed from *Liternum* by Duke Stephen II of Naples, to be redeposited in a church dedicated to

---

[40] Even the report of a recent excavation at the three-aisled basilical church of San Giacomo, Calvizzano, already attested through documents in 951, concentrated on underlying Roman remains and not on the church itself (Caputo 1989). Early Christian churches, later in Lombard territory, have been excavated in recent years at Avella (excavations by G. Pescatori Colucci) and Alvignano (*Compulteria*; excavations by E. Laforgia), the latter apparently having become derelict by the time of Pope Gregory (*Ep.* IX. 93–4).

[41] On the tradition of San Costanzo, perhaps patriarch of Constantinople in 666–670, see *AA.SS.* III: 375; Fatica 1992.

[42] On the reuse of a Roman cistern, and parallels, see Vaes 1989: 301.

[43] Aside from that published by Monti (1980; 1989; 1991), see also D'Agostino and Marazzi 1985; Guarino, Mauro and Peduto 1988.

her at the monastery of San Gaudioso, on the acropolis at Sant'Aniello a Caponapoli. The church at *Liternum*, built of *spolia* and paved with basalt blocks of the *Via Domitiana*, was a small rectangular building with two apses, one of which may have contained the tomb of the saint.

The Byzantine *castra* must all have also been served by churches. The best examples survive at Cuma, where the two Greek temples on the acropolis were converted to churches around the fifth century (Christern 1977: 216–25). The upper temple, sited on the highest point and dedicated to Jupiter, probably became the cathedral. It was transformed into a five-aisled church, containing a circular baptismal font revetted with white marble and once surmounted by a *tugurium* with six marble columns. It may have survived up to 1207, and an inscription recording Saint Maximus, said to be from *Apamea* and possibly martyred locally, was found amongst its ruins (Maiuri 1958: 124–5; Calvino 1960; D. Ambrasi, 'Massimo', in *BiblSanct.* 37–9; *BHL* 5846).[44]

The temple of Apollo, sited further down the slope, may have been dedicated to Saint Giuliana, an eastern martyr of fourth-century date. Her remains were later given by Bishop Fortunatus of Naples to Pope Gregory and placed in the cemetery of San Ciriaco at Rome. Little survives of the church erected above the temple on account of excavations in 1912, though it apparently reused the Roman cella walls (Gallo 1986). The entrance may have been to the southwest, though a large plinth in this area, possibly the base to a baptismal font, would seem to have partly obstructed access. If this were a baptismal font, later razed to the ground, it may be suggested that this temple housed the original episcopal church, later transferred to the temple of Jupiter. The distribution of the 90 tombs cut into the podium might suggest that the altar was placed not at the end of the cella, but three-quarters of the way along the nave, as in many early churches. Christern considered both churches to form part of a pilgrimage centre, suggesting that they were distant enough from the lower city of *Cumae* to have been of little use in routine liturgy (Christern 1977: 223–5). This takes no account of the fact that most of the lower city seems to have been abandoned by the time of the Gothic War at the latest, and the buildings should be regarded fundamentally as the regular episcopal and parochial centres of congregation. Mention

should also be made of a letter of Pope Gregory, dated 591, which refers to a monastery near *Cumae* dedicated to Saint Erasmus (Greg. *Reg.* I. 23).

On the outskirts of *Puteoli* lay the church of San Gennaro, by the crater of the Solfatara and close to where the saint was martyred. The removal of his spoils to Naples between the years 413 and 431 is a good indication of the waning importance of the site.

Also on the outskirts of the town, *in contrivio* (at a crossroads), lay the *praetorium Falcidium* with the adjoining basilica of Santo Stefano, possibly its first cathedral (D. Ambrasi, 'Gennaro', in *BiblSanct.* 141). The texts inform us that the early fourth-century Puteolean martyrs, Proculus, Eutychetes and Acutius, were killed and buried near the church (Fig. 4:14). The site plausibly may be identified with the Roman cemetery that lies at the junction of the three Roman roads of Via Celle, Via Campana Antica and that to Cigliano. The archaeological evidence indicates the continued use of a series of early Imperial mausolea for inhumation burials into late antique times, as well as the presence of a probable funerary basilica, *hospitia* and baths (De Caro 1999: 227). Dubois identified the *praetorium Falcidii*, presumably an estate-centre, with a villa of the Falcidii, a Roman family attested at *Puteoli* (Dubois 1907; *CIL* VI: 1944). He claimed to have seen the remains of two early Christian churches, though the only surviving evidence is an early Christian funerary inscription of C. Nonius Flavianus. By the sixth century a monastery had been founded on the site. By 600 it

Fig. 4:14. The ninth-century painting of Saint Eutychetes and Saint Proculus of Puteoli, *companion martyrs of Saint Ianuarius, in the catacombs of San Gennaro (photo: P.C.A.S., courtesy of G. De Pasquale).*

---

[44] On the conversion of temple to church see also Christern 1967.

was virtually abandoned because of the insecure conditions at the time, and Pope Gregory attached it to the Greek monastery of San Sebastiano in Naples (*Ep.* X. 61). The remains of the local martyrs were also removed to Naples save, perhaps, for parts of Proculus that presumably went to the church of San Proculo, founded within the *castrum* of *Puteoli* over the splendid temple of Augustus. Unfortunately, the church is not recorded in the texts until 1206, and excavation and restoration of the temple have removed virtually all traces of the early Christian building. It was later known as the *maior ecclesia putheolana*, having probably become the new cathedral during the fifth century (Annecchino 1960; Russo Mailler 1976; Christern 1977: 215).

Even less is known about the Church outside of the Phlegrean Fields, though towards the end of the millennium both urban and rural churches must have abounded throughout Neapolitan territory. However, the economic difficulties of the sixth century brought about the disappearance of a number of bishoprics. It is to be doubted that any rural churches were founded at that time, or for some time afterwards. Those that existed already are likely to have been private foundations annexed to late Roman villas or *praetoria*.[45] The later, medieval, rural or village church does not usually, I believe, reflect continuity of occupation from late Roman times, but rather reflects a gradual reorganization of the countryside and the creation of new parishes or *plebes*. If the results of Paolo Peduto's excavation of churches at Altavilla Silentina and Pratola Serra in Lombard Campania are emblematic, the phenomenon may have begun as early as the later seventh century (Peduto 1984a; 1992; see also below, Chapter 5).

Many small cult centres certainly existed, and should come to light through local surveys. Amongst these, mention may be made of the relatively few cave-churches in the territory of Naples, when compared to the abundant examples located in the more suitable limestone terrain of Apulia,

Basilicata, Sicily, and even the province of Salerno. In Campania these often found origin in heremitic dwellings as early as the fifth century (Kalby 1975: 155).[46]

However, near Naples, the only site studied to any degree is the exceptional monumental pilgrimage centre at Cimitile (Fig. 4:15).[47] In Roman times it was the cemeterial area of *Nola*, from which it takes its name. Its first claim to fame was as the burial place of Saint Felix in the third century. Other burials were placed around his tomb, forming a substantial martyrium, and in 313, under Constantine, an apsed basilica was erected over it. The complex rapidly became an important religious centre, visited by pilgrims from far and wide, and its bishops were both influential and wealthy. This is a prime example of the process so clearly illustrated by Peter Brown of the transference of interest from the 'city of the living' to the 'city of the dead', where new and reliable *patroni* were to be found in the Christian martyr and in his representatives on earth, the bishops, during the unsettled times of late antiquity (Brown 1981: 38–40).[48]

Cimitile's second claim to fame was as the seat of Bishop, later Saint, Pontius Meropius Paulinus, born in Bordeaux around 353/354. He had been proconsul of Campania and hereditary estate *dominus* at *Nola*, where one of his ancestors was acclaimed as *patronus ex origine*. Not only his culture and breeding, but also his position within the late Roman aristocracy, permitted him to expand Cimitile's renown. Though his ordainment shocked the Senate, he kept closely in touch with members of the aristocracy and seems to have continued in his role as aristocratic *patronus* within the sphere of the Church (Brown 1981: 53–4; also Frend 1969; Lienhard 1977).

Cimitile possessed a fragment of the Holy Cross, a gift from the wealthy and influential Melania, who had brought it over from Jerusalem, as Paulinus noted in an inscription to his friend Sulpicius Severus (Paulinus *Ep.* XXXII. 3).[49] The tomb of Saint Felix was further graced through the

---

[45] Such a site, which does not appear to have survived the fifth century, is known on Mount Finnochiaro, near Carinola in northern Campania (Arthur 1991a: 91).

[46] A hermit living 'in praerupta rupe', close to the city, or the church of *Sancta Maria de illa spelunca*, at the foot of Mount Vesuvius, is an example. See also the life and temptations of Saint Martin, who lived in a cave on Monte Massico, in northern Campania (Arthur 1991a: 91–2).

[47] Much has been written about Cimitile. See, for example, on its architecture Goldschmidt 1940; Venditti 1967: 530–42. On the remains of the cemetery see Chierici 1957; and Pani Ermini *et al.* 1993, for the recent excavations. See also Pani Ermini 1978a; Testini 1978; Belting 1978. A thoroughly new and detailed study of the whole complex remains an urgent priority, and is promised by Lehmann (1990; 1993).

[48] When Augustine became bishop, in 412, he found himself managing 'property twenty times ... greater than he had ever owned himself' (Brown 1981: 39).

[49] Melania visited Jerusalem with Rufinus of Aquileia in 373.

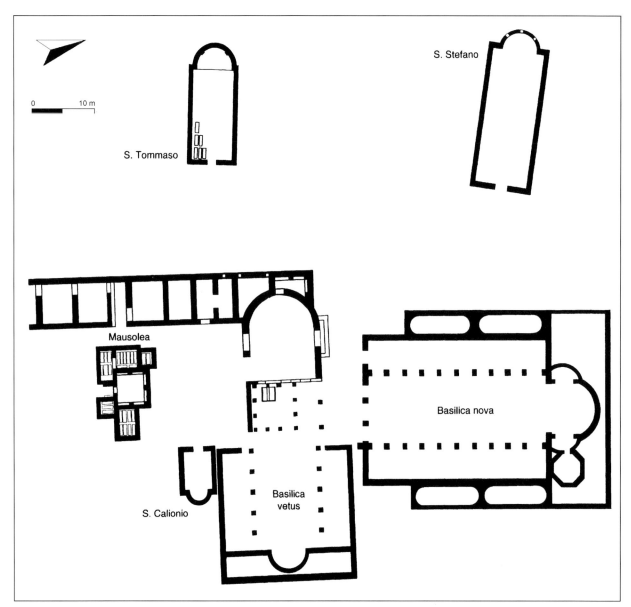

Fig. 4:15. Plan of Cimitile as it may have been in the sixth century (after Lehmann 1990: fig. 1, modified).

addition of relics of Saints Gervasius and Protasius, discovered by Ambrose of Milan and given to his friend Paulinus at Cimitile.[50] Paulinus's own prodigious contribution not only included a series of poems, the *Carmina Natalicia*, but an extensive building programme carried out on the site between 394 and 410. He restructured the church of San Felice, adding the *basilica nova*, a three-aisled basilical building, at right angles to it. The building was somewhat singular for its triconch or *cella tricora*, reflecting a new concept

and form of the triclinium as both seat and audience-hall of the *dominus/patronus*, as found in late Roman villas such as Piazza Armerina in Sicily and Desenzano near lake Garda (see, for example, J.B. Ward-Perkins 1981: 460–5).[51] It was richly decorated with *opus sectile* and wall-mosaics, partly ascribed to Sulpicius Severus by Paulinus. Paulinus was not new to the architectural developments in the houses of the aristocracy, and he may have wished the building to express his position as *patronus* in the sphere of his ecclesi-

---

[50] See Jones 1964: 959, on Ambrose's discovery of the otherwise unknown martyrs in 386, considered by some to have been a hoax on his part.

[51] Other examples include the triclinia of the villas of Patti Marina, Sicily, and Porto Saturo, Leporano (TA) (Lattanzi 1973; Voza 1977).

astical client relationships (Lavin 1962). It is said that the architectural form derived from north Africa and Egypt, where the strikingly similar, though perhaps later, basilica at Denderah may be cited (Venditti 1967: 534, 735, n. 349; Krautheimer 1975: 207).[52] The funerary church of San Tommaso and the church of Santo Stefano were both sixth-century additions.

The complex remained in Byzantine hands until, under Duke Grimoald in the mid-seventh century, it was absorbed by the territorial expansion of the Lombard duchy of Benevento. It was, indeed, in Lombard times that Byzantine architectural influence seems to have been particularly strong. A small basilica, dedicated to San Calionio, was restored by Bishop Leo III of *Nola*, in the early eighth century, and he also adapted an earlier Roman mausoleum so as to create the church of the Holy Martyrs. Some splendid examples of marble carving are attributed to Bishop Lupenus in the ninth century, at much the same time that the cult of Saint Faustillus was added to Cimitile's list of dedications. The transference of the bishopric back to a restored *Nola*, in 1372, both sealed the decline of the sanctuary and confirmed the economic revival of the neighbouring town.

CONCLUSIONS

In concluding this chapter, we may briefly return to within the city walls. The spread and consolidation of Christianity is recognized as one of the processes that helped to transform the classical town. But what changes in the organization and layout of early medieval Naples did ecclesiastical building create, and when?

Despite the limitations of the sources, it can be concluded that the major changes probably took place in late antiquity, when the major churches were erected. Building activity seems to have been fairly constant from Constantine through to the mid-sixth century, with an average of four churches being built per century. A period of about 200 years then elapsed before a new church is attested

in the eighth century. Only four churches are attested in the ninth, to be followed by a tenfold increase over the next 100 years. The tenth century thus appears to have been a period of great economic expansion and, if the number of new churches then gradually dropped, it may be argued that this was less to do with declining capital than the existence of a veritable glut of church buildings. By the later tenth century, some of the churches of the later attested 22 minor parishes were already in existence.

There is no evidence to suggest that churches were erected over classical temples prior to the building of San Paolo above the temple of the Dioscuri, between 801 and 816. However, some form of enforced sale or property confiscation, perhaps through the mediation of the civil administration, may have taken place, aided undoubtedly by availability of space following on from depopulation. Indeed, the lack of population pressure in late antique and early medieval times opened up possibilities in new urban planning that had not been available since the early Empire. This seems to follow a trend common to most of Italy. The earliest example of reuse in Rome dates to 609, when Pope Boniface IV (608–615) received permission from Emperor Phocas to convert the Pantheon into a church (*Lib. Pont.* I. 317). However, the temple of Augustus at Fondi had already been converted into the church of Sant' Andrea by the end of the sixth century (Greg. *Dial.* III. 7), and the *Athenaion* on the island of Ortigia, at Syracuse, had been converted in 595–596 (Agnello 1952: 37–52).[53] This is in stark contrast to the eastern part of the Empire, where reuse of ancient religious buildings took place much earlier. Campania, however, also provides the few exceptions to the rule in the West. They include the conversion of the two principal temples on the acropolis of *Cumae* into churches, perhaps in the fifth century, and possibly also the conversion of the temple of Augustus at *Puteoli* into the church of San Proculo around 600. The Neapolitan church of the Sant'Apostoli, built in 468, was supposedly sited upon a temple of Mercury.

[52] Sicilian *cellae trichorae* have been discussed by Wilson (1990: 307–8). Krautheimer stated that the right-hand lobe of the apse served as the prothesis for the preparation of the Eucharist, and the left one as a chapel for meditation. It is quite likely that the lateral apses were 'service areas', as probably the open apses or 'ambulatories' around the apses of churches like San Giovanni Maggiore and San Giorgio Maggiore (see above, p. 66), and the enclosed triconch at Venosa (Salvatore 1991). Again, the parallels with triclinia are striking, with necessary spaces for preparation and distribution of the banquet, as is that between the dinner offered by the late Roman *patronus* and the Eucharist officiated by the early Christian bishop. In this light, it is possible to understand the *mensa funeraria* and the martyria that take the form of *cellae trichorae*. The altars were the equivalent of tables or triclinia for the banquets offered by the *patroni/domini*. Banquets at tombs are attested from the third century in pagan contexts (*ILCV* 1570 from Mauretania, cited by Brown 1981: 23–4), and have a long history stretching back much further.

[53] See, in general, Ward-Perkins 1984: 91.

Fig. 4:16. One of the ninth-/tenth-century chancel screens from the church of Sant'Aspreno (photo: L. Pedicini).

Other churches also made use of pagan buildings. Both Sant'Aspreno and Santa Maria Donnaregina were apparently constructed within abandoned Roman baths.[54] The walls of the small barrel-vaulted proprietary church of Sant'Aspreno, built by Kampulus and his wife Costanza on the traditional site of hermitage of Saint Aspren, which now lies below ground on account of a raised ground level, are covered with white plaster bearing rudimentary painted festoons and other designs (Venditti 1967: 501–6). Amongst the few objects preserved are a simple altar and two marble chancel screens decorated with peacocks, griffins, leopards and other animals, enclosed by lattice-work (Fig. 4:16) (*MND* I: 157; Coroneo 2000: 159–60). The decorative style appears to be no later than the tenth century and perhaps imitated imported oriental cloths.

It is notable that many Neapolitan churches were oriented north–south, quite clearly following the street alignment and making use of earlier structures, as in the case of San Paolo Maggiore. The major churches were aligned on the principal roads: San Giorgio Maggiore on the lower *plateia*, Santa Maria Maggiore on the median *plateia*, San Paolo and San Lorenzo on the forum and the median *plateia*, Santa Maria Donnaregina on the upper *plateia* and San Giovanni Maggiore on the main road to the port, recalling the hypothesis of Jules Beloch of Greek divinities and temples associated with the three *plateiai* (Beloch 1989: 86). If San Paolo Maggiore is excluded, by virtue of the fact that it is not attested prior to the early ninth century, the five principal churches within the walls of late antique Naples were San Giorgio

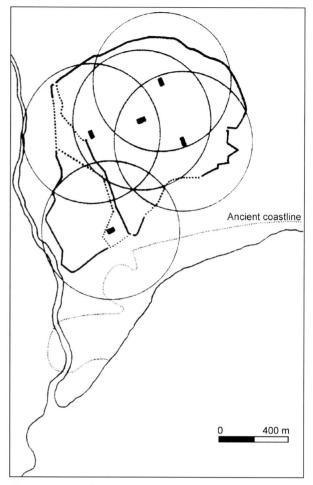

Ancient coastline

0   400 m

Fig. 4:17. The major basilical churches, built between the fourth and sixth centuries, circumscribed by hypothetical congregational areas of 400 m radius (drawn by author).

Maggiore, Santa Maria Maggiore, San Giovanni Maggiore, San Lorenzo Maggiore and Santa Restituta. All were standing by the later sixth century. If a circle with a circumference of 800 m is drawn around each of them, there was not one point within the walls that lay more than about 400 m from at least one of them (Fig. 4:17). Furthermore, the church of San Lorenzo Maggiore lies almost exactly in the centre of the town, echoing the centrality of the antique *agora*/forum. It lay, at most, some 700 m from the furthest point of the wall-circuit, to the southwest. The southwestern area of the town was the last to acquire a major church, San Giovanni Maggiore, in the third quarter of the sixth century. The 800 m circle circumscribing it is the only one to substantially transgress the limits of the walls, so as to have reached the population serving port facilities and

---

[54] Santa Maria Donnaregina was excavated by G. Vecchio and G. Mollo, who kindly gave me this information.

inhabiting the area where Narses appears to have expanded the wall-circuit (see above, Chapter 3). All told, the positioning of major churches seems to have been based on the concept that within about five minutes walking distance the entire population of the city could be served or controlled by the Church.

Their siting had some effect on subsequent urban topography; none more so than the cathedral, which created a new focal point within the city, competing in importance for a while with the site of the ducal palace, which was, however, to change function after the coming of the Normans. The cathedral was presumably built on public land, though it stands well clear of the Roman forum, still in use under the Ostrogoths. Not much later, the church and the market-place are found to be almost inextricably linked.

Some churches were founded by the dukes of Naples, the largest being San Paolo Maggiore. However, the dukes, and their wives, seem to have been more inclined to found monasteries. Five were created, and one renovated, by them during the ninth century, three under the Bishop-Duke Stephen II. Many of the smaller buildings, however, must have been on private land. Some private *tituli* probably existed, as in Rome, and in Naples we know of the foundation of churches dedicated to both Saint Mary and to Saint Sebastian in houses. Private chapels and proprietary churches, of course, were not unknown, as is shown by the surviving church of Sant'Aspreno, built by Kampulus and his wife (see below, Appendix II). Kampulus was probably from Gaeta, where the name appears frequently (Skinner 1995), and I wonder whether the fact that the small church was sited close to the port reflects the family's maritime interests. Church-owning families include the Isauri, Millusi, Carazzuli and Ferrari. The last were blacksmiths, and may indicate the beginning of corporate interests in the erection of churches. Be that as it may, many other minor churches may have been private foundations, but unfortunately we just do not possess the documentation.

5

TERRITORY

If we are to maintain that Naples remained both urban and a city-state throughout the early Middle Ages, it is necessary to understand the territory and the agricultural base that could permit it. In the absence of external capital it is difficult, if not impossible, for a township to survive unless sustained by a surplus agricultural production from a dependent hinterland.

In Roman times the *ager Neapolitanus* was severely limited in size. The sea boarded the territory to the south, which included the islands of Capri and Ischia. Marshy flats extended to the southeast, forming a natural boundary with the territories of the Vesuvian towns. To the north and west it was ringed by volcanic hills and craters rendering communications with the Phlegrean Fields and inland towns somewhat laborious. Apart from water transport, contact with *Puteoli* was *per colles* (over the hills), until Augustus provided a road *per cryptam*, cutting some 705 m through the hill at Fuorigrotta (Johannowsky 1952).[1]

With the decline of *Puteoli* through the fifth and sixth centuries the Phlegrean Fields passed under the administrative control of Naples. Following the Lombard invasion of 568 and the creation of a duchy at *Beneventum*, most of northern and southern Campania was lost, including much of the papal patrimony, leaving Naples as a Byzantine enclave. Some land, particularly *Liburia* to the north, was soon subjected to an unusual form of judicial rule that integrated holdings of the Neapolitan militia with those of the Lombards, creating an unusual border zone (Richards 1980: 128; Martin 1992: 268–73).

The sources referring to *castra* and to the fortification of old Roman towns indicate that the early medieval territory of Naples was substantially larger than the 17 km^2 or even the 50 km^2 upon which the town is variously said to have depended in earlier times (Lepore 1969: 146–8; also Miranda

1991: 223). It is more probably to be estimated in the order of 1,500 km^2 during its period of maximum extension. From the hills around the southeastern part of the Campanian plain the Lombards possessed a view reaching out towards the sea and broken only by the cone of Mount Vesuvius and the gentle heights of Naples and the Phlegrean Fields, rimming the core of the duchy of Naples. On clear days, of which there are many in this land, substantial movement, military or otherwise, across the intervening flat lands could be monitored and checked. Later medieval castles and towers often still mark the vantage points. However, there has been no archaeological study of Byzantine *castra* in this area, unlike other parts of Italy, and the pattern of territorial defence needs to be examined through fieldwork (Martin 1992: fig. 1; see Brogiolo and Gelichi 1996b; Zanini 1998).

By the sixth century, distinct Neapolitan territory contained the Roman towns of *Liternum*, *Cumae*, *Misenum*, *Puteoli*, *Acerrae*, *Atella*, *Nola*, *Surrentum* and *Salernum*. These were either abandoned or became dependent *castra* during the course of the century. Pope Gregory's letters illustrate some of them. Apart from safeguarding the network of surviving bishoprics and the large amount of land still subject to the seat of Saint Peter, and presumably organizing the redistribution of agricultural surplus from periphery to centre, they acted as fortified outposts and administrative satellites of Naples (Fig. 5:1). Martin Frederiksen appears to have viewed this development as that of refuge sites with the rural 'population retiring at need into [the] fortified *castra*'. A few of them remained substantial settlements, as archaeological evidence from *Cumae* and *Misenum* would suggest (Frederiksen 1984: 45). In other words, once typically urban, they developed into very specific military and administrative units designed to manage Naples's extended territory, declining,

---

[1] The only tunnel recorded by the *Tabula Peutingeriana*.

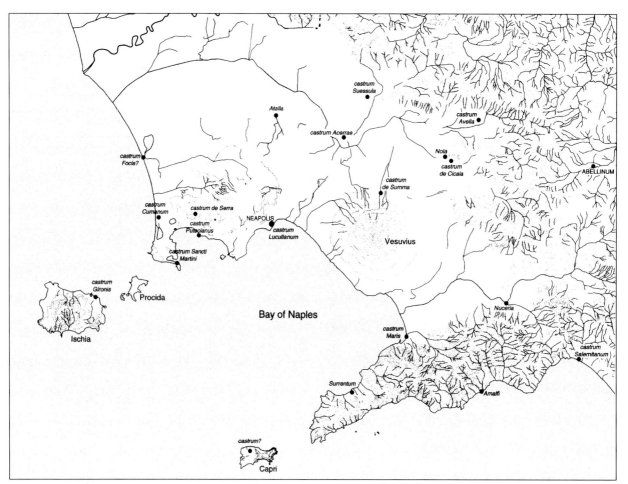

Fig. 5:1. The castra *around Naples (drawn by author on the base map in Frederiksen 1984: end papers).*

population-wise, with respect to their Roman forebears. There is now little doubt that the period saw the transition from an urban cultural pattern to a substantially rural one. The land that in Roman times had seen an affluence of greater and lesser urban territories developed into the hinterland of the sole surviving fully urbanized centre of Naples. The territory of Naples may be conveniently viewed as eight distinct portions, of which the first is by far the best known archaeologically:

1. the Phlegrean Fields;
2. the land from *Atella* to *Liternum*;
3. *territorium Cymiterense et Nolanum*, around Cimitile and *Nola*;
4. *territorium plagiense*, extending along the coast south of Naples, past the river Sebeto, as far as the river Sarno;
5. the environs of Naples;
6. the Surrentine peninsula, including Sorrento and, for a time, both Amalfi and Salerno;
7. the islands, principally Ischia and Capri;

8. the coastal town of Gaeta and its dependent territory.

The duchy is thus divisible into a core zone (Naples and its immediate surroundings), peripheral core areas (*Cumae*, Cimitile/*Nola*, etc.) and the countryside. Below we shall consider the peripheral core areas and the countryside.

THE PHLEGREAN FIELDS

The area presents a striking geomorphology through its recent vulcanism. Large craters intersect, the fertile soil has led to luxuriant vegetation, and the diverse rocks and slope patterns have led to differential erosion, all making for a varied and by no means unattractive environment. This greatly aided its development in Roman times, as the land was sought for agriculture, whilst the coast was exploited for luxurious retreats and the construction of commercial and military ports and harbours.[2]

---

[2] For a good general survey of the whole area see Amalfitano 1990.

From Naples, the Phlegrean Fields were accessible either along the old Via Antiniana, which crossed the hills of the Vomero, or through the *crypta Neapolitana*, cut by Augustus. A hamlet almost certainly existed at Fuorigrotta, at the northern exit of the tunnel, and an early medieval marble chancel screen was found in building debris near the San Paolo football stadium in 1985 (pers. comm. Deodato Colonnesi). A *casalium* of Antignano also existed, beneath the hills of the Vomero.[3]

The old Roman road from the *crypta Neapolitana* ran past the early Imperial baths and vicus at Via Terracina (Laforgia 1981). Before crossing the hills at Bagnoli to drop down to *Puteoli*, a diverticulum led northwards to the Roman spa at Agnano, which put to good use natural springs and steam vents. This amazing complex seems to have continued in use into the Middle Ages, as Pope Gregory tells of Saint Germanus, bishop of Capua, who visited the baths. They were perhaps still recommended by Peter of Eboli in 1471. Largely excavated in 1898, they show late modifications, including the blocking of some of the doors. The coin series runs up to Justinian. There is then a substantial gap until the presence of an issue of Charles I of Anjou (1266–1289) (Macchioro 1912).[4]

To the west lay the major Roman settlements of *Puteoli*, *Baiae*, *Misenum* and *Cumae*. Apart from *Baiae*, these sites appear to have hosted *castra* by the end of the sixth century, though were probably militarized earlier, and *Misenum* had been home of the Roman fleet.

The severely diminished political and economic importance of *Puteoli* after the fourth century has already been noted, and it must be significant that the city was not mentioned by Procopius in his *de Bello Gothico*, which treats events at both Naples and *Cumae* in some detail. Fifth-century artefacts are known and, though little has been published, they seem to represent a thin veneer over a much larger quantity of earlier material. Though once an independent municipality, *Puteoli* gave way to the increasing political importance of Naples to fall under its control perhaps by the end of the fifth century. The

reasons for its submission may be explained both by coastal bradyscism and by its lesser tactical strength, with the absence of a circuit wall (see above, Chapter 1). Until the mid-sixth century, the site seems to have retained a bishopric.[5] At the end of the century a monastery at *praetorium Falcidii*, founded outside of the town and to which the basilica San Stephani may have been annexed, was abandoned by its monks, who joined the monastery of San Sebastiano in Naples. On this evidence, it may be suggested that the town was effectively abandoned during the course of the century, when a *castrum* was perhaps established on Rione Terra around the *maior ecclesia putheolana* or San Proculo, which accepted the spoils of the martyr removed from the *monasterium Falcidis* (Fig. 5:2) (see above, Chapter 4). Both a *curtis* and a *palatium comitis* are attested at the site, reinforcing the idea of its continued official standing (*MND* II: 183). Maritime contacts into the late sixth or seventh century are indicated by the discovery of a wreck site in the bay yielding seven amphorae from around Samos, perhaps providing evidence for directional trade (Van Ingen 1933: 65, pl. XLII, no. 5; see also below, Chapter 7). The rest of the millennium is virtually an historical blank, though the celebrated baths in the area were still active when, in the summer of 866, Emperor Louis and Engelberga found time to stop off there (Cassandro 1969: 84; Kreutz 1991: 41).

Fig. 5:2. The site of the Castrum Putheoli, *on the promontory of Rione Terra (photo: author).*

---

[3] *Antinianum, ad illa Conucla* (possibly a Roman mausoleum) (R. 449, 520, 576). A church dedicated to Saint Menna existed along the road from Naples to the village (Capasso 1895: 215, n. 1).

[4] Coins of Justinian are a *nummus* and a *pentanummus*, as well as a bronze coin identified as being of Justinian and Athalric (527–534).

[5] See *CIL* X: 3299 for the tombstone of a bishop deceased in 511. A further bishop, Geminus, is attested in 558–559 (Pelagius *Ep.* IX).

In 1026 *Puteoli* fell briefly into the hands of Pandulph IV of Capua, and by the early twelfth century it had gained a certain measure of autonomy from Naples.[6] These events suggest that towards the end of the millennium the settlement was regaining importance, perhaps in the wake of Campanian economic expansion. Dated tombstones of 1021 to 1130 indicate the presence of an Arab community (Scerrato 1967: 145–9, 151–2, nos. 314, 316, 318). In the thirteenth century *Castrum Putheoli* appeared as *locus [...] mari montibusque inaccessibilibus circumquaque conclusum* to Niccolo Jamsilla (cited by Ruggiero 1975a: 58). Such can only refer to Rione Terra, reinforcing the belief that the promontory represented the focus of activity throughout the Middle Ages.

The promontory of Rione Terra, rising on the eastern side of the bay of Pozzuoli, is reputed to be the site of the Roman colony founded in 194 BC and of the earlier Greek foundation of *Dikearchia* in 528 BC (Gialanella and Sampaolo 1981). Excavations should furnish a great deal of information about this site, as the Roman remains appear to be exceptionally well preserved beneath *c.* 5 m of infill below the level of the temple of Augustus on the high point of the promontory. Along Via San Proculo, a Roman *taberna* was converted after the beginning of the third century into a bakery with donkey-mills. It survived until about the Gothic War, and was backfilled between the seventh and eighth centuries (De Caro 1994: 661).[7] Earlier excavations, following the fire of 1965 that devastated the overlying cathedral, laid bare the remains of the temple and brought to light eighth-/ninth-century pottery.[8] What is particularly striking is that, although this pottery has been found at Rione Terra, I am not aware of any from the rest of the Roman city, despite numerous excavations.

After the few words on its late fourth-century tranquillity by Symmachus (Pontieri 1977), neighbouring *Baiae* faded into obscurity. Cassiodorus, perhaps through hearsay, was able to praise the climate and spas of the small bay in the early sixth century (Cass. *Var.* IX. vi. 6). According to John D'Arms, 'something more fortified', beneath the late medieval castle, may have ensured continuity between Roman and late antique settlement (D'Arms 1981: 92–3). Procopius did not mention

Baiae in his account of the Gothic War, suggesting that it was substantially defunct by that date. However, by 921 a monastery, called Sant' Archangeli, *qui vocatur ad balane*, lay in the area (R. 9).

Though much archaeology was removed by Maiuri's clearance operations, underwater research at Punta Epitaffio has revealed a nymphaeum with late antique burials in its ruins (Gianfrotta 1987). A Justinianic coin hoard found there in the 1970s may suggest that the area was not totally unaffected by the conflicts of the Gothic War.

Roman *Misenum*, also scarcely known, sat largely beneath the promontory of Capo Miseno and its two port basins (Fig. 5:3). It housed the *classis Praetoria Misenensis* until the fifth century (Chatot 1896; Gigli 1946; Sirago 1984; also Cass. *Var.* V. 16–17). A decline in its importance may have begun somewhat earlier, though the harbour must have continued in use throughout the Middle Ages. To some extent protected by *Cumae* further up the coast, with the Lombard invasions refugees from the town are attested as having fled as far as Sicily (Richards 1980: 98). At the close of the sixth

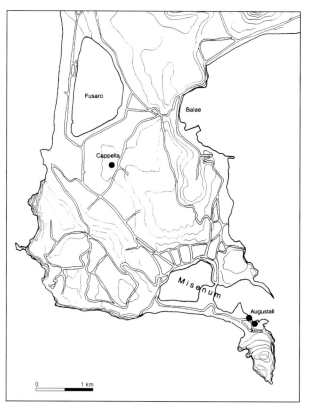

Fig. 5:3. Misenum *(drawn by author).*

---

[6] For references and possible continuity in Lombard control of *Puteoli* see Cassandro 1969: 219.

[7] The understanding of the nature and genesis of the infill is in itself an important issue for the late antique and medieval history of the site. It recalls that found alongside the *macellum* in Naples (see above, Chapter 3).

[8] Little has been published. See de Franciscis 1981.

century, Pope Gregory decided to defend the site with a *castrum*, perhaps to protect the profitable papal patrimony that had existed in the area since Constantine (*Lib. Pont.* I. (*vita Sylvestri*)). On the death of Bishop Liberius of *Cumae*, Bishop Benenatus of *Misenum* was delegated to govern both sees. He was funded by the pope to construct the *castrum*, though subsequent correspondence between the pope and the subdeacon Anthemius suggests that in 599 Benenatus attempted to embezzle funds (Fig. 5:4). Not long after the removal of Benenatus, Fortunatus II, bishop of Naples, became Visitor of the Church of *Misenum*, awaiting the election of a substitute (Greg. *Ep.* IX. 80, 121, 163).

An episcopal see appears to have been in existence as early as the beginning of the fourth century, going by the tradition of the martyr Sossius, deacon of the town, who was executed under Diocletian (Calvino 1969: 58; 1976). The first named bishop is Concordius (Mansi VIII: 236; *MGH, Auct. Antiq.* XII: 433, 18; 454, 44), who attended a Rome synod in 501–502, whilst a Bishop Peregrinus was sent on a mission to Constantinople (Mansi VIII: 412–16), along with Bishop Ennodius of Pavia, by Pope Ormisda in 517. A letter from Pelagius (554–560) informs us of Bishop Constans (*Pelagii I papae Ep.* XXII). A further bishop, Maximus (Mansi X: 1167), attended a synod at Rome in 649, and a Bishop Agnellus (Mansi XI: 299) is recorded as having been present at a council in the city in 680 (Calvino 1969: 67).

It is likely that the cathedral was sited in the area of Torre di Cappella, where the toponym 'il Vescovado' (bishopric) is attested.[9] A Roman cemetery with tile-tombs and two early Christian funerary inscriptions has been found there. One records the presbyter John, and is probably from the late sixth century. The other, of seventh- or eighth-century date, refers to Bishop Pacificus (Minasi 1890; Cautela and Maietta 1983: 160–3).

After severe damage during an Arab raid in 846, the church goods of *Misenum* were transferred to Naples under Duke Sergius I through intercession of his son, Bishop Athanasius II (Capasso 1895: 87, 212). In 906 the remains of Saint Sossius were also removed. The account of the transference, by John the Deacon, is revealing both for its literary style and for the image that it evokes of an abandoned Roman town (John the Deacon, *Translatio Sancti*

Fig. 5:4. The site of the castrum *of* Misenum, *on the promontory of Monte di Procida (photo: author).*

Sosii, MGH; Gay 1917: 229; also De Rossi: 1998). John described his search for the tomb of Sossius amongst the brambles covering the site. Now and again, his search was interrupted by glimpses of the ruins, abraded or broken inscriptions and a particularly fine window still in place high in a wall.

A document of 1129 attests a *castrum Sancti Martini* that, Cassandro suggested, was erected on Monte di Procida (Cassandro 1969: 216). Perhaps this was the same as that mentioned by Pope Gregory. Two monasteries are known in the area of *Misenum*. One, not named in the surviving sources, lay inside the *castrum*. Given the fort's name, it may have been dedicated to Saint Martin of Tours, whose cult was made popular through the *Vita* written by his friend Sulpicius Severus. The other, dedicated to Saint Pancras of Rome, lay between the *castrum* and a lake, which could be either one of the two interconnecting basins now known as Mare Morto and Porto di Miseno (*portus misenate*) (Cilento 1969b: 660). The dedication of the monastery to the Roman martyr Saint Pancras is telling in that the saint is nowhere else found venerated in Neapolitan territory, whilst having been made popular in Rome under both Symmachus and Pope Gregory. It may be suggested that the latter had some hand in the monastery's foundation on pre-existing papal land, as he is certainly attested as having founded or endowed monasteries elsewhere (Richards 1980: 256, for example).

The safest site for a *castrum* was Capo Miseno, more so than Monte di Procida. It rises to 167 m above sea level to dominate the sea route to Naples from the west. It is beneath Capo Miseno, towards the old Roman port, that an early medieval pottery workshop has been found. A large cistern, part of a second-century bath-building, lies on its northern

---

[9] See De Rossi 1998 for the cathedral.

slopes. One kiln has been found within the cistern, whilst others may lie nearby. Amphora fragments, datable to the eighth or ninth century, abound (see below, p. 122). Near the port basin, the Roman *sacellum* of the *augustales* seems to have been back-filled with rubbish from the sixth to the eighth centuries.[10]

Belisarius 'sent to *Cumae* as large a garrison as he thought would be sufficient to guard the fortress there, for there was no stronghold in Campania except those at *Cumae* and at Naples' (Proc. *Bell. Goth.* V. xiv. 2). With this passage, Procopius has confirmed *Cumae* as a *castrum* or military base in the first half of the sixth century, during the Gothic War (Fig. 5:5). With the taking of Benevento by the Lombards in 570, it effectively became the westernmost Byzantine nucleated site in the territory of Naples and thus of some strategic significance. It guarded an area of certain economic importance. In Republican times it was known for its fruit and vegetables (especially apples and cabbages), wine, fishing activities, pottery manufacture and grain from the southern part of the Campanian plain. Though the silting of its port may have led to decline in early Imperial times, this has sometimes been overstressed by scholars interpreting *ad litteram* Juvenal's rather rhetorical claim that the city appeared deserted (Juv. III. 2; Beloch 1989: 182–3).[11] The construction of the *Via Domitiana* in AD 95, linking *Cumae* with northern Campania, presumably facilitated traffic and the local economy. Indeed, the rebuilding of the immense Cumaean *capitolium* and its adornment with colossal statues and the construction of the 'Masseria del Gigante', all in the late first or early second century, does not suggest local economic hardship.[12] A wide belt of land to the north of the town, though marshy in the Middle Ages, had probably been drained by the Romans and may have provided port facilities.

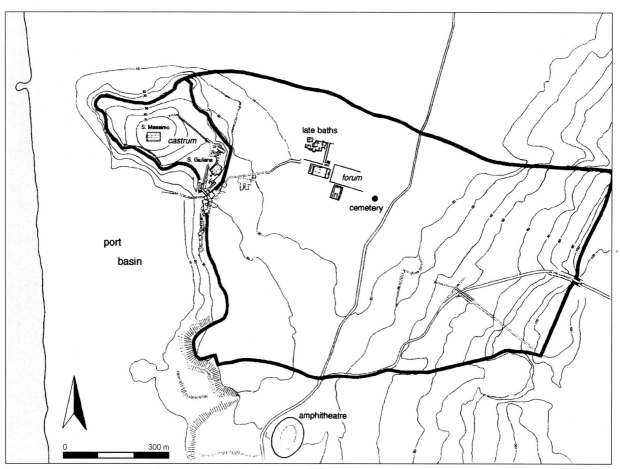

Fig. 5:5. Cumae *with its hypothetical wall-circuits (after Caputo* et al. *1996: inside cover; modified by Giuseppe Gavili).*

---

[10] I should like to thank Paola Miniero, Gianluca Soricelli and Carlo Rescigno for this information. See Miniero 2000.

[11] Frederiksen (1984: 225) wrote of 'the continual drift of coastal sand, gradually filling the shallow harbour of the old Greek city and reducing the facilities to no more than a fishing port'. See also De Caro 1993: 685. For the port see Vecchi *et al.* 2000.

[12] On Roman *Cumae* see Amalfitano 1990. On early Christian *Cumae* see De Rossi 1996.

Procopius told of the importance of *Cumae* during the Gothic War. It saw repeated action. Afterwards, the surrounding land appears to have remained economically important, even if many farmers moved within the town walls, probably to the acropolis that may have been restored by Flavius Nonius Erastus in 558 (see *CIL* X: 328, possibly fake). One local landowner was so wealthy that, in 559, he could afford a revision of his copy of *De Trinitate* (Riché 1962). Not much later, however, following the demise of Bishop Liberius, the bishopric was united with that of *Misenum* because of its diminishing congregations (Greg. *Ep.* II. 42).

The continued strategic importance of *Cumae* is shown both by the efforts of Romuald II of Benevento to capture and hold it in 715/716, though his domination lasted barely a year, and by the raids of Sicard in the territory after 830. Its *castrum* is attested as late as 1044 under Count Marinus (R. 36), whilst a document of 937 records Theophilactus as the resident *comes* (R. 480). The site was finally abandoned in 1205, following a Neapolitan raid.

Meagre archaeological evidence from the lower city seems to indicate parts of the central area of the town as having been a rubbish dump and quarry for *spolia* during the fifth century. A large limekiln has been found in front of the *aula sillana*, by the forum, probably dating to the sixth or seventh century.[13] Five coin hoards found in the Forum Baths contain coins no later than the early sixth century.[14] However, sometime after the abandonment of the baths, a new and modest bath-building was erected within the old Roman cisterns, suggesting that not all of the lower city had been abandoned in favour of the acropolis (additional information kindly provided by Elena Mariconda). Indeed, burials found at the 'Masseria del Gigante' may hint at the presence of a church in the area.

By the time of the Gothic War, the acropolis probably housed the major public buildings and had developed into a refuge for the population of the lower city and the surrounding countryside. Early medieval painted wares are to be found there, whilst similar pottery and ovoid lamps datable to the eighth century have come from the fill of a Roman cistern on the western side of the so-called 'cripta romana', excavated by Giuliana Tocco in 1984. The 'cripta romana' itself may have been largely blocked during the Gothic War, as is suggested by a coin hoard, deposited about 549–552, recovered from the fill (Miraglia 1986). Some of the pottery, in particular broad-line painted jugs, is similar to that produced near the amphitheatre around the sixth to seventh centuries, perhaps using clays quarried from the lake of Licola.[15] Possible evidence relating to episodes of the war include the buttressing of the ancient walls with brick-faced concrete and what appears to be a rectangular siege-gallery aimed at undermining the defences, which has been interpreted as the work of Narses.[16]

Not surprisingly, little of monumental scale survives from early medieval *Cumae*. Both classical Greek temples on the acropolis were converted into churches, indicating the existence of a substantial local congregation. The podium of the lower temple, dedicated to Apollo and converted perhaps into the church of Santa Giuliana, is riddled with graves long since emptied. Other, though fewer, graves also appear cut into the upper temple, of Jupiter, which had probably become the cathedral, dedicated to Saint Maximus.[17] Both of the classical tunnels cut through the tuff hill, the so-called Grotta della Sibilla and the 'cripta romana', were reused as catacombs. The marble revetted baptismal font at San Massimo gives an idea of the investment involved during the construction of the church. A sixth- or early seventh-century inscription to a local dignitary, Brunculus, probably comes from one of the two buildings, and one of them has yielded a further inscription attesting to the restoration of the oratory, perhaps following the Lombard sack of Romuald II in 715/716 (Calvino 1960; Parma 1989).

Finally, to the list of *castra* encircling the Phlegrean Fields should be added *castro de Serra*, sited above the pass of Montagna Spaccata, permitting access to the area from the plain of Quarto to the north. The *castrum* housed a church of San Nicola donated to the bishop of Pozzuoli by the Norman Prince Robert I in 1119 (De Blasiis 1915).[18]

---

[13] Excavations by Giovanna Greco and Stefania Adamo Muscettola.

[14] The latest datable coin from the hoards is of Athalaric (526–534) (Miraglia 1994b).

[15] The pottery is not published. For a photograph of one of the jugs see Amalfitano 1990: 307.

[16] On the buttresses see Maiuri 1954; Peduto 1976: 3. On the mine see Pagano 1986. A similar gallery, attributed to Belisarius, has been found in Naples, see Napoli 1959: 210, n. 74; Johannowsky 1960: 490–2.

[17] Some of these appear to be unexcavated. See Soprintendenza archives C16/19 for 21–4 May 1927.

[18] This is perhaps the only well-preserved early medieval defensive site in the Phlegrean Fields.

THE LAND FROM *ATELLA* TO *LITERNUM*

This was the southernmost part of *Liburia*, a territory which may largely be identified with the old *ager Campanus*, stretching south of the river Volturno (Cassandro 1969: 216–18). Most of *Liburia* fell into the hands of the Lombards in Capua. The river *Clanis* and its formidable surrounding marshes most probably formed an original frontier-zone between Lombard and Neapolitan territory. An environmental history of this area and the effect of the environment on settlement has still to be written, though deteriorating conditions might already be signalled under the Empire by partial desertion of the town of *Acerrae*, to the east of *Atella* (see Lepore 1952: 301, n. 1). However, much of *Liburia*, part of the large granary that had been the *ager Campanus*, was still hailed as being fertile towards the end of the millennium and thus quite understandably was contested by both the Neapolitans and the Lombards (Erchempert, *MGH, Ss. Rer. Lang. et Ital.* 60; Alex. *Tel.* III. 12). The original Neapolitan part of *Liburia* was known as the *pars militie*, presumably referring to its role as buffer-zone between Naples and Benevento. By the eighth century, documents show that there was an intermingling of Lombard and Byzantine properties in *Liburia*, as well as land in joint ownership, and it is wrong to believe that precise frontiers can be found or that they ever existed (Cassandro 1969; Martin 1992).

A glance at present-day settlements and territorial morphology seems to indicate the agricultural primacy of the area. The whole swathe of land stretching between *Liternum*, on the coast, and *Nola* is marked by a high density of -ano place names which, on current toponomastic interpretations, suggests that there was a good measure of continuity in land use through early medieval times (Calzolari 1994). For instance, *Turiniano*, deriving from *Torinius*, is described as a field in *locus Centura* in 968, and as a locus with its church of San Angelo 'in finibus Caudiense', on the edge of *Liburia*, in 991–992 (*CBenev* 14, doc. 5; Calzolari 1994: 98). A certain continuity is both further and eloquently supported by the surviving traces of the Roman centuriation around Naples, particularly in the old *ager Campanus* (Fig. 5:6). Ongoing excavations of an area of some 70 ha at Gricignano, in advance of a new military base, should help us to understand continuity in four *centuriae*. Already, two rooms of a modest farm building and adjoining orchard, perhaps dating to the sixth century and abandoned no later than the seventh, have been examined.[19] It sat upon a fill dating to the second half of the fifth century, which obliterated ditches associated with the 20 × 20 *actus* grid of the first half of the second century BC.

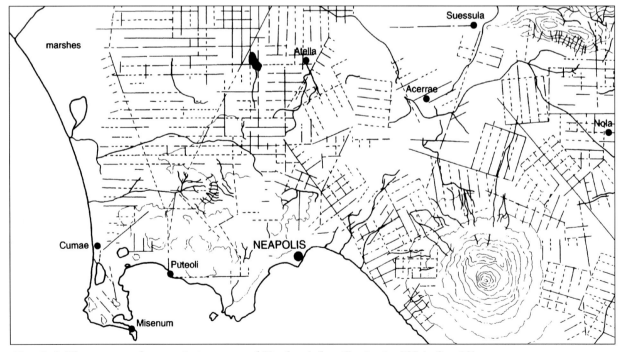

Fig. 5:6. The proposed centuriation around Naples (after Caniggia 1984: fig. 18).

[19] I am grateful to Silvana Iodice for this information. See Iodice and Soricelli 1996.

The major settlements in *Liburia* were *Liternum* on the coast, and *Atella* and *Acerrae* inland. *Liternum* was in decline during the late Empire and was abandoned in early medieval times, to be resettled as a fishing village by the eleventh century (Frederiksen 1984: 45). Remains of the site may be seen near Lago di Patria and, indeed, the town seems to have assumed the name of *Patriensis* during late antique times. A letter of Pope Pelagius I, dated 558–559, attests to the 'clerum vel cives ecclesiae Pa[t]riensis' in a dispute with the church of *Volturnum*, only 12 km up the coast (Pelagius *Ep.* 9; Calvino 1969: 76–8). A bishopric is attested up to 768. Jean-Marie Martin has placed a *castrum Focis* in this area (Martin 1992: fig. 1). A neighbouring diocese, cited solely in the aforementioned letter of Pelagius, lay at *Vicus Feniculensis*, probably later *Vico di Pantano* and now Villa Literno. *Pantanum* first appears as a toponym in 703 (Federici 1925: 135–6), indicating the existence of a marshy environment, perhaps deteriorating since late Roman times with the lack of maintenance of surface drainage systems (Calvino 1969: 75–80; Frederiksen 1984: 45).

In the 1960s William Tobias carried out excavations of *tabernae* by the forum of *Liternum* on behalf of the NATO Archaeological Society.[20] None of the many identifiable coins found ran past the fifth century, though some so-called 'minims' may date to the early sixth century. It was around this time that inhumation burials, containing African red slip ware lamps and imitations, were inserted to one side of the *capitolium*, which may have been converted into the episcopal church under the later Empire (Chianese 1938: 28). It is interesting that this central area does not seem to have been occupied after the early sixth century. Further tile-tombs and fourth- or fifth-century burials in African amphorae were destroyed during building works in 1987 in front of the Istituto Nazareth (personal observation).

A little to the south of the town the church of Santa Fortunata was erected around the fifth century. With almost complete desertion of the area by the end of the eighth century, Bishop Stephen II of Naples transferred the saint's remains to a church at the monastery of San Gaudioso within the city (Pagano 1989; see also above, p. 72).

Much less is known about *Atella* and *Acerrae*, though with the decline of *Puteoli*, the old Via Campana lost importance to the Via Atellana, which passed through the former town to connect Capua with Naples, as may be seen on the *Tabula Peutingeriana*.[21] *Castrum Acerrae* is attested at the end of the millennium (Cassandro 1969: 220).

TERRITORIUM CYMITERENSE ET NOLANUM, AROUND CIMITILE AND NOLA

Spread out in an arc to the northeast of Naples, lining the foothills of the Apennines, lay the Roman towns of *Abella, Calatia, Nola* and *Suessula*. Despite severe decline, they appear to have been fortified or strengthened in late antiquity, prior to the Lombard invasions. Even later, some of them lined the fluid border areas between Naples and the Lombard interior and were partly replaced by new sites in stronger strategic positions. *Comes* (counts), in charge of *castra*, are attested for *Abella, Nola* and *Suessula*, though only between the eleventh and early twelfth centuries (Cassandro 1969: 220, 386, n. 135–8).

The *territorium Cymiterense et Nolanum* included the old Roman town of *Nola*, perhaps stretching as far as *Suessula* (Cancello), to the northwest, and the developing religious centre of Cimitile, the site of a Roman cemetery where Saint Felix had been buried (see above, Chapter 4). Under Pope Pelagius I, *Suessula* seems to have been in severe decline, such that John, bishop of *Nola*, asked permission of the pope to sell its plate in order to meet the running costs of the parish. Pelagius replied that *Suessula* should be made a *titulus* of *Nola*, and that the Nolan clergy should run the church and its lands (Jones 1964: 900). It later became a Lombard *gastaldate* and bishopric, until its abandonment around the turn of the millennium in favour of the hilltop site of Arienzo (Kehr VIII: 476; IX: 125). The few early medieval finds from the site include seventh-century burials found within an early Imperial bath-building excavated at Via Santa Maria a Cancello (additional information obtained pers. comm. during the 1998 Taranto conference).

---

[20] I am grateful to Yvonne Morrison and William Tobias for information on the excavations.
[21] At Aversa (*ad Septimum*), burials of the sixth to seventh centuries have been found above the surface of the Via Campana.

Both Roman *Abella* (later Avella) and *Calatia* (later Maddaloni), in the hills to the northeast of *Nola*, seem to have fallen fast to the Lombards of Benevento, and to have become strategic sites defending the passes to the interior and perhaps acting as control points for the movement of goods. *Abella* guarded the valley pass of the river *Clanis*, the route to Avellino, Benevento and across the Apennines to Apulia. At the beginning of the fifth century it was still able to restore its aqueduct, thereby supplying *Nola*, as a devotion to Saint Felix (Luciano *et al.* 1980).[22] It appears to have been occupied through early medieval times, though it lost its bishopric with the arrival of the Lombards. The castle on the hills above, with its double *enceinte*, appears to be relatively late, though Paolo Peduto has dated its upper elliptical enclosure and towers to Lombard times, perhaps the first half of the seventh century. With the *divisio ducatis* it was assigned to *Salernum*, though in 887 it was briefly held by Athanasius II of Naples (Peduto 1984b: 395–8; Coppola and Muollo 1994: 18–23).

By the first half of the eighth century *Nola* itself appears to have been absorbed by the territory of Lombard *Beneventum* (Cassandro 1969: 149). Little is known about the archaeology of *Nola* during late antiquity and early medieval times. Pottery from the ring-road site does not appear to go past the sixth century.[23] The medieval street-plan totally disregards the original Roman layout, and I would suspect that, even if never totally abandoned, the town had become a mere shadow of its former self in early medieval times. Part of the population may have moved to the developing centre of Cimitile, whilst Landulph Sagax, writing in the tenth to eleventh centuries, reported that Belisarius sent some of its inhabitants to repopulate Naples (Landulfi Sagacis, *Historia romana* XVIII. 14 (see Crivellucci 1913); von Falkenhausen 1992: 10).[24] Another part may have populated *Castel-cicala*, attested in 1017 as a *castrum* guarding the pass to Avellino (*RNAM*: 304).

In the territory of *Nola*, a Roman villa has been excavated in località Saccaccio (Sampaolo 1986: 114–15). Originally built in the second century BC, it survived into the fifth century, when it seems to

have been badly damaged by an eruption of Mount Vesuvius, perhaps that of 472. Later buildings, pottery and a coin of Justin or Justinian I suggest reoccupation into the first half of the sixth century.

TERRITORIUM PLAGIENSE, EXTENDING ALONG THE COAST SOUTH OF NAPLES, PAST THE RIVER SEBETO, AS FAR AS THE RIVER SARNO

From around Mount Vesuvius and down along the coast south of Naples, past the river Sebeto, and as far as the river Sarno, lay the *territorium plagiense*. Much of it was flat, and some marshes existed along the coast, though it was backed by Mount Vesuvius. It included much of the land devastated by the eruption of AD 79. None the less, it was reoccupied shortly afterwards, as is indicated by villas at Ponticelli and *Pompeii*, and many other finds dating down to the late Empire.[25] Indeed, it may have been the lesser eruption of 472 that eventually caused more havoc to agriculture, as it came about during a period of general recession. We have yet to discover evidence for prompt reoccupation of the areas damaged at that date. A likely treasure, now represented by an intact silver casket imitating wickerwork (Fig. 5:7), possibly dating to

Fig. 5:7. Silver casket found near Herculaneum *(photo: Pedicini).*

---

[22] Erroneously cited by Frederiksen (1984: 52, n. 83) as 'Pietro *et al.* 1980'.

[23] I wish to thank Valeria Sampaolo for having shown me the pottery from excavations in and around *Nola*.

[24] However, the account of Landulph has been put in doubt: for example, Cuozzo and Martin 1995: 8–9. Of Cimitile, nothing is known outside of the religious complex illustrated in Chapter 4.

[25] On the finds see Renna 1992: 59–62, n. 224. The site near *Pompeii* that has yielded material dating to as late as the fifth or early sixth century has been excavated by Ernesto De Carolis. Frederiksen, to whom much of the evidence was not available, considered the area to have been long abandoned (1984: 45–6).

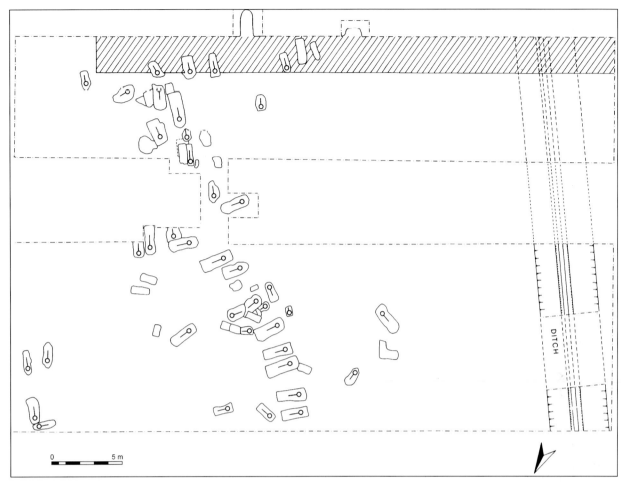

Fig. 5:8. The late Roman cemetery at Via Botteghelle, Ponticelli (after De Stefano and Carsana 1987: fig. 29).

the fifth century and reputedly from the area of *Herculaneum*, is none the less an indication of the existence of someone of wealth in the area in late antiquity (Pedicini and Pedicini 1986: 214–15, no. 64).[26] With the destruction of *Pompeii*, *Herculaneum* and *Oplontis* in AD 79, the major settlement in the Sarno valley became *Nuceria* (Nocera), which appears to have contracted in late Roman times to be lost to the Lombards in 593 (Johannowsky 1980; also Varone 1994).

Minor settlements are known in the area, along the coast and on the foothills of Vesuvius, several of which are likely to have been of Roman origin (Schipa 1892: 593). The church of Santa Maria at Pugliano near Ercolano, first attested as *Pulianum* in 921, contains two Roman sarcophagi, likely to have been gathered nearby and reused as altars with bilingual Latin/Greek inscriptions probably dating to the late tenth century (R. 7; Cavallo 1993: 277, 281).

At Ponticelli, attested since 804, an excavation has revealed the cemetery of a rural population at Via Botteghelle, with some 52 inhumation burials dating between the fourth and first half of the fifth centuries (Figs 5:8 and 5:9) (De Stefano and Carsana 1987: 18–23; see below, Chapter 6). There is little doubt that it included a Christian community, in part emphasized by the use of tiles stamped SPES DEI in a foot-shaped frame. The inclusion of jugs, one of which contained an egg, in two of the burials, may express the persistence of die-hard Roman practices, occasionally found to this day (de Martino 1987, for example).

To the west of Vesuvius lay *Turris de Octabo* (Torre del Greco) and *castrum Maius*. The former is attested in a document of Duke Sergius VII, dating to 1129 and stipulating freedom of commerce and navigation to the people of Gaeta and to all inhabitants of the territory of Naples (Cassandro 1969: 216). There is no evidence that

---

[26] Pedicini and Pedicini described the object as 'alto-medievale' and 'certamente dalla Regia di Portici'.

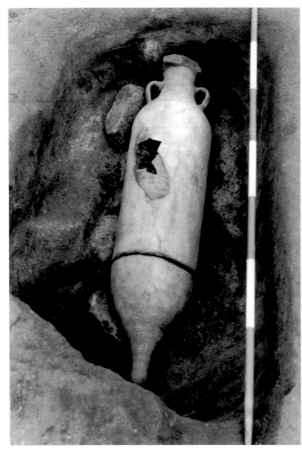

*Fig. 5:9. A child burial at Via Botteghelle, Ponti-
celli, in a Tunisian amphora of form Keay VII,
dating from the fourth to early fifth centuries
(photo: author).*

this was a fortified site of early Byzantine date.
Castrum Maius is attested under Duke Theodore,
in 775, as lying between the island of Capri and the
patrimony of Naples (*MND* I: 49). It could be
earlier, and it might be the same site as *castrum
Maris* or *Castrimaris*, later Castellammare (see
below, p. 95), though in neither case do we possess
archaeological evidence.

To the north of Vesuvius lay the settlement of
Sant'Anastasia, dedicated to the Diocletianic
martyr from *Sirmium* whose remains had been
transferred to Constantinople. Roman settlement
in the area does not appear to have been any more
substantial than agricultural villas. An early
church was revealed during the construction of a
building at the angle of Via Giuglielmo Marconi
and Via Primicerio, though it was not documented
(additional information kindly provided by A.
Parma). Two cemeteries have been uncovered.
One, of early Imperial origin, revealed late Roman
amphora burials and inhumations without grave-
goods, whilst the other was of sixth-century date
(Parma and Gifuni 1987).

Further to the east of Sant'Anastasia was *Castro
de Summa* (Somma Vesuviana). Lying on the
northern foothills of Mount Vesuvius, it was
perhaps intended to control access to Naples from
the Lombard territories to the east, around
Avellino, and to the south, towards Salerno. It is
only attested towards the end of Naples's independence when, in 1119, it was governed by a
senior (Cassandro 1969: 219).

Towards the northwest and west of Vesuvius lay
the *casale* of *Tertium* (Terzo), known in the tenth
century for its water-mills (see below, Chapter 6).
On Mount Vesuvius itself was the monastery of
Santa Maria, associated with a cave (R. 82). San
Pietro a Scafato lay on the southern limit of the
territorium plagiense bounded by the river Sarno
and takes its name from the *scafo* or ferry that was
used to cross the river. It was perhaps a settlement
located on the frontier between Neopolitan and
Lombard territories, strategically sited at the river
crossing.

Early medieval burials have been found at
various places around Sarno (*Terravecchia*), only
just in Lombard territory (Iannelli 1988). Of
particular note are five tombs explored in località
Villa Venere – San Vito. Oriented east to west,
with heads to the west, they were all roughly built
of reused stone. Only one yielded grave-goods,
consisting of a pair of gold earrings and a penan-
nular bronze brooch with zoomorphic terminals
and the inscription +LU[PU] BIBA. It is one of a
group found widely distributed in southern Italy
and dated to the later seventh and eighth centuries
(Salvatore 1979).

THE ENVIRONS OF NAPLES

A number of settlements lay in the area of
Capodichino (*caput de clivo*), the good cultivable
land above the ridge to the northeast of Naples, overlooking the marshes and flatlands that ran down to
the sea (Capasso 1895: 203). Field survey within the
airport suggests that the land was heavily cultivated
in Roman times (Arthur 1990b). *Caput de clivo* is
attested in a lease of 938, which also mentions a
place called *Nepetianum* (R. 42). The largest settlement was perhaps the *casalium* of *Paternum* (San
Pietro a Patierno), already attested in 932. The
church of San Pietro was a proprietary church of a
certain John *miles*. Duke Sergius donated a piece of
land in the *terra* of the *casalium* to the Neapolitan
monastery of San Salvatore in insula maris (R. 22,
113; also Skinner 1995: 43–5; Archivio Storico
Napoli – Monasteri soppressi: volume 138).

To the west is Capodimonte (*caput de monte*) with the settlement of *Ianula*, attested between 982 and the thirteenth century (Capasso 1895: 210). The adjoining hills of the Vomero held the settlements of *Costigliola* (San Potito), *Corrillianum*, with its two churches of Sant'Arcangelo and San Vito, *Babulia*, *loco Piscinule* (*Piscinola*) and *Toricli* (tower?) (Capasso 1895: 215–16).

At Marano, in the woods of Pietra Spaccata, above Masseria Faragnano, a small abandoned cave-church dedicated to Santa Maria is cut into the volcanic tuff, on the edge of a valley (Fig. 5:10). Heavily reworked, perhaps in the seventeenth century, it appears to have been of simple Byzantine type with a domed nave and an apse, behind which runs a semicircular ambulatory, accessible from either side of the apse. An inhumation burial has been found behind the altar, indicating that the deceased was of holy status or, more likely, that he/she was the object of remembrance of a proprietary church.[27] Remains of a mosaic floor near the building suggest that it might have had its origin in late Roman times, perhaps annexed to a villa.[28] The parallel with the 'South Church' of San Vincenzo al Volturno is striking, where a similar ambulatory also contained a tomb of special significance. The 'South Church' may likewise have begun in late Roman times as a funerary chapel (Hodges and Mithen 1993: 180–3).

THE SURRENTINE PENINSULA, INCLUDING SORRENTO AND, FOR A TIME, BOTH AMALFI AND SALERNO

Much of this territory, the southernmost of the duchy of Naples, was lost in the 770s, when Arechis II of Benevento conquered it to establish a principate at Salerno (Delogu 1989). It was composed essentially of a limestone peninsula that formed the southern rim and barrier of the bay of Naples. Access to the bay from the south was by sea, either through the narrow passage (*c.* 5 km across) guarded by the island of Capri and Punta della Campanella, the tip of the Surrentine peninsula, or through the pass at the eastern end of the peninsula, from Cava dei Tirreni into the Sarno valley. The four major settlements were *Stabiae*, *Surrentum*, Amalfi and *Salernum*.

Stabiae, medieval *Castrimaris* and modern Castellammare di Stabia, was a thriving settlement in Roman times, badly hit by the eruption of Vesuvius in AD 79. Archaeological evidence for late antique and early medieval *Stabiae* is provided by an early Christian cemetery unearthed next to the cathedral in 1879 and 1931–1933 (De Rossi 1879; Di Capua 1935: 170). Two pieces of forum ware from the site appear to indicate activity around the eighth to tenth centuries.[29] Various inscriptions were found, including one dated 401, whilst the burials apparently continued into the sixth century. Another inscription of 535 is known from the nearby hill of Varano (*CIL* X: 786). A small settlement may have been sited at the foot of the hill around the cave-church of San Biagio, perhaps originally dedicated to San Giasone e Mauro, whose paintings begin in the eighth century (Ferraro 1991; Bertelli 1994: 131–5; 1996). It would appear to have been a dependency of the

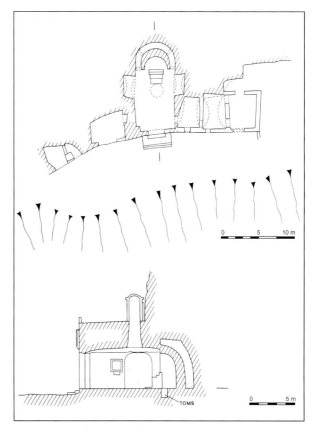

Fig. 5:10. The cave-church at Marano (courtesy of Antonio Guarino).

---

[27] The principle is the same as that which lies behind the apsidal architecture of the churches of San Giorgio and San Giovanni Maggiore in Naples, and may be found in middle Byzantine cave-churches such as that of San Gregorio at Matera (Venditti 1967: 345, fig. 217). I owe the information regarding the site to Catello Pasinetti and Michele Varchetta.

[28] Recent survey in the area of Faragnano has located six Roman sites within less than 1 km from one another, to the east of the church of Santa Maria (Boenzi *et al.* 1995). Site A, in particular, has yielded abundant pottery that runs into the early sixth century, though it is wrongly dated in the article (see especially nos. 25, 32, 33, 57).

[29] These are in the Stabia Museum. I should like to thank Domenico Camardo for this information.

Benedictine monastery of San Renato of Sorrento. The site was probably already in existence in late Roman times, as is suggested by the discovery nearby of a cemetery and African red slip ware lamps of the later fifth to early sixth centuries. Edrisi attested *Stabiae* as a well-defended port with good resources of water and food (Schmiedt 1978a: 176). The nearby island of Robiliano or Reviliano (Roman *Petra Herculis*) housed a Benedictine monastery by the early tenth century (*RNAM* I: doc. XXX; Camardo and Ferrara 1990). If this may be identified with the island of *Eumorphiana* mentioned by Gregory the Great (*Ep.* I. 48), then a monastery existed there already at the end of the sixth century.

Further to the south lay *Surrentum* (Sorrento). Continuity at the town seems confirmed by the survival of much of the ancient street-grid (De Caro and Greco 1981). However, surprisingly little is known about its archaeology, even for classical times. The source material is richer. By Pope Gregory's time it was a bishopric. Later it became a duchy (Sangermano 1988).[30] Edrisi attested it as having had a port with a shipyard, of difficult access (Schmiedt 1978a: 176). According to Giulio Schmiedt, the channel was the passage between the island of Capri and Punta della Campanella, the southernmost entrance to the bay of Naples (Schmiedt 1978a: 176).

Lesser sites in this area include *Planities* (Piano di Sorrento), *Massa Aequana* (Vico Equense) and *Massa Publica* (Massalubrense). If these last two have origins in late antique *massae* (Vera 1986b: 430), we may conclude that ample agricultural use was made of this bountiful northern coast of the Surrentine peninsula. Indeed, wine was exported from the area in the tenth century, following an earlier tradition (R. 257).[31] The *Massa Publica*, first attested in a document of 938, may have derived from old *ager publicus* (Filangieri di Candida 1974: 97–103). It possessed a port, close to which are the remains of a Roman villa, as well as the church of Santa Maria della Lobra, supposedly of early Christian origin and built over a classical temple. However, as with both *Massa Aequana* and *Planities*, there is no clear archaeological evidence for late Roman or early medieval times.

Amalfi, on the southern coast of the Surrentine peninsula, together with Salerno, guarded the southernmost territories of Naples. It is attested as a *castrum* in 596 in a letter of Pope Gregory warning the inhabitants and its bishop against living or conducting affairs outside its boundaries (Greg. *Ep.* VI. 23).[32] It is not heard of again until 812 when, upon the request of the governor of Byzantine Sicily, it had enough ships to participate in ousting Arabs from Tyrrhenian waters. It appears to have gained its independence shortly afterwards, in 839, after which it rapidly became important as an international trading state, its merchants being attested at centres such as Alexandria and Constantinople.[33] In 1073 it capitulated to the Normans. There is no archaeological evidence available for Amalfi's early medieval settlement, in contrast to that at neighbouring Salerno.

Salerno lies beneath Mount Bonadies, gripping a narrow strip of coast between the hills and the sea to the south. It is delimited by two torrents, of the Fusandola to the west and the Rafastia to the east.

The original Byzantine *castrum* has been reconstructed as a quadrilateral fort covering some 6.5 ha within the area of the present town centre, though little clear evidence is available to support this (Amarotta 1989: 68–70, fig. 19). Others see an early date, at least by the sixth century, for the foundation of the castle visible above the town, where a curtain wall and tower have been assigned to Narses, during the Gothic War (Alfano and Peduto 1992: 507; Romito and Peduto 1996: 6–7). That *Salernum* was garrisoned and already dependent upon Naples in the early seventh century is indicated by a letter of Pope Honorius I (625–638) requiring the *magister militum* of Naples to sentence a murderer amongst the soldiers stationed there (Kehr VIII: 67). Not much later, probably in 640 during the reign of Arechis I, it was unified with the southern Lombard state of *Beneventum*.

Archaeological evidence, however, is slowly accruing to permit a vision of the town's vicissitude through late antiquity and the early Middle Ages. In late antiquity it appears to have suffered the

[30] I should like to thank Mario Russo for having discussed the archaeology of Sorrento with me.
[31] Early Imperial production is attested through the sources (Tchernia 1986) and by the discovery of kiln wasters of form Dressel 2–4 wine amphorae (additional information, Carlo Rescigno).
[32] Also George of Cyprus (Gelzer 1890: 28, 543).
[33] Much has been written about the economic fortunes of Amalfi. Citarella's studies (1967; 1968; 1977) are seminal. See also the important study by Del Treppo and Leone (1977), whilst Kreutz (1991: 79–93) has examined the question more recently. See also Gargano (1992) on the town's topography.

general urban decline of many Italian towns, apparently aggravated by periods of massive land slips. Between the late fourth and early fifth centuries, Arrius Maecius Gracchus was recorded on a statue base as having repaired the town to its original splendour after a disastrous land slip (*CII.* X· 520; Peduto *et al.* 1989: 34). The event seems to be attested through excavations. A wealthy late Roman *domus* and adjoining street, excavated in Via Mercanti, as well as a bath-building by San Pietro in Corte, near the walls overlooking the sea, were buried by colluvial soil in the late fourth or fifth century (Peduto *et al.* 1989: 11–12). Similar soil deposits appear to have been unearthed in Via Giudaica (Iannelli 1992).

These areas were used for burials during the seventh to eighth centuries, and have also yielded traces of wooden houses and debris from a blacksmith who worked both iron and bronze. Indeed, during this period a number of old intramural areas appear to have become vacant, suggesting population decline.

Salerno seems not to have fared well until the reign of Arechis II, under whom it was virtually refounded in the 770s to 780s by the enlargement of the defensive circuit and the erection of a *palatium* (*Ep. Lang.* III. 696–7).[34] Excavations at San Pietro in Corte, where seventh-century burials were found, have brought to light spectacular remains of part of the palace of Arechis, and the palatine chapel of San Pietro e Paolo. During the tenth or eleventh century, baths were built in the area now occupied by the late medieval chapel of San Salvatore de Fondaco, to the immediate southeast of San Pietro in Corte (Peduto *et al.* 1989; Di Muro 1998).

The town became independent of Benevento under the principate of Siconulph (840–849), whose authority was proclaimed in a coinage initially based on Byzantine gold coinage (Mangieri 1991: 13–14). It clearly continued to develop in the ninth century, when as early as the 870s renowned doctors, such as Jerome, sowed the seeds of its internationally famous medical school (Oldoni 1988: 13–14). Documents in the *Codex Diplomaticus Cavensis*, attest to a thriving countryside. It fell to the Normans in 1085.

THE ISLANDS, BEING PRINCIPALLY ISCHIA AND CAPRI

The islands in the bay of Naples, as many elsewhere, seem to have acted as refuge sites, partly through a spontaneous movement of people and partly through the official creation of *castra*. The concept of 'refuge site' has been developed amongst archaeologists concerned with the Aegean islands in late antiquity, especially during the period of the Slav invasions of Greece (Hood 1970). In effect, it has been used to explain the rise in importance of certain Adriatic islands during early medieval times, such as the rise of Grado hand in hand with the decline of Aquileia, and the rise of the Torcello/Rialto/Venice complex following on the decline of coastal sites such as Altino (Leciejewicz, Tabaczynska and Tabaczynski 1977; Schmiedt 1978b: 80–82; Schultz 1991: 419–21).

It would appear that similar population movements took place elsewhere in Italy, including Campania. In one of Pope Gregory's letters, he was quite concerned that the sudden arrival of new inhabitants or refugees on the island of *Eumorphiana* could pose a serious threat to the godliness of the monks already living there. His solution was to banish the women, quite clearly the major distraction, to alternative refuge sites (Richards 1980: 98).

Four principal islands lie around the bay of Naples; Ischia, Procida/Vivara, Nisida and Capri. No sites are known on the smaller islands, though on Procida the monastery of Sant'Angelo was already in existence by 1026 (R. 408). The major islands of Ischia and Capri, in their respective positions at the western and eastern entrances to the bay of Naples, were both garrisoned.

The *castrum Gironis*, attested on the island of Ischia (*insula maiore* or *Iscla*) in the tenth century, though probably built somewhat earlier, was presumably a planned establishment (Hofmeister 1924: 251–4, 267–8; Cassandro 1969: 216). The actual fortified site has not been located. Don Pietro Monti has rejected the idea that a Byzantine *castrum* could have been sited above Lacco Ameno, on Monte Vico, despite its abundant early medieval remains (pers. comm., 15 May 1991). Alternatively, it is possible that a *castrum* lies beneath the castle at Porto d'Ischia, though the modern port basin, carved out of a volcanic crater, may still have been a land-locked lake in antiquity.

---

[34] The principal study of the early medieval history of Salerno is Delogu 1977. See also Kreutz 1991: chapter 6.

During Republican and early Imperial times, *Cartaromana* seems to have been the principal settlement on the island, though there is evidence to suggest that it had declined by the sixth century (additional information, Ida Attolini). Instead, from late antiquity the site of *Lacco Ameno* flourished. Excavations beneath the church of Santa Restituta have revealed an abundance of archaeological evidence, with a concentration of material dating to the sixth and seventh centuries (Monti 1980; D'Agostino and Marazzi 1985; Guarino, Mauro and Peduto 1988). The excavations have yielded pottery wasters dating perhaps from the sixth to eighth centuries, including some of transport amphorae. Iron smelting was also practised. The sheer quantity of material could support the hypothesis that, despite the felicitous strategic position of Naples, Ischia became something of a refuge centre, hosting refugees from the Phlegrean Fields and elsewhere.

Capri, instead, has no clearly attested *castrum*, though, on the basis of tenth-century documents, it has often been supposed that a Byzantine fortification lies beneath the castle of Barbarossa at Anacapri (for example, Cantone, Fiorentino and Sarnella 1982: 8, n. 35). It may have been for defensive purposes that Duke Theodore of Naples leased the island with the monastery of Santo Stefano and *casalia* from Pope Gregory II in the first half of the eighth century (*MND* I: 49; see Brown 1984: 101–2). In 866, however, it was appropriated by the Carolingian emperor, Louis II, who gave it to Amalfi in recognition of its help in liberating the Neapolitan bishop, Athanasius, who had been imprisoned at Castel dell'Ovo (Camera 1881: 109–10; Galasso 1980: 514).

GAETA

Gaeta, some 100 km along the coast to the north of Naples, was separated from it by a large stretch of land in Lombard hands. To the north it bordered the papal state. In early Byzantine times Gaeta was perhaps annexed to the territory of Rome. The site had been safeguarded by the Byzantine government, much like Terracina, on account of its strategic position across the Via Appia and along the sea route to Rome. It may have become dependent on Naples in 727, during the iconoclast controversy (Cassandro 1969: 223). Its economic

strength later permitted its development into an autonomous, nominally Byzantine, duchy. The effective break from Naples is probably to be dated from about 787–788, following Charlemagne's campaign in southern Italy, when the town, surrounded by papal territory, found a nominal *rapprochement* with Rome more convenient (von Falkenhausen 1978a: 13–14; Guiraud 1982). Lip-service to Naples continued for many years, as is shown by a Gaetan document of 839 that records Andreas II of Naples as 'domini Andree eminentissimo consul et duci nostri', despite the substantial measure of independence under its new *hypatoi* (Gay 1917: 21; Cassandro 1969: 223). Not long after, under Docibilis I (867–*c*. 910), the small city-state seems to have broken away from any remaining Neapolitan hegemony and a ruling dynasty was formed that survived, more or less, into the eleventh century.[35] It eventually fell to Pandulph IV of Capua in 1032/1033 (Cassandro 1969: 316).

DISCUSSION

Much ink has flowed in explaining the collapse of the Roman urban settlement pattern. In Italy alone it was based on 372 towns, being on average one to every 800 km^2. In fertile areas like Campania, urban settlement was far denser. By the seventh century a third of the towns had vanished. It seems clear that amongst the principal reasons for the disappearance of the Roman town are lowered early medieval productivity, first and foremost agricultural, and declining trade, together with untoward fiscal policies that hastened the gradual breakdown of the state.[36] It is likely that population decline resulted, exacerbating the situation. The crucial centuries to our understanding of settlement transformations and population decrease and migration are the fifth and sixth, although the transitions brought about in the preceding centuries are not to be underestimated in the construction of any general model. Until recently the archaeology of early medieval settlements was hampered by the lack of datable artefacts.

Recent excavation, both in Naples and elsewhere, has begun to shed light on the ceramics circulating after the demise in the importation of African red slip ware, the archaeologist's principal

---

[35] For the most recent and fascinating political history of Gaeta see Skinner 1995.
[36] Amongst the many archaeological works, readers may be referred to Hodges and Hobley 1988; Reece 1988.

dating evidence for late antique contexts.[37] It is thus now possible to date contexts, with a fair degree of certainty, to individual centuries spanning much of the first millennium. This breakthrough, combined with the information gleaned from the written sources, permits the identification of a series of sites with late antique and early medieval occupation, and the exclusion of those probably abandoned by late Roman times. However, the main problem in identifying continuity seems to rest not so much on the recognition of ceramics that succeed African red slip ware, but on the possibility that on many sites fewer ceramics were in use after the sixth century, with an increase in the use of wooden vessels (see Moreland 1993: 99–101). If this is the case, then only very careful excavation will really provide us with an index of the scale of early medieval rural occupation.

Through ceramic dating, recent field survey in the Phlegrean Fields, conducted by Project EUBEA, shows that almost 12% of the rural sites in existence during the early Empire were probably still in use by the early sixth century (Fig. 5:11).

However, the number of rural sites and the close-knit distribution of *castra* in the Phlegrean Fields implies, to my mind, that a fair proportion of agricultural land remained under cultivation near Naples, and was possibly still in the hands of medium-sized landowners up to the sixth century. On, albeit slim, archaeological evidence, most of the surviving villa sites seem to have been maintained by peasant families or relatively modest tenants, though they may have been owned by relatively well-to-do proprietors. Indeed, the rarity of archaeological evidence of discreet living standards suggests that such proprietors did not live on the land.

This by no means conflicts with the view of an increasing ruralization of late and post Imperial culture, including the towns. First of all, late Republican and early Imperial villas in areas like coastal Campania quite blatantly displayed the attributes of Roman urban culture, and their rurality consisted in their setting and function more than in any social attribute. Even so, great changes had already taken place by the mid-Empire, with

	Puteoli suburbs	Hinterland up to Monte Spaccata	Plain of Quarto	Northern Campania
Roman Imperial sites	176	43	131	138
Sites with post-fourth-century pot	2	12	27	27
Sites with post-sixth-century pot	1	1	2	3

Fig. 5:11. The number of rural sites around Puteoli *counted during the 1988–1989 Project EUBEA field survey, compared to those known in northern Campania (sources: Arthur 1991a; Miraglia 1994b: 59–60).*

The data from territory gravitating on the bay of Naples at this time compares closely with the results from a field survey of some 100 km² conducted in northern Campania, 50 km to the north of Naples. There, around 19% of sites survived the fifth and early sixth centuries, whilst only three have recognizable early medieval pottery. This contrasts with the even more drastic reduction in inhabited rural sites in other areas of Italy during the later Empire stressed by various scholars on the basis of field surveys and excavations conducted up and down the peninsula (as summarized in Lewit 1991: chapter 3). Despite the difficulties in dating post-sixth-century sites, and the probability that more will be recognized in future, the decline in inhabited sites and in overall cultivation was probably a very real trend.

the disappearance of the classical slave-based holdings, and by the late Empire villa settlement had reduced drastically. What survived, as far as we can tell, was quite different to what there had been. Many of the earlier, wealthy, absentee landowners had disappeared or become evermore absent, as the distribution of capital within the Empire changed radically. With them, 'urban' comforts in rural contexts eventually disappeared, and there was almost certainly a proportionate rise in the peasant class both within and outside the increasingly blurred town limits. There is little evidence for what we might suppose to be the centres of large holdings or *latifundia*, save the toponyms referring to *massae*, and no recognizable praetoria, unless we count Paulinus's Cimitile and the unexcavated *praetorium Falcidii* near *Puteoli*.

[37] On African red slip ware see principally Hayes 1972; 1980. Fentress and Perkins (1988) have charted its demise. On later wares in southern Italy see Arthur and Patterson 1994.

However, at the turn of the fourth century, land magnates such as Symmachus possessed properties near Naples. The apparent absence of estate-centres might be explained by a lack of archaeology. However, it is possible that throughout the late Empire both the abundance of towns in the area that could accommodate the functions of praetoria, and a certain continuity in the fractioning of the highly fertile land that rimmed the bay of Naples, effectively stunted the processes of estate agglomeration indicated for other areas of Italy (see Vera 1995).[38]

After the Gothic War, Imperial holdings may have passed into the hands of the Byzantine provincial administration. Many also went to the Church and remained in the hands of local bishops, churches and monasteries right through early medieval times. Byzantium, however, confiscated many papal properties in 732, and Pope Hadrian was still trying to retrieve them 30 years later (Marazzi 1992). As regards the property market, little is known about it until the appearance of documentary sources towards the close of the millennium. A singular inscription in stone (Fig.

5:12) documents the sale of the *casalium* of Memorola, close to *Cumae*, by the *honesti viri* Sisinius and Leopardus to the *honesti* Barbarus and Florentinus, during the seventh century (Barone 1918). This is an interesting early example of what appears to be a rural settlement, though the term *casalium*, often equated with village and its dependent land, is in this case probably a farm. Continuous references to landholdings in the texts imply that there was a premium on agricultural property around Naples, despite the troubled times.

Though none of the sites in the Phlegrean Fields have been excavated, two villas closer to Naples, at Marianella and at Ponticelli, have. They suggest what the material from the survey sites might actually represent.[39] The earlier of the two, at Cupa Marfella, Marianella, in the hills behind Naples, is a farm of classical Vitruvian type, with rooms grouped around three sides of a square courtyard. It dates from the first century AD, and has yielded broad-line painted pottery dating to the seventh or eighth century. The only associated structures were two pits and a number of post-holes. A simple adult inhumation burial without

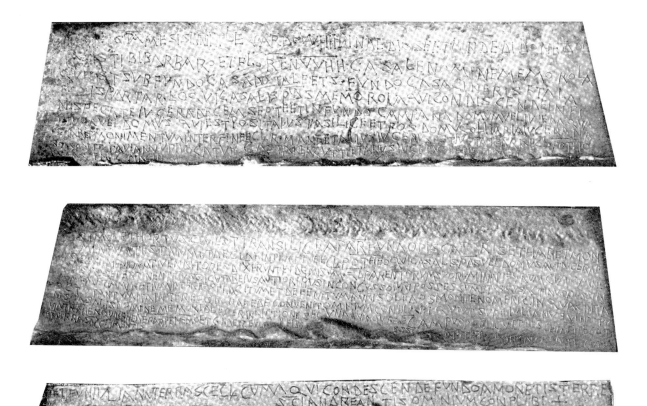

Fig. 5:12. Document in stone recording the the sale of the casalium *of Memorola, near* Cumae *(from Barone 1918) (courtesy of the Archivio di Stato di Napoli).*

---

[38] On the *praetorium Falcidii* see above, pp. 76–7. For late Roman properties around the bay see D'Arms 1970: 226–9.
[39] A note on these is in De Stefano and Carsana (1987: 61–9). Information on Marianella was provided by G. Miraglia.

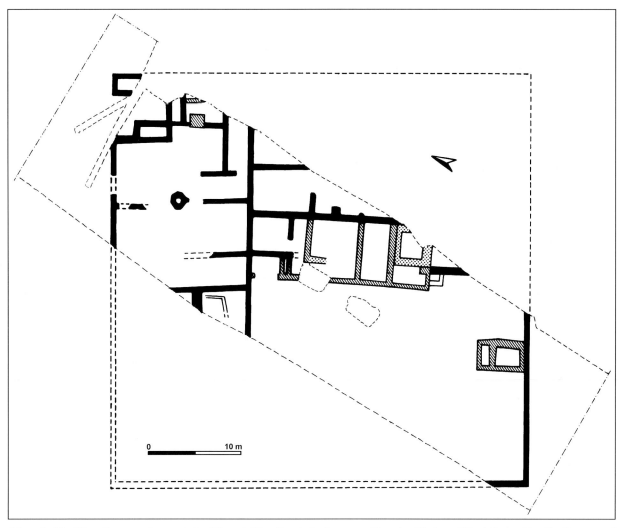

Fig. 5:13. The Roman Imperial villa at Via Bartolo Longo, Ponticelli (modified from De Stefano and Carsana 1987: fig. 130).

grave-goods was found inserted into the rubble of the Roman building. Though there was evidently continuity or reuse at the farm, farming activity was clearly of a different nature and greatly reduced in scale when compared to earlier times. It may be hypothesized that final abandonment was occasioned by the shift of the inhabitants to the budding village of *Piscinola*, attested as *loco Piscinule* in 1058 (R. 490).

At Ponticelli (Via Bartolo Longo) a late Republican villa was destroyed by the eruption of Mount Vesuvius in AD 79 and buried beneath pyroclastic debris, to be replaced by a totally new structure in the second century, probably occupying an area of about 2,000 m² (Fig. 5:13). This survived into the early sixth century, as is shown by the discovery of African red slip ware and local pottery types, and was almost certainly not used any later (De Stefano and Carsana 1987: appendix 1). Some 300 years passed before the first surviving

reference to *casale Ponticellum*, in 804, probably lying at some distance from the villa, close to the river Sebeto.

In central Campania, the dense dispersed settlement of 'Roman type' had totally disappeared, according to archaeology, after the first half of the sixth century. Most of the Roman villas and farms that had survived up to then were abandoned. They gave way to a small number of nuclei in prominent geomorphological locations, such as the acropolis of *Cumae* or the promontory of Rione Terra at Pozzuoli. These are the *castra* whose formalization was principally a result of the Lombard invasion of Italy in 568, speeding along the abandonment of the surviving undefended rural sites around Naples. Undoubtedly this would also have led to changes in the agrarian regime, but not to the wholesale abandonment of cultivated land. The farmer or tenant perhaps no longer lived on his holding, but cultivated it from the town or *castrum*, defining a pattern that is still typical of much of southern Italy (Blok 1969). We might, indeed, view the *castra* as defended agro-towns. In contrast to other areas of Italy, widespread cultivation continued without apparent interruption through the second half of the first millennium, as is implied by the remarkable survival of Roman centuriation both in Lombard and Neapolitan territories (Fig. 5:6) (Valerio 1983; Caniggia 1984: 86).

The discrepancy between the apparent abandonment of most rural sites by the early sixth century and the development of *castra* during the latter part of the same century needs to be explained. Perhaps the most likely hypotheses are:

1. that occupation of the rural sites continued up to the end of the sixth century, and perhaps even beyond, but remains as yet unrecognized because late African red slip ware rarely reached the sites, and knowledge of other late sixth-century pottery is still limited;
2. that the shift to nucleated sites took place slightly earlier, though they did not officially become *castra* until the end of the century.[40]

Abandonment of rural sites during the long drawn-out Gothic War is a tempting assumption, though it needs to be proved. Why people did not return to their properties afterwards also needs to be examined. *Per contra*, some of the *castra*, such as *Cumae*, almost certainly saw immigration during the conflict, though they may not have been established as permanent *castra* until the arrival of the Lombards. Indeed, during the deployment of Justinianic forces under the command of Belisarius, Procopius explicitly stated that there were no Gothic strongholds in Campania, save Naples and *Cumae* (Proc. *Bell. Goth.* V. xiv. 2). This would seem to underline the continuing strategic and, I suppose, economic importance of the bay of Naples well into the sixth century, continuing as it did to represent a stepping-stone on the eastern route to Rome, and it may be remembered that Gothic presence is otherwise little attested in southern Italy. Only the garrisons of Syracuse and Naples seem to have been of any standing, both being strategic ports on the routes to Africa and the East.[41] It may be noted, however, that Benevento possesses a pentagonal prow-tower of Byzantine type, which

may have been erected prior to the arrival of the Lombards (see above, Chapter 3). Though the walls of Naples were refortified from the reign of Valentinian III, the first mention of a fort in the suburbs dates to the campaigns of Belisarius in 536.[42]

Under Justinian, the role of *castra* was perhaps seen as little more than temporary, necessitated by the war. By the end of the century, Pope Gregory's letters indicate that the papacy was aware of the need for permanent fortified settlements, as they demonstrated both pressure being brought to bear on local authorities and the desire to provide financial assistance. From the later sixth century Naples had to contend with the Lombard duchy of *Beneventum*, which, at the time, was almost incessantly active against Byzantine interests. On one occasion, in 596, Duke Arechis invaded Neapolitan land, taking a number of prisoners, both freemen and slaves. Pope Gregory was involved in obtaining the ransom through his Neapolitan subdeacon Anthemius, not only, it seems, for ecclesiastical dependants or slaves, but also for tenant farmers (Greg. *Ep.* VI. 32; I. 410–11; Recchia 1978: 71–2). It is therefore not surprising that he was also concerned with strengthening the defensive system of both the city and its countryside, particularly in view of the important papal possessions at *Misenum* and on the island of Capri. The Empire, at the time, was governed by Maurice, whose policy marked a turning-point in the transition from the late Roman administrative structure to that of medieval Byzantium. In the West, he founded the exarchates of Ravenna and Carthage, with both military and political powers in the hands of the exarchs, and through them attempted to render the West capable of self-defence (Ostrogorsky 1968: 69–70). His will even arranged for the installation of a western government based in Rome under his younger son, Tiberius, though plans were dashed by the usurpation of Phocas (602–610), Gregory's ally. Maurice's regard for the western part of the Empire and his policy of militarization may well have added further fuel to Pope Gregory's own policy. Though the two men were never great friends, Gregory maintained a sober diplomatic relationship with the eastern government, contrasting his attrition with the eastern patriarchate (Haldon 1990: 42).

[40] Such shifts certainly took place elsewhere. They are well-documented in Liguria (Christie 1990) and Provence (Chapelot and Fossier 1980: 194). As regards *castra*, care is needed in the interpretation of terms. During the tenth century the word *castrum* was used to indicate a town in antithesis to the village though, of course, both town and village need themselves to be defined (von Falkenhausen 1978a: 145–6).

[41] The only other garrisons or *praesidia* known were sited at *Beneventum*, *Aceruntia* in Basilicata, *Roscianum* in Calabria and *Panormus* (Palermo) in Sicily.

[42] For Valentinianic fortification see *CIL* X: 1485; Christie and Rushworth 1988. For Justinian see Proc. *Bell. Goth.* V. viii. 5.

The military system on the ground, as it had developed by the seventh century, echoes certain principles of eastern Byzantine military policy, paralleled elsewhere in Italy. These include defence in depth, troops deployed in fortified centres within the hinterland and active participation of the civilian population in guarding and repairing fortifications (Brown 1978. 325). The combination of textual and archaeological evidence seems to illustrate a defensive system around Naples based on *castra* of varying size and importance, many of which, however, are not attested until after the year 1000 (Martin 1992: 268–73). Whether this is due to the vagaries of the sources, or because some of the sites are effectively later in date, we do not know yet. However, unlike other areas, such as Liguria or the Via Armerina corridor between Rome and Ravenna, there seems to have been little new fort building, but rather adaptation of old classical towns.

The development of *castra* was, according to Frederiksen, sparked off by the need for refuge centres into which the rural population could retire when necessary (Frederiksen 1984: 45). This concept might well be applicable to their early days, though archaeology suggests that after the sixth century much of the rural population lived permanently within the walls. Thus they were far more than refuge sites, and perhaps should be compared with the settlements of some of the late Roman *limitanei*. Similar sites seem also to have developed in Lombard territory, separated from Naples by frontier land cultivated by both Lombards and Neapolitans from at least the eighth century. It is possible that a number of smaller sites were set around Naples to guarantee further the security of the city. Once again, archaeology is severely wanting and, as in Byzantine Liguria, material evidence is anything but evident (Christie 1990: 238–9).

A further series of *castra*, not all dependent on Naples, may have lined the Tyrrhenian coast so as to protect coastal traffic between the various Byzantine holdings of Sicily, north Africa and the East, on the one hand, and between Rome and far-flung papal possessions on the other (von Falkenhausen 1992: 18–20). These sites scattered along the coast in defensible positions, safeguarding maritime communications, vary from urban centres to possible military *praesidia* such as that found at Cosa in Tuscany (Fentress *et al.* 1991). Between Rome and the bay of Naples the only clearly identifiable site is Gaeta, which, in effect, was far more than a *castrum*. To the south of

Naples and Salerno, there was probably a handful of such sites. One was Agropoli. A letter of Gregory the Great suggests that Felix, bishop of *Acropolis*, had fled there from *Paestum* by 592, and was given charge of the coastal sees still in Byzantine hands (Greg. *Ep.* II. 42; Richards 1980: 100). The site appears to have yielded ceramics of probable Neapolitan manufacture, dating to the early sixth century (Cantalupo 1981). Another was almost certainly the actual town of Policastro, betrayed by its name (Natella and Peduto 1973: 508, 520). Yet another may have been *Tropea*, where excavations in Piazza del Castello indicate substantial activity during the sixth century (Di Gangi, Lebole Di Gangi and Sabbione 1994), and at least one ceramic jug of Neapolitan manufacture has been found. Future excavation and study of these sites should help to show in what measure they might have been connected to Naples and how they may have aided communications with the East.

According to the sources, by the ninth century a new rural settlement pattern, based in part on the *casalia*, had come to the fore. Plotted on a map (Fig. 5:14), these appear in a wide swathe from the north and west of Mount Vesuvius, northwards into *Liburia*, with very few in the Phlegrean Fields and along the coast north of *Cumae*. Their rarity in the Phlegrean Fields is perhaps to be explained by the predominance of *castra*, whilst northwards the marshes may have impeded agglomeration.

Some of these settlements were already in existence from the early eighth century, such as those that Duke Theodore of Naples leased along with the island of Capri, and there seems to have been at least one seventh-century example near *Cumae* (see above, p. 100). The *curtis* and the villa are also occasionally attested in the written sources. *Artianum* (Arzano: first attested in 937) and *Mairanum* (Marano: first attested in 942), both perhaps significantly praedial toponyms, were presumably estate-centres. However, the majority of peasant labourers, going by site-types attested in the sources, did not inhabit the estate-centres but the scattered villages or *casalia*. Indeed, it was by the end of the millennium that most of Italy was characterized by a plethora of village communities unlike anything that had been seen before (De Seta 1984). Evidence is lacking for the foundation dates of these new communities that, according to some, may have had their origins in late antique estate-villages. None have been excavated yet.

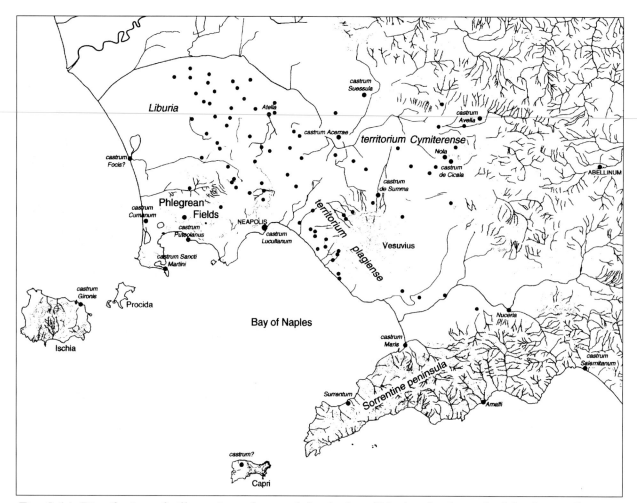

Fig. 5:14. Distribution of villages in and around the duchy of Naples, by the end of the first millennium (based on Frederiksen (1984) base map with data from Capasso 1895).

Analogies help provide working hypotheses for the transition of Roman villas and farms to villages. Evidence from Gaul has suggested a developmental sequence from an abandoned villa to the deposition of burials in its shell and, from this, to the constitution of an associated church or chapel and eventually to the growth of a village around the rural religious focal point (Percival 1992). Whilst John Percival has stressed the schematic nature of the hypothesis and variations on its theme, it does provide ideas that may be examined through excavations in appropriate areas of both surviving and abandoned medieval villages.

As in Gaul, many villa sites in various parts of Italy were used as focal points for cemeteries and churches.[43] Some of the villas may have possessed private churches or chapels (*oratoria*) as part of their function, whilst other villas may have been abandoned and later reused for the siting of a rural church.[44] Closer to Naples, the church of San Costanzo, Capri, was built over Roman remains during the fifth century (Arthur 1992), and that of San Giacomo, Calvizzano, was erected over a villa (Caputo 1989).[45] Whereas in the first case the church is late Roman and there is evidence for continuity down to the present, in the latter the church is probably medieval and no evidence for continuity has been presented. A monastery was built at the *praetorium Falcidii* at *Puteoli*, another (San Severino) was founded on a private estate around the *Lucullanum* near Naples, and Paulinus sited another on his estate at Cimitile near *Nola* (see above, Chapter 4). In internal

---

[43] For Avicenne in the province of Forti-Cesena, see D'Angela 1988, to cite one of the few well-published examples with a seventh-century cemetery.

[44] See Fiore Cavalieri (1988) for an oratory within a late Roman villa at Fara Sabina, not far from Rome.

[45] For San Giacomo, Calvizzano, note the praedial toponym. A similar story may explain the positioning of the seventh-century church of San Lorenzo, Altavilla Silentina, where abundant Roman pottery has come to light (Peduto 1984a).

Campania various medieval villages attested by the eleventh or twelfth century seem to have developed upon sites of Roman villas, though again no evidence of continuity has been shown. These villages often appear to be identified through their churches, with early saintly dedications, to which praedial toponyms were added (Franciosi 1978: 158–9).[46] Examples in the area of Naples appear to be San Giorgio a Cremano, attested as a *locus* in 955,[47] and San Pietro a Patierno, *locus* from 960, with its proprietary church of John *miles* (see below, p. 94).

Through the combined evidence, a four-stage development from Roman dispersed settlement to villages may be suggested (Fig. 5:15). From the late Empire, down to the sixth century, in the context of a still relatively strong and organized agricultural economy, the countryside appears to have been dotted with surviving villas and farms radiating out from their associated towns. The latter still served as market centres, continuing the tradition of the Roman *nundinae*.

During the course of the sixth century, a further proportion of the surviving rural settlement was abandoned, as farmers gravitated towards more secure *castra* or immigrated to Naples itself, which appears to have expanded. With the abandonment of much previously farmed land, farmers either travelled between their holdings and the central places or reverted to sheep rearing, as may be indicated by the proportionate rise in sheep/goat in Neapolitan faunal assemblages. Only parts of a few Roman villas and farms continued to be occupied, though by reduced populations, and agricultural surplus was severely diminished. There may well have been a rise in the proportion of free peasantry, both because of difficulty in the control of manpower and because of the meagre returns that could be had from tied labourers or tenants.

By the eighth century, landlords, including the church and monasteries, attempted to re-establish control of the land and rural manpower by founding rural churches that acted as focal points both for daily exchange and seasonal markets, as well as, of course, for the celebration of Mass. These churches may appear to be isolated, but actually lay at the centre of an area of scattered small farms. They were sometimes erected over abandoned Roman buildings so as to economize in materials and labour. They are identified both by

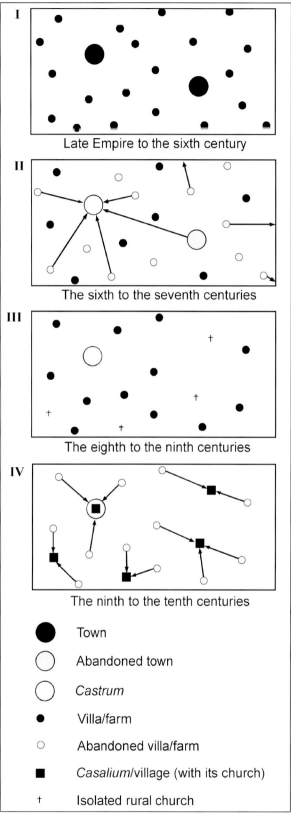

Fig. 5:15. Hypothetical changing settlement patterns in and around the territory of Naples (drawn by author).

[46] Unfortunately, the sites in question are not named, aside from Santa Maria di Fontigliano, near Nusco, in the province of Avellino.
[47] A church of San Giorgio is no longer attested at the site.

their dedications and by the area in which they are sited, which may take the name of a previous Roman *fundus* or of a distinguishing natural or artificial feature.

During the ninth and tenth centuries the inhabitants of the scattered farms shifted their abodes towards the churches. The benefits to peasants of such a shift included factors such as the desirability to be close to the church/market, the necessity to pool resources for land clearance and the sharing of implements such as mills, ploughs and ploughteams. Also, we must not underestimate the basically gregarious nature of humans. All this stimulated surplus production, leading to population growth and a developing market economy. The *castra* may or may not have survived as focal points, whilst the more successful *casalia* eventually developed into the agro-towns of the later Middle Ages and modern times.

Jean-Marie Martin, arguing from sources for Apulia, also believes that churches appeared before *casalia* or villages (Martin 1993). Archaeology in Italy has not yet revealed sufficient scattered farmsteads to confirm the model, though preliminary evidence for such a scenario appears to be coming from work in Tuscany. Small farmsteads, probably single family units have been excavated at Poggio al Tesoro and San Quirico e Pace (Castelnuovo Berardenga), and appear to date from the sixth to the middle of the seventh centuries. Nearby, in the municipality of Poggibonsi, such scattered settlement seems to have been followed by the construction of a church at Galognano, and then by the foundation of a village at Poggio Imperiale.[48] Even as far away as England, archaeology seems to show that in some areas Saxon settlement consisted of a scatter of farms with an isolated church between them until at least the time of the *Domesday Book*, when nucleated villages were established (Aston 1985: 69; Lewis, Mitchell-Fox and Dyer 1997: chapter 3).

If this basic model is correct, and numerous variations should be expected, it can be seen how place-names survived from Roman times without indicating survival of multi-family population groups. Thus toponomastic survival may be seen as one indication of the appearance of the medieval village, albeit on lands that had probably never been completely abandoned by the farmer.

The appearance and spread of villages has, alternatively, been seen as the nucleation of peasants or *coloni* within the context of a changing system of late antique agricultural management (Vera 1983: 511).[49] In this case, the village dwellers would have been dependent on a 'villa' or estate-centre, perhaps run by a bailiff and owned by an absentee landlord. It is his name that is now preserved in the numerous Latin-root place-names distributed throughout much of the western Empire. The existence of such estate-villages, evermore independent of declining towns and central authority, as *curiales* or likely municipal candidates fled to the country, may furthermore have stimulated the growth of rural markets and fairs in opposition to the *nundinae*, a direct emanation of a system based on urban markets. It is interesting that the medieval town of Sala Consilina developed at the site of a major fair attested by Cassiodorus (Cass. *Var*. VIII. xxx; see below, Chapter 6). The toponym is composed of the Lombard term *saal* (farm) and the name of the abandoned Roman town of *Consilinum*, lying not far away. The villa need not have been situated in or near the village and, of course, it may eventually have been abandoned, to be reused as a focus for burial or for something else, leaving the village structure intact and thus able to continue and develop through medieval times.[50] This may explain the genesis of some medieval villages.

Hypotheses can run riot with the present state of knowledge and the absence of a 'small-town and village archaeology', as opposed to the consolidated rural and urban archaeology. In the final analysis, we should perhaps hypothesize various combinations of the models.

The opening-up of land abandoned since Roman times is suggested by documents dating from the tenth to the twelfth centuries that refer to *exauda terra* or rendering the land workable (R. 154 (AD 966), 663 (AD 1135).[51] Furthermore, the common toponomastic prefix casa-, attested in the

---

[48] Excavations by Riccardo Francovich and Marco Valenti. See Cambi *et al*. 1994: 198–200, 211; Valenti 1995: 84–7. See also Valenti 1996: 365–9. He defines the period from the Gothic War to the establishment of new and dependent villages through the course of the later seventh and eighth centuries as 'chaotic', and sees it as characterized by free peasantry living in isolated farmsteads.

[49] See also Garnsey (1978: 225) for north Africa. See Salway (1970: 12) for Britain.

[50] See the suggestions of Agaché (1970: 207) for northern Gaul.

[51] On the term see Du Cange: *exaudinare/excaudicare*.

territory of Naples by the tenth century, seems also to be indicative of new settlement (Galasso 1982: 28).[52] Some such toponyms are certainly earlier, though again the sites remain to be examined archaeologically. Casanova, in northern Campania, is quite explicit; Caserta, neighbouring the old Roman Capua, has now become a major city. Both were in Lombard territory, whilst already by 967 a *Casacelere* lay in the border area of *Liburia* (R. 163).

Finally, mention should be made of one of the features that typifies much of central Italy from around the year 1000, and sometimes before; the development of small fortified central places. These may represent either a strengthening of control from a central power over the dependent territory, or even a fractionalizing of power in the hands of families that later crystallize into the medieval nobility, especially under the impulse of feudalism. In any case, the appearance of these centres of *incastellamento* would indicate, if not a regeneration of the countryside, its populations and its markets, at least a rationalization of production and redistribution.[53] The territory of Naples, due to its particular political structure, does not seem to follow models of *incastellamento* drawn up for other parts of Italy, or even for the neighbouring Lombard territories, that often date from the ninth or tenth century. On the military side, as has been shown, a clear defensive framework was already in existence by early Byzantine times and, in a sense, perpetuated part of a settlement distribution, at least as far as major sites, already in existence in Roman times, are concerned. This makes me recall Wickham's words (1989: 275):

> probably, in richer zones with a marked survival of large late antique estates (*aziende*) continuity may have found more favourable conditions in respect to other situations; I am now thinking of a site like Mola di Monte Gelato, and even the plain of Lucca, where there is certainly continuity, no type of shift and a market economy centred on the town.[54]

There is even little evidence that the *casalia* or villages of early medieval foundation later fell under the 'protectorate' of feudal lords. For the whole of the period under consideration, power and control seems to have been centred on Naples itself, with a degree of decentralization following the Norman conquest (Figliuolo 1993: 70). Indeed, as far as I can tell, the lack of overt pre-Norman *incastellamento* may have been based on a desire of the dukes of the city to avoid the potential growth of independently powerful rival families. Naples had only to remember that its own ruling dynasty had come to power in 840, with the accession of Sergius I, count of *Cumae*. This pattern is in marked contrast to that found in the Lombard territories of Capua, Benevento and Salerno. There, fragmentation into local units of power is clearly marked. This may be seen by the development of *gastaldates* from the eighth century and by the appearance of *castelli* encircling Neapolitan territory or guarding access to the hinterland at the mouths of the rivers Volturno and Garigliano.[55]

Thus, in sum, the Roman urban settlement pattern, sustained by a well-balanced network of dispersed agricultural settlement, survived into the early sixth century. This pattern cannot be traced any later. However, of the 50 or so minor settlements listed by Schipa as having existed in the territory of the duchy of Naples not one has been examined archaeologically, though certain indications are to be found in documents, particularly in leases (Schipa 1892: 592). Few of the sites are attested earlier than the beginning of the tenth century, though that is not to say that they were not in existence earlier. Indeed, many of their names, some 50%, have -ano suffixes, seemingly indicating some form of continuity. The very abundance of minor sites, if nothing else, suggests that land was fairly densely occupied and worked towards the end of the millennium, and an objective for future years will be to establish when, in early medieval times, this pattern of dispersed settlement appeared.

The difficulty comes for the archaeologist who attempts to identify rural sites, let alone land use, on the ground. Judging from the evidence for the Phlegrean Fields, to the immediate west of Naples, corroborated by recent field survey, Roman rural

---

[52] See the list of casa- toponyms in the index to *MND* II: 291.

[53] Very little work has been done on the *incastellamento* of the area around Naples. Toubert (1995: III, chapter 3) has dealt mainly with Monte Cassino and northern Campania.

[54] The site at Mola di Monte Gelato has now been published by Potter and King (1997).

[55] A good survey of castles, towers and other fortifications is still lacking for much of northern Campania. For inland areas see Coppola and Muollo 1994. Southern Campania is the subject of continuing research by Paolo Peduto at the University of Salerno. See also Kreutz 1991: 134–5.

sites were occupied into the sixth century. There is then a distinct break, and few early medieval sites have been identified archaeologically though, it has to be said, none have previously been looked for. The explanation for the apparent dearth of such sites probably lies not only in insufficient archaeology, but also in a process of nucleation that came to a head during the sixth century, on account of the disruptions of the Gothic War and of the Lombard invasions. First came the *castra*. When conditions were more settled, perhaps from the eighth century, these were followed by the many villages or *casalia* that lay behind, and now lie beneath, the foundations of the numerous agro-towns typical of the later medieval and modern hinterland of Naples.

6

ECONOMY

There is little to suggest that late Roman and early medieval Campania was any less fertile than was the classical *Campania felix*. Such catastrophic events as scorched-earth policies during the Gothic War, or the eruption of Vesuvius in 472 or prior to 507–511, which effectively destroyed crops and led to famine, probably had short-term effects on harvests. In the latter case the level of destruction was such that Theoderic considered applying tax-relief to Campania for a few years (Cass. *Var*. LXX).

Long-term effects were probably the result of climatic change, though there is little evidence that this seriously influenced crop yields. Naples's greatest shortcoming was its own restricted territory, the limitations of which must have been felt following the Lombard invasion and the interruption of stable commerce with much of the surrounding region. This had been regulated through daily markets and gave access to the rich crops of the *ager Campanus* to the north, which gravitated towards Capua (Frayn 1993: 79–83, fig. 8). The loss of agricultural land, probably more than considerations of a strategic nature, led to the tenacious hold of the flat lands of *Liburia*.

However, the greatest single factor influencing production may have been rural population decline. This would have led to decline in both food producers and non-food producers (and thus in demand). Decline of the latter would have led to a qualitative and quantitative decline in craft production and specialization, which, indeed, is what we find when the evidence is appraised.

Examination of production and trade should therefore begin with the produce of the land as, in such a densely inhabited area as the bay of Naples, intensive agricultural exploitation must have been a prerequisite for both stability and development.

AGRARIAN PRODUCTION AND ANIMAL HUSBANDRY

Much has been written about the fertility of Campania, and of how its soils and climate have provided a hardy and luxuriant vegetation, so much so that it is doubtful that there were any prolonged periods of economic instability due to crop failure. None the less, there is a certain amount of evidence to show that the environment around Naples changed significantly through classical times. We read, for instance, of the cutting of forest around the crater of lake Averno by Agrippa to supply the shipyards of the imperial fleet (Strabo V. iv. 5), whilst marshes between *Cumae* and *Liternum* were drained by Domitian and others.[1]

Late Roman and early medieval population decline must have led to a certain amount of abandonment of the heavily worked classical countryside, and to the regeneration of woodland in some of the less valuable agricultural areas. Climatic deterioration, beginning in later Imperial times, must also have favoured regeneration of the marshes in low-lying zones. This may have been particularly so to the east of the city and around the river Savone near *Liternum*, where the toponym *Pantanum* first appears in 703 (*Chronicon Vulturnense* I: 135–6 (see Federici 1925); Arthur 1991a: 89–90). The latter was a marginal area of the duchy, a contested frontier zone though, at times, an area where Neapolitans and Lombards worked side by side, as is made clear through the documents referring to *Liburia* (see above, Chapter 5). These same documents suggest that land drainage, which was completed only in the last century, was again taking place before the end of the tenth century. The foundation of Norman Aversa in 1058 is perhaps a sign that the lands of *Liburia* had been substantially reclaimed and made to yield extensive

---

[1] For example, that around the *Via Domitiana* (Frederiksen 1984: 20).

crops, though some parts had probably been farmed since classical times. None the less, one of the claims of the government of Don Pedro di Toledo, in the sixteenth century, was the restoration of this part of the Terra di Lavoro. Indeed, one chronicler ventured to call it 'the healthiest land in the world' (Braudel 1975: 71). It is now visibly fertile, with canals cut through the loamy soil, sludgy in winter and dusty during the hot dry summers.

Remnants of forests are known along the coast north of *Cumae* in the twelfth and thirteenth centuries. Others are attested in and around the Phlegrean Fields, by Pozzuoli (*difesa Puteolana*: 1269), Quarto (1269, 1282–1283) and Giuliano (*difesa Collinaria*: 1269), whilst much of the Sorrento peninsula was probably continuously wooded (Cascella 1991: 90). However, there is no evidence to suggest that local wood was a resource heavily exploited by the urban inhabitants of medieval Naples. Indeed, the regenerated trees were probably less useful than the wood of more mature forests of inland areas towards Benevento.

Little is known about grain supply and consumption. The area around Naples probably never produced a particularly large yield. By about 1970, the yield of the province was 6.7% of Campania's total, whilst the flat lands of Caserta, to the north, produced 27.6% (Ruocco 1970: 104). With the Lombard conquest, most of northern Campania, including the old *ager Campanus*, one of the richest granaries of Italy, was lost to the imperial administration.[2] However, both north Africa and Sicily, until the Arab invasions, remained important sources. Importation of grain to Naples from north Africa might be indirectly indicated by the continued importation of African ceramics and oil amphorae well into the seventh century, after they had stopped circulating in many other areas of Italy (Soricelli 1994; Reynolds 1995). This supply may have been in the hands of the *commerciarii* in Tunisia, whose seals are known as late as the reign of Constantine IV (668–685) (Diehl 1896: 500–2). Importation of surplus from Sicily or other areas of southern Italy is not explicitly attested after the early sixth century, though that is not to say that it did not occur, perhaps especially from the substantial papal estates of Saint Peter (see Recchia 1978:

154).[3] Even Egypt, until it was lost to the Empire in 640–645, might have provided occasional supplies, as it did to Rome during a period of famine under Pope Benedict I in 579 (*Hist. Lang.* V. 11).

After the seventh century more effort had probably to be invested locally, especially in the flat lands to the southeast of Naples and in *Liburia* (Frederiksen 1984: 20–1). The latter area was divided with the Lombards, and it is more than likely that its grain was one of the mainstays of commerce between Naples and Lombard Capua. Continuity in the use of these lands may be suggested by the relatively good rate of survival of Roman centuriation down to the present day, as well as by the pattern of scattered villages and hamlets that seems to have its origin in early medieval times.

Within the city, early medieval layers have yielded wheat, barley, millet and pulses (Fitt 1988). A text refers to donations of 210 *modii* of wheat and 200 jars of wine per annum to the *diaconia* of Saint Ianuarius in 680, and towards the end of the first millennium tenants are found paying wheat to monastic landlords (Tutini 1681: 85).[4] By then, improvements in agricultural techniques, such as the greater use of the horse, better ploughs and more articulated crop rotation, may have ensured good harvests, though the only direct evidence from Naples for a developing agricultural regime, at the moment, comes from documents. Water-mills, for instance, are attested from the middle of the tenth century, especially in the low land between the city and the river Sarno.[5] One with its leat (*fossatum*) existed at *Tertium*, to the west of Vesuvius, according to a document of 1016, which also stipulated the quantities of wheat (*Triticum*) to be given by tenant farmers to the monastery of San Sergio e Bacco on holy days (R. 367). In 949, two other mills, also at *Tertium*, were exchanged between Duke John III and Abbot Peter, of San Severino e Sossio (*MND* II: ii, *Diplomata et chartae* 3). Their appearance is testimony to substantial capital outlay. In 1009 Duke Sergius of Amalfi sold a water-mill (*mola acquaria*) to Archbishop Leo of Amalfi for 300 *soldi*, at a rate of four gold *tarì* to the *soldus*, so as to recover expenses for the defence of the town against the Arabs (Cassandro 1969: 210).[6]

---

[2] For Campanian grain in Roman times see Rickman 1980.

[3] Cassandro (1969: 255) has affirmed that grain was also imported from the Roman Campagna.

[4] At least in Byzantium, barley was considered a poor substitute for wheat, whilst millet was used as a last resort (Teall 1959: 99–100).

[5] For the growth in the use of water-mills see Duby 1975: 237–8; Harvey 1989: 128–33. The *Domesday Book* registered the existence of 6,000 in Britain in 1086.

[6] On the complexity of mill ownership in Campania, and particularly at Gaeta, see Skinner 1995: 73–8.

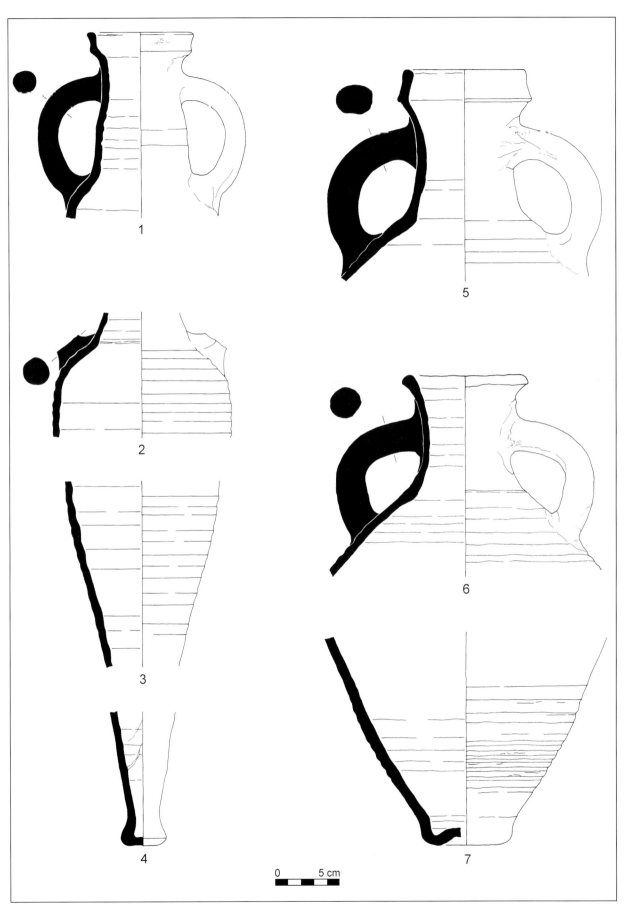

Fig. 6:1. Local Neapolitan amphorae of fifth- and sixth-century date (drawn by author).

The area of the bay of Naples was known for its wine from Roman times. It included *Amineum* from the hills behind Naples, *Trebellicum*, and the lesser-known *Gauranum* from the Phlegrean Fields.[7] Continued production during late antiquity and the course of the Middle Ages is hardly in doubt, though both quality and quantity need to be ascertained. Archaeology and the sources indicate that in no other period of antiquity or the early Middle Ages did the production of surplus wine in Italy reach the quantities produced during the last two centuries of the Republic and in the early Empire. In much of the country, surplus production declined notably from the latter half of the first and early second centuries. None the less, local amphorae show that Campania, including Naples, continued to export smaller quantities into the fourth century and beyond. Though a hiatus in the evidence exists for the later fourth and most of the fifth centuries, archaeology may well close the gap. Local amphorae are known for the later fifth and early sixth centuries (Fig. 6:1). Their forms relate them to Calabrian and eastern Sicilian amphorae, which were widely distributed around the Mediterranean, particularly in Rome and Marseilles (Arthur 1989c). No examples of the Neapolitan amphorae have yet been identified outside the city, which suggests limited exportation.

Another gap exists in the sequence between the early sixth and the later eighth centuries. That is not to say that wine was no longer exported. One of Pope Gregory's letters specifically refers to wine from the island of Procida, whilst the papacy's tenacious hold of land around *Misenum* may well have been dictated by the potential supply from that area (Greg. *Ep*. IX. 53).

Unlike most parts of Italy known to have produced wine for export in Roman times, the bay of Naples can be shown to have continued to produce amphorae into the eighth and ninth centuries (Fig. 6:2).[8] Wasters from kiln sites at both *Misenum* and Ischia indicate their local provenance. They are likened to finds from the area of Rome, some of which may be imports from the surviving papal patrimony around the bay of Naples (Arthur 1993). This type is found in Naples and Pozzuoli, at a deserted medieval village near

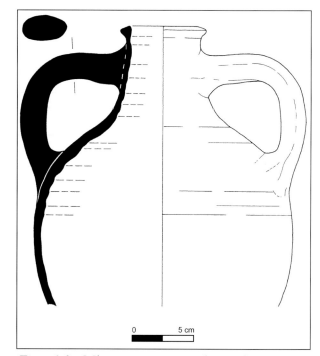

Fig. 6:2. Misenum-*type amphora from Rione Terra, Pozzuoli.*

Mondragone (Albarella, Arthur and Wayman 1989: fig. 7, no. 20) and, more significantly, at the Crypta Balbi, Rome (Paroli 1992b: 359–64), and also in Sicily (Ardizzone 2000). Though the identification of products carried in these vessels is debatable, their form suggests it was wine. It is worth noting that Duke Theodore, in stipulating a 29-year lease on Capri with Pope Gregory II in the eight century, agreed to pay him 100 amphorae of wine per year (*MND* I: 49).

The sources indicate wine circulating locally in *horna* (pottery containers) up until the beginning of the eleventh century (*MND* I: 190). Eventually the wooden barrel supplanted the ceramic amphora as an export container, and it is becoming clear that this happened in different areas at different times.[9] Amphorae were used in the East up to Ottoman times and in Apulia until the thirteenth century. There is no evidence for Neapolitan amphorae after the ninth century, and casks had certainly supplanted them after the end of the first millennium. Accordingly, it is possible to suggest that wine exportation continued after the disappearance of local amphorae.[10] Wine from Sorrento circu-

---

[7] For the amphora evidence, see Panella 1989; Arthur and Williams 1992; and, in particular, Tchernia 1986, which is by far the most complete account of viticulture in Roman Italy.

[8] Grape pips have come from a seventh-century context at Carminiello ai Mannesi and eighth- to ninth-century layers at Santa Patrizia (see below, p. 114). Pat Hinton kindly identified the carbonized seeds from Carminiello ai Mannesi (context US II 5).

[9] The seventh-century Farmer's Law refers to the cask (*bouttion*) for storage of wine in the East (Ashburner 1912: 69).

[10] See Hayes (1992: chapter 9) for eastern amphorae, and Arthur (1992) for the Apulian examples. The Neapolitan barrel has been discussed by Zug Tucci (1978). It may be observed that a cooper is attested in Naples in 974 (R. 201).

lated in the late tenth century (R. 257), whilst at Pozzuoli local production is attested again by the early eleventh (R. 375). Various qualities were recognized during early medieval times, and two documents cite a *vinum graecum* (R. 375, 409).

The use of olive oil is illustrated in late antique Naples by abundant oil amphorae and lamps found in excavations. Importation of oil amphorae continued into the seventh century, though in ever-decreasing numbers. African lamps were locally imitated from the later fifth century. By the seventh century, a new south Italian/Sicilian form had made its appearance, though apparently it did not outlive the eighth (Garcea 1987; 1994).

Thus, evidence suggests increasing rarity in the use of oil during early medieval times, with subsequent changes in dietary patterns. Though olives grow well in Campania, they may not have been exceedingly common in antiquity on account of an overspecialization in other crops, especially vines (see Arthur 1991a: 78). When African supply ceased, no later than the fall of Carthage in 698, Naples had to rely mainly on her own capabilities, until oil was perhaps again imported from southern Italy and Arab territories from the early eighth century (Kreutz 1991: 51). Thus, with the disappearance of the African supply, olive oil perhaps became scarce enough to explain the decrease in the use of oil lamps. This also might explain the increasing importance attached to the production of alternative and less costly wax candles, through which it seems to have been possible to have obtained a healthy income in early ninth-century Byzantium, and of soap, whose manufacture was already regulated by a guild in Naples by 599.[11] Constans II was soaping and not oiling his body when he was murdered in the baths at Syracuse (*Lib. Pont.* 344). Tallow candles were perhaps also produced using animal fat. The rise in the proportion of cattle also suggests a greater possibility of the use of butter to compensate for the decline in oil, whilst the cultivation of flax could have provided linseed oil. It may further be noted that no early medieval pottery vessels appear to replace the 'frying-pans' of Imperial times, also found in Naples (see Bettini and Pucci 1986).[12] Oil, none the less, did not disappear from use in diet, and it is possible that, quite aside from the Maghreb, quantities were later imported from Lombard areas or from the Byzantine south. The sources refer to

olive cultivation around Naples by the end of the millennium, though there is no indication of quantity. Now olives are rarely to be seen around Naples, and the nearest available sources are towards Avellino or on the Sorrento peninsula, whilst Campanian production is concentrated in the province of Salerno (Ruocco 1970: 134–6). Olive pits are not common in excavations, though they have been found at Santa Patrizia.

Some palaeobotanical evidence is now available for Naples, where soil conditions allow for good preservation of carbonized and mineralized seeds.[13] The intramural orchards, represented by early medieval 'dark earth' layers at Via San Paolo and Vico della Serpe, indicate the availability of various fruits and nuts, including grapes, plums, walnuts and hazelnuts (Fitt 1988). The most rewarding site remains Santa Patrizia, where flotation of early medieval layers has revealed abundant remains dating from the eighth to the ninth centuries (Fig. 6:3). Context 807 is one in a sequence of near-contemporary dumps, totalling 1.20 m in depth, around the medieval monastery. It has yielded abundant cabbage and fat hen, the latter having, though a wild plant, broad-toothed leaves that can be eaten rather like spinach. Whilst the list of species present is telling both as regards plant contributions to the diet and the economy, and the range of spontaneous plants, if the soil that contained them was brought to the site, we have no way of telling where they were grown.

However, given the identification of Neapolitans as 'leaf-eaters' (*mangiafoglie*) up to the sixteenth and seventeenth centuries, when the association was gradually supplanted by *maccheroni*, it may be suggested that cabbages and other greens had become staples because of the abundant orchards (Sereni 1981). Patricia Skinner has picked up on this, noting that the cultivation of greens appears in Neapolitan documents, the earliest of which, dating to 1033, lists greens, onions and leeks paid as rent to the monastery of San Gregorio Armeno (Skinner 1997: 6).

Much of the fruit identified was probably produced within or around the walls, whilst the grapes must have come from the vineyards in the territory. Apples recall the *mala cumana* exported in Roman times. Citrus fruit seems to be attested by the ninth century, and is certainly mentioned in a document dating to 1125. Though some say that

[11] On the profession of *keroularius*, see Lopez 1959: 72; for the soap-makers, see R. 101, 197.
[12] Though many examples were possibly made on Aegina, other clay fabrics are known, including a local Campanian one.
[13] The evidence is based on studies conducted by Jane Fitt and Marina Ciaraldi. For mineralization, see Green 1979.

	Family	Genus/species	Common name	Whole	Fragments
Cereals					
	Graminaceae	*Setaria* spp.	Millet	5	4
	Graminaceae	*Hordeum murinum?*	Wall barley	2	3
	Graminaceae	*Agrostis* spp.?	Bent	7	37
	Graminaceae	spp.	Grasses	4	15
Legumes					
	Papilonaceae	*Vicia/Lathyrus*	Vetch/vetchling	28	16
	Papilonaceae	spp.		1	1
	Papilonaceae	*Lotus corniculatus*	Lotus	3	0
	Papilonaceae	*Medicago* spp.	Medick or alfalfa	1	1
Fruit and nuts					
	Vitaceae	*Vitis vinifera*	Grape	2	6
	Rosaceae	*Prunus cerasus*	Morello cherry	2	2
	Rosaceae	*Prunus* spp.		1	0
	Juglandaceae	*Juglans regia*	Walnut	0	9
	Moraceae	*Ficus carica*	Fig	9	5
Other plants					
	Chenopodiaceae	*Chenopodium album*	Fat hen	534	200
	Cruciferae	*Brassica campestris*	Cabbage	347	20
	Cruciferae	*Brassica* spp.	Cabbage	1	0
	Cruciferae	*Sinapis* spp.	Charlock	1	0
	Urticaceae	*Urtica dioica*	Nettle family	2	0
	Caprifoliaceae	*Lonicera* spp.	Honeysuckle family	1	0
	Umbelliferae	*Conopodium majus*		1	2
	Umbelliferae	*Apium graveolens*	Celery	3	0
	Umbelliferae	spp.	Carrot family	2	0
	Urticaceae	*Urtica urens*	Nettle family	12	3
	Linaceae	*Linum catharticum*	Flax	4	0
	Linaceae	*Linum usitatissimum?*	Cultivated flax	0	1
	Labiatae	*Satureia* or *Origanum*	Savory or origan	5	3
	Labiatae	spp.		2	0
	Campanulaceae	*Legousia* spp.?	Bellflower family	8	5
	Boraginaceae	*Myosotis* spp.	Borage family	1	0
	Caryophyllaceae	*Silene (gallica?)*	Campion/catchfly	9	5
	Caryophyllaceae	*Stellaria* spp.	Chickweed	4	1
	Caryophyllaceae	spp. (*Cerastium* type)	(Mouse-ear)	2	1
	Papaveraceae	*Papaver rhoeas* or *dubium*	Poppy	6	0
	Onagraceae	*Epilobium* spp.?	Willowherb	12	4
	Scrophulariaceae	*Veronica polita/hederifolia*	Figwort family	1	0
	Euphorbiaceae	*Euphorbia peplus*	Spurge	0	2
	Resedaceae	*Reseda* spp.	Mignonette	0	2
	Polygonaceae	*Rumex Sanguineus*	Wood dock	2	1
			Totals	**1025**	**349**

Fig. 6:3. Plant remains from an eighth-/ninth-century context (US 807) excavated at Santa Patrizia, based on analyses conducted by Marina Ciaraldi.

the Sicilian Arabs introduced them, lemons were known in early Imperial Italy (De Seta 1981: 34; Salza Prina Ricotti 1987: 112–13). Chestnuts, boiled following a Roman custom, may also have been used to make the poor man's chestnut flour, common in Naples during the shortages of the Second World War (R. 321; Pliny *NH* XV. 93–4).

If we consider the environmental potential of the area, this evidence for fruit must represent a small portion of what was locally available, though there is no evidence whatsoever to indicate that any of it was exported. None the less, alongside vegetables, it played a part in local transactions and appears in rent payments (Skinner 1997: 8).

Cloth, instead, was certainly an item of long-distance commerce. The city produced important items of silk, including tapestries or veils (*vela chrisoclava*), such as those that were hung between the columns of the *Stephania* by Duke Sergius I and his wife in the ninth century, or the altar coverings donated by Bishop Athanasius. Athanasius II offered similar objects for the altar of Sant'Aniello (Rotili 1978: 57). Indeed, by the end of the eighth century, the city seems to have been noted for its purple-dyed cloth (*blatin neapolitano*), clearly an élite production, as its use, since Roman times, had been reserved for the imperial court (*Lib. Pont.* II. 30). The dye itself may have come from the East. Perhaps the ninth-century bishop's mitre said to be of Bishop Paulinus of Capua (ob. 843), now in the cathedral treasury at Capua, is a Neapolitan product (Galasso 1967: pl. 18). Whether the silk itself was produced in Naples or imported from the mulberry plantations in Calabria or elsewhere is not known.[14]

Seeds of flax, whose stem fibres are used to produce linen, have been found in eighth-/ninth-century contexts in Naples. Later, there is textual evidence for the city's importance in the production and exportation of linen, and in the tenth century, the Arab geographer Ibn Hawqal knew the town by the name Nab,l al Kaltan (city of the linen cloth).[15] The spinners or *filiolarii* attested in the documents may have been involved in this industry (R. 181, 274, 352, 407, 451). It has been suggested that flax was produced in marshy areas (*fusari*) to the northeast of the city, as well as to the south, where the *Lavinarius* or public conduit met the sea (Capasso 1895: 186–7; De Seta 1981: 31). Indeed,

in linen production the fruiting flax plants had to be cut and impregnated with water, or 'retted', for a number of weeks so as to separate the fibres from the soft tissues, following which the fibres would be dried and bleached in the sun (Polunin and Huxley 1987: 112).

Timber was of great value. It may be recalled how the Byzantines rightly disapproved of traders who furnished war materials to their enemies, and how the Arabs desired the timber, tar and pitch, to be had in Neapolitan territory. Already in the 870s, Louis II had accused Naples of furnishing 'arma, alimenta et cetera subsidia' to the Arabs (Anon. Salern. *Chronicon* II. 2). Timber must have played a role in the development of local ship construction attested through the sources, and must have been widely used in the building profession. The ready supply of wood may have been decisive in the conversion from the ceramic transport amphora to the Neapolitan wine barrel, assumed in later medieval times as a standard measurement throughout Italy (Zug Tucci 1978). Timber was also available from the Surrentine peninsula, behind Amalfi, perhaps at first exploited by Naples, though later a significant item in the merchandise of the small city-state (Citarella 1977). It may also have been obtained through Benevento, surely always a fairly heavily forested area, far more so than the land of the coastal city-states.

It is also worth remembering that Pope Gregory ordered 24 *sellae plectiles* from a Neapolitan craftsman (*Ep.* IX. 17, 52). They may have been chairs of intertwined canes or reeds, obtained presumably from the local marshes. Another product of the brackish marshes and lagoons may have been salt, which sources mention as an item of commerce in the eleventh and twelfth centuries (*MGH Scriptorum* (see Pertz 1826: ss. XVIII. 72); Galasso 1975: 102). The position of the city and its territory must have made its procurement easy, and there can be little doubt that it was obtained earlier, perhaps from the lagoons of Patria, Licola and Fusaro, near Cuma.

Far more evidence is available for the role of meat in the economy.[16] Considering meat available to excavated bone ratio, of the three principal domesticates raised for food, the pig seems to have been the preferred meat resource throughout Roman times. Roman faunal assemblages in Italy

---

[14] Skinner (1995: 284) regarded the silk in the West as having been brought from Constantinople.
[15] For growing of flax, see R. 81 of 953; Schipa 1893: 262; Citarella 1968: 546. Skinner (1995: 271–2) has suggested that 'the production of the cloth may have been a Neapolitan state monopoly'. For Ibn Hawqal, see Amari and Schiapparelli 1883: 95.
[16] On the sources, see Skinner 1997: 12–15.

are generally dominated by pig. The *Theodosian Code* tells us that *Lucania* provided Rome with pork in the fourth and fifth centuries (*Cod. Theod.* XIV. 4; Whitehouse 1983). A similar provision perhaps applied to Naples. In the faunal sequence from Santa Patrizia, which has so far provided the best evidence in the city, pig bones indeed dominate in the late fourth century (Figs 6:4 and 6:5). Between the fifth and the sixth centuries the quantity of sheep/goat bones rises sharply, and continues to rise until about the beginning of the seventh century, if not later. Subsequently, though, before the later eighth/early ninth century, the trend returns to the late Roman pattern. A check on this is provided by contexts at other sites. At the Girolomini site, for instance, a large late fourth-century group is clearly pig dominated, as are the mid-fifth-century contexts at Carminiello ai Mannesi. The large sample of the late fifth/early sixth century from the latter shows a marked increase in sheep/goat. This continues, though less emphatically, in the later seventh-/early eighth-century deposits. All later contexts, at Carminiello ai Mannesi, Via San Paolo and Santa Patrizia, are again pig dominated. On the whole, the evidence suggests that consumption in the city was based primarily on pork until the later fifth century. Pigs were then supplanted by sheep/goat, as well as cattle, returning to a pattern similar to that of Roman times towards the end of the eighth century.

All this is of great significance, as the short-lived insurgence of a sheep/goat dominated economy may be interpreted both as a sign of increasing impoverishment, given the relative cost-effectiveness in their rearing with respect to pigs, and of ruralization of the urban habitat. Annie Grant, in discussing medieval England, has argued that the decline in relative proportions of pig to sheep and particularly to cattle may be a reflection of the return of much previously cultivated land to pasture (Grant 1988: 159). In this light, it is

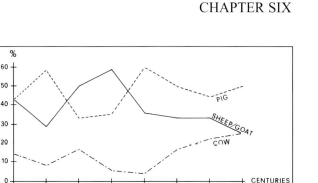

Fig. 6:4. The changing pattern of sheep/goat, pig and cow consumption in Naples (sources: Albarella and Frezza 1989a; 1989b; King 1994).

tempting to associate the rise in quantities of sheep/goat bones in Naples with the notion of *agri deserti* representing an increase of uncultivated or pasture land in late antiquity. This is followed by a resurgence of pig towards the later eighth century, perhaps representing an expansion in arable farming. Furthermore, it would seem that the sheep were killed at a fairly advanced age for their meat, after having been fully exploited for milk and wool. Though sheep and goat bones are not always easily distinguished, preliminary research also suggests that in Naples goats became relatively more common in early medieval times. In late Roman contexts at Carminiello ai Mannesi the late Roman sheep/goat ratio seems to have been in the order of 3.5:1, whilst the ratio in later fifth-/early sixth-century contexts alters to 1.5:1. Goats produce about four times as much milk as sheep and are far more adaptable, not requiring a strict transhumance system, so their relative increase in numbers might signal a breakdown in traditional systems of mutton supply. Drovers, with their flocks from the hills of the Abruzzi, still appeared around *Nola* during the winters of the early fifth century, though such movement was probably restricted during the period of the Gothic War and following the Lombard invasions.[17]

Centuries	1–4	late 4	late 4	mid-5	late 5–6	late 5–6	late 6–8	6–12	16–20
Contexts	CM	SP 258	GI 52	CM	VSP	CM	CM	VSP	VSP 263
Pig	65	79	58	61	49	35	42	42	37
Sheep/goat	31	20	36	33	33	56	50	17	19
Cattle	5	2	7	6	18	9	9	41	44

Fig. 6:5. Relative percentages of the three principal taxa calculated on the number of identified fragments (sources: Albarella and Frezza 1989a; 1989b; King 1994).

---

[17] Paul. *Carm.* 511–67, where the shepherds are described as receiving Christian charity during the feast of Saint Felix. The tradition of transhumance from the Abruzzi is still kept alive by the appearance of shepherds in Naples at Christmas time, playing their flutes and bagpipes in the hope of earning an extra lira or two. The end of a transhumance route in the Phlegrean Fields might be indicated by the toponym Val di Pecora, though it is not known when it was first used.

By the later fifth to the sixth centuries, there appears also to have been a rise in proportions of cattle. Unlike pigs, they do not compete with man over food resources, thriving quite well on grasses, straw, chaff, leaves and garbage, whilst producing milk, excellent fuel in the form of dung, by-products such as leather and horn, and can be used for traction (Harris 1985). Of the domesticates they are, none the less, the least efficient in converting energy to meat. Particular broken cattle bones suggest that marrow was regularly extracted.

Returning to pigs, it is worth noting that the fifth-century faunal assemblage at the *Schola Praeconum* excavations in Rome was also pig dominated (Whitehouse 1983). This has been linked both to Cassiodorus's statement about pork supply to the city, and to finds from the late Roman rural site of San Giovanni di Ruoti in Lucania. At San Giovanni, 40% of animal bones in midden A (*c.* AD 375–425) were of pig, with the proportion rising to 65% in midden B (*c.* 460–525) (White-house 1983). Similarly, numerous pigs seem to have been reared at the late Roman rural site of San Vincenzo al Volturno (Hodges 1993b: 262).[18] Midden B at San Giovanni seems to have gone out of use not long after sheep/goats began to dominate over pigs in Neapolitan archaeological contexts. Though I do not wish to suggest a direct link between San Giovanni and Naples, an indirect correlation may be hypothesized in the breakdown of traditional systems of pork supply to the city, following patterns in Rome.

A story from 533 told of a demon, in the guise of a sow, inhabiting a rubbish heap where the church of Santa Maria Maggiore was to be built. Why the poor beast should incarnate a demon is hard to say, though it may be linked to a view, common in the hotter climes of the Mediterranean, that it was an unclean animal (Harris 1985). Indeed, pigs can be scavengers and pick up various diseases, such as trichinosis, through their promis-cuous eating habits, and perhaps such a risk was greater in the degraded environment of early post-classical Naples. In the late fourth-century dumps at Santa Patrizia, when the animal was still preferred to sheep/goat, even pig's feet, one of its less palatable components to many cultures, were found as food remains.

Amongst the domesticates, few donkey and mule bones have been identified between the late fifth and the eighth centuries (King 1994: 402; Albarella, pers. comm.), whilst being fairly common on some sites, such as at the late Roman rural complex of San Giacomo degli Schiavoni, Molise (Albarella 1993). Though never a great food resource, it is interesting that the animals do not seem to have been used on any significant scale for their energetic potential in the city, particularly as transport, for which they have been used in relatively recent times. Horses are also present, though, again, they are not particularly common.

As regards hunting, sixth- and seventh-century faunal assemblages from the city yield occasional bones of fallow deer (*Cervus dama*), roe deer (*Capreolus capreolus*) and hare. Scarce remains of tortoise suggest that it too might have been eaten on occasion. Faunal assemblages from late Roman and early medieval rural sites are totally lacking. However, the emphasis on hunting in early medieval literature and the appearance of royal hunting grounds in later times, such as the *Real Caccia del Savone*, might indicate that such a form of food supply was significant for the rural populace (see, for example, Fumagalli 1988).

Of the various animal by-products, bone was certainly worked into objects. The site of Carminiello ai Mannesi has provided bone off-cuts dating to the early sixth century and a bone spatula of the same period, perhaps related to the pre-paration of skins (Di Giovanni 1994: 364–5).

Fifth- to sixth-century archaeological contexts indicate that fishing was significant, and there is no reason to doubt that this was not so throughout early medieval times (Rhodes 1994; Frezza 1995). As now, the smallest fish were probably consumed bones and all. Bass, cod, conger eel, gilthead bream, grouper, sea bream and tunny are all repres-ented in fifth- to sixth-century contexts. Excava-tions at Santa Patrizia have also yielded sea urchin spines in an early medieval context. Shellfish are well-represented (Cretella 1994), particularly oysters (*Ostrea edulis*) and spiney or thorny oysters (*Spondylus gaedoropus*), in the late fifth and the sixth centuries, though by then the systematic commercial cultivation established in late Repub-lican times seems to have been abandoned.[19]

---

[18] See also the arguments made by Barnish (1987).

[19] See D'Arms (1970: 136–7) for Roman oysters, particularly from lake Lucrino, near *Puteoli*, and Camodeca (1981: 99–100, n. 126), for their continuing economic importance for fourth-century *Puteoli*. Cassiodorus (*Var.* I. 2) told how the murex industry was still thriving at Otranto around AD 507. Harvey (1989: 170–1) has discussed the importance of fish to the Byzantine diet.

Fishing rights related to both coastal and fresh waters. The monastery of San Salvatore, for example, is found leasing a tract of 'mare piscatorio' or fishing sea (ASN *Catasto di S. Pietro a Castello*, R. CCLXIII; Castellano 1975: 189–90), whilst rights of the monastery of San Severino e Sossio regarding Lago di Patria, on the north-western edge of Neapolitan territory, are known from 988 (*MND* I: *Diplomata* 18).

There is perhaps nothing that illustrates Naples's increasing commercial role through the Dark Ages better than its involvement in the slave trade. This is attested as early as 599. In Pope Gregory's letters we find imperial officials in Naples commissioning Jews to acquire slaves in Gaul, much to the disdain of the pope, not over the question of slavery itself, but over the subordination of Christian slaves to Jewish merchants (*Ep.* IX. 104, 111; Brown 1984: 202–3). The Neapolitan treaty of 836 with Benevento also regarded, *inter alia*, commerce in slaves. Towards the later first millennium, other sources indicate that by then they were largely of Lombard extraction, sometimes put on the market by the Lombards themselves, and even sold to Muslim masters (Croce 1944: 22). Though they do not appear frequently in the sources, in the tenth century they could belong to land-based *coloni*, and were occasionally freed through testament (R. 44, 164, 196, 329).

URBAN MANUFACTURE

There is a certain amount of information, both textual and archaeological, for urban manufacture. The division between rural (primary) and urban (secondary) production blurred in early medieval times, hand in hand with the ruralization of the town. However, the affirmation of Naples as capital of the duchy led to the development of certain professions, which were fundamental to her position. Shipbuilding sustained her role as a budding commercial and military power, and it would be interesting to know where the wood came from (Surrentine peninsula, Benevento?), whilst building professions and certain artists and craftsmen were necessary to reinforce her political

status. It may be recalled that the Church fed the builders and painters, whilst the ruling families patronized jewellers and moneyers. Towards the close of the first millennium there is evidence for some organization of craftsmen and traders, with professions often concentrated in particular streets or areas.[20]

Ceramic production could be either urban or rural, depending more often than not on available clay sources. In the area of Salerno, for example, *lutifuguli*, who dug clay to purify and sell it to potters, are indicated by the sources at the turn of the first millennium as working along the river Bonea, near Cava dei Tirreni and Vietri (Peduto 1982: 17). The potteries may well have been located nearby, and Vietri, in more recent times, has risen to fame for its ceramics. Of course, such divisions of labour were not always necessary, dependent upon resource location. Potters in the area of Naples are attested at *Cumae*, *Misenum* and Ischia, all close to clay deposits, whilst there is no evidence for production in the city itself, despite the fact that pottery was made there in Roman Republican times, presumably from imported clays.

Professional blacksmiths, at least until the end of the millennium, may have been located mainly within the major settlements, as their raw material had either to be imported or obtained as local scrap, and might thus have been expensive until the opening up of commerce.[21] Little archaeological evidence is available concerning the production of metal objects in Naples through the Dark Ages, and in part this is probably because of a reuse of metals in a period when little could be discarded. The humble ironwork found regularly in excavations is likely to be largely of local manufacture. Ischia, since Greek times, had been a centre of iron processing, and archaeological evidence from excavations at *Lacco Ameno* have revealed abundant slag dating to the sixth century AD (Monti 1989: 77). Somewhat later, the sources refer directly to *ferrarii* or blacksmiths in Naples. Indeed, during the tenth century, three apparently interrelated families of smiths, Cicino, Corbulo and Pantaleoni/Papalone, lived and worked in *vicus Sancti Georgii* (Skinner 1994: 291–4).[22]

---

[20] For this and trades in general in Naples, see also Skinner 1994: 294–5. Even now, some trades are traditionally linked to streets and areas, such as Via San Biagio ai Librai and 'gli orefici'.

[21] Iron-working is attested around the eighth century in a small settlement near Mondragone, though perhaps this was linked to San Vincenzo's particularly dispersed economic system. See Albarella, Arthur and Wayman 1989; Hodges 1994.

[22] The road has been located, and future archaeology there should search for traces of smithing.

Archaeology demonstrates that even small rural villages such as that found near Mondragone, in Lombard territory to the north of Naples, had their own smelting furnaces, at least towards the end of the millennium (Albarella, Arthur and Wayman 1989).[23] Naples's shipbuilding activity must have required fairly competent blacksmiths, capable of producing more than the general run of agricultural implements. Excavations have yielded only small items, including various iron nails and miscellaneous iron fragments, as well as two arrowheads of simple flat-leaf types, from Carminiello ai Mannesi and Piazza Bellini, the latter with barbs (Feugère 1994). No tools of any sort are known. If there was a scarcity of iron in the second half of the first millennium, as seems to have been the case both over much of Europe and in the Byzantine East, we should perhaps expect the metal to have been used predominantly for weapons, essential structural elements and heavy-duty tools (Harvey 1989: 124–5).

A few items of bronze have also been recovered during excavations. These include a simple seventh- or early eighth-century cast buckle from excavations at Santa Patrizia, of a type originally developed amongst the peoples of central Europe and paralleled at Lombard Cividale (Fig. 6:6), and a late fifth- or early sixth-century strap-end from the site of Carminiello ai Mannesi.[24] To these may be added the Byzantine bronze reliquary crosses with incised decoration dated to the seventh or eighth century, now in the Museum of Capodimonte (Galasso 1967: 38, pl. XIV).

As far as regards costly jewellery, the only fairly certain Neapolitan find is that of a seventh- or eighth-century gold earring with semi-precious stones, of Byzantine type, in the Sambon collection (Rotili 1978: 57–8, pl. 77). However, it is similar to another gold earring, probably from a burial in the area of *Herculaneum* (Breglia 1941: 57, pls XXV.7, XXXVIII.1, no. 224).[25] Both bear coin impressions on the reverse. The former has an unidentified coin type, whilst the *Herculaneum* example bears the impression of an Oscan denarius of C. Papius Mutilus, struck in the years 91–88 BC. This singular characteristic is the

distinctive feature of type 4 of Melucco Vaccaro's typology of 'orecchini a cestello' (Melucco Vaccaro 1972: 12–13). The renowned treasure from Lombard Senise, composed of earrings, a disc brooch, a gold cross and a ring, was found in a late seventh-century burial. The earrings also bear coin impressions, of solidi of Constantine IV (668–685), likening them to the Sambon and *Herculaneum* earrings. They could all have been made in a Neapolitan workshop, as was the Benevento brooch, and may well be products of 'court' artisans as, though they have been assigned to Benevento, they are of late Roman-Byzantine tradition (De Rinaldis 1916; Galasso 1967).[26] The display of the jewellery and its subsequent deposition may, furthermore, indicate the adoption of Byzantine prestige goods as a means of furthering the status of the non-Byzantine élite.

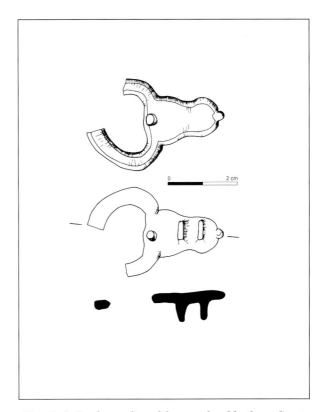

Fig. 6:6. Early medieval bronze buckle from Santa Patrizia, of seventh- or eighth-century date (drawn by Michele Varchetta).

---

[23] For the archaeological evidence of an eleventh-century smithy at nearby Salerno, see Iannelli 1992.

[24] Compare the Santa Patrizia buckle with that from Cividale (Tagliaferri 1990: 443, 446, no. X.118a). See also the buckle from Celimarro (Castrovillari) (D'Angela 1980: tav. V, no. 2). For the strap-end see Feugère 1994: 357–9, fig. 153, no. 11.

[25] Perhaps the two gold earrings published by Breglia (1941: 98, pl. XLIII.3, nos. 1007–8) come from the same site (Siviero 1954: n. 532, tav. 248; Melucco Vaccaro 1972: 13, fig. 29).

[26] See also the interesting discussion by Lipinsky (1973: 1398–402). The production of the filigree decorated gold disc brooches from Castel Trosino has been assigned hypothetically to Ravenna (for example, Melucco Vaccaro 1988: 161).

The only jeweller attested during the duchy is the Greek *aurifex* or goldsmith Nicephorus, at the service of Duke Sergius VII, in 1131 (*MND* II: 81). It would not be at all surprising if the working of gold and other valuables was monopolized by the dukes, both to reinforce their power and status and to supply the administration with goods for political exchange. The model existed in late Roman times and was quickly adopted by certain societies peripheral to the Empire, hand in hand with an evolving and marked social stratification. Naples was also known for its book production, principally in the hands of the monastic scriptoria though, at times, clearly patronized by leading noble families.

Professions in building and the arts are also indicated through evidence of architecture, painting, mosaic production and sculpture. The use and production of building materials has been discussed in Chapter 3, where it has been shown that little fresh material seems to have been manufactured after the sixth century, though a lot of work must have gone into systematic demolition of ancient buildings. Both demolition and construction presumably took place throughout the entire second half of the first millennium, as the list of ecclesiastical building suggests (Appendix II). Local pozzolana continued to be used in mortars, which suggests continuity in quarrying, and it may, indeed, have been an item of export to Carthage into late antiquity, perhaps being shipped out of the bay as ballast in the ships that had brought over African oil and grain (Williams 1984).[27]

Very little painting is known to date after the fifth-century works in the catacombs of San Gennaro and San Severo (Bertelli 1992). Remains of early medieval painting, carelessly imitating marble, were brought to light in 1986 on a pier separating the apse from an external ambulatory during excavations at the church of San Giovanni Maggiore, though they have not been published. Other fragments were found during excavations of the church of San Costanzo, Capri, in 1990 (Arthur 1992), whilst painting imitating marble was also present at the church of Santa Fortunata, at *Liternum* (Chianese 1938; Pagano 1989). The large urban church of San Paolo was apparently richly painted between 801 and 817, though none of this survives (Capasso 1895: 109). An inter-

esting document of 1036 records the intention of the count of Ischia, Marinus, and his wife, Theodora, to paint their monastery of Santa Maria 'sita in monte qui dicitur Cementara' with images of Christ, the Virgin, Saint Benedict, Saint John and Saint Restituta, patron saint of the island (R. 458). The lack of extant examples, only partly explained by the inherent fragility of early medieval plaster, is largely due to the numerous episodes of church redecoration carried out by later medieval and Renaissance artists.

Mosaicists worked on a fairly large scale in late antique times. What has survived is limited mainly to part of the pavement of the basilica of San Lorenzo Maggiore (Hirpinus 1961: 15–16, figs 13–15), the decorated cupola of the baptistery of San Giovanni in Fonte, some pieces at Santa Restituta, and four *arcosolia* and other remains in the catacombs of San Gennaro. Fragments of tomb covers in mosaic from the catacombs are similar to north African examples, such as those on display in the Bardo Museum, Tunis, and suggest African influence.[28] Through Procopius we know that a huge mosaic of Theoderic once existed in the area of the forum (Proc. *Bell. Goth.* V. xxiv. 22). Under Bishop John II (533–555) a mosaic depicting the Transfiguration was set up in the apse of the *Stephania*. The discovery of glass paste tesserae (blue, green or translucent clear glass examples covered with gold foil) indicates that the apse of the basilica of Santa Maria Maggiore, constructed in 533, was also decorated with rich mosaics, as must have been the other near-contemporary basilicas. The mosaicists's art seems to have declined during the sixth century, probably yielding to the cheaper technique of painting, whilst floor mosaics were in part substituted by *opus sectile*, in which great use was made of reworked Roman revetment marbles. The only examples yet known from Naples are the fragments in the apse of San Giovanni Maggiore, datable to the original construction of the church by Bishop Vincent (555–578).[29] In Campania, however, one may cite the splendid pavement of the church of San Menna, at Sant'Angelo dei Goti, near Benevento, the remains from the palace of Arechis II at Salerno and fragments at Cava dei Tirreni, all of early medieval date (Peduto *et al.* 1989).[30]

[27] I suspect that pozzolana was also used in the mole at Thapsus, Tunisia, though such use would undoubtedly have been early Imperial in date (personal observation). See also Panella 1993: 634.

[28] I should like to thank Mara Amodio for this information, which will form the subject of her thesis.

[29] Revealed during excavations in 1986 and not published yet.

[30] It has been suggested, though with little reason, that these craftsmen, who laid the foundations for later Cosmatesque art, were brought over from Constantinople (Farioli Campanati 1982: 257, cat. no. 87).

A very competent school of sculptors, versed in Byzantine craftsmanship, was active in Naples during the sixth century, as may be illustrated by various pieces in the churches of Sant'Aspreno and of San Giovanni Maggiore. Little then exists until the later ninth century, when Bishop Leo III carried out large-scale work at Cimitile for the foundation of the church of the Holy Martyrs (Venditti 1967: 530–41). The work is very competent and may probably be attributed to Neapolitan hands. It is possible, on the basis of the surviving remains, to argue continuity in craftsmanship and tradition. Great professionalism is also to be noted in the field of inscribers, as may be exemplified by the epitaph of Duke Bonus, dating to 832–834, in the cathedral of Naples.[31]

Evidence for glass manufacture is provided by abundant cullet and other fragments from sixth- and seventh-century contexts excavated at the site of Carminiello ai Mannesi (Miraglia 1994a). Amongst the vessels represented at the site are hanging lamps with triangular handles rising vertically from the rim. This type is rare, otherwise attested only at San Giovanni di Ruoti (near Potenza), Belmonte in Apulia, San Vincenzo al Volturno and Ischia, and may be a local product (Stevenson 1988; Guarino, Mauro and Peduto 1988: fig. 17d–f; Miraglia 1994a). Indeed, it is possible that the production represents a continuing tradition from Roman times, when the sands around *Cumae* and *Liternum* were exploited, and that local products were exported in south-central Italy.[32]

Afterwards, glass tends to become rare in archaeological contexts, and indeed little has come from the pottery-rich layers of eighth- and ninth-century date at Santa Patrizia. This is probably an indication of decline in usage rather than of more efficient recycling systems, and a similar pattern is apparent in Rome (as at the Crypta Balbi (Saguì 1993b: 117)). Even after the Norman conquest, glass is still rather uncommon in medieval archaeological contexts, though fragments in an opaque red fabric, possibly imported from Apulia, and some rather rare pieces of stained blue window glass with fleur-de-lis

motifs, of twelfth-century date, have come from excavations at Santa Patrizia (Fig. 6:7).[33]

Neapolitan commercial activity was such that the city required a flourishing shipbuilding industry. We may remember how the port was important enough for Narses to have enclosed it with defences by the mid-sixth century. By the end of the century, Pope Gregory had reason to complain about Bishop Paschasius of Naples, who not only spent too much of his time building ships, but lost 400 solidi through his activity (*Ep.* XIII. 29). Gregory's letter is particularly precious as an indication of the possible scale of ecclesiastical investment in commerce, even if Paschasius seems to have gone overboard with his enthusiasm. Shipyards are also attested at the end of the first millennium on both toponomastic and documentary grounds: and at a later date Edrisi's geography further attests such yards at Sorrento and Amalfi.[34] By that time, the few sources for the matter seem to indicate that the activity was in private hands, apart, perhaps, from the construction of warships (Galasso 1965: 101–2).

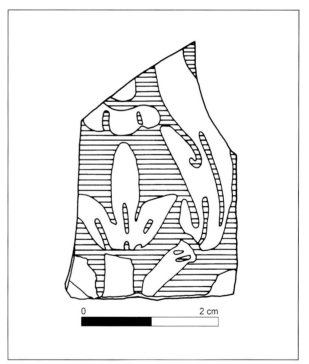

0   2 cm

Fig. 6:7. Stained glass from Santa Patrizia (drawn by Michele Varchetta).

[31] On this, and on the literary content of other funerary epigrams, see Cilento 1969a: 537–50.

[32] For Campanian glass production in Roman times, see Pliny *NH* XXXVI. 194.

[33] Apart from northen European contexts, such glass seems also to have been current at Constantinople by the early twelfth century, going by finds from Kariye Camii and from the church of Christ Pantocrator at Zeyrek Kilise Camii (Megaw 1963: 348).

[34] See Cassandro (1969: 237, 252–3) for tenth-century documents.

CERAMICS

Of all the items that should be considered in a discussion of the economy of Naples, pottery is without doubt the most eloquent from an archaeological point of view because of its ubiquity. The ceramic sequence from Naples covers much of the second half of the first millennium, though precise dating has not always been obtainable. Mass production of pottery, by what I call the 'late Roman ceramic industries', ceased during the first half of the sixth century, together with the disappearance of a pervasive regional market system based on *nundinae* (Arthur and Patterson 1994; Arthur 1998a). Archaeological contexts dating to this period are the latest to yield standardized fine wares in any quantity, sometimes imitating the African red slip ware imported from the area of present-day Tunisia (Fig. 6:8) (Hayes 1972). From about the mid-sixth century, by far the greatest proportion of pottery used in and around the town was doubtless manufactured around the bay of Naples. There is, in fact, evidence in the area for three kiln sites, at Cuma, Miseno and Ischia.[35]

The first two lie in the Phlegrean Fields, an area reputedly poor in workable clays, though it is possible that raw material was obtained from the deposits accumulated within the infilled lagoon of Licola, immediately to the north of Cuma (Arthur *et al.* 1991: 10). A further clay source may have been the crater of Solfatara, above Pozzuoli, which was noted for its kaolin (Frederiksen 1984: 27).[36] Indications of a kiln site at Cuma are provided by the discovery of various wasters found near the amphitheatre. Only two ceramic forms are represented so far, both jugs, distinguished by the presence of either one or two handles. They bear broad-line arcs painted in red or brown on the body and rough bands down the handles. The vessels are of a type common in various sixth- and early seventh-century contexts excavated within Naples.

For *Misenum* the evidence is more eloquent (De Rossi 2001). A varied stratigraphy has been revealed within the shell of an abandoned Roman brick-faced concrete cistern. What appear to be layers of silt are intercalated with layers of ash and dumps containing abundant ceramic fragments, including wasters, broad-line painted pottery and lamps of the 'ciabatta' type (Garcea 1987). A damaged structure found within the cistern appears to be part of a simple circular kiln. Though the pottery has still to be published, amongst the products is a type of transport amphora that would appear to date to the eighth century or thereabouts (Fig. 6:2). If the kiln was used for amphorae, it seems to confirm the picture of a declining technology, already suggested by the discovery of simple circular pedestal kilns at Otranto, used for the production of amphorae and cooking wares during the seventh or eighth century (Arthur *et al.* 1992).[37]

Evidence for pottery production on the island of Ischia comes from the excavations carried out by Father Pietro Monti around the church of Santa Restituta at *Lacco Ameno* (Monti 1980; Guarino, Mauro and Peduto 1988: pls I–III, fig. 8).[38] There are few wasters, though transport amphorae, similar to those produced at *Misenum*, seem to be local. A mould for lamps of a type imitating African lamps of form Hayes II, which occurs in Neapolitan archaeological contexts, has also been recovered.[39] The manufacture of pottery seems to date principally from the sixth to the eighth centuries.

The production of pottery up to the sixth century is attested on a significant scale around the *ager Falernus*. Unlike the three known sites near Naples, this area produced a whole series of African red slip ware imitations and colour-coated wares. The northern Campanian products are very similar to finds from two substantial late fourth-century contexts and one of mid-fifth-century date unearthed in the town. It is quite possible that at that time Naples was partly supplied by these kilns, lying only some 50 km up the coast, though confirmation will have to await petrological analyses.[40]

---

[35] Unfortunately, none of these discoveries have been published adequately.

[36] This is unlikely ever to have been a particularly fertile clay source. I should like to thank Marcello Schiattarella for having shown me the remnants of the deposits.

[37] Roman amphora kilns were far more impressive and articulated (Peacock 1982: 67–73).

[38] However, I have doubts as to the assignment by Guarino, Mauro and Peduto of vessels tav. II, nos. 1, 3, 6 (and possibly 2 and 5) to early medieval times.

[39] The reasons that led Guarino, Mauro and Peduto (1988: 460–2) to conclude that the mould was a modern forgery appear to be unfounded, as the form is well paralleled. The 'approximate' decoration occurs on other local imitations of north African lamps, and the absence of an interlocking mould for the bottom of the lamps is explained by the fact that they were often finished by hand.

[40] For products of the north Campanian kilns, see Cotton 1979 (in particular the late Roman hard red coarse-ware and the colour-coated ware); Cotton and Metraux 1985 (colour-coated wares); Arthur 1998a. The late fourth-century contexts in Naples are Girolomini context 52 and Santa Patrizia contexts 258 and 263, whilst that of the mid-fifth century is Carminiello ai Mannesi area III.

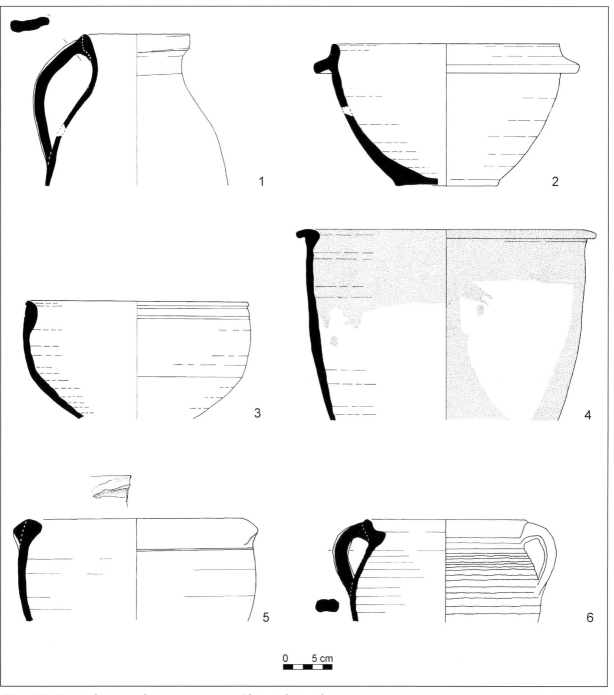

Fig. 6:8. Neapolitan sixth-century wares (drawn by author).

Most of the information concerning early medieval pottery production around Naples, however, derives from the excavations carried out within the city itself in the 1980s. During the course of the fifth century, colour-coated or slipped wares similar to the *ager Falernus* products started to lose ground, first to pottery that was only partially immersed in slip and then to regular, broad-line, painted wares, which are typical of the sixth and much of the seventh centuries. Other classes also made their appearance, like the red burnished pottery that runs from, at least, the mid-fifth to the mid-sixth centuries.[41] Because of its distinctive nature, it is a useful guide in exploring the commercial contacts between Naples and other areas at the time (Iannelli 1985: 719–24; Arthur 1994: 210–12). Indeed, it has been found at Ischia (information kindly supplied by Don Pietro Monti),

---

[41] Earlier burnished wares appear in the late fourth-century contexts cited in the note above, although they are less frequent and the forms differ.

Capri (Arthur 1992), *Abellinum* (Colucci Pescatori 1986), *Nola* (information kindly supplied by Valeria Sampaolo), Agropoli (Iannelli 1985), and even further south, as far as the important late Roman site of *Tropea*, in Calabria.[42]

The seventh-century broad-line painted wares are somewhat cruder than their early sixth-century predecessors, and include jugs and large deep basins. Trefoil-mouthed jugs are characterized by the presence of painting along the lip, and parallels may be cited from Pratola Serra in the province of Avellino, associated with a coin of Heraclius, and from Pozzuoli (Peduto 1984a: pl. XIII, no. 5).[43] Other examples have already been found in areas far from Naples, such as at the seventh-century Lombard cemetery at Vicenne, Molise (Genito 1988: fig. 18). By the eighth century, painted pottery seems to have become finer, with thinner walls and more carefully painted and elaborate decoration (Fig. 6:9). This included painted bands less than 10 mm in width, triangles, arcs and spots, often combined. Though precise dating of the ware is limited by the absence of secure chronological pegs, parallels are to be found amongst material from excavations at the Crypta Balbi site in Rome (Arthur and Patterson 1994: 415–19, figs 3–6).[44] Furthermore, it appears to have been contemporary with the appearance of the so-called lead-glazed forum ware (*ceramica a vetrina pesante*).[45] An interesting feature is the appearance of small closed vessels with elongated nozzles or tubular spouts, also paralleled at the Crypta Balbi, and at Santa Maria in Civita, in the Biferno Valley (Patterson 1985: 90, fig. 4:3, nos. 8–9), as well as amongst Carolingian finds in France.[46]

The characterization of ninth-century pottery is difficult, as no certain contexts of that date have yet been identified in Naples. Though some of the layers at Santa Patrizia may belong to the ninth century, we have to turn to the excavations at San Pietro in Corte and San Salvatore in Fondaco,

Salerno, for an idea of Campanian wares of that period. A striking feature of the pottery from Salerno and Benevento is the appearance of broad-line painted graffito wares, where the decorative incisions were applied after firing, over the painted decoration (Pastore 1995: 257–62; V. Carsana and C. Scarpati, in Lupia 1998). Similar wares have been found at the church of San Marco a Rota, Mercato San Severino. This ware seems to be datable solely to the late eighth and ninth centuries, thus perhaps providing some evidence for an economic distancing between Lombard Benevento and Salerno on the one hand, and Naples on the other. Later painted wares from Naples and Salerno, especially from the eleventh and twelfth centuries, are much more similar to each other, and are characterized by narrow-line painted decoration, often forming spirals.

In much of Italy, plates, bowls and cups are rare in archaeological contexts after the sixth century (Arthur and Patterson 1994: 419, fig. 6). This is presumably a result of the increasing use of wooden substitutes. Excavations of a well at San Martino Valle Caudina, near Benevento, for instance, have revealed lathe-turned wooden bowls alongside painted ceramic jugs with wooden bungs, all dating to the seventh century or later.[47]

As regards cooking wares, the range of forms in late Roman times seems more varied than those that became established from the sixth century. Casseroles or open forms, which often recall the north African forms Hayes 23 and 197, tended to disappear in favour of small one-handled cooking pots of a type that survived into later medieval times.[48]

Another form that makes its appearance is the *clibanus* or *testum*, which was a portable oven, apparently for the baking of bread and heating of other foods (Fig. 3:20) (Cubberley, Lloyd and Roberts 1988). The vessel, known since prehistoric times, is still in use along the Dalmatian coast,

---

[42] The finds from *Tropea* come from tomb no. 34 at the cemetery excavated in Largo Duomo (additional information kindly supplied by Claudio Sabbione). For the importance of *Tropea*, see Noyé 1988: 89–90, and for the excavations, see Di Gangi, Lebole Di Gangi and Sabbione 1994.

[43] For the Pozzuoli jugs in the British Museum, see Arthur 1994: 483, pl. 68.

[44] A bowl of this class comes from Pratola Serra (Saporito 1992: 200–1, 216–17, fig. LX, no. 103). See also Santa Maria Capua Vetere (Arthur and Patterson 1994: fig. 5, no. 7). A painted jug, of eighth- or ninth-century date, is in the museum of the catacombs of San Gennaro. For Crypta Balbi, see Romei 1997.

[45] On forum ware, see Paroli 1992a. For local early medieval glazed pottery, see Arthur and Capece 1992. Vittoria Carsana tells me that more forum ware has since appeared in Naples, particularly from excavations at San Marcellino. See also Carsana 1996: 144–5; Giampaola, Fratta and Scarpati 1996: 130, n. 59.

[46] This form is perhaps somewhat later in Sicily. See Isler (1994: fig. 12) for an eleventh- or twelfth-century example from Monte Iato.

[47] I should like to thank Carlo Franciosi, the site director, for this information.

[48] On cooking wares in general, see Carsana 1994; Reynolds 1995.

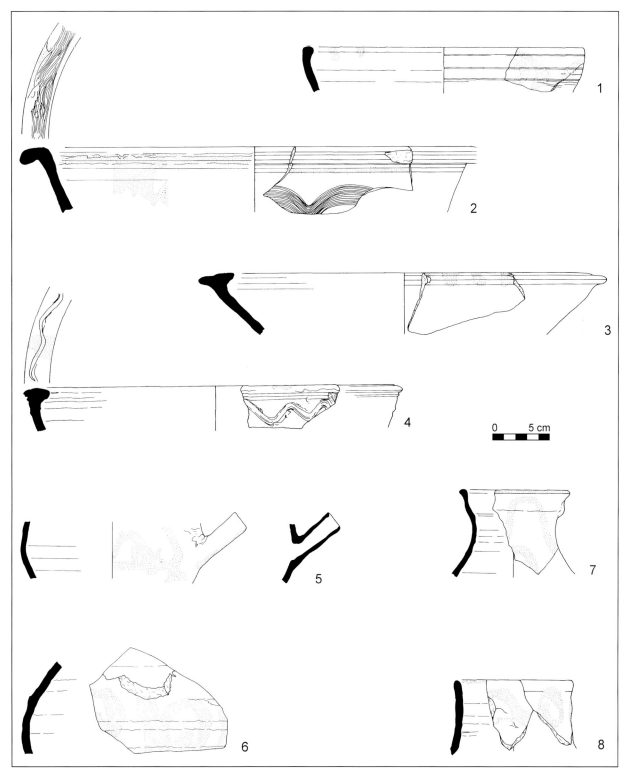

Fig. 6:9. Neapolitan eighth-century wares (drawn by author).

where it is known as the *crpnja*, and in Rumania, where it is known as the *tsesta*. It appears restricted to rural areas where centralized bakeries do not exist or are insufficient to meet demand (Carlton 1988; Nandris 1988: 130–1). Thus, I believe it may be concluded that the *crpnja/tsesta* is basically a rural vessel conceived for domestic use by small, relatively isolated or markedly agrarian population groups.

If one turns to examine the archaeological evidence in Italy for the contexts and distribution of the *clibanus*, the rudiments of a pattern seem to emerge. Although more evidence needs to be gathered, *clibani* appear in Campania in both urban (*Pompeii* and Naples) and rural (the *ager Falernus*, the Francolise villas) contexts during the Republic. Their use seems to continue predominantly in rural contexts during the early and mid-Empire, even being produced in the *ager Falernus*. In Naples, they reappear during the fifth to the sixth centuries, to survive until at least the end of the millennium (Carsana 1994: 243, type 68), whilst even in northern Italy the form makes a comeback in early medieval times (Brogiolo and Gelichi 1996a: 226). Thus a model may be proposed whereby the *clibanus* was commonly in use during the Republic, until centralized baking became the norm in Roman towns. Their use was then limited to rural societies. When centralized baking became evermore restricted during the late Empire, the *clibanus* once more appeared in towns. If this is confirmed by future research, it may be possible to use the form as an indicator of rural practices emerging within towns during the early Middle Ages.

Thus a major change in pottery types appears to occur towards the end of the fifth or the early sixth century, in tune with an increasing regionalization of production and supply throughout central and southern Italy (as discussed by Patterson 1985: 102–5). Afterwards, ceramic styles in Naples remained particularly static until the eighth century. This is important in the light of other evidence that suggests the economy started to pick up during the century, and probably in the latter half (see below, Chapter 7). The quality of both fine painted and cooking wares, and the tentative introduction of the technology of glazing during the course of the eighth century suggest that manufacture remained in the hands of professional potters, whether working full-time or not. Household production, if any existed, was certainly extremely limited in Naples, though perhaps more so than in far-flung rural areas.

References to *figuli* (potters) appear from about the tenth century in southern Italy. A certain Cesarius *figulos* is mentioned at Monte Cassino in 918. In 1009, Iohannes and Stephanus, 'filii Ursi fictilario', from Nocera, rented lands near the abbey of Cava dei Tirreni. The earliest attested *fictiliarii* in Naples are John and Peter, in 1120 (Ballardini 1964: 215; Donatone 1967: 583, 590; Peduto 1993). Though the absence of earlier references to potters is probably to be related to the scarcity of documents antedating the tenth century, it was during the later eleventh or twelfth century that Neapolitan ceramics were quite clearly influenced by an increase in the number of imported wares and by greater mobility and specialization of craftsmen. This led to a greater premium being put on ceramicists who were able to produce decorative pots and tiles that could be used in architectural decoration and as prestige items. The widespread use of lead glazing is the most evident technological advancement (Fig. 6:10) and is first found on a series of hooked-rim basins, which clearly imitate vessels from the Maghreb, probably mediated through copying of similar Sicilian productions (Arthur 1986c: 546–

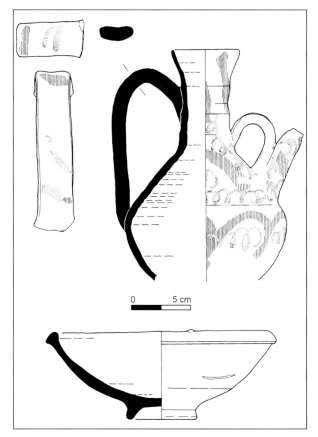

Fig. 6:10. Lead-glazed wares of late eleventh- to twelfth-century date from Santa Patrizia (drawn by author).

8, fig. 2).[49] They bear an internal green lead glaze, which also covers the rim, and sometimes display simple dark brown to black underglaze decoration. Many of these basins were found at Santa Patrizia, which also yielded a jug of the same ware, similar to a brown painted vessel from Pylos in Elis, Greece (Coleman 1986: 147–8, pl. 53, no. F40). The basins are amongst the first medieval Neapolitan ceramics to have enjoyed an extra-regional market. In Pisa examples have been found used as decoration in the façades of the church buildings of San Sisto (1131–1133), San Silvestro (1118) and Sant'Andrea (early twelfth century) (Berti and Tongiorgi 1981), whilst similar products appear in the bell-tower of Santa Maria della Luce (1099–1118) in Rome (Mazzucato 1976: 34–40). On this basis, we might surmise that the technique started to be used systematically by Neapolitan potters by the late eleventh century.

By the later twelfth or early thirteenth century, production further diversified, and the quality of Campanian lead-glazed products notably improved. Spiral ware basins, decorated with green and brown painted overlapping spirals, beneath a lead glaze, were possibly produced in the territory of Salerno,

alongside rarer jug forms. The territory of Naples itself may have produced rather shiny yellowish lead-glazed vessels, often cups, with polychrome painted decoration, often in red, green and brown.[50]

The most eloquent archaeological data for commodity importation consists of transport amphorae, of which a good series, dating from the late fourth through to the later seventh centuries and beyond, exists from archaeological contexts in Naples. Phase VI deposits, dated to the mid- to third quarter of the fifth century, in the excavations of Carminiello ai Mannesi, yielded an average 35% of coarse pottery to 65% amphorae.[51] By the late fifth to early sixth centuries the proportion of coarse pottery rises to almost 50% in respect to amphorae, whilst by the late sixth to seventh centuries coarse pottery drops to 32% against 68% amphorae. The latest context (US II 5), datable to the late seventh to the eighth centuries, sees a drastic rise in the proportion of coarse pottery to 69%, against 31% of amphorae, some of which may be residual.

The discussion that follows is based on percentages of recognized amphorae against all amphora fragments found in the contexts taken into consideration (Fig. 6:11). A large quantity of fragments

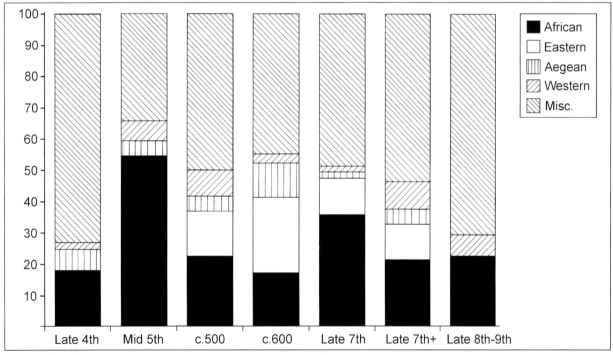

Fig. 6:11. Fluctuations through time of amphorae in Naples, grouped by area of provenance (drawn by author).

---

[49] Ada De Crescenzo informs me that the bowls are also fairly common at Salerno.

[50] The most detailed account of later medieval ceramics in Naples remains Fontana and Ventrone Vassallo 1984. For spiral ware, see Vitelli and Riley 1979; Fontana 1984: 119–28.

[51] Coarse pottery includes what Italian archaeologists know as 'ceramica da cucina o da fuoco' and 'ceramica comune', but not fine table-wares such as *sigillata*.

has not been identified, many of which may represent vessels from areas of Italy/Sicily and the East (Fig. 6:12). It is possible that certain importing areas are not represented, through use of biodegradable containers (southern Gaul, north Italy?), and that the available assemblages are not truly representative of the relative quantities of amphorae imported into the city, but instead reflect use and depositional factors.[52] None the less, I believe that the excavated contexts permit a general view of changes in importation over a crucial period stretching from the later fourth to the ninth centuries and beyond.

In the late fourth century a large variety of imported amphorae may be recognized, particularly from the excavations at Girolomini and Santa Patrizia. They come from Tunisia, Tripolitania, Spain, Chios, Crete, the Meander valley of Asia Minor, possibly the Dodecanese and southern Calabria.[53] No vessels have been recognized as coming from the Near East, despite a healthy production of wine recorded along the Levantine coast. The relative proportion of African goods reaching Rome and Ostia by the late fourth and early fifth centuries seems to have been much higher than that reaching Naples (Anselmino *et al*. 1986; Carignani and Pacetti 1989; Martin 1989; Panella 1993: 637), perhaps indicating a greater dependency of the capital on imported grain and oil and, *per contra*, a greater measure of Campanian self-sufficiency. In the capital, African amphorae comprise virtually half of the imported examples, whilst in Naples they reach barely a quarter. Almagro type 51C amphorae represent the last significant Spanish imports, with arrivals probably trickling into the first half of the fifth century. The 1.4% of Italian vessels, including Calabrian fabrics, seems to mark the beginning of a trend, witnessed during the course of the fifth century, of a rise in proportion of Calabrian, Campanian and possibly Sicilian containers.

By the mid-fifth century, African amphorae had risen from the 17.6% of the late fourth century to 44.4%, thus reaching the Rome/Ostia proportions, despite the negative judgement that scholars have

attributed to the economy of north Africa following the Vandal invasion.[54] There is also a significant decline in unidentified amphorae, suggesting that goods were now arriving predominantly from a select number of key agricultural areas. Perhaps the rise in African vessels may be read as responding to a crisis in the productivity of Campanian staples that reached a head during the fifth century (Ruggini 1961: 151–2). It might also be suggested that the mid-fifth-century alignment between the data from Rome and Naples is the result of other factors such as:

1. state regulated importation to Naples not taking place to any great extent until the fifth century;
2. a general self-sufficiency until about the mid-fifth century, when conditions changed, perhaps partly on account of an imbalance caused by immigration from north Africa and from *Puteoli* and the surrounding countryside;
3. the sources of supply represented by the miscellaneous amphorae declining.

By the end of the fifth to the early sixth centuries, the proportion of African amphorae had dropped again, though Africa continued to represent the single most important source of imported olive oil. There was also a slight rise in western vessels, mainly from southern Calabria/eastern Sicily and of local origin, and a significant rise in amphorae coming from eastern areas, probably all wine containers.[55] The two trends may be linked, with eastern ships loading Sicilian/Calabrian goods whilst sailing through the straits of Messina (Reynolds 1995: 134). At this time, the Gothic garrison in Naples, at least, seems to have received the *annona*, and trade through the port was managed by the *comites* of the city. However, vagaries in supply may have been occasioned not only by the Vandal presence in Africa, but also by the government's difficulty in assuring control of *navicularii*, contrary to earlier times.[56]

Archaeological contexts in Rome also show a halving in the proportion of African amphorae when compared to the mid-fifth century (Panella 1993: 650). Though this may have been a belated

---

[52] Note the observations by Wickham (1988a). I am not as good at playing chess as he suggests, though, on the other hand, I believe that he is unduly pessimistic about the potential of quantitative studies.

[53] Meander Valley: Late Roman Amphora 3 (= LRA 3), for which see Peacock and Williams 1986: 188–90. Chios: LRA 2, which is often confused with other globular amphorae and still requires close study (see Riley 1979: 217–19). There are also some fragments of amphora form Richborough 527, the kilns of which have been identified on the island of Lipari. Madeleine Cavalier, who sent me the information, suggested that they might have contained alum.

[54] Ostia, Terme del Nuotatore: 45.1% in the fourth century (Anselmino *et al*. 1986: 66, table 2). Rome, Schola Praeconum I deposit: 42.5% by the middle of the fifth century (Whitehouse *et al*. 1982).

[55] On the Calabrian/Sicilian types, see Pacetti 1998. The local vessels are discussed above.

[56] See De Salvo (1986) on an interpretation of Cassiodorus.

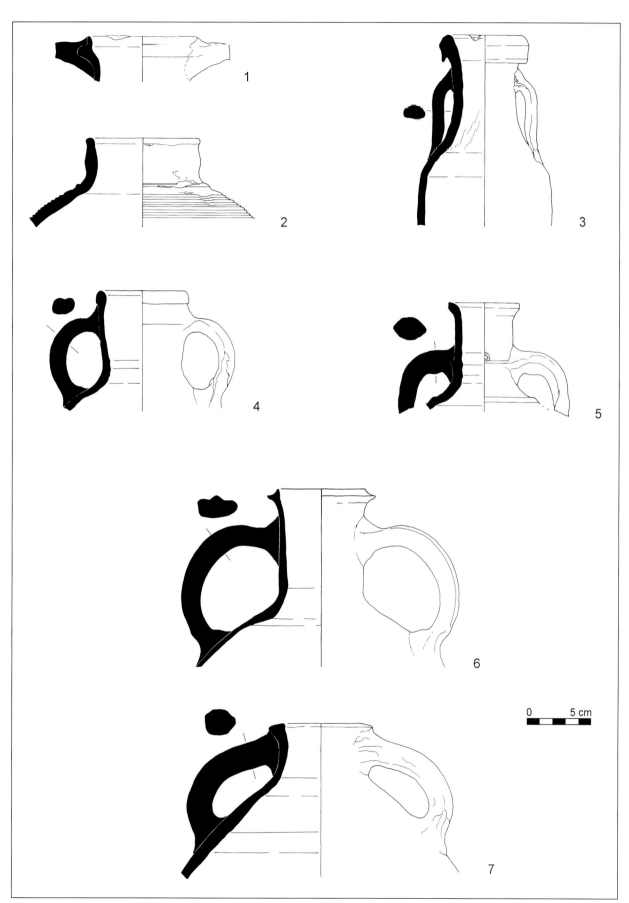

Fig. 6:12. Amphora types imported into Naples. 1–2 Palestinian; 3 north African; 4 Greek; 5 Nubian; 6 Calabrian; 7 probably Sicilian. All are fifth- to sixth-century, save for no. 3, which dates to the sixth to seventh centuries (drawn by author).

effect of the Vandal occupation of north Africa, most of the eastern amphorae appear to have been wine containers, thus not representing any direct economic rivalry with African oil. None the less, a distinct impression that the East was becoming of greater significance to Naples and the West in general is indicated by the fact that the amphorae were accompanied by minor quantities of eastern table and cooking wares (Soricelli 1994; Carsana 1994; Reynolds 1995: 23, 93).[57] The East is represented above all by amphorae from the Gaza/Askalon strip, which would have contained a noted wine mentioned in the sources.[58] They make up 6.7% of all amphora fragments. They are followed by vessels from Cyprus/Cilicia/northern Syria, the Meander valley, Palestine, Chios, possibly Icaria and Egypt.[59] Most of them probably contained wine, whilst some were perhaps non-commodity specific. The Cypriot/Cilician/northern Syrian container, known as Late Roman Amphora 1, is a case in point, with both wine and olive oil regularly suggested as contents (Panella 1993: 665–6). An example from Carminello ai Mannesi bears a *titulus pictus* in Semitic or Syriac whose translation seems to be either 'spices 10 (?) for the creditor' or 'purple (dye) 10 (?) for mantle'.[60]

Unfortunately, Naples has not yet provided contexts of mid-sixth-century date from which to judge importation of goods in amphorae. However, by the end of the century, the proportion of eastern amphorae had doubled, whilst that of African vessels had continued to decline, reaching 17.5%, close to late fourth-century percentages. Though north Africa was still the single area most represented, it was closely followed by Gaza/Askalon, which reached 14.5%. There was also a significant rise in the proportion of amphorae from Cyprus/Cilicia and Chios, virtually matched

Fig. 6:13. A late sixth- or seventh-century 'Samos cistern type' amphora from Santa Maria la Nova (photo: E. Emilio).

by an amphora type from Samos (Fig. 6:13). This last is scarce in the western Mediterranean, appearing at key sites and emporia such as Otranto, Rome, Ravenna, Brescia and Carthage, and in the small coastal village of Kaukana, near Camarina, Sicily. Its distribution may suggest that trade was directional. The wide range of eastern mediterranean amphorae found in the city is atypical when compared to Carthage, Marseille and Spanish sites.[61]

---

[57] Pantellerian ware is not as common as Reynolds has stated (1995: 93), as the types found at Naples are mostly Campanian.

[58] See Glucker (1987: 93–4) for the sources. The amphora type has been well treated by Riley (1979: 219–23). Kilns for the type have recently been found at Askalon, and may have existed as far south as Ashdod and el-Arish.

[59] Cyprus/Cilicia/north Syria has been discussed best by Empereur and Picon (1989: 236–43) and Riley (1979). For the Meander valley LRA 3, see Arthur 1998b: 165. In Palestine these include both LRA 5 and an amphora known as Agora M334 (see Riley 1979: 223; Johnson 1988: 209–10, respectively). For Chios LRA 2, see Arthur 1998b: 168–9. For Icaria, see Adamschek 1979: 117, RC22 according to *tituli picti*. See also Fulford and Peacock 1984: 127–8, no. 39, fig. 38, nos. 48–48bis. For Egypt LRA 7, see Riley 1981: 121.

[60] I should like to thank Giancarlo Lacerenza for allowing me to read his report on the *titulus pictus* (Lacerenza 1987). Purple-dyed cloth (*blatin neapolitano*) is attested as a local speciality in the eighth century (see above, p. 115).

[61] On the Samos type, see Arthur 1990a; Panella 1993: 664; Saguì 1993a: 412, fig. 7, from Rome; Zanini 1998: 312, 315. I should like to thank Brunella Bruno for information on a find at Brescia. In the East, further examples have been recorded at Istanbul (Hayes 1992: 67–9, fig. 23, no. 1), Side, Turkey (Baths Museum) and Ostrakine, northern Sinai (excavations conducted by Eliezer Oren). Few examples are present in the Bodrum Castle Museum (personal observation), making rather unlikely Panella's suggestion that they might have come from Halikarnassos. With the unification of the Byzantine navy by Constans II, Samos became the headquarters of the Byzantine naval theme, until the later creation of the *théma Samos*, centred at *Smyrna* (Toynbee 1973: 261, 324–5). On the atypicality of the Neapolitan finds, see Reynolds 1995: 133–4.

In the seventh century, Naples was still importing amphorae, containing primarily oil and wine from north Africa and the Levant, with perhaps lesser quantities from Asia Minor and the Aegean. The African amphorae, reaching 35% in context US 600, appear to be either very large cylindrical containers (essentially form Keay LXI) or very small vessels (*spatheia*) in a cream coloured fabric.[62] There is, however, a rise in the quantity of amphorae from Chios, from 1.7% in the early sixth century, to over 5% by the early seventh, after which the classic form disappears from circulation (Reynolds 1995: 76).[63] The Samos amphora type accounts for another *c.* 5% of the total amphora fragments by the late sixth to the early seventh centuries. Both types appear to have contained wine and, alongside Constantinople-type cooking wares, emphasize close supply links with the eastern capital.[64] Gaza amphorae drop to some 5%.

By the end of the sixth century 'annonae et consuetudines' were taken for granted, so much so that their suspension was a cause of complaint by Pope Gregory to the praetorian prefect of Italy (Greg. *Ep.* X. 8; see Jones 1964: 898–9). As accumulating evidence from around the Mediterranean suggests that the open market had dwindled by this time, and as amphorae seem to have been imported to Naples in fair quantity through the sixth and seventh centuries, it may be that some form of forced supply continued to buttress Naples for quite some time after Gregory's remonstration.

Much of the eighth century is absent from the archaeological record, though late eighth- or early ninth-century layers have been identified at Santa Patrizia. They yielded a small number of local amphorae, produced in kilns at Miseno, Ischia and elsewhere. Alongside them were a few imported vessels. As in the seventh century, it may be argued that they were produced predominantly around the Aegean, and perhaps in Sicily and other surviving areas of Byzantine domination.

Amphorae are also rare in contexts between the ninth and eleventh centuries. Also at Santa Patrizia

five contexts have yielded 244 sherds, 90 (37%) of which were residual, principally of the fifth to seventh centuries.[65] The remaining 63% were not identifiable, though a few fragments appear to represent types produced around Ganos, on the Sea of Marmara.[66]

By the eleventh century, port taxes were partly paid in wine amphorae (R. 378) and, indeed, a discrete number, particularly 'amphores a cannelures' of Fatimid type, once again appear in archaeological contexts. Produced between Palermo and Marsala, they may be subdivided into two main forms (Fig. 6:14) (see Ardizzone 1999).[67] Shared traits are the reddish, white-speckled, fabrics, red or brown painted bands and ribbed bodies. The long-necked form may have held a sweet wine, whilst cane sugar may be suggested for the other. The latter was a recognized export from western Sicily under the Arabs (Purpura 1985:

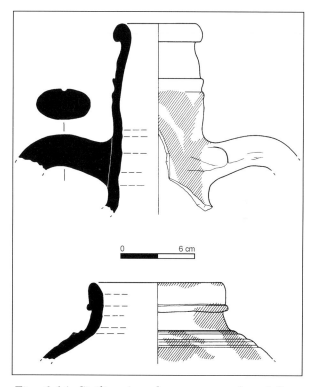

Fig. 6:14. Sicilian 'amphores a cannelures' from Santa Patrizia and Sant'Aniello a Caponapoli (drawn by author).

---

[62] This appears to match data from Marseilles and elsewhere (Bonifay and Piéri 1995: 97, 106). For the large African vessels, see the comments of Paroli *et al.* (1996: 128–9).

[63] The later Chian type, at Emporio, has been presented by Boardman (1989: 96–7).

[64] On Constantinople type cooking pots, see Carsana 1994: 254–5. Panella (1993: 654–69) has presented a general discussion of this period.

[65] The contexts examined are US 716, 720, 739, 760 and 770.

[66] For a whole example from Castellabate, in the province of Salerno, see Cianfarani 1995. For Ganos, see Günsenin 1993.

[67] In thin section the fabrics of examples from Naples present calcareous voids, with angular to sub-angular grains of quartz and orthoclase feldspar, compatible with samples of tiles collected in northwestern Sicily. I should like to thank Marco Fuscaldo for this information.

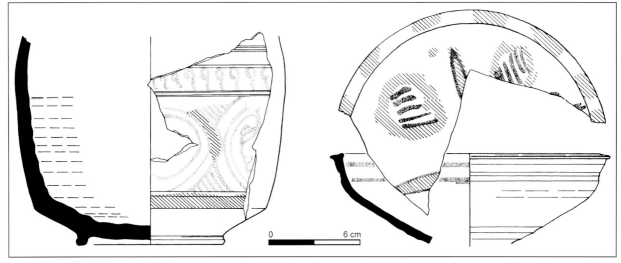

Fig. 6:15. Imported wares from north Africa in Naples (drawn by author).

134).[68] In Naples, the amphorae occur in contexts dating from the later eleventh or twelfth to the first half of the thirteenth centuries.[69] Other examples have been found in the province of Salerno, as well as at Benevento.[70] Such a quantity may represent the growth of trade with Sicily, following the Norman conquest of the island, though I know of no amphorae from Campania later than the twelfth century, when the wooden barrel had probably substituted most ceramic transport containers.

It is significant that excavations in the city have yielded one of the latest series of African red slip tablewares found outside Carthage (Fig. 6:15), seemingly aligning the supply of Naples in the seventh century with that of Rome. Most of the vessels were found at Santa Patrizia, with some pieces from Carminiello, including Hayes forms 99c, 105, 108 and 109 (Soricelli 1994: 149–50). A few examples of seventh-century cooking pots come from the Aegean (Carsana 1994: 254–5). From the Alpine area, are three vessels in *pietra ollare* or soapstone, dating to the sixth and seventh centuries, which also appear as far south as Otranto.[71]

By the end of the seventh or the eighth century, archaeologically attested imports from the East are almost absent. Occasional amphorae still arrived, perhaps indicating sporadic trade, though their precise source of manufacture is not known.[72] Instead, links with northern and central Italy might have increased marginally. Excavations in the city, above all at the site of the monastery of Santa Patrizia, have also yielded small quantities of a regional production of the lead-glazed pottery known as forum ware, which now seems unlikely to date earlier than the mid- to later eighth century (Christie 1987).[73] There is no evidence that this class of pottery survived in Naples into the twelfth century, when local hooked-rim basins make their appearance. As this class of pottery is common around Rome, one may ask whether its appearance in Naples indicates the import of agricultural goods from Rome, especially grain. The Roman Campagna at this time was undergoing some measure of reorganization, with the foundation of the *domuscultae* in lieu of lost papal properties in Sicily (Wickham 1978: 177). In this context, it is also worth noting the discovery of an imported

---

[68] Sugar cane (*Saccharum officinarum*), native to New Guinea, was known to Pliny (*NH* XII. xvii. 32), though it does not seem to have been used in the Mediterranean until it was introduced along with the spread of Islam (Watson 1983). It was then regularly produced both in the Holy Land and on Cyprus by the Latin states.

[69] They are found at the sites of Santa Patrizia, Via San Paolo, Girolomini chiostro, Sant'Aniello and the Duomo.

[70] For Altavilla Silentina, see Bisogno and Guarino 1984: 103–4, 108–9, pls XXVII–XXVIII, both forms. For Capaccio Vecchia, see Maetzke 1984: 144–5. Additional information about Salerno (form 1) was kindly provided by P. Peduto. For Salerno (form 2) and Fratte, see Pastore 1995: 262–4. The example from Agerola was found by Tommaso Wenner in a cave. Additional information about Benevento was kindly provided by Caterina Scarpati.

[71] The Naples examples come from CM US II 5 (Arthur 1994: 351–2), VS US 237 and PB (residual). For Otranto, see Sannazaro 1994. For an example from *Abellinum* (Atripalda), erroneously dated in Arthur (1994: 351), see Colucci Pescatori 1986: pl. LXXXII, no. 39. For the production see Bagolini *et al.* 1987.

[72] See, for example, the amphora published in Arthur 1989a (fig. 5).

[73] For forum ware from Naples, see Arthur and Capece 1992. It may also have a Carolingian connection, as very similar glazed pottery has been found in France and Germany, dating from the ninth century (Rouaze 1988: 335–6, no. 405 (from Saint Denis, near Paris); Ballardini 1964: 144–5, figs 189–90 (in the Kaiser Friedrich Museum, Berlin)).

amphora, apparently similar to an example from the Roman church of Santa Maria in Cosmedin, dating to no earlier than the pontificate of Hadrian I (772–795) (Mazzucato 1977: fig. 67).[74]

The later eleventh or twelfth century witnesses an explosion in the quantity of imported pottery. The majority appears to be of Sicilian origin, including *ceramica sicula-maghrebina* and the 'amphores a cannelures' discussed above. Sicula-maghrebina ware is characterized in Naples by hooked-rim bowls in a white to yellowish fabric with an overall green lead glaze, often with black/brown underglaze decoration. Petrological analysis, revealing the presence of volcanic inclusions, suggests that it could come from eastern Sicily.[75] It was soon imitated around the bay of Naples. Local products are somewhat less fine than the originals and are distinguished by the lack of a lead glaze on the exterior surface. True maghrebina ware, produced in Islamic north Africa, has been found mostly at Santa Patrizia. Almost without exception it is in a reddish clay fabric also encountered amongst amphorae imported from Tunisia in Roman times. The commonest form is the hooked-rim bowl with an overall green glaze and underglaze decoration in black/brown and yellow.

Byzantine glazed wares are quite rare in Naples and along the Tyrrhenian coast of Italy. The earliest imported ware may be that which Gabriella Maetzke has termed *vetrina verde giallo brillante su pasta bianca*, probably to be identified with the 'glazed white ware' recognized at Constantinople. A few scraps have been found in Naples, as well as at Benevento, Salerno, Capaccio and Otranto (Maetzke 1976: 92–3; Iannelli 1992: 22–4).[76] Fragments of twelfth-century graffito ware have come from excavations at Santa Patrizia (Arthur 1986a: fig. 3), Vico della Serpe (De Stefano and Carsana 1987: 35, no. 67) and the Policlinico (Genito 1985: 177, n. 64), whilst it is totally absent amongst the abundant thirteenth- and fourteenth-century material from San Lorenzo Maggiore (Fontana 1984).[77] A particularly fine basin, in the

Museum of Capodimonte, may have been produced in the Aegean and imported as a luxury object in the twelfth century, though there is some doubt as to its provenance (Donatone 1967: pl. 217). The general scarcity of Byzantine pottery in Naples might indicate sporadic commercial contacts with Byzantium both before and after the Norman conquest (Lovecchio 1989).[78]

COINAGE: PRODUCTION

The control of the public economy of Naples was in the hands of the joint civil and military administration, under the government of the duke, first as representative of Byzantium and, after the mid-eighth century, as autonomous ruler, paying lip-service from time to time to the emperor in the East. The bishop of Naples provided a parallel authority. A small series of seals, those of the secular authority in Greek, and those of the ecclesiastical authority in Latin, provide material evidence for both (*MND* II: 243–5).[79] However, the true material indicator of economic authority should be provided by numismatics.

The first coins struck in Naples, many centuries after the closing of the Greek mint, may have been under Totila, during Ostrogothic times, so as to have paid troops engaged against the Byzantine forces during their reconquest of Italy (Wroth 1966: 83).[80] According to Ricotti Prina, the first Byzantine coinage of Naples was struck by the Byzantine forces in the field in 552/554, under Justinian (1972: 20–1). The issue, of gold folles bearing the exergue letter P, was presumably intended as an emergency measure to stabilize the political situation during and just after the siege of Cuma, which had been in the hands of Teia's Goths. This was, furthermore, just one of the episodes during the rather contracted war that must have left its toll on the bay of Naples. The army had to be paid, a certain amount of reconstruction was necessary, and what could not be requisitioned had to be bought. Furthermore, state finances must have been so drained that the imposition of extra

---

[74] The amphora was incorporated within the church structure. The church of Santa Maria in Cosmedin was built under Hadrian I, and restored under Nicholas I (858–867).

[75] Petrological analyses by David Williams.

[76] Some of the 'plain white ware' vessels from Otranto appear to be of the same fabric (Patterson and Whitehouse 1992: 163–6).

[77] The pottery from Vico della Serpe, and all but one of the fragments from Santa Patrizia, appear to be of the same type and possibly belong to the class represented by Batch O in Megaw and Jones (1983). Arthur 1986a: fig. 3, no. 16, appears to be of fine sgraffito ware (see Hayes 1992: 44–5, fig. 17, no. 5).

[78] See Berti and Tongiorgi (1981: 276) for the similar situation of Pisa.

[79] In general, on Byzantine seals in Italy, see Laurent 1962.

[80] It may be noted that the majority of bronze coins from one of the Cuma hoards is attributed to Totila, from his mints at Turin and Rome (Miraglia 1986). Could some be local?

taxation, as far as was reasonably possible, would presumably have further contributed to the cash flow.[81] Indeed, coins of Justinian are reasonably common in the area, and were present in a hoard of gold solidi, *semissis* and *tremissis* from Punta dell'Epitaffio, Baia, found over twenty years ago.[82] Various bronzes of the emperor are known from hoards at *Cumae* itself (Miraglia 1986), possibly buried on the occasion of sieges during the war, and as scattered finds in Naples (where *pentanummi* have been found in the excavations at Santa Patrizia), at the Roman and medieval baths at Agnano (a *nummus* and a *pentanummus* (Macchioro 1912: 38)) and at *Cartaromana*, Ischia (a *decunummus* (Monti 1980: 326, fig. 138)). A bronze coin of Justin (518–527), or Justinian, also comes from a Roman villa near *Nola* (Sampaolo 1986: 114, n. 9). Up until Justinianic times, if not later, circulating coinage in Naples comprised a mix of contemporary or near-contemporary issues, including Vandal emissions of Baduela, as well as earlier Roman bronzes.[83]

A permanent local mint was not opened in Naples until Duke Basilius, appointed by Constans II, presumably received permission directly from the emperor during his visit to the city in 663. The money was perhaps issued to support the new administration and its financial policy, which included the little understood western *nauticatio*, a tax probably levied on the import and export of goods to Byzantine territory, principally by sea (Danstrup 1946: 167). Emissions were of bronze twenty *nummi* (half follis) pieces with the mint mark NE (Morrisson 1970: 366; Pannuti and Riccio 1984: 2, nos. 1, 2). They are by no means common, in contrast to the imported five *nummi* bronzes of the same emperor. Denominations of half folles of copper, and possibly some debased gold from the times of Constantine IV, Justinian II and Leontius, continued up to about 695 (Grierson 1968: 48–9, 500, 620 (Leontius); Morrisson 1970: 413).[84] Of Justinian II we also possess bronze twenty *nummi* coins on rectangular flans, always with the mint mark NE (Ricotti Prina 1972: 66, pl. 14, nos. 28–9). A single half follis and a possible solidus have been attributed to the Emperor Leo III, taking local coinage into the first half of the eighth century, whilst Cécile Morrisson has also tentatively assigned some solidi of Anastasius II (713–715) and Theodosius III (715–717) to the Naples mint (Morrisson 1970: 421, 444, 447; Pannuti and Riccio 1984: 5).

Fig. 6:16. Coins of the duchy of Naples: anonymous issue (no. 1), Duke Stephen (nos. 2–3) and Duke Sergius II (no. 4) (© Copyright The British Museum; reproduced courtesy of The British Museum).

---

[81] On the expenses of military expeditions see Hendy 1985: 221–4.

[82] The hoard is perhaps represented by a single *tremiss* from recent excavations (Gianfrotta 1987: 109).

[83] Two coins of Totila/Baduela have been found in the Santa Patrizia excavations.

[84] On debasement, see O'Hara 1988. On gold of Constantine IV and Justinian II, see Hahn 1981: 155, 169; Donald 1995: 28 (a halved solidus of Justinian II).

	Santangelo	Fiorelli	Total	%
Anonymous (Saint Ianuarius types)	3	15	18	30.5
Stephen (755–800)	9	21	30	50.8
Emperor Basil I (867–886)	0	1	1	1.6
Sergius II (870–878)	1	5	6	10.1
Athanasius II (878–898)	1	3	4	6.7
Total			**59**	

Fig. 6:17. Ducal coins in the National Archaeological Museum of Naples. Santangelo and Fiorelli collections (Fiorelli 1866–1872).

Shortly after the fall of Ravenna in 751, control of the production of coinage was assumed directly by the dukes under Stephen II. It is after this that the mint is first attested in the sources (Fig. 6:16) (see above, Chapter 2).[85] The sole denomination appears to have been a twenty *nummus* piece. One type, classed as a civic issue by The British Museum, though of uncertain attribution, bears the bust of Saint Ianuarius holding the gospel and an accompanying legend on the obverse and the legend +/NEAPOL/IC on the reverse (Fig. 6:16). The few known specimens are partly die-linked, suggesting that they belong to a somewhat limited issue (Pannuti and Riccio 1984: 5).[86] Duke Stephen's issue, bearing the bust of Saint Ianuarius on the reverse and a stepped or Calvary cross on the obverse, seems to have been the most common of all ducal coins (Figs 6:16 and 6:17).[87] The sheer crudity of these types is striking, and suggests that professional die-cutters were not available, though their quantity may indicate that authorities were attempting to regularize exchange in the context of a developing economy.

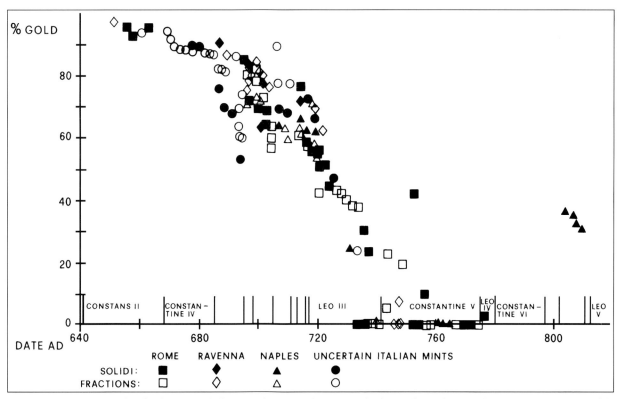

Fig. 6:18. The standard of gold solidi in Italy from the seventh through to the ninth centuries (after Oddy 1988: fig. 3; reproduced courtesy of The American Numismatic Society, New York).

[85] For the first reference in the sources, see *MND* I: 262 (for the year 763: *in platea que ad Moneta dicitur*).
[86] One example exists in The British Museum collections (55–6–12–239), whilst further single pieces have been illustrated by Grierson (1991: 86–7) and Monti (1980: 293, fig. 129). I should like to thank Lucia Travaini for information on die-linkage.
[87] This is the commonest early medieval Neapolitan coin in The British Museum collections, totalling thirteen pieces, virtually all from different dies. I am grateful to Sig. De Falco, Naples, for information about coins on the market.

Succeeding coin output seems to have been miserly by comparison. Naples continued to mint bronze folles and half folles during the ninth century, notably under Sergius II (870–878), though also under Athanasius II (878–898), neither of whom hesitated to display their portrait on the opposite side to Saint Ianuarius (Fig. 6:16) (Pannuti and Riccio 1984: 7).[88] Interestingly, gold solidi seem to have been issued by the dukes under the names of Emperors Nicephorus I and Stauracius (803–811), and Theophilus, Michael II and Constantine VII (829–842), when imperial gold was no longer being produced in peninsular Italy (Fig. 6:18) (Grierson 1961: 41–2, 47; Morrisson 1970: 498, 502, 531; Hendy 1985: 423).[89]

Naples may also have struck a silver *miliaresion* of Theophilus, Michael II (and Constantine VII), if the identification of a coin found at Matera is correct (Salvatore 1986: 124). During the reign of Basil I (867–886), the city also seems to have issued some silver denarii, following an initiative of *Beneventum* in taking up the Carolingian standard, perhaps pointing to developing relations with the Lombards (Martin 1983: 187; Pannuti and Riccio 1984: 9).[90] Virtually nothing is known of Neapolitan coinage after the ninth century. Excavations at Santa Patrizia have yielded a silver bracteate coin which bears a monogram within a pearl border, perhaps reading Iohannis (Fig. 6:19). The reverse is blank. Though the piece appears to be unique, it may have been issued under the authority of Duke John II (915–919) or John III (928–969).[91]

Fig. 6:19. Silver coin from Santa Patrizia with a monogram reading Iohannis, perhaps of Duke John II (915–919) or John III (928–969).

0   1 cm

The Neapolitan coin series is not recognizably continuous or articulated, though this might be due to our lack of knowledge concerning local issues, which were probably never numerous (Sambon 1912: 44–5). It is, of course, one matter what was being struck, and quite another what composed the pool of money in circulation. What is notable, however, is that after Stephen II the coins are distinctly modelled on eastern Byzantine coinages, underlining an attempt to imitate monetary policy and stressing continued economic links. Lombard *Beneventum* also copied eastern coinage. However, initiated under Duke Gisulf I (689–706), it seems to have been abundant and more articulated than that of Naples (Grierson and Blackburn 1986: 66–72).

COINAGE: CIRCULATION

No systematic study has been conducted yet on coin circulation in Campania, and few coin lists are available. The lack of fully published excavations makes it almost impossible to build up a general picture of circulation though, as will be shown, coins all but disappear after the first half of the sixth century.[92]

The Roman villa of Minori, on the Sorrento peninsula, provides a sample of 79 coins stretching from the late Republic to late fourth-century issues of Valentinian II and Honorius, after whose reigns the site might have been abandoned (Fig. 6:20) (Mangieri 1988).

The high percentage of third- and particularly fourth-century coins is striking, and suggests higher coin loss and greater on-site circulation in late Roman times. Though difficult to interpret without more evidence, this might suggest that a certain amount of market-place activity was leaving the towns by the third century. However, despite the small quantity of coins found in Naples (Fig. 6:21), fourth-century coins from the city form 50% of the coins found for the same time-span as that covered by the series from Minori.[93] A rather similar trend to that noted for Naples may be seen

[88] The five examples in The British Museum collections are listed, probably erroneously, under Sergius II.

[89] The gold standard of these coins, from 30 to 37%, is quite high when compared with the Italian Imperial issues of the previous 100 years (Oddy 1988: 141). Could the metal have derived from trade with Egypt?

[90] There is some doubt as to the attribution.

[91] I should like to thank Lucia Travaini for the suggestion. The coin, from context US 642, weighs 0.40 gm.

[92] The possibility of circulation of earlier coin must not be ignored, though it is unlikely to have played a great part in exchange. The problem may be tackled in two ways: firstly, by the analysis of all coin finds significantly earlier than the context in which they have been found, including burials, though the percentage of other sorts of residual material must be taken into account so as to judge the likelihood of casual intrusions; and, secondly, by the study of the reuse of earlier coins in datable jewellery, as has been done in Britain (Rigold 1974).

[93] On the gradual shift of much market activity from towns to the countryside during the Empire, see Vera 1995: 339.

Period	No.	%
Republican	1	1.3
First century	2	2.5
Second century	3	3.8
Third century	17	21.5
Fourth century	56	70.9
Total	**79**	

Fig. 6:20. Quantities of coins listed by centuries from the Roman villa of Minori.

in the coin finds from Corinth (Edwards 1933).[94] Again, there is a high number of fourth-century coins, though, unlike Naples, the proportion drops considerably in the fifth century. In both cities, coins are virtually absent through the later seventh and eighth centuries, whilst in Corinth numbers start picking up again during the course of the ninth century. Revival of circulation in Naples is, instead, a phenomenon of later medieval times.

Though late Roman, earlier Byzantine and 'Vandal' coins are found with a certain frequency around Naples, all coins post-dating the emissions of Justinian are rare, excluding the imported copper issues of Heraclius and Constans II from a single hoard at Carminiello ai Mannesi (Sgherzi 1994). Excavations at Santa Patrizia have yielded two bronze *nummi* of Totila (541–549) from the mint of *Ticinum*, and three *pentanummi* of Justin II (565–578) from Ravenna. A bronze coin of Tiberius II (578–582) comes from a burial at Via San Paolo,

whilst another comes from the catacombs of San Gennaro.[95] Ischia has yielded a piece of Justin II.[96] A locally struck twenty *nummi* piece of Constans II comes from the Neapolitan site of Sant'Aniello (Cantilena 1987). Another seventh-century hoard of 129 Byzantine gold coins was discovered in a pot at *Lacco Ameno*, Ischia, and contained imported issues of Heraclius and Constans II (De Petra 1895). A limited circulation of these coins in internal Campania may be indicated by the discovery of a follis of Constans II at Gargani, Roccarainola (Capolongo 1987).[97] Only one coin of the independent duchy, a follis of Duke Athanasius II (878–898), has been found during excavations in Naples (from Sant'Aniello a Caponapoli (Cantilena 1987)). However, a possible issue of Duke John II or III comes from Santa Patrizia, whilst a bronze follis attributed to Duke Stephen II is known from Monte Vico, Ischia (Monti 1980: 293, fig. 129). Finally, from the city we may also count a tenth-century bronze of Constantine VII (950–959) (from Sant'Aniello a Caponapoli (Cantilena 1987)). From outside the Byzantine or local sphere are a coin of Charlemagne from Ischia (Monti 1980) and a hoard of gold coins, allegedly from Naples, comprising six Beneventan *tremisses* and one *semiss* and one *tremiss* of Heraclius.[98] Perhaps this is just the tip of an iceberg. The role of coins in daily exchange during the early Middle Ages is far from certain, and it may be asked whether they were used in paying some form of lip-

Period	CM	SP	VS	PT	VSP	SA	POL	Total	%
Republican	0	0	0	0	0	0	0	0	0
First	3	1	0	1	0	0	2	7	11.8
Second	0	0	0	0	0	0	1	1	1.7
Third	2	1	1	0	0	0	0	4	6.8
Fourth	8	3	1	0	0	0	0	12	20.3
Fifth	11	1	1	0	0	0	0	13	22.0
Sixth	7	9	0	0	1	0	0	17	28.8
Seventh	(32*)	0	0	0	0	1	0	1 (+ 32)	1.7
Eighth	0	0	0	0	0	0	0	0	0
Ninth	0	1	0	0	0	1	0	2	3.4
Tenth	0	0	0	0	0	1	0	1	1.7
Eleventh	0	0	0	0	0	1	0	1	1.7

*Fig. 6:21. Quantities by century of coins from excavations conducted in the city of Naples. For site abbreviations see Appendix I. * Single hoard of mid-seventh-century date.*

[94] See also the graph in Randsborg 1991: 134, fig. 73.

[95] Neither are published, though the second is on display in the museum of the catacombs of San Gennaro.

[96] This is a five *nummi* piece from *Cartaromana*, Ischia (Monti 1980: 326, fig. 138).

[97] Note the discovery of a gold coin of Arcadius in the woods behind Gragnano, to the south of Naples (Cosenza 1907: 309).

[98] The Naples hoard, found in 1896 and now in the Museo Nazionale delle Terme, Rome, is, unfortunately, of dubious provenance (Arslan 1994: 508, n. 90).

service to a die-hard tradition of monetary circulation. If we knew more about their use and status, we might be able to say more about the places in which they have been found.

Whilst middle Byzantine coinage is all but absent in Naples when compared to southern Apulia, Basilicata and Calabria, it probably circulated in the nearby Lombard town of Salerno. Bronzes of Emperors Romanus I (920–944) and Constantine VII (950–959) were used as flans for both Lombard and Norman coins struck there (Mangieri 1991: 20–1, 41).[99] I doubt if any base metal Byzantine coin circulated later, to judge from the coins found in Calabria and eastern Sicily, which terminate by this time. The last reference to Byzantine coin in Naples is the twenty *soldi* of Bithynian gold cited in a document of 1026 (*MND* I: 255, n. 406), whilst the first reference to the Arab *tarì* in Naples dates to 935 (*MND* I: 84, n. 23).[100]

Given the rarity of early medieval coin finds, I suggest that a waning monetary economy continued up to the reign of Justinian or Justin II, and that conditions supported limited monetary exchange for another 100 years, up to about the time of Constans II.[101] Even so, it was often necessary to draw upon substantially earlier issues, as may be deduced from coin hoards. By the later sixth, and, perhaps particularly, in the seventh centuries, both old and contemporary gold and bronze coins were quite regularly perforated in Italy to be used as pendants or inserts in jewellery. This suggests a radical change in the concept of coinage, which may assume a purely symbolic value of wealth, as in the case of more recent Bedouin and Berber monetary jewellery. Furthermore, it may be no coincidence that imported ceramics, including amphorae, are well attested into the first half of the sixth century and gradually tail off by the end of the seventh, perhaps indicating the collapse of a complex stratified market system. Though the mint of Naples continued production after Constans II, and up to and throughout the period of the independent duchy, output seems to have been so limited as to negate its use in day to day exchange. It may, however, have served a limited function at élite levels and in a local

system of tax collection.[102] The great differences in coin types encountered from area to area in southern Italy and Sicily, in the absence of regulated exchange systems such as we have today, will have negated the efficient functioning of coin in the market. It is possible that a mixture in the use of old bronze coinage (though we do not know how long bronze could circulate at the time), limited locally minted bronze (though how limited this really was, we do not know) and barter could cater for any necessary minor transactions. The tendency of the population, however, was towards individual self-sufficiency, which partly explains the growth of numerous private orchards within the city walls and changes in the composition of faunal assemblages. Such a system probably survived until the reintroduction of a fully-fledged monetary economy during the later Middle Ages (Martin 1983).

Only large transactions, including property, seem to have been regulated through the use of gold (Martin 1983: 192–3). In the ninth century, going by the documents, use was made of Beneventan gold in Naples and other parts of southern Italy. Indeed, von Falkenhausen postulated a relative well-being of southern Italy through the strong economic influence of Byzantium, when the rest of Italy and western Europe was represented by a silver standard (von Falkenhausen 1978a: 18–19).[103] Whilst agreeing about the relative wealth of the area, I find it hard to believe that this was due more to Byzantine influence than autonomous development, linked with the opportunities provided by Arab expansion in Sicily and elsewhere. It may be noted that even taxes such as the *portuaticum*, perhaps a development of the earlier *nauticatio*, paid by ships entering the ports of Naples, could be paid in kind as late as the eleventh century (*MND* II: 235–6, 378; Casssandro 1969: 207). A document of 1018 contests the payment for a ship, belonging to the monastery of San Sergio e Bacco, entering the larger port of the city, of a *modius* of grain, a jar of wine, half a *modius* of salt and two quarts of incense. A payment of a *modius* of salt and two quarts of incense was required for entrance to the smaller port (R. 378).

---

[99] A bronze coin of Constantine VII and Zoe (913–919) has been found at Capaccio Vecchia, above *Paestum* (Delogu 1976: no. 3).

[100] It is possible that the six gold coins from Arab Sicily in the Museum of Naples, of which the earliest dates to 841–857, come from the city (Scerrato 1967: 159).

[101] Indeed, the mint of Catania was opened to coin small bronze early in the reign of Maurice, around 582–583, and seems to have survived until about 630. Arslan (1994: 509) has stated that the real crisis began at the time of Heraclius.

[102] It has been suggested (for example, Haldon 1990: 119) that the paucity of coin after Constans II is a result of 'the state increasingly financing its forces with produce, equipment and so forth in kind'.

[103] She noted a singular dicovery of a hoard near Bologna, significantly composed of gold coins of Lombard Benevento (Arechis II: five examples), of Abbasid provenance (eleven) and from Byzantium (Leo II–Nicephoros I: 23 examples (Frati 1857)).

COMMERCE AND EXCHANGE

Roman Naples appears to have been a fairly typical antique 'consumer city'. Apart from some wine produced in her hinterland and accompanying black-glazed pottery under the Republic, there is no evidence of any production for an 'international' market that would place her in a different position to the majority of Roman consumer centres. Indeed, given her limited territory, she was presumably less productive than most other Campanian towns, from which grain and other produce was to be had in abundance. She was, none the less, able to feed partly off the enormous market generated at neighbouring *Puteoli*. Though I do not intend to enter into the thorny debate of the economic standing of Roman towns, I would stress that it was *Puteoli*, and not *Neapolis*, that was an exception to the general rule.[104] *Puteoli* was also a 'consumer city', but she developed a singular role as a major entrepôt within the Roman commercial structure (Frederiksen 1984, for example). Even if her role was less marked under the later Empire, though still stressed by the provisions of *annona* during the fourth century, what remained of *Puteoli*'s position was inherited by Naples through the fifth century. My argument is thus that Naples passed from being one of many Roman 'consumer towns', with productive activity geared essentially to meet local needs, to a city-state with, albeit limited, market production and the functions of an 'international' emporium, also serving a Lombard hinterland. To use a model developed from geographer's analyses of exchange systems, early medieval Naples might be defined as a dendritic central-place system, in which a monopolistic market (gateway community) occurred on the edge of a region to control exchange in prestige items (dyed purple cloths, jewellery, books and high-quality craftsmanship and know-how) and other valuable goods (timber, slaves, wine, weapons, linen), as well as the production of limited commodities for external distribution.[105] This role was perhaps also critical to the status of *Beneventum* in early medieval times.

What is also important here is the continuing, if not indeed strengthened, rapport that the city had with the countryside, perhaps indicated by a discrete survival of Roman centuriation in the hinterland. Though much of the reduced urban population may have been largely self-sufficient through the cultivation of the land plots within the partially abandoned Roman insulae, the Church, the monasteries and their dependent poor, and the civil and military community, depended on agricultural estates, with their larger and more varied yields, for sustenance, if not for the creation of a tradable surplus. This much seems clear from the rich Neapolitan archives (for example, Cilento 1969b: 666–8). Furthermore, from the seventh century, the economic base that ensured the survival of the militia was created through the assignation of land plots and no longer through any great centralized system of taxation, accountancy and payment (Brown 1984; Wickham 1988b: 108).

We might examine exchange processes on two levels, that of internal exchange within the territory of the duchy itself, and that of 'international' exchange. The first will show how there was relatively little isolation of town and countryside within the duchy, unlike other parts of early medieval Europe, and thus how it maintained a rather unusual strength and cultural cohesion. The second will demonstrate even more how Naples was able to survive as an urban complex, to become a decisive force in later medieval Italy.

In Roman times, quite aside from the permanent shops of Naples, much exchange with the Campanian hinterland and neighbouring regions functioned through the system of *nundinae* (Macmullen 1970; Frayn 1993). These were pre-established market-days that took place at a series of towns through a rotating system based on a public calendar. The travelling distances between the market centres was usually reasonable, for example, *Neapolis–Puteoli* = 12 km, *Neapolis–Cumae* = 16 km, *Neapolis–Nola* = 24 km, whilst *Nola* to *Cumae* was around 40 km. The sites in the Phlegrean Fields and the Sarno river area could also be reached by sea, as also, necessarily, could the islands. It would seem that the system broke down in late Roman or early post-Roman times. Though direct evidence is missing to date its collapse, future work on the distribution of ceramics may help to resolve the matter. Indeed, in a recent study, the decline of the late Roman pottery industries in southern and central Italy through the later fifth and the first half of the sixth centuries has been linked to the demise of the *nundinae*. This is based on the argument that the industries, though generally rurally based, served predominantly urban markets through the exchange system (Arthur and Patterson 1994).

---

[104] On this question, see Jongman's (1988) provocative *Pompeii* paradigm, to which I am indebted for certain ideas.

[105] For this and other models, see the discussion and references in Hodges 1982: chapter 1.

With the regression in commerce and exchange, the system of the *nundinae* seems to have been partly replaced by seasonal markets or fairs, suggesting a reduction in the scale of exchange. It seems also that trade and pilgrimage frequently went together, echoing the function of pre-Roman and early Roman Republican sanctuaries (Barnish 1989: 388). The famous sanctuary of San Felice at Cimitile lay at the junction of the main east–west route from Avellino and Benevento to Naples, and the north–south route through Campania. It was also at the end of a transhumance route, and gathered worshippers from as far as the Val di Tanagro, where an important fair was sited. It had probably become the centre of a major fair itself, attracting shepherds in the lambing season, peasants with their meagre surplus products, peripatetic craftsmen, merchants and, of course, pilgrims. The fair may have lasted throughout much of early medieval times, though it was but one of a series of seasonal fairs for which evidence in southern Italy is gradually accumulating.[106] The parish church of Santa Maria at Nocera, for example, held a smaller fair. It took place in a field, on the other side of the road from the church, 'in quo annualiter in festo sancte Marie de mense septembri mercatum peragitur'. From the beginning of the ninth century, transactions had also been conducted 'in atrio sancte Marie' (Ruggiero 1975b; *CDC* I: v. 6; I: lxxix. 102–3; I: xcix. 126–8).

Thus, quite aside from its role in the buttressing of holy status, the early Christian search for prestigious relics and traditions was probably also oriented towards the creation of places of exchange. The evident expenditure on the sanctuary of Cimitile can, indeed, be explained through prospects of an effective economic return, and who better to develop it in its early days than Paulinus, a retired estate owner. No one can deny the scale of commerce instigated by the pilgrimages and crusades to that holiest of sites, Jerusalem, and it is likely that Suger's famous abbey of Saint Denis, on the outskirts of Paris, was partly built from the funds generated by similar activity.[107]

In addition to regular commercial activity held within the walls, Naples had its own extramural fair. Amatus of Monte Cassino told how the 'fair and market' were opened to the Normans in the eleventh century on the outskirts of the city, in a marshy area, rich in spring water (Amato II. xv. 307). Might the sanctuary of San Gennaro have acted as such in earlier times?

The distribution of certain bronze items in southern Italy, such as the bronze 'Lupu biba' incised brooches, often extremely similar to one another in type and manufacture, suggests the existence of itinerant craftsmen (Fig. 6:22) (Salvatore 1979).[108] They appear mainly to have been produced by a single workshop and, if so, the only other likely way that their archaeological distribution may have been formed is through the work of itinerants. They presumably frequented fairs as well as travelling between surviving centres.[109]

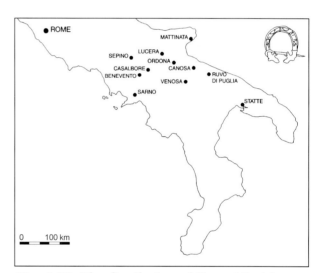

Fig. 6:22. The distribution of 'Lupu biba' bronze fibulae (drawn by author and Sally Cann).

Apart from the development of fairs, one of the results of the breakdown of the Roman exchange system and of the network of *nundinae* was that trade was forced progressively towards the coasts, leading to desertion of part of the ancient road

---

[106] One of the best attested fairs is that of Leucothea, held on Saint Cyprian's day, at the site of *Marcellianum*, near the old Roman town of *Consilinum*, Val di Tanagro. It is significant that the settlement of Sala Consilina (in the province of Salerno) subsequently developed at the site, suggesting its continued importance from when the fair was first attested, by Cassiodorus (*Var.* VIII. 30), through Lombard and later times.

[107] On the tight interaction between pilgrimage and trade, see, for example, Stopford 1994.

[108] Other examples are from Sarno (Iannelli 1988: esp. fig. 4), Ordona (Mertens 1995: 352, fig. 354), località Beneficio, Monte Marano, Benevento (Franciosi 1982: 445–6), Casalbore (additional information kindly supplied by Roberto Padrevita).

[109] This would resolve the issue posed by Salvatore (1979: 347–8), who noted that the brooches bear both Lombard and Roman names, apparently inscribed by the craftsmen on commission. Rather than the various clients travelling to the workshops, the names could have been applied at the moment of sale during the craftsmen's tour of the fairs.

system. Indeed, there is little evidence that roads themselves were systematically maintained after the fifth century, even when still used. The decline in internal traffic is reflected in the fall off through time of African red slip ware and, slightly later, by the limited find-spots of Byzantine coins. Though the published evidence is still insufficient for us to be able to attempt regression analyses, it is clear that the distribution of African red slip ware diminished markedly in the sixth century, as in much of Italy. The latest, seventh-century, forms have been recognized only in Naples itself and a few other select areas (Fentress and Perkins 1988).

After the sixth century, the little professional commerce that did continue within land-locked areas, or between the coast and the interior, was probably of two sorts. Major commerce was represented by the search for slaves, wood and other valued items. It was probably largely this that kept open both commercial and political links between land-locked Benevento and Naples. Such goods, upon reaching Naples, could then be shipped out to Rome or even to north Africa and the East. The other form of exchange was at gift level, reinforcing political ties. Perhaps the Senise gold jewellery, possibly made in Naples and found in the Lombard territory of Benevento, testifies to such a mechanism. It may also have involved expert craftsmen for one-off commissions in building, wall-painting and the like.

However, the most striking feature of production is that it seems to have been geared above all towards self-sufficiency. This appears evident from the lower levels of provisions, from gardens and orchards, to the upper levels of institutions and powerful families where the distribution of landholdings in varied terrains could guarantee the appropriate circulation of all manner of products of the land (Grierson 1959: 128, for example). Apart from those of the papacy, one may recall the numerous holdings of monasteries such as San Vincenzo al Volturno, distributed not only in Naples, but throughout southern Italy (*Chronicon Vulturnense passim*). Only the lowest social classes were excluded from this mechanism, and the Church, in particular, attempted to provide for them, in true Christian spirit.

The archaeological evidence presented earlier in this chapter demonstrates brisk exchange in primary commodities, even with the East, into the seventh century, unlike many other areas of Italy. Well into late antiquity, a relatively free open market seems to have existed. The same commodities, though clearly in varying percentages, could be found throughout the urban communities of the Mediterranean and beyond. From the mid-sixth century, the particular composition of many imports to Naples, represented above all by pottery, suggests that processes of directional trade were being reinforced by central government, by the Church and by landowners. After 600, alongside African imports, there were amphorae and pottery from eastern areas gravitating around Constantinople. In the western Mediterranean, the Samos cistern amphorae seem to have been directed towards Naples, Rome, Ravenna, Otranto, Syracuse (?) and Carthage, around which there seems to be some evidence of a fall off.[110] The proposed model of directional trade might be recognized 'by break-of-bulk operations (storehouses, organizational systems, waste materials) and by signs of preferential supply in large quantity. In favourable cases, both of these will result in a higher frequency of finds and hence in a departure from the monotonic decrease effect encountered with non-directional trade' (Renfrew 1984: 150). The late antique centres mentioned above, to paraphrase Colin Renfrew, were being 'supplied preferentially (with respect to their neighbours)', outside of a strictly commercial cost-profit mechanism (Renfrew 1984: 149). It is argued that much of this material, because of its singular nature with respect to finds from other contemporary Italian sites, may, in effect, represent 'doles from other parts of the Empire' upon which Naples may have depended into the second half of the seventh century, if not later (Lopez 1959: 72).

A certain amount of private enterprise clearly continued. As long as trade was remunerative, we may imagine wealthy merchants engaged in tramping the coasts between important markets.[111] The early seventh-century Yassi Ada ship, which sunk around 625, looks to be ecclesiastic (Bass and Van Doorninck 1982), whilst the mixed composition of cargoes from shipwrecks, such as that found off Cefalù, Sicily, may well be the result of buying and selling from port to port (Purpura 1983).

---

[110] It is interesting to find both Naples and Ravenna involved in a preferential Byzantine supply mechanism by the seventh century, as precursors to the later development of Amalfi and Venice as powerful trading states with more than an economic foothold in Byzantium. Indeed, one of the most potent factors in the development of the maritime city-states and their commercial strength must have been the traditional links with the Byzantine East.

[111] This is the French 'navigation de cabotage' (Ahrweiler 1978: 276).

However, despite Toynbee's belief that the Arab naval offensive of 649–678 did not paralyse maritime trade, these were difficult times for Byzantium, and lasted until about 747, with the defeat of the Arab fleet off Cyprus (Toynbee 1973: 45).[112] Though this much seems to be illustrated by the growing body of archaeological evidence from the eastern Mediterranean, traffic never totally ceased. The Anglo-Saxon monk, Willibald of Wessex, later bishop of Eichstatt, travelled widely during these difficult years (Holder-Egger 1887; Talbot 1954; Tobler 1974). During his pilgrimage to Jerusalem he stopped off in Paphos in 723, only to remark that the island was 'inter Graecos et Saracenos'. After Constantinople, he visited Lipari in 729, and was in Rome the next year, having doubtlessly passed through Naples.[113] He recorded a ship from Egypt harbouring in the city in the 720s. Later, the difficulties in communications may have relaxed and, in 787, we find that a certain Gregory from Rome, alongside various Sicilian bishops, had attended the second ecumenical council of Nicea to discuss the iconoclast heresy (Sauget 1968; Ostrogorsky 1968: 162).[114] In 820, Saint Gregory Decapolite travelled from Reggio to Rome on a ship from Naples (Dölger 1953: 358–9).

None the less, it may well have been the loosening of eastern control and diminishing supplies that prompted Naples's secession by the second half of the eighth century, after the loss of Ravenna. As Toynbee wrote (1973: 281),

> the Italian city-states that were nominally under East Roman sovereignty — particularly Venice, Amalfi, Naples and Gaeta — were the beneficiaries from the economic war between the East Roman Empire and the Umayyad Caliphate that was started by the East Roman Imperial Government during and after the second Arab siege of Constantinople in 717–18.

Restrictions were placed on Byzantine traders, and their activity was never held in great esteem in the East. This opened the way for the small western maritime powers who, as middlemen between the Empire, the Muslims and the West, were able to build up economic fortunes. One need only remember the 1,200 pounds of gold left on the death of the Venetian merchant-doge Giustiniano Partecipazio in 829 (Cessi 1942: 95).

During his stay in Italy, Constans II reorganized western Byzantine territories and introduced taxation on maritime traffic (*nauticationes*) controlled by the *kommerkiarioi* or customs officials, as in the eastern Empire (Ahrweiler 1961). This would hardly seem to be a sign of cessation in mediterranean-wide trade, even if its volume had been severely reduced. This much is demonstrable archaeologically. Whilst material evidence for later centuries is scarce, there is not much doubt that commerce continued to be important to Naples's well-being throughout the Dark Ages. By the mid-eighth century, the documents contain references to *negotiantes* or *negotiatores* (for example, Cassandro 1969: 250–6). Furthermore, the *naukleroi* of Byzantine times were not the same as the tied *navicularii* of late Roman times. With the breakdown of compulsory guilds, they were able to manage their own affairs without the debilitating pressure of central government. Neapolitan ships plying the Tyrrhenian coast are attested even more from the ninth century, though they are curiously absent in sources referring to Italian traders in the East. However, it is quite unlikely that Naples did not engage in commerce with the East, or attempt to tap the rich Muslim world. Perhaps her interests were largely disguised, in that they may have been attended to above all by Amalfi and by Amalfitan traders resident or trafficking in the city: Pope Hadrian I, in the late eighth century, spoke of 'Amalfitani ducati neapolitani' and 'optimates Graecorum sedentes in Neapolim' (Galasso 1965: 111).[115] Neapolitan interests in commerce are, furthermore, evidenced by a treaty of 836, the *Pactum Sicardi*, between Naples and Sicard of Benevento. It demonstrates concern about, in particular, the obtaining of slaves from Lombard areas not, I believe, for use in Naples, and is contemporary with the city's emission of gold coinage. Already by this time, Amalfi, as a dependency of Naples, seems to have possessed a fundamental role as intermediary, which is shown in the treaty by an entire chapter dedicated

---

[112] For the archaeological evidence, see the summary by Sinclair Hood in Ballance *et al.* 1989: 7–8.

[113] Frederiksen (1977: 125, n. 28) remarked on the standard route from Sicily to Rome, passing through the Aeolian islands, Naples/Pozzuoli, Gaeta and Terracina. See Proc. *Bell. Goth*. III. vi. 14–18. The importance of Lipari and its adjoining isles is well supported with archaeological evidence (Bernabò Brea 1988).

[114] Gregory was probably part of a legation from Rome that had really travelled east to beg from Constantinople the restoration of papal patrimonies confiscated after the fall of Ravenna (Every 1962: 95).

[115] The trading professions were not highly regarded by the Byzantines. 'The attitude of the emperor Theophilus when confronted with the mere possibility of being considered a *naukleros* ... contrasts so beautifully with the clear and contemporary operation of the Imperial hypatos and doge, Giustiniano Partecipazio, as an actual and habitual investor in overseas trading ventures' (Hendy 1985: 169).

to her status and entitled *De Amalfinis qualiter pera-gantur* (Galasso 1965: 108–12). Above all, the form of the treaty appears to indicate Naples's conscious exploitation of the possibilities that Amalfi was able to offer. In part this may have been because a substantial part of Naples's overseas commerce was in the hands of Oriental merchants who found it increasingly difficult to maintain their contacts with the Levant and north Africa following Arab expansionism. This may have been further exacerbated by the Arab conquest of Sicily and the politically difficult position in which Naples, as a nominal Byzantine duchy, found itself in respect to trade with an erstwhile Byzantine theme. We might recall how the Byzantines, not surprisingly, disapproved of traders who furnished war materials to their enemies and, indeed, in the 870s, Louis II had accused Naples of furnishing 'arma, alimenta et cetera subsidia' to the Arabs (*Anon. Salern.*, *Chronicon* II. 2). Amalfi might have been regarded as conveniently out of all this, and there is no doubt that the small coastal settlement made the most out of her position, particularly after gaining her independence from Naples in 839. Furthermore, it appears to be a point of fact that her vigorous development as a mediterranean-wide commercial power coincides both with the Arab conquest of Sicily and with the decline in Neapolitan direct overseas involvement.

Citarella cited the main products for Venetian exchange in north Africa and the East, during the tenth and eleventh centuries, as slaves, timber, iron and agricultural products (Citarella 1968: 537). We have seen how the Neapolitan treaty with Benevento regarded slaves, and how Naples still produced a surplus of wine in the eighth century and linen right through the Dark Ages. It might have obtained wood from the Surrentine peninsula, if not from Benevento itself.[116] Thus, there can be little doubt that the city had goods to trade with the Arab world.

In 839 the Lombards of Benevento took Amalfi, and this may have been the point that signalled the decline of Neapolitan hegemony. By the tenth century, Neapolitan maritime power, whether private or public, seems to have become a shadow of its former self, and Campanian mediterranean-wide commerce seems to have passed into the hands of Gaeta, to the north, and Salerno and, in particular, Amalfi, to the south (Galasso 1965: 108). On the archaeological side, it may be noted that there is little evidence of imported or exported pottery until the later eleventh or twelfth century. This seems typical of other contemporary sites and thus cannot be used in the evaluation of Naples in isolation, or as a true index for the innumerable perishable goods that were objects of trade. Continued construction within the city, if not increased investment in the sector, does suggest that, despite an apparently weaker control over maritime commerce, a certain economic solvency was maintained.

It is by no means insignificant that by the later ninth and tenth centuries many transactions in coastal Campania were made in imported Arab coin, which, it may be noted, was of a higher gold standard than local currency. In 977, Ibn Hawqal judged Naples second only to Amalfi as a commercial centre, and this source must not be underestimated. By the mid-eleventh century, commerce with the Arab world seems to have been thriving sufficiently to have permitted the growth of a resident Arab community. This much is suggested by three tombstones inscribed in Kufic from the city (Scerrato 1967: 150–7, nos. 317, 320, 323). The earliest may be dated to 1054, and records the sepulchre of a judge, doctor and imam, possibly from Islamic Spain. Scerrato has suggested (1967: 150–1) that another, dated 1073, may record an exile from Sicily, which had fallen to the Normans the previous year . Thus, though Naples appears to have had an openly hostile policy towards the Arabs in the period immediately before and after the destruction of their colony, at the battle of the Garigliano in 915 (Skinner 1995: 38), commercial relations appear to have been maintained more or less continuously from the ninth century, if not earlier, when the city had broken away from Byzantine control.

As little other evidence exists at present to evaluate Naples's role at this time, I feel that too much weight has been placed on the scale of her decline, arguments being *ex silentio*. Naples's elaborate port facilities were well used by Amalfitan traders up until the decline of Amalfi from the late eleventh century.[117] The advantage of her position had also been recognized by other maritime city-states. Indeed, not long afterwards, Pisan traders showed great concern over Norman hegemony of coastal Campania, and not least Naples.[118]

---

[116] Wood was always a prized commodity in the Mediterranean (Braudel 1975: 239).

[117] On this section, and particularly on the changing fortunes of Amalfi and of emigrated Amalfitan merchants, see also Figliuolo 1993: 78–81.

[118] On Pisan traders resident by the port, see Galasso 1965: 116. Fuiano (1972: 44–8) discussed the concern of Pisan traders about Roger's conquest of Naples. This is supported archaeologically by the distribution of Neapolitan glazed ceramic bowls (*bacini*) in Pisa from the early twelfth century (Berti and Tongiorgi 1981).

THE BIRTH OF A CAPITAL

In September 1140, after some 60 years of political and physical struggles, the Normans led by King Roger II de Hauteville entered the city of Naples, putting an end to its autonomous rule. Roger did not find an essentially Byzantine population or culture group, as his kinsmen had encountered in the Terra d'Otranto, but a rather cosmopolitan society, reflecting centuries of the city's involvement in international affairs. Alongside remnants of a Graeco-Roman society, were Byzantine Greeks, Syrians, Jews, Arabs, Lombards, descendants of the Ostrogoths and various western Europeans. The presence of this motley crowd partly explains the relatively rapid disappearance of Greek cultural elements in Naples when compared to the theme of *Langouvardia*, where Byzantine culture was far more deeply rooted (Guillou 1977: 61).[1]

It has been argued that the Norman administration was detrimental to Naples's economic development. Though Naples undoubtedly took second place to Palermo in Norman affairs, reflecting its later submission to the new power, the little archaeological evidence that is available for the Norman period does not confirm a view of economic recession. Indeed, paradoxically, it may have been the Norman conquest of Sicily from the Arabs, sealed by the foundation of the *regnum Siciliae* by Roger in 1113, that aided the commerce of Naples, as it did for much of the western Mediterranean.

To understand Naples's position after the year 1000, and to understand what she represents today, it is necessary to attempt a synthesis of the archaeological evidence for the period stretching across the second half of the first millennium. Of eighteen sites excavated in the city in the 1980s, ten yielded evidence concentrating between the late fourth and the seventh centuries, though one excavation in particular, Santa Patrizia, also provided abundant material of the eighth and early ninth centuries. The story presented here takes its lead from the pattern seen to be emerging from these recent excavations.

During the early Middle Ages we may identify various changes in the city when compared to earlier times. It often has been stressed how the near-perfect survival of the street-grid is quite unique, even when compared to towns in northern Italy where the phenomenon is decidedly more common, and is in itself indicative of some form of settlement continuity since classical times (see above, p. 38). Within the insulae, late antiquity saw a substantial abandonment, or change in function, of Roman buildings and spaces, both public and private. During the fifth and sixth centuries, a large insula block (Fig. 0:1, CM) was abandoned by its inhabitants and used, in turn, for burning lime, retrieving *spolia* and dumping rubbish, leading eventually to the blocking of a *cardo* or *stenopos*. By the tenth century, the *cardo* seems to have been known as Vico Clusa. Other *cardines* by the forum and beneath the modern cathedral were likewise blocked with rubbish. Rubbish also blocked drains and festered, thus helping to create the conditions that saw a proliferation of black rats, the type known to be a carrier of the plague. The greatest urban changes, however, came about during the sixth century, rather than the fifth. Both the *odeion* and the *macellum* were abandoned, reusable marbles and tiles ripped off, and perhaps the earliest burials within the *pomerium* were inserted into their fabrics. During the reign of Justinian and in the years of restoration that immediately followed the end of the Gothic War, three major churches were built over old Roman buildings, only one, San Lorenzo, certainly on erstwhile public space, by the forum. This activity was followed by an hiatus of almost two centuries in monumental building, which can be compared with Rome, where, between 590 and 772, the erection of only three churches is attested. In Naples, what evidence does exist for building, aside from meagre historical sources, is limited to adjustments made to standing structures. It was also in the sixth and early seventh centuries that layers of dark

---

[1] C.D. Fonseca pers. comm.; A. Jacob pers. comm.

earth began to form in various areas between walls. This soil type appears to represent the existence of substantial cultivation within and between former structures. If our attention is turned to the countryside, it is again the fifth and early sixth centuries that see the most dramatic changes according to the archaeological evidence. Though, unlike many other areas of Italy, the Roman rural settlement distribution survived to a fair degree up to the early sixth century, with about an eighth of the villa and farm sites examined in the Phlegrean Fields yielding late Roman pottery, there are no signs of later activity. It is hard to escape the conclusion that there was a partial shift of agricultural activity to within the walls of Naples, stimulated by the farmers' sense of insecurity, and made possible by a very real population decline in the preceding decades. Such processes may have affected the town of *Cumae*, whilst *Puteoli* and *Misenum* became small fortified *castra*.

The evidence of both faunal and ceramic remains reinforces this vision of the ruralization of the urban habitat of Naples. Roman faunal assemblages are essentially pig dominated. During the later fifth to sixth centuries sheep/goat began to dominate, and this pattern lasted, more or less, into the eighth century. Pottery also changed, not only from a Roman style 'factory' production to a simpler one, perhaps based on small part-time artisanal workshops, but also in the nature of the various forms. Cooking wares, in particular, now include portable bread ovens and a series of casseroles similar to those used today for simple rural recipes. Indeed, what little material culture survived stood in stark contrast to that of Roman times, suggesting the scarcity of an agricultural surplus able to sustain secondary manufacturing activities.

It is perhaps largely a modern construct to associate rural custom with poverty, though, in the case of late antique and early medieval Naples, such an association may not be far off the mark. No single archaeological element indicates poverty in itself, and here we may lament the scarcity of anthropological analyses, which can be telling as regards nutrition and health. However, a general impoverishment of the town is suggested by increased ruralization, lack of new architecture, widespread rubbish accumulation (itself leading to a decline in sanitary conditions), a simplified material culture and the virtual disappearance of a monetary economy, with all its possibilities.

On what may seem to be a more positive note, during the later fifth and sixth centuries, a period for which most Campanian towns have yielded little archaeological evidence of intense activity, some indeed appearing close to desertion, Naples was importing fair quantities of pottery and foodstuffs. Transport amphorae arrived from southern Italy, Tunisia and the eastern Mediterranean, some containing olive oil and many containing wine. Furthermore, it was one of the few areas of Italy that seems to have been producing its own transport amphorae, suggesting the creation of a minimum surplus, perhaps of wine, for export. By the seventh century, local amphorae seem to have disappeared, and the number of imported vessels appears to have declined, most by then coming from the eastern Mediterranean, though their relative quantity still remained significant in contrast to that at most other old Roman towns. Some of this presumably represented market exchange though, as time passed, it may have increasingly represented imposed directional trade (*dirigisme*), mainly by central government and ecclesiastical authorities, institutions still strong enough to make long-distance shipping viable. This interpretation may be supported by two further archaeological phenomena: a presence of Byzantine bronze coinage that might have lasted until Constans II, and the reconstruction of the town walls with the provision of typical Byzantine pentagonal prow-towers, probably dating to after the refurbishment that took place under Valentinian III.

Archaeology has thus highlighted various social and cultural changes in Naples and its surrounding territory. Depopulation of the city is indicated by the abandonment of living areas and their conversion to activities traditionally held outside the walls, such as rubbish disposal, burial and agriculture. The rise in sheep/goat consumption and the change in some cooking ware types, including the appearance of the portable bread oven, and the creation of cultivable land within the city walls, is an indication of increasing ruralization of the urban habitat, and perhaps also an indication of urban impoverishment. However, capital expenditure is marked by the construction of a number of extravagant churches, as at Rome and Ravenna, and the refitting of the walls, which, it may be recalled, were about 4.5 km in length. The circulation of coinage and the importation of goods, even from the eastern Mediterranean, if not also from the Far East, also suggest some form of long-distance exchange.[2]

---

[2] See, for example, the Indo-Pacific Tridacna shell from Carminiello ai Mannesi (Cretella 1994). Cassiodorus was aware of these shellfish from the Indian Ocean (*Var.* I. 35).

The lesser quantity of archaeological evidence after the mid-seventh century shows, none the less, the local production of transport amphorae and of good quality ceramics in the later eighth and ninth centuries, and suggests, once again, that the territory of Naples was producing some exportable surplus and, perhaps, creating new capital. A gradually increasing 'cash-flow' would have led to greater exchange and the resurgence of professions, of which that of the potter is best illustrated through the reappearance of finely made wares, with very close parallels to vessels from Rome. Aside from occasional eastern amphorae, imports now included some worked stone vessels from Alpine areas and a little pottery from the area of Rome itself. The faunal remains revert back to the 'Roman style' pig-dominated pattern that had gradually disappeared during the fifth and sixth centuries. We may suggest that this is an indication of a gradual reurbanization of the city and transference of much rural activity, once again outside the walls, confirmed slightly later by the new *casalia* or villages of the documents (see above, p. 93). Despite the appearance of good historical source material that suggests a boom in building activity by the tenth century, physical evidence for new construction in and around the city is slight. It includes a bath-building erected, probably, sometime around the year 1000, and the conversion of the small basilical church of San Costanzo, Capri, into one with a Byzantine quincunx plan. Whatever their precise date, I doubt that they can be placed after the Norman invasion of the city.

I believe that this summary does some justice to the available archaeological evidence. The final effort of this essay is to attempt a reconstruction of historical processes through a combined reading of archaeological and historical source material.

Naples is traditionally seen as having had an economy orientated towards the sea. This is by no means true for the beginning of the early Middle Ages. The sea alone could not support the population of such a substantial urbanized community and, with the waning of maritime trade from the sixth century, the city was increasingly reliant on its fertile hinterland. Naples was, however, fortunate in that it had inherited a large territory formed through the dissolution of surrounding Roman towns, and that this territory was one of the most economically productive in the whole of the mediterranean basin. Its hold and exploitation of the land, far more successful than that managed by hundreds of other old classical towns, is partly indicated by the longer survival of dispersed agricultural settlement in central Campania. When this disappeared, also by the mid-sixth century, it was not because of an abandonment of the land in agricultural terms, but simply because of a redistribution or retreat of manpower to within the security of fortified *castra*, such as the acropolis of *Cumae* and Rione Terra, Pozzuoli, or within the city of Naples itself.

The ability to stave off the Lombards, and at the same time to maintain a 'satisfactory' level of agrarian production, guaranteed the city's survival throughout the difficult years of the seventh and eighth centuries, without having to rely to any great extent on the sea. Paradoxically, this very success may have stunted the city's development as a maritime power. Indeed, it was the far smaller settlement of Amalfi, significantly lacking in good or extensive landed territory like Genoa or Venice, that, for a time, was able to take the lead in this sector.

The fairly rich material and documentary evidence now available, the mere existence of which is telling, evokes an articulated scheme of growing urban development and political influence.

1. By the fourth century, *Neapolis* was a coastal town, but not of any great consequence, having lost its prime commercial position to *Puteoli* during the late Republic. It was, none the less, involved in the mediterranean-wide exchange network, and well-linked to the rich agricultural hinterland of the *ager Campanus* and the area around Vesuvius. Nearby *Puteoli*, on the other hand, was still important to maritime commerce and to the supply to Rome, and *Misenum* still housed the imperial fleet.

2. Through the later fifth and sixth centuries, with *Puteoli*'s inexorable decline, Naples became evermore important as a strategic centre and, by virtue of this fact, attracted the interests of government as a central place. This led to its development, both in economic and political terms, first under Rome and later under the Ostrogothic administration. It may be shown to be involved in directional trade, together with Rome and Marseilles, through the distribution of southern Calabrian and eastern Sicilian wine amphorae.

Though slightly later, increased taxation by the Byzantine government, after Justinian's reconquest of Africa and Italy, may have bled certain areas dry: key strongholds, such as Ravenna, Syracuse and Naples, might have been affected positively as recipients of the entries. But there is more. The Justinianic policy of reconquest was probably not intent on reuniting the whole of Spain and Gaul with the rest of the Empire simply for the meagre returns of an ideology, but rather aimed to consolidate the old and rich agricultural power base of which Campania formed a significant part.

As a result of reconquest, the new Byzantine western frontier, up until the Lombard and Arab invasions, may be seen as being the Alps, the Tyrrhenian coast of Italy and the coast of the Maghreb. Strategic points had to be buttressed if there was to be any hope of holding the Empire together, along with the collection and redistribution of local agricultural surplus, keeping open the principal centres for taxation and maintaining Rome as a symbol of imperial power. Indeed, the mention of refortifications in inscriptions and texts, and the construction of *castra* indicate the importance attached to Naples. It was certainly not defended purely for its own sake, and was clearly sought out as a defensible site with a rich agricultural hinterland along a strategic communication and supply route to Rome.[3] The considerable effort spent on safeguarding Naples and other areas, both by the Byzantine government and by the Church, highlights the vital importance of this artery. The Church had already assumed a good measure of authority and responsibility with the breakdown of central government in the West, and this is particularly evident after Justinian and the Lombard conquest, and especially during the papacy of Gregory the Great.

None the less, increasing evidence regarding dark earth layers, certain ceramic forms and farmyard animals roaming the town seems also to indicate an increasing blurring of the distinction between town and country, which had been so evident in Roman times.

3. Thus, with the increasingly difficult hold that Constantinople had on Italy, the strongholds of Ravenna, Rome, Naples and southern Italy were courted. Naples's increasingly important role, seen during and after the Justinianic campaigns of reconquest, is again highlighted by the visit of Emperor Constans II to Byzantine domains in Lombard Italy, in the mid-seventh century.[4] He established a local mint in Naples, and the first direct nomination in a long line of stable, and eventually hereditary, dukes. There is also some evidence to suggest that the city and its *castra* continued to receive imported goods,

even from the East, up to the end of the century, even if the latter half of the century was also a period of relative neglect by Byzantium, hard pressed as it was by the Arabs. In Roman times taxation by central government had stimulated free trade. The breakdown of taxation, or rather of a balanced system of taxation, along with the breakdown of central government, had dealt a decisive blow to the open market. Indeed, the material evidence seems to confirm that, with the breakdown of external stimuli to production, people reverted back to producing only what they needed.

Though rural settlement declined drastically, this happened later than in other parts of Italy, and is perhaps to be accounted for more by political than by economic factors. Indeed, in Raymond Lopez's words, 'if the core of the Empire did not suffer too much from amputations at the periphery, readjustment was hard for those maritime towns whose hinterland fell under barbarian rule. Thessalonica, Cherson, Carthage, Rome and Naples were the most notable among such towns in the seventh century' (Lopez 1959: 72). The Lombard invasions represented the clash of a chiefdom-based society with what now approached an early state society. This created positive feedback to Lombard culture, and, at first, negative feedback to an already weakened classical culture, thus hastening the final disintegration of the classical world system in Italy. But, I will argue, it was the emerging Lombard state of Benevento that eventually guaranteed Naples's survival after the later sixth- and seventh-century depression.

Without the strong external interests, or rather the protectionist policy shown by Byzantium, the city would probably have reached the low point seen in so many other areas of coastal and inland Italy. Between the later seventh and mid-eighth centuries, it had certainly reached the lowest point in its own economic history.[5]

4. As a direct result of Byzantium's loosening hold and lack of aid to Italy, culminating in the capitulation of Ravenna to the Lombard king Aistulf in 751, Naples had to fall back on her own resources to survive. This may be seen by the later eighth century, if not earlier, when the Neapolitan economy seems to have been picking up under its own steam, signalled by the city's decisive move

---

[3] The same policy also resulted in the relatively short-lived development of Ravenna as an administrative core.

[4] See the comments by Zanini (1998: 143–5).

[5] Galasso (1965: 67) saw Naples touching the bottom of the barrel somewhat earlier, during the sixth century. It was perhaps mainly during the seventh and early eighth centuries that pottery from Lombard Benevento was least like that from Byzantine Naples (see above, Chapter 6).

towards administrative independence from Constantinople. This was aided and abetted by the emergence of new and powerful, semi-dynastic, families, who grafted onto the Byzantine administrative hierarchy, and who were also able to limit, and eventually to absorb, ecclesiastical authority by the creation of family ties. At this point in time, Naples might be defined as a dendritic central-place system, to use a geographer's term, functioning as a gateway community sited on the edge of Campania and controlling exchange, including that of prestige goods, as well as producing a limited number of commodities for external distribution.

Samuel Barnish is undoubtedly right in maintaining that one of the principal features that kept alive towns in northern Italy, Syria and Palestine, and, we might add, a couple of centres on the northern Black Sea coast, was their continued role as gateway settlements and economic mediators. 'Where trade continued to pass through a city, or to be carried in its ships, tolls could still be exacted, and nobles still be tempted to reside in the hope of exotic luxuries and opportunities for their display' (Barnish 1989: 394). Lombard Benevento especially had to rely partly on Naples for external communications, at least until Salerno gained independence in the 770s–780s under Arechis, and Amalfi established its own autonomy in 838/839. Even after this date, bad relations between the various Lombard states may have reinforced Naples's role as intermediary from time to time, and the city was, geographically, a far more natural outlet for Benevento than either Salerno or Amalfi.

The growth of Naples's own economy and polity must be compared with the contemporary Carolingian 'renaissance', about which much has been made.[6] The coincidence is too strong to be fortuitous, though whether the causative factor was Carolingian expansion and its effects on European economic development, or whether one should look elsewhere for the stimulus to Neapolitan and Campanian growth, is debatable. Little is known about relationships with the Carolingian Empire. In 826, Naples sought aid from Louis the Pious against the Lombard expansion of Benevento, though, not long after, Francia seems to have supported Amalfi in favour of the duchy (Sancti Iohannis Damasceni, *Epistola ad Theophilum Imperatorem*).[7] It should be stressed, however, that the Frankish invasion of Italy did not really include the south, even if Lombard Benevento briefly became a tributary state.

Instead, on a pan-mediterranean level, the relative autonomy of the Italian city-states enabled them to take advantage, as privileged intermediaries, of the trade block between Byzantium and the Umayyad Caliphate created after the second Arab siege of Constantinople in 717–718. A slow economic growth, even if still tentative through much of the early eighth century, already involved Naples's satellite settlement of Amalfi, as well as, of course, Venice. Later, with the rise of Genoa and the growth of Arab economic power, these city-states created a competitive, entrepreneurial, sea that was to survive in much of its original form until the Ottoman expansion of the fifteenth century and the Hapsburg rise to power. Indeed, we may identify the multiplier effect taking place within the context of a new mediterranean and, dare I say, European wide exchange system, transcending cultural boundaries.

During the first half of the ninth century, Naples struck coinage in gold, possibly already made available through trade with the Arabs who had, during the course of the century, gained the monopoly of Sudanese reserves (Grierson 1961: 41–2, 47; Hendy 1985: 423; see also above, Chapter 6). A surplus of wine was produced and exported. Animal husbandry was, perhaps, becoming more profit oriented. A political and commercial pact, regarding, above all, slaves, was signed with Benevento in 836. However, and perhaps solely because of the chronological limitations of the Neapolitan documents, it was not until the following century that various churches and scattered village settlements seem to make their debut. In fact, they probably began to make their appearance earlier, and I would correlate the growth of Naples's economy and increasing reurbanization with the development of the countryside, which assumes, once again, its own particular characteristics. All told, things appeared to be on the up. Evidence thus seems to be accumulating to show that the Neapolitan city-state enjoyed a period of relative prosperity, perhaps during the second half of the eighth and certainly from the first half of the ninth centuries. Aside from the blow dealt by the declared autonomy of Amalfi, there is little evidence to show that it declined substantially thereafter. One need only recall the words of praise for Naples's linen towards the end of the tenth century by Ibn Hawqal, who was, after all, a merchant from

---

[6] See particularly the thesis of Hodges and Whitehouse (1983).
[7] This is an apocryphal text. See the discussion by Hendy (1985: 669).

Baghdad. Though much of this trade was probably at first limited to luxuries, it helped to define a power base from which a more articulated economy would develop.

Developments in the Arab world itself may thus help to explain the south Italian revival. Already, in the second half of the seventh century, the expanding Islamic world had shown interest in the prospects offered by Byzantine Italy. In 668–669, the Ummayad governor of Egypt, Abd-Allah ibn Qaïs, raided Sicily (Vasiliev 1959: 63). But despite this Islamic aggression, coming to a head with the Arab siege of Constantinople in 717–718, monk Willibald of Wessex records an Egyptian ship in the port of Naples in the 720s. Indeed, the city may have continued to foster links with the Near East through its role as a major stopover for pilgrims to and from the Holy Land.[8] Towards the middle of the eighth century, Egypt began to show signs of a development that was relatively independent from the old centre of Arab power in the Middle East. Indeed, with the shift of the Arab capital from Damascus, first to Qasr b. Hubayra, and eventually to Baghdad from 750 onwards with the takeover of power by the Abbasids, Egypt became peripheral to the centre of Islamic power. Much of Abbasid trade indeed spurned the Mediterranean in favour of resources in the Far East and Africa (Whitehouse 1987). In Egypt, archaeology has demonstrated the continuous production of commercial transport amphorae from Imperial times into the eighth century (Spencer and Bailey 1982: 16–20). Historical material provides evidence for the prosperous rule of the Abbasid governor Ahmad b. Tulun (868–884), 'an independent ruler in all but name' (Hodges and Whitehouse 1983: 151). He created a suburb north of Fustat that aped Samarra and its great mosque (Kennedy 1986: 316).[9] In the following century, the Fatimid dynasty of Ifriqiya came to power and, by 959, a market of the Rum (Byzantines) is first attested at Fustat — who exactly these Rum traders were, we do not know. By 978 Amalfitans are documented at Cairo (al-Qahira) under Caliph al-'Aziz, the new capital founded three miles north of Fustat only nine years

earlier (*CDC* II: 300; Cahen 1955; Kreutz 1991: 82–3). We should probably not doubt that these traders were already established in Egypt under the father of al-'Aziz, the great Fatimid Caliph al-Mu'izz, whose gold coins were even copied by Salerno and who entertained links with the Byzantine court (Stern 1950).[10] Egypt was probably one of the wealthiest areas bordering the Mediterranean by the end of the first millennium. Quite apart from the fertility of the Nile valley, gold reserves were to be had in Nubia, and the country lay as intermediary for prestige goods from the Indian Ocean, China and east Africa, such as textiles, pepper and other spices.[11] The sources that recognize Campanian exchange with Egypt, however few they may be, not surprising given the delicate political equilibrium, are enticing enough as to suggest that such trade was a very lucrative activity for all concerned.

5. By the tenth century, a new market economy lay clearly on the horizon. Perhaps the more frank autonomy of Amalfi had led it to usurp Naples's primacy in mediterranean trade by the later ninth century, after the latter had been briefly called to order during Emperor Basil's reconquest of southern Italy.[12] Indeed, Byzantium, at times, was a stone around Naples's neck. As in later oriental empires, Byzantium 'suffered from the consequences of having a centralized authority which insisted upon a uniformity of belief and practice, not only in official state religion, but also in such areas as commercial activities and weapons development' (Kennedy 1987: xvi; also Lewis and Runyan 1990: 33). It was this historical heritage that Naples never entirely shed.

Whatever the precise causes of the city's relative failure in respect to the other Italian city-states, it is Amalfi that figures in tenth- and eleventh-century documents as the Campanian commercial power in the East, at Cairo and Constantinople, as well as in the central and western Mediterranean. Indeed, it has been shown that 'during most of the eleventh century, the Italian city-states, with the exception of Venice, Lucca, Salerno and Amalfi, were still outside the horizon of the Geniza papers' (Goitien 1967: 40).[13]

---

[8] On the potential scale of such traffic, see Stopford 1994.

[9] The excavations that should shed light on these problems are being conducted by the American School of Oriental Research.

[10] A bronze coin of al Mu'izz is even attested at inland Matera, in Basilicata (Salvatore 1986).

[11] On the wealth of Fatimid Egypt, see Kennedy 1986: 343. See also Hourani 1995.

[12] This view seems now to be supported by archaeological evidence such as the ample distribution of early medieval (late ninth-century +) lead-glazed pottery from Salerno (Paroli *et al.* 1996: 125).

[13] This contradicts the view of Lopez (1975: 83), who claimed that Amalfi was not able to eliminate the competition provided by Naples, Gaeta and Salerno.

Amalfi retained its prominent position only so long as its limited resources permitted it to manage a relatively large share of the commercial traffic in the Mediterranean. As traffic and exchange increased within the context of an expanding market economy, Amalfi's share declined proportionately, and her power, significance and monopoly waned. It may well be that Amalfi represented Naples in the East, and was synonymous with Campanian trade. Naples's elaborate port facilities had been well used by Amalfitan traders (Skinner 1995: 269–72), thus facilitating the city's procurement of Arab merchandise, which its openly hostile policy, both before and after the defeat of the Arabs at the battle of the Garigliano in 915, would otherwise have made rather difficult. Whilst a case can thus be made for Amalfi's role as commercial intermediary, by the end of the millennium Naples's decline was more apparent than real. Within the space of a couple of centuries, under Angevin rule, the city reached its prime position in southern Italy, which it retains to the present day.

Naples's fortune during the period of worldwide economic expansion at the end of the first millennium was due to its strategic position, maritime prowess and ability to act as commercial mediator between productive areas, rather than on the possibility of marketing any particular surplus product of its own. Thomas, indeed, was right in noting the exceptional case of Naples, stating that the 'civitas survived by resuming its pre-Roman character of a trading city-state' (Thomas 1967: 334). Furthermore, if one accepts Hammond's distinction between the town and the city, in that the former did not 'extend its influence or control to any great extent outside of the agricultural area necessary to maintain its self-sufficiency', one might argue that Naples developed from a Roman town into a medieval city (Hammond 1974: 6). All this goes against Edith Ennen's extreme view that the population of Naples was composed only of landed proprietors (Ennen 1978: 77). The evidence does not support this, and her view was probably influenced by the undoubted supremacy of Amalfi and other city-states towards the end of the millennium. Naples quite clearly had many landowners, including religious communities, but it may be argued that concentration of land was not only due to donations or gradual absorption of common and wasteland, but also to investment of capital acquired through commerce. Profit from such activity invested in agriculture would create a mechanism whereby old Roman lands were slowly reclaimed, leading once more to the production of a surplus, perhaps in particular wine, and the development of secondary manufacturing activities. This enabled it to hold its own against other potentially competitive trading states.

Naples thus developed into a privileged centre of production and exchange, almost an emporium, during early medieval times though, perhaps because of a policy somewhat similar to that of Byzantium itself, it was eventually overshadowed towards the end of the first millennium by Amalfi, as Byzantium was by Venice.

Appendix I

EXCAVATIONS CONDUCTED IN AND AROUND NAPLES DURING THE 1980s

Some eighteen new archaeological excavations were conducted in the city of Naples during the 1980s, many as a result of the major earthquake that struck Campania in November 1980 (De Stefano and Carsana 1987). One old excavation, started in the 1960s at San Lorenzo Maggiore, was also continued from time to time (De Simone 1985).[1] Only three of these sites have been fully published so far — Sant'Aniello Caponapoli, Palazzo Corigliano and Carminiello ai Mannesi — as well as the late Roman and Byzantine church of San Costanzo, Capri. However, the data from many of the others are now systematically archived and form part of a database, produced by Project EUBEA and housed by the Soprintendenza Archeologica delle Province di Napoli e Caserta. If, and when, they are all published will depend largely on Italian government financing.

In the meantime, because of their overall importance for understanding the archaeology of Naples, summary results and bibliographies are presented here. The excavated sites, located in Fig. 0:1, apart from those outside the area of the antique city, are as follows.

1. SS   Via Santa Sofia (1983).
2. VS/VSg Vico della Serpe (1985)/Vico della Serpe (giardino) — Santa Maria d'Agnone (1986–1988).
3. CM   Via Carminiello ai Mannesi (1983–1984).
4. GI   Girolomini (1984).
5. GIc   Girolomini — chiostro (1984).
6. SGP   San Giovanni in Porta (1986).
7. SP   Santa Patrizia (1983–1986).
8. VSP   Vico San Paolo, 42 (1984–1986).
9. PT   Pietrasanta (Santa Maria Maggiore) (1984–1985).
10. SMN   Santa Maria la Nova (1983).
11. BE   Piazza Bellini (1984).
12. SMA   Santa Maria Antesaecula (1983).
13. PC   Palazzo Corigliano (1982–1984).
14. SA   Sant'Aniello a Caponapoli (1982–1983).
15. CSA   Chiesa di Sant'Aniello (1979).
16. POL   Policlinico (1983).
17. DG   ex De Giaxa property, Via L. Armanni (1985).
18. DR   Donnaregina (1988).
19. SGM   San Giovanni Maggiore (1987).
20. SC   San Costanzo, Capri (1990).
21. VB   Via Botteghelle, Ponticelli (1986).
22. PBL   Via Bartolo Longo, Ponticelli (1986).
23. SL   San Lorenzo Maggiore (various dates).

Note: Some excavation contexts are cited in the text. These are prefixed by the abbreviation US = *unità stratigrafica*/stratigraphic unit.

1. VIA SANTA SOFIA (1983)

Period I.   A small length of drystone wall in squared blocks of local yellow volcanic tuff came to light outside the modern building (see period IV). Associated black-glazed pottery suggests a date for its use towards the end of the fourth or the early third century BC.

Period II.   A series of layers, over 1.5 m thick, containing abundant finds of about Claudian date was found within the cellars of the modern building. These covered part of a Roman cistern that could not be examined. There is no evidence of further construction until the seventeenth- to eighteenth-century building was erected on the site in period IV.

Period III.   The period I wall went out of use by the end of the second or beginning of the third century AD, as is shown by a layer of clay that covered the structure and contained African red slip ware (TSC A) of that date.

Period IV.   Dumps of building debris, pottery and bone, datable to the seventeenth to the eighteenth centuries, accumulated, probably created for the construction of the present standing building.

Excavation was financed by the Commissariato Straordinario di Governo as part of the post-seismic reconstruction of Naples and directed by the writer for the Soprintendenza.

Bibliography: De Stefano and Carsana 1987: 29–30 (interim report).

---

[1] See also Hirpinus 1961; Johannowsky 1961; Recupido 1984. See Fontana and Ventrone Vassallo (1984) for the important collection of medieval ceramics from the excavations. Vittoria Carsana kindly informed me (October 1997) that she is continuing excavations at the site.

2. VICO DELLA SERPE (1985)/VICO DELLA SERPE (GIARDINO) — SANTA MARIA D'AGNONE (1986–1988)

Period I. Roman Imperial. Construction of a building that was largely unexcavated.

Period II. First half of the sixth century AD. Razing of the period I building and dumping of rubbish and earth, possibly for the intentional creation of agricultural land. Amongst the finds was a group of amphorae including a good proportion of forms LRA 1 and LRA 4.

Period III. Sixth to thirteenth centuries. Agricultural use of the area, with a consequent build up of 'dark earth'. This deposit, about 3 m in thickness, contained highly fragmented artefacts dating throughout medieval times and terminating with thirteenth-century material including Angevin coins.

Period IV. Thirteenth century. Construction of the road, whose alignment still survives, and perhaps of a building fronting the road to the south. The door opening onto the road was blocked in the sixteenth century, given the date of a coin placed within a socket of the threshold block.

Period V. The period IV building suffers structural damage, perhaps caused by an earthquake.

Period VI. Eighteenth century. Levelling of the period IV structures and use of the area for a series of vats of uncertain use.

Period VII. Nineteenth century. Backfilling of the vats and creation of a small piazzetta, which still existed at the time of the excavation.

Excavation was financed by the Commissariato Straordinario di Governo as part of the post-seismic reconstruction. The first season was directed by the writer, and later seasons were directed by Giuseppe Vecchio for the Soprintendenza.

Bibliography: Arthur and Vecchio 1985: 421–2 (interim report); De Stefano and Carsana 1987: 33–8 (interim report); Ferulano 1991 (site development).

3. VIA CARMINIELLO AI MANNESI (1983–1984)

Period I. Second to first centuries BC. Construction of a well-appointed building (*domus*?) with at least one black and white mosaic floor.

Period II. First half of the first century AD. Features, including a well containing a Dressel 2–4 wine amphora, that may be related to the period I building.

Period III. Late first century AD. Demolition or backfill of period I structures for the construction of an insula or apartment block in brick-faced concrete and *opus reticulatum*, with associated bath-building, to the east side of the *cardo/stenopos*.

Period IV. Second to fourth centuries. Minor restorations to building. Adaptation of two lower floor rooms into a mithraeum.

Period V. First half of the fifth century. Lime burning, followed by abandonment and deposition of silt in at least one of the lower-floor rooms.

Period VI. Middle to later fifth century. Stripping of reusable materials from the building, including marble and bricks. Beginning of systematic dumping of rubbish within the building.

Period VII. End of fifth to first third of the sixth centuries. Further rubbish dumping. Discovery of numerous bones of black rat (*Rattus rattus*).

Period VIII. Late sixth or early seventh to later eighth centuries. Levelling and reuse of area, and creation of a terrace dividing the period III complex into two distinct parts. Various rooms beneath the terrace were reused, with higher floor levels, perhaps as habitations. Further dumps. Burial of seven infants (plague victims?) within the period III fountain room.

Period IX. Thirteenth century. Dump of waste within the period III fountain room, containing thirteenth-century ceramics. Original construction (?) of Santa Maria del Carmine ai Mannesi, known in the literature as a sixteenth-century church.

Period X. Post medieval.

Period XI. Twentieth century.

Excavations were directed by the writer for the Soprintendenza, with Gianluca Soricelli acting as site supervisor.

Bibliography: Arthur 1994 (final excavation report).

4. GIROLOMINI (1984)

Period I. Possibly third to second centuries BC. Construction of a building in large squared tuff blocks. This was found already excavated in 1984, and it was not possible to continue examination of the structure.

Period II. First century BC to first century AD. Partial demolition of the period I building and construction of another building (a *domus*?), which included a large cistern, with three aisles divided by six piers and adjacent structures in *opus reticulatum*, with a floor in *opus signinum* containing scattered white limestone tesserae. Much of the stratigraphy had been removed by the unpublished excavations of 1984.

Period III. Late fourth century AD. Abandonment of the period II structure. A large pit was dug through the floor of the cistern and its fill (US 52) included a considerable quantity of pottery, glass, faunal remains, bone hairpins and other artefacts. Of particular interest are the abundant fragments of decorated wall- and ceiling-plaster, perhaps coming from the latest phase of the period II building.

Period IV. 1592–1619. Construction of the Girolomini monastic complex. Curiously, a female skeleton with an engraved silver reliquary cross above the ribcage was found in an earthen deposit apparently associated with the construction. The sprawled position of the skeleton suggests that the body did not have a regular burial and may have been the result of a murder or plague epidemic.

Salvage operations were directed by the writer for the Soprintendenza.

Bibliography: Arthur and Vecchio 1985: 421 (interim report); Albarella and Frezza 1989b (Project EUBEA archive report: faunal remains).

5. GIROLOMINI — CHIOSTRO (1984)

Trench A. Semicircular Roman Imperial vat lined with *opus signinum*, associated with a channel and floors, cut by a pit containing fifth- to sixth-century ceramics. Later covered by a sequence of layers of organic brown earth (US 77a–d) containing mixed medieval pottery, possibly no later than the early thirteenth century, including lead-glazed wares and Sicilian 'amphores a cannelures'.

Trench B. Part of a late medieval building dating to around the thirteenth century.

Excavations were directed by Giuseppe Vecchio for the Soprintendenza, with Marialaura Raimondi as site supervisor.

Bibliography: Arthur and Vecchio 1985: 421 (interim report).

6. SAN GIOVANNI IN PORTA (1986)

Site of the tenth-century church of 'San Iohannis evangelistae in vico triafata' (Capasso 1895: 126–8).

Scarse remains of medieval tuff block ashlar walls, possibly relating to the external walls of the church. The interior of the structure was found to be gutted and contained building rubble. The church is attested as having been demolished in 1856. The excavation was not completed, due to continual vandalism of the site.

Excavation was financed by the Commissariato Straordinario di Governo as part of the post-seismic reconstruction and directed by Giuseppe Vecchio for the Soprintendenza, with Giuliana Miraglia and Maria-laura Raimondi as site supervisors.

Bibliography: not published.

7. SANTA PATRIZIA (1983–1986)

The site was divided into nine areas, based on a division formed by the foundations of the standing building within which the excavation took place (Fig. 4:10).

Period I. First half of the second century AD. Areas i–iii: construction of a large Roman building in brick-faced concrete, possibly a podium, with an infill consisting of building rubble (fragments of *opus quasi reticulatum* and *latericium*) and rubbish (pottery, bones, etc.). The northwest angle and some 14 m of the building's western side were exposed, though it appeared to continue southwards. Part of a pavement in *opus signinum* was revealed to the west of the building.

Period II. Late fourth century. Area vii: large dumps of urban rubbish containing ceramics that are almost identical to and contemporary with a pit group from the Girolomini excavations (US 52).

Period III. Late sixth century. Area ii: beginning of the formation of dark earth layers, which seems to continue up to the end of the first millennium.

Period IV. All areas: construction of a rectangular hall (7.5 m × >11.5 m) with central piers and a small atrium. The eastern wall reused the Roman brick-faced concrete structure of period I. These remains

are interpreted as being part of the early medieval monastery of San Nicandro e Marciano (later Santa Patrizia) attested in this area of the city.

Period V. Eighth to ninth/tenth centuries. Abandonment or modification of part of the monastic complex, with raising of floor levels, particularly in area ix.

Period VI. Tenth to eleventh centuries. Area ii: deposition of five adult burials, above dark earth layers, with the following ages: tomb 1: male? 37–45; tomb 2: female 44–52; tomb 3: male? 40–5?; tomb 4: male? 20–39; tomb 5: male? 40–52.

Period VII. Twelfth to early thirteenth centuries. Area ii: construction of a vaulted cellar and other structures, abutting the outer north wall of the period I brick-faced concrete building, containing a backfill of twelfth-century ceramics, save for the uppermost layer with protomaiolica. Area vii: construction of a building with work surfaces and a basin.

Period VIII. 1864. The convent is dissolved and becomes the barracks of local militia.

Excavations were directed by the writer for the Soprintendenza, with Vittoria Carsana, Gabriella Gasperetti and Bianca Sgherzi as site supervisors.

Bibliography: Arthur 1984 (interim report); Arthur 1986c (later medieval ceramics); Garcea 1987 (lamps); Arthur and Capece 1992 (forum ware); Arthur and Patterson 1994 (early medieval ceramics); Project EUBEA archive reports; Carsana 1995 (postgraduate thesis); Frezza 1995 (fish remains).

8. VICO SAN PAOLO, 42 (1984–1986) (Fig. I:1)

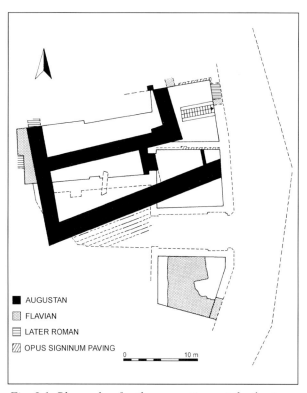

AUGUSTAN
FLAVIAN
LATER ROMAN
OPUS SIGNINUM PAVING

0   10 m

Fig. I:1. Phase plan for the excavations at the theatrum tectum *at Via San Paolo (after De Stefano and Carsana 1987: fig. 80).*

Period I. First to fifth centuries AD. Construction and use of the *theatrum tectum*.

Period II. Fifth to sixth centuries AD. Abandonment of building; removal of material for *spolia*; insertion of at least one burial, associated with a bronze coin of Tiberius II (578–582), cut into the structure of the building.

Period III. End of sixth/seventh to twelfth centuries. Development of 'dark earth' deposit, possibly used for agriculture.

Excavation was financed by the Commissariato Straordinario di Governo as part of the post-seismic reconstruction and directed by the writer, with Bianca Sgherzi as site supervisor.

Bibliography: Arthur 1989b (Project EUBEA archive report: excavation report); Albarella and Frezza 1989a (Project EUBEA archive report: faunal remains); De Stefano and Carsana 1987: 41–8.

9. PIETRASANTA (SANTA MARIA MAGGIORE) (1984–1985)

Period I. Late Republic, possibly later third or second century BC. Construction of a well-appointed *domus* in squared tuff blocks with traces of wall-painting. This structure, and those of the succeeding Roman periods, provide the original southern limit of the insula fronting Via dei Tribunali, and the eastern limit fronting the surviving *stenopos*.

Period II. Around the mid-first century BC. In front of the present church. Construction of a building in *semilateres* and *opus quasi-reticulatum*. One room contained two rectangular vats lined in *opus signinum*, one with the lower half of an amphora inserted at its base. Two adjacent rooms had *opus signinum* pavements with geometrically arranged black and white tesserae forming a series of rosettes. Mosaic floors, probably belonging to this building, have been found below the present church. Some of the squared tuff blocks of the period I building were re-employed in the building's foundations.

Period III. Around the later first century AD. Major modifications to the period II building, including the addition of new walls in *lateres*. Amongst the finds was an amethyst intaglio depicting an ithyphallic herm.

Period IV. AD 533. Construction of the basilical church of Santa Maria Maggiore by Bishop Pomponius. Traces of white marble paving and loose mosaic glass paste tesserae, both turquoise and translucent with gold foil, revealed beneath the central nave of the present church, close to the apse.

Period V. Early medieval? An adult skeleton was found carelessly buried above the Roman remains without a coffin or grave-goods.

Period VI. Probably twelfth century. Construction of the surviving bell-tower in reused Roman *lateres*. The inner wall of the arch beneath the campanile rests upon a wall of the Roman building, so that the bell-tower in effect projects over part of the street, none the less leaving a pedestrian passage.

Period VII. 1653. Total reconstruction of the church by Cosimo Fanzago.

Excavation was financed by the Ministero dei Beni Culturali and directed by the writer, with Gianluca Soricelli as site supervisor.

Bibliography: Arthur and Vecchio 1985: 417–20 (interim report).

10. SANTA MARIA LA NOVA (1983)

Period I. First century AD. Construction of a cistern in mortared volcanic tuff blocks, associated with a structure built of *semilateres*, both lined with mortar.

Period II. First to early second centuries AD. Construction of a building with walls in *opus reticulatum* faced with plaster, for which part of the period I building was demolished. An associated floor of flat tiles bore remains of tile-built *suspensurae*, indicating the presence of a hypocaust.

Period III. Late sixth to early seventh centuries. Abandonment of this part of the building with reuse of the spaces for the insertion of two burials: an inhumation of a very muscular adult male of around 34 years of age (stature 1.80 m) and a child burial in a 'Samos cistern type' amphora. Redeposited rubble, probably from the period II building, included painted wallplaster and marble revetments.

Period IV. Probably seventeenth century. Construction of the standing palazzo, seriously compromising the antique remains.

Excavation was financed by the Ministero dei Beni Culturali and directed by the writer, with Gianluca Soricelli as site supervisor. Examination of anthropological remains by Sarah Bisel.

Bibliography: King 1984 (faunal remains); Arthur and Vecchio 1985: 422–4 (interim report).

11. PIAZZA BELLINI (1984)

Period I. Fourth century BC. Construction of the Greek city wall in large rectangular yellow tuff blocks.

Period II. Various dump layers within the *emplecton* suggest readjustments in early medieval times. Finds include forum ware and a barbed iron arrowhead.

Excavation was financed by the Ministero dei Beni Culturali and directed by Giuseppe Vecchio, with Ciro Pierattini as site supervisor.

Bibliography: Vecchio 1985c (interim report).

12. SANTA MARIA ANTESAECULA (1983)

Located to the north of the ancient city, in the area now known as the Sanità.

Period I. Probable agricultural use testified by wellsorted light brown humic soil above the natural tuff bedrock, containing mixed pottery from neolithic to early medieval times. The latest datable ceramics include broad-line painted wares and forum ware of the eighth to ninth centuries.

Period II. Sixteenth century. Construction of the convent of Santa Maria Antesaecula.

Excavation was financed by the Commissariato Straordinario di Governo as part of the post-seismic reconstruction and directed by Giuseppe Vecchio, with Ciro Pierattini as site supervisor.

Bibliography: De Stefano and Carsana 1987: 31–2.

13. PALAZZO CORIGLIANO (1982–1984)

Period I. Sinking of some eight or ten wells immediately within the Greek walls, backfilled in period II.

Period II. End of third to beginning of second centuries BC. Construction of a rectangular building, a base ('massicciata') to support a new *stenopos*, following the alignment of Via del Sole, and a large drain. This is interpreted as evidence for the urbanization of this part of the town (Pelosi 1991: 9).

Period III. Second half of the first century AD. Dump of building rubble and waste, possibly consequent to an earthquake, in a large pit.

Period IV. Slight and undefinable traces of medieval activity.

Period V. Fifteenth century. Final filling of the Hellenistic drain (period II above), and construction of Piazza San Domenico Maggiore, following the earthquake of 1456.

Period VI. Sixteenth century. Construction of Palazzo Corigliano.

Excavations were directed by Bruno D'Agostino, assisted by Patrizia Gastaldi.

Bibliography: Bragantini and Gastaldi 1985 (interim report); Bragantini 1991 (part I of the final report).

14. SANT'ANIELLO A CAPONAPOLI (1982–1983)

Period I. Greek

Phase I. Fifth century BC. Construction of the town wall.

Phase II. Late fourth century BC. Reconstruction of the town wall.

Period II. Medieval.

Phase I. Fourteenth century. Construction of a surface and related contexts.

Phase II. Fourteenth century. Construction of the Angevin town wall reusing parts of the late fourth century BC wall.

Period III. Renaissance and modern.

Phase I. Sixteenth century. Layers created from levelling above the town wall.

Phase IIa. Sixteenth century. Construction of a cistern within the structure of the Greek wall.

Phase IIb. Seventeenth century. Use of the cistern and associated levels and contexts.

Excavations were directed by Bruno D'Agostino, with Annamaria D'Onofrio as site supervisor.

Bibliography: D'Onofrio and D'Agostino 1987 (excavation report).

15. CHIESA DI SANT'ANIELLO (1979)

Period I. Probably fourth century BC. Construction of double curtain wall as part of the defences of *Neapolis*.

Period II. First century AD. Construction of buildings in *opus reticulatum* over a platform created through backfilling of the Greek walls.

Period III. Uncertain early medieval. Discovery of a group of early medieval ceramics including a jug in scale-decorated forum ware (Arthur and Capece 1992).

Excavations were directed by Giuseppe Vecchio.

Bibliography: Vecchio 1985b (interim report).

16. POLICLINICO (1983)

Period I. First-century dump, possibly post AD 62 earthquake.

Period II. Late first century. Construction of a domed oven.

Period III. Around the end of the second century. Abandonment and partial destruction of the oven.

Period IV. First half of the thirteenth century. Dump covering Roman remains.

Period V. Post-medieval activity.

Excavations were directed by Bruno D'Agostino.

Bibliography: D'Onofrio 1985 (final excavation report).

17. EX DE GIAXA PROPERTY, VIA L. ARMANNI (1985)

Period I. Discovery of two backfilled wells, cut through the natural pozzolana and tuff, containing material dating to the sixth century BC, including a Greek commercial amphora and an *askos*.

Period II. First century AD. Dump of building material.

Excavation was financed by the Commissariato Straordinario di Governo as part of the post-seismic reconstruction and directed by Giuseppe Vecchio, with Marialaura Raimondi as site supervisor.

Bibliography: not published.

18. DONNAREGINA (1988)

Sited to the east of Via Duomo, on the *summa plateia*. Excavations were carried out within the church, which was apparently founded as Santa Mariae dominae reginae in 780.

Period I. Second to third centuries AD. Construction of a bath-building, of which part of a rectangular room with *suspensurae* (*caldarium*) and two rectangular apsed basins lined with *opus signinum* have been excavated. The supposed *caldarium* has a coloured geometrical mosaic pavement, and *tubuli* within the walls.

Period II. Modifications to the baths.

Period III. The excavated rooms of the baths were backfilled with pottery dating no later than the fourteenth century.

Period IV. 1620–1649. Construction of the church of Santa Maria Donnaregina Nuova.

Excavations were directed by Giuseppe Vecchio, with Giuseppe Mollo as site supervisor.

Bibliography: not published; see Mollo 1988 (brief archive report).

19. SAN GIOVANNI MAGGIORE (1987)

Period I. Third quarter of the sixth century. Construction of the basilical church of San Giovanni Maggiore. Excavation within the apse revealed the original *opus sectile* paving sealing a layer with pottery similar to that found at Carminiello ai Mannesi, period VII.

Period II. Early medieval painting imitating marble was noted in the intrados of one of the blocked arches forming the ambulatory.

Limited excavations were directed by Giuseppe Vecchio, with Giuseppe Mollo as site supervisor.
Bibliography: not published.

20. SAN COSTANZO, CAPRI (1990)

Period I. Undefined prehistoric occupation.
Period II. Second half of the second to mid-first centuries BC. Construction of a Roman villa or farm.
Period III. Roman Imperial. Objects found out of context suggest continuing use of the period II building, until its (partial?) destruction for the construction of the period IV church.
Period IV. Fifth century. Construction of a small basilical church in *semilateres* with reused columns (Fig. 4:13).
Period V. Probably tenth century. Conversion of the original church into a Greek cross-in-square plan church.

Excavation directed by the writer for the Soprintendenza.
Bibliography: Arthur 1992 (final excavation report).

21. VIA BOTTEGHELLE, PONTICELLI (1986)

Building construction revealed a cemetery composed of at least 52 inhumation burials, datable between the fourth and first half of the fifth centuries (Fig. 5:8). Some 45 individuals were recovered. Many infants were contained in African and Tripolitanian amphorae, three were in Iberian amphorae of form Keay XXIII, whilst adult burials consisted of tile-tombs (*a cappucina*) and simple inhumations. Some of the tiles were stamped SPES DEI. A wide V-sectioned ditch to the west of the burials may have formed part of a cemeterial enclosure.

The anthropological data yield a mean age at death of *c.* nineteen years, influenced by a high sub-adult mortality of 60%, with 48.1% (thirteen individuals) less than one year old. Adults comprised eleven males and seven females, with a high percentage of mature adult males. Indeed, six were in the 45+ age range.

Excavation was financed by the Ministero dei Beni Culturali and directed by the writer.
Bibliography: Arthur and Vecchio 1985: 422 (interim report); De Stefano and Carsana 1987 (interim report). The anthropological report by Pieropaolo Petrone is not published. I should like to thank Trevor Anderson for his comments on the report.

22. VIA BARTOLO LONGO, PONTICELLI (1986)

During building works a villa complex was brought to light in Via Bartolo Longo, Cupa Pironti, Ponticelli, on the lower slopes of Vesuvius.
Period I. First century BC? Construction of a villa. Of particular note was the discovery of a structure that appeared to be a T-shaped 'corn drier' (Fig. I:2), unique to Italy, though similar to examples known in Britain (see Morris 1979: chapter 2).
Period II. AD 79. Total destruction and burial of the period I villa during the eruption of Mount Vesuvius. The area was subsequently abandoned for about a generation.

Fig. I:2. T-shaped corn drier from the Roman villa at Ponticelli (photo: author).

Period III. Second century. A square building with massive foundations, possibly a monumental tomb or a tower, was erected over the site of the villa.
Period IV. Second century. A totally new villa complex, within a roughly square enclosure, that occupied an area of some 2,000 m² (Fig. 5:13), was constructed at Cupa Pironti, incorporating the period III structure. The southwest angle of the enclosure appears to have been open space, either a courtyard or garden. Living quarters appear to have occupied the eastern range of buildings, whilst the northern range was devoted to work facilities, including a cistern, a *torcularium*?, and a vat lined with *opus signinum*. To the east of the enclosure was a cemetery with at least 23 burials (fourteen children within amphorae, four tile-tombs and five probable wooden coffin burials).
Period V. Third century. A rectangular block of rooms was erected in the centre of the enclosed area, overlooking the walled courtyard/garden. One room revealed a simple black on white floral mosaic. It is suggested that the block was two-storeyed, and it is interesting to note that its ground dimensions are similar to those of the later apsidal hall found in the villa of San Giovanni di Ruoti (in the province of Potenza) (Small and Buck 1994: chapter 9).
Period VI. Fourth to fifth centuries. Minor structural additions.

The villa survived into the early sixth century, on the evidence of African red slip ware and local pottery types paralleled at Carminiello ai Mannesi (period VII). There was no evidence for later occupation, though after desertion the villa was stripped of reusable materials.

Excavations were directed by Giuseppe Vecchio, with the assistance of the writer, and Gianluca Soricelli as site supervisor.
Bibliography: De Stefano and Carsana 1987 (interim report).

23. SAN LORENZO MAGGIORE

Excavations were directed at various times by W. Johannowsky, G. Vecchio and A. De Simone.
Bibliography: De Simone 1985.

Appendix II

ECCLESIASTICAL BUILDING IN NAPLES UP TO 1140

The aim of this appendix is to provide basic information about ecclesiastical building in Naples, including all manner of churches, monasteries and *diaconiae*. In particular, a *terminus ante quem*, usually based on the first reference in the sources, is given. Presumably some were already in existence by the time they were first mentioned, though only archaeology is likely to confirm this. A lot more work could refine the list. Source material is also seriously wanting for the central years of the early Middle Ages. Despite its shortcomings, the list should help to gauge roughly economic expenditure in Naples from the later Roman Empire through to the end of the duchy of Naples.

It is not always possible to distinguish ecclesiastical churches from proprietary churches or chapels, or to define the scale of construction and investment. Major churches are signalled, as are lay constructions, when possible. Suburban foundations are also included, such as the constructions at the *castrum Lucullanum* or at the complex of San Gennaro at Capodimonte, when they appear to gravitate directly upon Naples. Ecclesiastical building dependent upon *castra* in the territory of Naples, or rural foundations, many of which seem to lie at the foundations of later rural settlements (for example, San Pietro a Patierno), are not included in the list.

Capasso (1895) discussed the chronologies of most of the foundations, with the majority of the documents having been presented in *MND*.

I am particularly indebted to Brunella Bruno who has compiled the following list of ecclesiastical foundations, by means of a computerized database.

MAJOR CHURCHES (MAGGIORI)

After 314 – Reference to the basilica of Santa Restituta, built under Constantine between 314 and 335, dedicated to the Saviour (Salvatore) and the Holy Apostles (Sant'Apostoli) until the eighth century (*Lib. Pont.* I (*vita Silvestri*); Capasso 1895: 66–7).

After 367 – Bishop Severus (367–386) erected the basilica of San Giorgio Maggiore (*Gesta Ep.* 405 (Severus); Capasso 1895: 79–81).

468 – Bishop Soter erected the basilica of Sant'Apostoli on, as legend has it, a temple to Mercury (*Gesta Ep.* 408 (Soter); Capasso 1895: 81).

After 499 – Bishop Stephen I built a second basilica dedicated to the Saviour (the *Stephania*) between *c.* 499 and 502. In 795 it was destroyed by fire and rebuilt (*Gesta Ep.* 408 (Stephen I); Capasso 1895: 67).

533 – Bishop Pomponius erected the basilica of Santa Maria Maggiore (*Gesta Ep.* 408 (Pomponius); Capasso 1895: 82–4).

After 539 – Bishop John II (539–559) built the basilica of San Lorenzo Maggiore. Probably the same as 'San Laurentii in platea Augustali' (R. 29 (AD 935); *Gesta Ep.* 410–11 (John II)).

555 – Bishop Vincent erected the basilica of San Giovanni Maggiore (*Gesta Ep.* 411 (Vincent); Capasso 1895: 84–6).

By 816 – Duke Anthemius converted the temple of the Dioscuri into San Paolo Maggiore between 801 and 816 (R. 43, 211, 273, 307, 377; Capasso 1895: 109–10).

OTHER CHURCHES

c. 344 – Bishop Fortunatus I was buried in a church 'foris urbem quasi ad stadia' (*MND* I: 163; *Gesta Ep.* 404; Capasso 1895: 206; Cilento 1969b: 721).

c. 360–408/410 – Reference to the basilica 'beati Ianuarii martyris', at Capodimonte, outside the walls (*MND* I: 174; Capasso 1895: 207; Cilento 1969b: 721).

c. 363–408 – Bishop Severus was buried in the church founded by him 'foris urbem' (*MND* I: 166; Capasso 1895: 206; Cilento 1969b: 721).

Fourth century? – Reference to the church and catacombs of Bishop San Efebo or Eufebio (Libellus miracollorum San Euphebi = *MND* I: 331; Capasso 1895: 204).

c. 444 – Bishop Nostrianus was buried in the church of 'Gaudiosi Christi confessoris, foris urbem euntibus ad sanctum Ianuarium martyrem, in portico sita' (*MND* I: 171–2; Cilento 1969b: 721).

486/489–498 – Bishop Victor erected a church 'ad nomen beatae Eufimiae' outside Porta San Gennaro (*MND* I: 174–5; *Gesta Ep.* 408 (Victor); Capasso 1895: 205–6).

486/489–498 – Reference to the church of 'sancti Agrippini confessoris', sited in the San Gennaro complex (*MND* I: 174; Capasso 1895: 208; Cilento 1969b: 721).

486/489–498 – Bishop Victor founded the church, 'foris civitatem, ad nomen beati Stephani levitate et martyris' (*MND* I: 174; Capasso 1895: 208; Cilento 1969b: 721, 750–63). Calvus, bishop of Naples, erected the church of 'San Sossio, ad area' (Capasso 1895: 204–5; Cilento 1969b: 721).

Seventh century? – Reference to the church of Santa Barbara, in the *castrum Lucullanum* (Capasso 1895: 226).

Earlier than 834 – Duke Bonus (ob. 834) was buried in the church of 'Santa Mariae ad plateam' or 'Santa Marie de Merulo comite', a minor parish (Capasso 1895: 107).

Before 849–872 – Duke-Bishop Athanasius I conceded 'beate ecclesiam Lucie martyris in perpetuum' to the monastery of 'San Salvatore in insula maris', within the *castrum Lucullanum* (*Vita San Athanasii = MND* I: 217; Capasso 1895: 225).

876 – Reference to the 'oratorium San Laurentii in porticu ante illam sito' (basilica of San Gennaro outside the walls) (*Acta translationis San Athanasii ep. Neapolitani = MND* I: 285; Capasso 1895: 208).

876 – Probable reference to the basilica of San Ianuarii, perhaps built by Duke-Bishop Athanasius I (*Vita San Athanasii = MND* I: 217; Capasso 1895: 209–10).

Early tenth century – Reference to the church of 'San Bicenti Christi martiris sita in insula maris' (R. 687; Capasso 1895: 234–5).

920 – 'Maru et Barbaria monaca, mater et filia', of the Isauri family, possessed 'Eufimia martira Christi', in the district 'duos amantes iuxta murum publicum' (R. 6; Capasso 1895: 123–4; Skinner 1994: 291).

924 – First reference to the church of 'archangeli Michaelis, sita a foris sub muro publico regione portenobense' (R. 11; Capasso 1895: 98–9).

927 – 'Scauracio ven. medico filio q.d. Gregorii et Drosum seu Maru germanis filiis q. Basilii et Marie' possessed the church of 'Ianuarii sacerdotis et martiris, sita inter plateam, que appellatur trea fata, et inter vicum qui vocatur duodecim putea, regione porte San Ianuarii' (R. 14; Capasso 1895: 104–5).

About 936 – Reference to church 'Arcangeli Michaelis situm in mercatum' (same as the church of 924 above?) (R. 33; Capasso 1895: 100).

955 – Reference to San Silbestri, a minor parish church (R. 87; Capasso 1895: 112).

960 – Reference to San Nicolaus, a minor parish church (R. 111; Capasso 1895: 109).

961 – Reference to the Greek church of 'San Iohannis Baptiste, site in vico, quod dicitur clusa, regione Furcillense' (R.118; Capasso 1895: 105).

964 – Reference to the church of 'San Archangeli ad signa' (R. 137; Capasso 1895: 100–2).

964 – Reference to 'San Thomae ad Capuanam in regione Termense', a minor parish church (R. 137; Capasso 1895: 114–15).

968 – Reference to the church of 'Santa Marie, que nominatur at media'. In 988 the female monastery of 'Santa Marie que vocatur at media' was attested (R. 168, 257; Capasso 1895: 166).

970 – The Ferrari family founded 'sancti Petri situm at illos Ferrarios', a minor parish church. Possibly 'San Pietro ad Aram', an early Christian church with three naves divided by eight columns (R. 187; Capasso 1895: 110–11; see San Petri ad area, below (AD 1104)).

988 – Reference to the church of 'San Petri Christi apostoli, que ponitur at media' (R. 257; Capasso 1895: 111).

997 – Reference to church of 'San Cipriani, sita nella regione Furcillense' according to Capasso (R. 302; Capasso 1895: 102).

By 999 – During the reign of an unspecified emperor Basilius, Gregorio de Orreu gave the church of 'Santa Mariae in vico Formelli' to the monastery of San Severino e Sossio (R. 647, II. 1, Capasso 1895: 130).

By 999 – John III, consul and duke, gave the church of Santa Caeciliae to the monastery of Monte Cassino. The church was sited in 'la via detta delle Palme' (Capasso 1895: 120–1).

By 999 – Reference to the church of 'sancti agrippini de regione furcillense' (R. 656; Capasso 1895: 97–8).

By 999 – 'Sant'Aniello a Caponapoli', no later than the tenth century, probably earlier. Possibly the church of the monastery of the same name, mentioned in 1058 (below).

Tenth to eleventh centuries – Reference to the church of San Venere, in the *castrum Lucullanum* (*MND* II: 172; Capasso 1895: 226).

1011 – Reference to the church of 'San Dei genitricis Mariae que nominatur de domino Atriano' (R. 340; Capasso 1895: 108).

1012 – Reference to 'San Iohannis qui vocatur in curte', a minor parish church (R. 347; Capasso 1895: 105).

1012 – First reference to 'Santa Marie ad sicule', a minor parish church (R. 344; Capasso 1895: 107–8).

1019 – Reference to the church of San Felicis, a minor parish church, sited upon a tower of the city wall (R. 383, 514; Capasso 1895: 103–4).

1025 – The Amalfitani family owned the church of 'Santa Mariae ad circulum', in the *castrum Lucullanum* (R. 402; Capasso 1895: 223–5).

1026 – The de Moneta family owned the church of Santa Marie (R. 409; Capasso 1895: 108–9).

1038 – Reference to a church, near the forum, of 'San Simeonis, quam quidam fecit ven. recordationis d. Iohannes Consul et Dux' (R. 468; Capasso 1895: 113–14).

1054 – Reference to the destroyed church of San Pauli, of the monastery of 'San Sebastiani de Neapoli, positam intus destructum *castrum Luculanum*' (R. 488; Capasso 1895: 225).

1071 – Reference to the church of 'San protomartiris Stephani de Arco Roticorum' (R. 507; Capasso 1895: 112–13).

1075 – Reference to the church of San Severini, grange of the monastery of San Teodoro e Sebastiano (Capasso 1895: 141–2).

1104 – Reference to the church of 'San Petri ad area', outside the walls (R. 584; Capasso 1895: 200; see 'sancti Petri situm at illos Ferrarios', above (AD 970)).

1130 – Reference to the church of 'San Cruci de regione forum' (R. 647; Capasso 1895: 102–3).

1136 – Reference to the church of 'San Iohannis et Pauli de regione augustale' (R. 666; Capasso 1895: 105–6).

1137 – Reference to the church of San Rufi. It is probably the same as San Rufi et Carponi attested in 1016 (R. 360, 668; Capasso 1895: 111–12).

1142 – First reference to 'Santa Maria ad cancellum', a minor parish church. It may already have been in existence in the eleventh century (*Notam. instr. San Gregorii* no. 391; Capasso 1895: 106–7).

MONASTERIES

363–c. 408 – Bishop Severus founded the female monastery of San Potiti (*Gesta Ep*. 405; Capasso 1895: 172; Cilento 1969b: 721).

363 c. 408 – Bishop Severus was buried in the church founded by him 'foris urbem' (*MND* I: 166; Capasso 1895: 206; Cilento 1969b: 721).

492–496 – Barbara built the 'monasterium in honorem San Severini Noricorum apostoli', in the *castrum Lucullanum* (*MND* II: 172; Capasso 1895: 218).

591 – First reference to the monastery of 'San Petri basilicam, in Lucullano castro' (Greg. *Ep*. L. i. 24 = *MND* I: 183; Capasso 1895: 220).

591 – First reference to the monastery of 'San Archangeli, in Lucullano castro'. In 977 it is called 'ad circum' (Greg. *Ep*. L. i. 24 = *MND* I: 183; R. 213; Capasso 1895: 221).

599 – First reference to the male Greek monastery of 'San Theodori et Sebastiani quod appellatur Casapicta situm in viridiarium' (R. 654; Capasso 1895: 153–4).

Before 599 – In 599 the male Greek monastery of San Sergii et Bacchi was joined with the monastery of San Theodori et Sebastiani. It was sited in the *castrum Lucullanum* (Capasso 1895: 153, 225).

Sixth century – Reference to the 'monasterium Gratterense, quod situm in Plaia', later Santa Mariae at Cappella, attested in 996 (Greg. *Ep*. L. x. 61 = *MND* I: 183; R. 293; Capasso 1895: 239).

Seventh century – Reference to the Greek monastery of 'San Salvatore in insula maris' (Capasso 1895: 226).

763 – Eufrosina was abbess of the female Greek monastery of San Marcellini et Petri. At the beginning of the ninth century, Theodonanda, wife of Duke Anthemius, renovated and enlarged the monastery. In 1016 it was sited 'ad patricciana, regione Portobensis' (R. 366; Capasso 1895: 160–3).

Eighth century – Stephen II, bishop and duke, founded the female Benedictine monastery of San Festi et Desiderii (Capasso 1895: 156–8).

Eighth century – Stephen II built the church, dedicated to Santa Fortunata, in the Greek female monastery of San Gaudiosi. In 1132 it was attested as 'monasterii San Gaudiosi Xpi confessoris et Santa Fortunate virginis' (R. 655; Capasso 1895: 158–9).

Eighth century – Stephen II, bishop and duke, founded the female monastery of 'Salvatoris nostri Iesu Xpi et San Pantaleonis'. In 1009, Duke Sergius IV joined it with 'San Sebastiani atque Gregorii' (R. 166; Capasso 1895: 170–1).

c. 811 – Anthemius, consul and duke, and Theodonanda founded the male monastery of San Cyrici et Iulicte (Capasso 1895: 148–9).

Early ninth century – Euprassia, daughter of Stephen II, bishop and duke, and wife of Duke Theophilactus, founded the female Benedictine monastery of 'Santa Maria situm at Albina' (Capasso 1895: 165–6).

Before 849–872 – Duke-Bishop Athanasius I conceded 'beate ecclesiam Lucie martyris in perpetuum' to the monastery of 'San Salvatore in insula maris', within the *castrum Lucullanum* (*Vita San Athanasii* – *MND* I: 217; Capasso 1895: 225).

849–872 – Duke-Bishop Athanasius I founded a monastery by the church of 'sanctissimi ac beatissimi martyris Ianuarii' (*Vita San Athanasii* = *MND* I: 217; Capasso 1895: 209; Cilento 1969b: 722).

877–898 – Athanasius II shifted the male monastery of San Severini, within the city walls (Capasso 1895: 152–3).

914 – First reference to the female monastery of San Nicandri et Marciani. In 1065 it is attested as 'San Nicandri et Marciani atque Patritiae' (R. 2, 497; Capasso 1895: 168–70).

916 – Reference to the female monastery of San Martini. It was sited near the walls (R. 4; Capasso 1895: 168).

917 – Reference to the male Greek monastery of San Dimitrii or Demetrii, sited 'in regione Albinensi'. In 1016 it was attested as 'San Dimitri atque Benedecti' (R. 5, 366; Capasso 1895: 149).

921 – Reference to the female Benedictine monastery of 'San Archangeli qui vocatur ad balane' (R. 9; Capasso 1895: 156).

930 – First reference to the female monastery of 'San Sebastiani atque Gregorii'. In 1009, Duke Sergio IV joined it with the monastery 'Domini et Salvatoris nostri Iesu Christi atque Pantaleoni'. Later known as 'San Gregorii majoris and San Gregorio Armeno' (R. 17; Capasso 1895: 159–60).

935 – First reference to the male Greek monastery of 'San Anastasii et Basilii at media', under the *igumenus* Iohannes (R. 29; Capasso 1895: 145–6).

937 – Male Benedictine monastery of Michahelis archangeli, sited 'in vico qui vocatur fistula fracta'. Probably to be identified as 'San Archangeli de illi Morfissa' attested in 967 (R. 37, 163; Capasso 1895: 147–8).

967 – First reference to the male monastery of 'San Gregorii quam de Regionarium'. It was sited at 'Cimbeum regione Furcillense' (R. 160, 433; Capasso 1895: 149–51).

981 – Reference to the male monastery of San Pellegrini. In 1132 it became a female monastery in 'regione foru' (R. 230, 652; Capasso 1895: 171–2).

988 – Reference to the female monastery of 'Santa Marie que vocatur at media' (R. 257; Capasso 1895: 166).

992 – Reference to the male monastery of 'San Pauli Captolicae maioris' (R. 273; Capasso 1895: 152).

Tenth century – Febronia was abbess of the female monastery of San Samone, Guritae et Abibii (Capasso 1895: 172–3).

1025 – Reference to the male monastery of 'San Martini ad monacorum'. Perhaps this is the same monastery as founded by Bishop Severus (363–409) (R. 402; Capasso 1895: 151).

1025 – Reference to the female monastery of 'Santa Mariae de domina Aromata', founded, probably, by the Domina Aromata family (R. 402; Capasso 1895: 166–7).

1026 – Reference to the Greek female monastery of San Vincentii. Perhaps this is the same as that attested in 944 and 949 (R. 52, 409; Capasso 1895: 173–4).

1050 or 1065 – Marinus, a monk, founds the male monastery of San Sepulchri (*MND* II: 98; Capasso 1895: 173).

1054 – Reference to the destroyed church of San Pauli, of the monastery of 'San Sebastiani de Neapoli, positam intus destructum castrum Lucculanum' (R. 488; Capasso 1895: 225).

1058 – First reference to the male monastery of 'beatissimi Agnelli' under abbot Peter (R. 490; Capasso 1895: 144–5).

1076 – First reference to the male monastery of 'San Andreae ad Jrculum', corruption of Erculem (R. 523; Capasso 1895: 146–7).

1076 – Reference to the female monastery of 'Santa Maria de domina Regina'. This is probably the same as that attested in 780 with the title of 'San Pietro de monte de domina regina' (R. 523; Capasso 1895: 167–8).

1078 – First reference to the female Benedictine monastery of 'Sant'Agate que nominatur ad Pupulum' (R. 529; Capasso 1895: 154–5).

1130 – First reference to the Greek female monastery of 'Santa Marie de Anglone'. Later it becomes Benedictine (R. 643; Capasso 1895: 163–5).

DIACONIAE

585 – San Andrea ad Nidum. It already existed in 585 if Saint Candida was buried there. It is attested in 713 when Theodimus was rector. In the ninth century it was no longer patrimony of Saint Peter's. In 1139 it is also attested as a hospital (Capasso 1895: 87–8).

c. 680 – Bishop Agnellus founded the *diaconia* of San Gennaro (*Gesta Ep.* 418; Capasso 1895: 88–9; Ambrasi 1985).

721 – Duke Theodore built the church and *diaconia* of San Giovanni e Paolo, where he was buried. Later called de Praetorio (Capasso 1895: 89–90).

937 – First reference to San Giorgio 'ad forum' or 'ad mercatum'. It was sited in the 'regione Augustale' near the forum (R. 37; Capasso 1895: 91–2).

941 – The *diaconia* of San Pietro is first attested. Perhaps 'San Pietro ad amphitheatrum' (R. 43; Capasso 1895: 95).

1018 – First reference to 'Santa Maria ad Cosmedin'. It probably existed before the ninth century (R. 377; Capasso 1895: 90–1).

1021 – First reference to 'Santa Maria ad presepe'. In a document of 1137 it is attested as 'Santa Marie que appellatur at rotunda' (R. 402, 669; Capasso 1895: 92–4).

Appendix III

CHRONOLOGICAL TABLE

Histories of early medieval Naples have been written from time to time, availing themselves of what is an impressive collection of source material when compared to that extant for most other contemporary urban settlements, such as Bari, Benevento, Reggio or Otranto.[1] Indeed, the only other near comparable source collections in southern Italy also regard Campania, focusing on the area around Salerno. Thus a stock of acquired knowledge exists for Naples, with which the histories constructed from the material evidence may be compared.

The following table is dedicated to an extreme synthesis of Neapolitan history, after the end of the Roman Empire in the West in 476, through the times of both the Byzantine and the later independent administration, until the Norman conquest of 1140.

476 – Emperor Romulus Augustulus exiled at the *Lucullanum* in Naples by Odoacer.
488 – Ostrogothic kingdom.
535–552/554 – Gothic War.
535 – Naples resisted Justinianic forces.
543 – city recaptured by Totila.
552 – city retaken by the imperial troops under Narses after the battle of Monti Lattari, near Mount Vesuvius.
568 – Lombard invasion of Italy.
570 – Lombards took *Beneventum*.
581 – Naples was attacked by the Lombards.
580s – a supreme command was established at Ravenna, effectively initiating the exarchate.
590 – Formia was abandoned to the Lombards, cutting off the land route between Naples and Rome.
592 – Pope Gregory urged Emperor Maurice and the exarch to send a duke to Naples.
593 – *Nuceria*, controlling the Sarno valley and the principal route into southern Campania, fell to the Lombards.
600 – Gudeliscus attested as *dux Campaniae*.
603 – Guduin first attested as duke of Naples.
616–617 – John of Conza seized power in Naples, proclaiming himself emperor.
661–666 – the threat of Lombard expansionism moved Constans II to invade southern Italy.
661/662 – appointment of Basilius as duke of Naples under Constans II.
674–678 – first Arab siege of Constantinople.

703/704 – Gisulf I of Benevento attacked Neapolitan territory. It is possible, though far from certain, that on that occasion the future Emperor Leo III was sent to Campania with 120 *dromones*, the swift Byzantine war ships.
715/716 – Romuald II took the *castrum* of *Cumae*.
717 – with the help of Pope Gregory II, Duke John recovered *Cumae*.
717–718 – second Arab siege of Constantinople.
723–724 – Pope Gregory II refused to support a tax census with which the eastern government, under Leo III Isauricus, would probably have further despoiled the Church and Roman territories.
731/732 – Leo III Isauricus annexed papal possessions to the Byzantine patriarchate.
751 – Ravenna fell to Aistulf, and the government of Naples was made to depend upon the *strategos* resident in Syracuse.
755 – a hereditary 'monarchy', which was to last for 77 years, began under Duke Stephen II.
758 – King Desiderius met the representative of Emperor Constantine V in Naples, so as to obtain the assistance of the Sicilian fleet in capturing Duke Liutprand of Benevento, in refuge at Otranto.
758–787 – reign of Arechis II at Benevento, capital of the sole remaining Lombard state in Italy.
763 – Duke Stephen II acknowledged the ecclesiastical supremacy of the iconodulist pope, perhaps thus underlining independence from Byzantium.
773–774 – the Lombard kingdom fell to the Franks under Charlemagne, crowned king at Pavia.
782 – Arechis II attempted to take possession of the territories of Naples and Amalfi.
786 – Arechis II and Duke Gregory II signed a treaty concerning the *tertiatores* of *Liburia*. They were tied tenants who, whilst paying a partiary rent of one-third of the produce of the holding, could be bought and sold like slaves. The treaty highlights the curious situation whereby many of them were jointly owned by Naples and Benevento, or by various nobles, monasteries and churches.
787 – Pope Hadrian laid claim to the old Campanian *patrimonium* at the Second Council of Nicea.
812 – Naples refused to supply a contingent to the eastern Byzantine fleet deployed in counter-attacks, on the occasion of a Muslim assault on Sicily.
812 – Ischia and Ponza were raided by Arabs.

---

[1] Most of this material is conveniently assembled in *Monumenta ad Neapolitani ducatus historiam pertinentia* (= *MND*), edited by Bartolomeo Capasso.

812 – peace was achieved between Charlemagne and Grimoald of Benevento.

820s – most of Byzantine Sicily fell to the Arabs.

821 – the *cives* overthrew Duke Stephen III.

826 – Stephen III requested the help of Louis the Pious against the threat of Lombard expansion from Benevento.

831 – Sico of Benevento attacked Naples and stole the relics of Saint Ianuarius from the extramural church and catacombs at Capodimonte.

835 – Naples employed Sicilian Arabs as mercenaries against Lombard Benevento.

836 – a five-year peace treaty (*Pactum Sicardi*) was stipulated between Sicard of Benevento and Duke Andreas. It seems to have been occasioned by fear of the Arabs. The treaty shows Lombard dominance in that it required a tribute to be paid by Naples. It also guaranteed the position of Neapolitans in Lombard territory and demonstrated particular respect to merchants.

840 – Duke Andreas travelled to France to renew his request to Lothar for Carolingian assistance against Benevento. The emperor sent to Naples a Frank named Contardus, with a contingent of troops, who assassinated the duke and took power in the city. This led to a local uprising and the capture and killing of Contardus, only a few days later, in the episcopal palace.

840 – Sergius count of *Cumae* became duke of Naples.

840–1137 – the Sergian dynasty of dukes.

842/843 – Naples furnished help to the Sicilian Arabs in capturing Byzantine Messina.

846 – Rome, *Misenum* and Ischia were sacked by Arabs.

849 – Caesar, son of Duke Sergius I of Naples, was called upon to lead a fleet against the Arabs who had raided Neapolitan territory and sacked Rome in 846. They were routed at the battle of Ostia.

861 – Pope Nicholas I attempted to barter his acceptance of the 'neophyte' Patriarch Ignatius with the return of the papal lands in southern Italy.

869 – the Saracen caliph, Seodan, last emir of Bari, 'crudelissimus, impiissimus et pestifer', led an attack on Naples.

870s – beginning of the Byzantine reconquest of southern Italy under Emperor Basil I.

871 – Salerno was besieged by Aghlabids from north Africa.

877 – Pope John VIII devolved 1,400 gold *mancusi* towards a succesful coup against the pro-Arab Duke Sergius II.

877 – the treaty of Traetto was drawn up between Pope John VIII and a coalition of Campanian city-states, which included the hiring of Amalfi's fleet to patrol Tyrrhenian waters against the Arabs.

881 – the monastery of San Vincenzo al Volturno was sacked by Arabs.

882 – Duke-Bishop Athanasius was excommunicated by the Church.

882 – upon ousting Arabs from the territory of Naples, Athanasius was readmitted to the Church. The Arabs were resettled at *Agropolis* (Agropoli) and Mons Garelianus. The Arabs of Mons Garelianus were effectively placed by Desiderius of Gaeta as a buffer against the Lombards of Capua.

883 – Arabs sacked the monastery of Monte Cassino.

885–886 – Naples was briefly rejoined to Byzantium and struck coins in the name of Basil I.

887 – Prince Atenulf swore an oath of fealty (*foedus gallicus*) to Duke Athanasius for a fixed term of fifteen months.

891–900 – Benevento was captured and held by Byzantine forces.

892 – first mention of the Byzantine theme of *Langouvardìa*, created as a bulwark against the Muslims in Sicily and their Bulgar allies in the Balkan peninsula.

900 – Benevento was recaptured by Prince Atenulf of Capua.

900–902 – the emir, Ibrahim ibn Ahmad, quashed a rebellion in Sicily, took Taormina, sacked Byzantine Reggio, and started to move up the peninsula.

903 – unsuccessful attempt by Duke Guy of Spoleto, with a coalition of Lombards and Neapolitans, to oust the Arabs at Mons Garelianus.

909 – Atenulf of Capua approached the Byzantine emperor, Leo VI, for help against the Arabs at Mons Garelianus.

915 – the Arab mercenaries of Gaeta at Mons Garelianus were defeated by coalition forces under the command of the Byzantine *strategos* Nicholas Picingli.

918 – Sicilian Arabs attacked Reggio.

924 – Sicilian Arabs again attacked Reggio, and exacted further tributes.

928 – Arabs attacked Taranto, Salerno and Naples, and came to terms after the stipulation of an annual tribute.

933–940 – the *Pactum Sicardi* was renewed under Duke John III.

949 – Naples attacked Byzantine *Sipontum*.

956 – the *strategos* of Calabria and Marianos Argiros, with an eastern expeditionary force, blocked the port of Naples, to bring the city once again under Byzantine suzerainty.

958 – Arabs attempted to free Naples.

973 – Naples, alongside Duke Manso III of Amalfi, aided Pandulf's cousin, Landulf of Conza, in a coup against Gisulf of Salerno.

974 – Gisulf retook Salerno with the aid of Pandulf, prince of Capua and Benevento.

981 – Manso III retook Salerno.

1025 – the Byzantine *catepan*, Boiannes, largely responsible for the Byzantine 'reconquest' of Italy, was called back to Constantinople by Constantine VIII, upon the death of Emperor Basil II.

1026 – the *castrum* of *Puteoli* fell to the Lombards under the command of Pandulf IV of Capua.

1027 – Naples was taken by Pandulf IV, and Duke Sergius IV fled to Gaeta.

1029 – Sergius IV retook Naples with the aid of Norman mercenaries and ceded Aversa to Rainulf Drengot.

1041 – at the Council of Melfi the Normans agreed upon their territorial subdivisions and moved to conquer the remaining Byzantine territory in Apulia and Basilicata. Around the middle of the century, other

Norman and French knights reached Italy, including both Richard Quarrel and Robert Guiscard de Hauteville: the latter was to consolidate Norman power in southern Italy.

1044 – last mention of a count of *Cumae*.

1048 – the Norman Richard Quarrel became count of Aversa.

1059 – an allegiance between the papacy and the Normans, including territorial subdivisions, was sealed at the Council of Melfi.

1062 – Richard Quarrel, prince of Capua, attempted to take Naples.

1073 – Amalfi broke away from Gisulf II of Salerno and opened its doors to Robert Guiscard.

1076 – Salerno fell to Robert Guiscard.

1077 – Robert Guiscard besieged Naples, though the siege was lifted following the death of his brother.

1085 – Robert Guiscard died off the coast of Cephalonia, after an abortive attempt to take Constantinople.

1130 – Pope Anacletus crowned Roger II king of Sicily, and granted him the 'honour' of Naples.

1132 – Roger was momentarily defeated by Prince Robert of Capua and Rainulf I, count of Aversa, with the aid of Sergius VII of Naples, at Nocera.

1137–1140 – interregnum in the government of Naples.

1140 – Naples succumbed to the Norman king, Roger II.

Appendix IV

CHRONOLOGY OF THE DUKES AND THE BISHOPS OF NAPLES

DUKES

The following list derives from *MND* II, Fedele (1903) and Cilento (1969a), with modifications. There is some uncertainty over dates.

BYZANTINE DUKES

Gudeliscus (*dux Campaniae*)	by 600
Guduin	*c.* 603
John of Conza (*Compsa*)	*c.* 616
Anatolius	between 625 and 638
Basilius	661/662–666
Theophilactus I	666/667–670
Cosmas	670–672
Andreas	672–677
Caesarius	677–684
Stephen I	684–687
Bonellus	687–695/696
Theodosius	695/696–705/706
Caesarius II	705/706–711
John I	711–719
Theodore	719–730
George	730–740
Gregory I	740–755

INDEPENDENT DUCHY

Stephen II	755–766
Gregory II	766–794
Theophilactus II	794–801
Anthemius/Antimus	801–816
Interregnum	816–821
Stephen III	821–832
Bonus	832–834
Leo	834
Andreas II	834–840
Contardus	840
Sergius I	840–865
Gregory III	865–870
Sergius II	870–878
Athanasius	878–898
Gregory IV	898–915
John II	915–919
Marinus I	919–928
John III	928–969
Marinus II	969–976/977
Sergius III	977–998
John IV	998–1002
John IV and Sergius IV	1002–1005
Sergius IV	1005–1027
Pandulf's Lombard rule	1027–1029
Sergius IV	1029–1033
Sergius IV and John V	1033–1038
John V and Sergius V	1038–1050
Sergius V	1050–1076
Sergius VI	1077–1090
Sergius VI and John VI	1090–1107
John VI	1107–1122
Sergius VII	1122–1137
Interregnum	1137–July 1139
Roger's Norman conquest	August 1139 (in September 1140 he took physical possession of the city).

BISHOPS AND ARCHBISHOPS

On the bishops' calendar, see Achelis (1930) and Mallardo (1947). The following chronology derives mainly from Cilento (1969b: 721–2). The established chronology has been criticized most recently by Bertolini (1970).

BISHOPS

Asprenus	first century
Epithimitus	?
Maronus	?
Probus	?
Paul I	?
Agrippinus	third century
Eustachius	third century
Ephebus	end of third to start of fourth centuries
Calepodius	uncertain seat *c.* 343
Fortunatus	*c.* 344
Maximus	*c.* 356
Zosimus	*c.* 356–362
Ursinus	366– ?
Severus	360s–408/410
Ursus	*c.* 410
John I	*c.* 413–432
Nostrianus	*c.* 444
Timasius	*c.* 455
Felix	fifth century
Soter	*c.* 465
Victor	486/489–498
Stephen I	499–502

Pomponius	514–532	Tiberius	821–841
John II	533–555	John IV 'the scribe'	c. 842–849
Vincent	555–578	Athanasius I	849–872
Redux	579–582	Athanasius II	
Demetrios	590–591	(also Duke from 878)	876–898
Fortunatus II	593–600	Peter	c. 898–903
Paschasius	600–615	Stephen III	903–911
John III	615–635	Athanasius III	911–960
Caesarius	635–639	Nicetas	known in 962
Graciosus	640–647	Gregory	known in 969
Eusebius	647–649		
Leontius	649–653	ARCHBISHOPS	
Adeodatus	653–671		
Agnellus	c. 671–693	Sergius I	990–1005
Julian	c. 693–701	John I	1007–1033
Lawrence	c. 701–717	Victor	attested around 1050
Sergius	717–746	Sergius II	attested in 1059
Cosma	up to 748	John II	attested from 1066 to 1076
vacant seat		Peter I	attested from 1094 to 1100
Calvus	750–763	Gregory	attested in 1116
Paul II	763–768	Marinus	attested from 1118 to 1151
Stephen II (Duke)	768/769–799/800	vacant seat	until no later than 1175
Paul III	c. 800–821		

BIBLIOGRAPHICAL ABBREVIATIONS

AA.SS.	*Acta Sanctorum.*
AE	*Année Epigraphique.*
Amato	Amato di Montecassino, V. De Bartholomaeis (1935) (ed.) *Ystoire de li Normant* (*Fonti per la Storia d'Italia*). Rome, Istituto Storico Italiano per il Medioevo.
ASN	*Archivio di Stato di Napoli.*
BHL	*Bibliotheca hagiographica Latina antiquae et mediae aetatis* (1898–1901, reprinted 1949). Brussels, Société des Bollandistes.
BiblSanct.	*Bibliotheca Sanctorum.*
CBenev	Bartoloni, F. (1950) (ed.) *Le più antiche carte dell'abbazia di San Modesto in Benevento (secoli VIII-XIII)* (*Regesta chartarum Italiae* 33). Rome, Istituto Storico Italiano per il Medioevo.
CD	*Chronicon ducum et principum, in MND.*
CDA	Filangieri De Candida, R. (1917) (ed.) *Codice diplomatico amalfitano.* Naples, S. Morano.
CDC	*Codex Diplomaticus Cavensis* (1873–1893). Naples/Pisa/Milan.
CIL	*Corpus Inscriptionum Latinarum.*
Du Cange	Du Cange, C. (1884–1887) *Glossarium mediae et infime Latinitatis.* London, D. Nutt.
Gesta Ep.	Waitz, G. (1878) (ed.) *Gesta Episcoporum Neapolitanorum, MGH Scriptores rerum Langobardicarum et Italiacarum saec. VI–IX.* Hanover, Hahn.
ILCV	Diehl, E. (1925–1931) (ed.) *Inscriptiones Latinae Christianae Veteres.* Berlin, Weidmann.
ILS	*Inscriptiones Latinae Selectae.*
Kehr	Kehr, P.F. (1935–1961) (ed.) *Regesta Pontificum Romanorum: Italia Pontificia.* Berlin, Weidmann.
Lib. Pont.	Duchesne, L. (1886–1957) (ed.) *Le Liber Pontificalis.* Paris, E. Thorin/De Boccard.
Mansi	Mansi, J.D. (1901–1927) (ed.) *Sacrorum Conciliorum nova et amplissima collectio.* Paris, H. Weller.
MGH	*Monumenta Germaniae Historica.*
MND	Capasso, R. (1881–1892) (ed.) *Monumenta ad Neapolitani ducatus historiam pertinentia* (2 vols). Naples, F. Giannini.
PLRE I/II	Jones, A.H.M., Martindale, J.R. and Morris, J. (1971) *The Prosopography of the Later Roman Empire* I, *AD 260–395.* Cambridge, CUP; Martindale, J.R. (1980) volume II. Cambridge, CUP.
R.	*Regesta Neapolitana, in MND.*
RNAM	Baffi, M. *et al.* (1845–1861) (eds) *Regii Neapolitani archivii monumenta.* Naples, Regia.

ABBREVIATIONS FOR REFERENCES

ArchMed	*Archeologia Medievale*
ASPN	*Archivio Storico delle Province Napoletane*
CollEFR	*Collection de l'École Française de Rome*
JRA	*Journal of Roman Archaeology*
MEFRM	*Mélanges d'Archéologie et d'Histoire de l'École Française de Rome. Moyen Âge et Temps Modernes*
NapNob	*Napoli Nobilissima*
PBSR	*Papers of the British School at Rome*

REFERENCES

Accorona, F., La Forgia, E., Schiavone Palumbo, E. and Ziviello, C. (1985) La fornace di Corso Umberto. In Pozzi (1985): 378–85.

Achelis, H. (1930) *Die Bischofschronik von Neapel.* Leipzig, Karl W. Hiersemann.

Achelis, H. (1936) *Die Katakomben von Neapel.* Leipzig, Karl W. Hiersemann.

Adamo Muscettola, S. (1985) Il tempio dei Dioscuri. In Pozzi (1985): 196–206.

Adamschek, B. (1979) *Kenchreai. Eastern Port of Corinth* IV. *The Pottery.* Leiden, Brill.

Addyman, P.V. (1989) The archaeology of public health at York, England. *World Archaeology* 21 (2): 244–64.

Agaché, R. (1970) *Détection aérienne de vestiges protohistoriques Gallo-Romains et médiévaux dans le bassin de la Somme et ses abords.* Amiens, Société de Préhistoire du Nord.

Agnello, G. (1952) *L'architettura bizantina in Sicilia.* Florence, La Nuova Italia.

Ahrweiler, H. (1961) Fonctionnaires et bureaux maritimes à Byzance. *Revue des Études Byzantines* 19: 239–52.

Ahrweiler, H. (1978) Les ports byzantins (VIIe–IXe siècles). In *La navigazione mediterranea nell'alto medioevo* (*Atti del 25 congresso internazionale di studi sull'alto medioevo*): 259–83. Spoleto, CISAM.

Albarella, U. (1992) Le ossa umane. In Arthur (1992): 53–7.

Albarella, U. (1993) The fauna. In U. Albarella, V. Ceglia and P. Roberts, San Giacomo degli Schiavoni (Molise): an early fifth-century AD deposit of pottery and animal bones from central Adriatic Italy: 203–21. *PBSR* 61: 157–230.

Albarella, U. and Frezza, A.M. (1989a) *I reperti faunistici di Via San Paolo.* Naples, Progetto Eubea. Unpublished archive report held by the Soprintendenza Archeologica delle Province di Napoli e Caserta.

Albarella, U. and Frezza, A.M. (1989b) *I reperti faunistici di GI52.* Naples, Progetto Eubea. Unpublished archive report held by the Soprintendenza Archeologica delle Province di Napoli e Caserta.

Albarella, U., Arthur, P. and Wayman, M. (1989) M179: an early medieval lowland site at loc. Arivito, near Mondragone (Caserta). *ArchMed* 16: 583–612.

Alchermes, J. (1994) Spolia in Roman cities of the late Empire: legislative rationales and architectural reuse. *Dumbarton Oaks Papers* 48: 167–78.

Alfano, L. and Peduto, P. (1992) Ceramiche a vetrina pesante di Salerno e provincia. In Paroli (1992a): 504–10.

Alfödy, G. (1974) *Noricum.* London, RKP.

Alisio, G. (1965) La chiesa e il campanile della Pietrasanta in Napoli (ii). *NapNob* 4: 42–52.

Almagro, M., Caballero, L., Zozaya, J. and Almagro, A. (1975) *Qusayr 'Amra, residencia y banos Omeyas en el desierto de Jordania*. Madrid, Ministerio de Asuntos Exteriores.

Altamura, A. (1974) (ed.) *Cronaca di Partenope*. Naples, Società Editrice Napoletana.

Amalfitano, P. (1990) (ed.) *I Campi Flegrei, un itinerario archeologico*. Venice, Marsilio.

Amari, M. and Schiapparelli, C. (1883) L'Italia descritta nel 'Libro del Re Ruggero' compilato da Edrisi. *Atti del Reale Accademia dei Lincei* 8, ser. 2.

Amarotta, A.R. (1989) *Salerno romana e medievale. Dinamica di un insediamento*. Nocera Inferiore, Laveglia Ed.

Ambrasi, D. (1980) Il cristianesimo e la chiesa napoletana dei primi secoli. In *Storia di Napoli* 3: 133–334. Naples, Società Editrice Storia di Napoli.

Ambrasi, D. (1981) Le diaconie a Napoli nell'alto medioevo. *Campania Sacra* 1: 45–61.

Ambrasi, D. (1985) Strutture civiche e istituzioni sociali nella Napoli ducale. *NapNob* 24: 19–29.

Andreassi, G. and Radina, F. (1988) (eds) *Archeologia di una città. Bari dalle origini al X secolo*. Bari, Edipuglia.

Andreucci Ricciardi, A. (1991) Forma Urbis e scacchiera ippodamea. In M. Rosi (ed.), *Napoli, stratificazione storica e cartografia tematica*: 14–23. Naples, Edizioni Giannini.

Andrews, D. (1991) Tower building and upwardly mobile elites in medieval Italy. In E. Herring, R. Whitehouse and J. Wilkins (eds), *The Archaeology of Power, Part 2, Papers of the Fourth Conference of Italian Archaeology*: 81–6. London, Accordia Research Centre (University of London).

Angel, J.L. (1947) The length of life in ancient Greece. *Journal of Gerontology* 2: 18–24.

Annecchino, R. (1960) *Storia di Pozzuoli e della zona flegrea*. Pozzuoli, Comune di Pozzuoli.

Anselmino, L., Coletti, C.M., Ferrantini, M.L. and Panella, C. (1986) Ostia. Terme del Nuotatore. In A. Giardina (ed.), *Società romana e impero tardoantico* III, *le merci, gli insediamenti*: 45–81. Rome/Bari, Laterza.

Ardizzone, F. (1999) Le anfore recuperate sopra le volte del Palazzo della Zisa e la produzione di ceramica comune a Palermo tra la fine dell'XI ed il XII secolo. *MEFRM* 111 (1): 7–50.

Ardizzone, F. (2000) Rapporti commerciali tra la Sicilia occidentale ed il Tirreno centro-meridionale nell'VIII secolo alla luce del rinvenimento di alcuni contenitori di trasporto. In G.P. Brogiolo (ed.), *II congresso nazionale di archeologia medievale*: 402–7. Florence, All'Insegna del Giglio.

Arslan, E. (1994) La circolazione monetaria (secoli V–VIII). In Francovich and Noyé (1994): 497–519.

Arthur, P. (1984) Rapporto preliminare sullo scavo a Santa Patrizia, Napoli. *ArchMed* 11: 315–20.

Arthur, P. (1986a) Archeologia urbana a Napoli: riflessioni sugli ultimi tre anni. *ArchMed* 13: 515–25.

Arthur, P. (1986b) Problems of the urbanization of Pompeii: excavations 1980–1981. *Antiquaries Journal* 66 (1): 29–44.

Arthur, P. (1986c) Appunti sulla circolazione della ceramica medievale a Napoli. In *La ceramica medievale nel mediterraneo occidentale*: 545–54. Florence, All'Insegna del Giglio.

Arthur, P. (1989a) Aspects of Byzantine economy: an evaluation of amphora evidence from Italy. In V. Déroche and J.-M. Spieser (eds), *Recherches sur la céramique byzantine* (*BCH Supplement* 18): 79–93. Paris, De Boccard.

Arthur, P. (1989b) (ed.) *Il Theatrum Tectum di Neapolis*. Naples, Progetto Eubea. Unpublished report held by the Soprintendenza Archeologica delle Province di Napoli e Caserta.

Arthur, P. (1989c) Some observations on the economy of Bruttium under the later Roman Empire. *JRA* 2: 133–42.

Arthur, P. (1990a) Anfore dall'Alto Adriatico e il problema del Samos Cistern Type. *Aquileia Nostra* 61: 281–96.

Arthur, P. (1990b) *Archaeological Study of the US Navy Zone — Capodichino Airport*. US Naval Support Activity Naples, archive report.

Arthur, P. (1991a) *Romans in Northern Campania: Settlement and Land Use around the Massico and the Garigliano Basin* (*Archaeological Monographs of the British School at Rome* 1). London, British School at Rome.

Arthur, P. (1991b) Naples: a case of urban survival in the early Middle Ages. *MEFRM* 103 (2): 759–84.

Arthur, P. (1992) (ed.) La chiesa di San Costanzo alla Marina Grande di Capri. Scavi 1990. In F. Tessitore (ed.), *L'Isola e il Santo* (*Quaderni di Civiltà del Mediterraneo* 1): 13–115. Naples, Editoriale Scientifica.

Arthur, P. (1993) Early medieval amphorae, the duchy of Naples and the food supply of Rome. *PBSR* 61: 231–44.

Arthur, P. (1994) (ed.) *Il complesso archeologico di Carminiello ai Mannesi, Napoli (scavi 1983–1984)*. Galatina, Congedo.

Arthur, P. (1995) The urban archaeology of medieval Naples: current trends and future prospects. In P. Urbanczyk (ed.), *Theory and Practice of Archaeological Research* II, *Acquisition of Field Data at Multi-strata Sites*: 227–52. Warsaw, Dabrowski.

Arthur, P. (1998a) Pottery in Naples and northern Campania in the sixth and seventh centuries. In L. Saguì (ed.), *Ceramica in Italia: VI–VII secolo*: 157–84. Florence, All'Insegna del Giglio.

Arthur, P. (1998b) Eastern mediterranean amphorae between 500 and 700: a view from Italy. In L. Saguì (ed.), *Ceramica in Italia: VI–VII secolo*: 491–510. Florence, All'Insegna del Giglio

Arthur, P. (1999) The 'Byzantine' baths at Santa Chiara, Naples. In J. DeLaine and D.E. Johnston (eds), *Roman Baths and Bathing, Part 1: Bathing and Society* (*JRA Supplement* 37): 135–46. Michigan, JRA.

Arthur, P. and Capece, B. (1992) Ceramica a vetrina pesante e 'forum ware' a Napoli. In Paroli (1992a): 497–503.

Arthur, P. and Patterson, H. (1994) Ceramics and early medieval central and southern Italy: 'a potted history'. In Francovich and Noyé (1994): 409–41.

Arthur, P. and Vecchio, G. (1985) Gli interventi di scavo recenti o in corso nel centro antico. In Pozzi (1985): 416–25.

Arthur, P. and Whitehouse, D.B. (1983) Appunti sulla produzione laterizia nell'Italia centro-meridionale tra il VI e il XII secolo. *ArchMed* 10: 525–37.

Arthur, P. and Williams, D.F. (1992) Campanian wine, Roman Britain and the third century AD. *JRA* 5: 250–60.

Arthur, P., Guarino, P.M., Jones, D.A. and Schiattarella, M. (1991) Applicazione integrata di metodologie geologiche in archeologia ambientale: l'esempio del Progetto Eubea. *Geologia Tecnica* 2: 5–13.

Arthur, P., Caggia, M.P., Ciongoli, G.P., Melissano, V., Patterson, H. and Roberts, P. (1992) Fornaci altomedievali ad Otranto. Nota preliminare. *ArchMed* 19: 91–122.

Ashburner, W. (1912) The Farmer's Law. *Journal of Hellenic Studies* 32: 68–95.

Aston, M. (1985) *Interpreting the Landscape. Landscape Archaeology and Local History*. London, B.T. Batsford.

Avetta, L., Marcelli, M. and Sasso D'Elia, L. (1991) Quote San Francesco. *MEFRM* 103 (2): 599–609.

Bagolini, B. *et al.* (1987) *La pietra ollare dalla preistoria all'età moderna*. Como, New Press.

Baldassare, I. (1986) Osservazioni sull'urbanistica di Napoli in età romana. In G. Pugliese (ed.), *Neapolis. Atti del 25 convegno di studi sulla Magna Grecia*: 221–31. Taranto, Istituto per la Storia e l'Archeologia della Magna Grecia.

Ballance, M., Boardman, J., Corbett, S. and Hood, S. (1989) *Excavations in Chios 1952–1955: Byzantine Emporio* (*Annual of the British School at Athens Supplement* 20). London, Thames and Hudson.

Ballardini, G. (1964) *L'eredità ceramistica dell'antico mondo romano*. Rome, Istituto Poligrafico dello Stato.

Balzaretti, R. (1991) History, archaeology and early medieval urbanism: the north Italian debate. *Accordia Research Papers* 2: 87–104.

Barnish, S.J.B. (1987) Pigs, plebians and potentes: Rome's economic hinterland, *c.* 350–600 AD. *PBSR* 55: 157–85.

Barnish, S.J.B. (1988) Transformation and survival in the western senatorial aristocracy, *c.* AD 400–700. *PBSR* 56: 120–55.

Barnish, S.J.B. (1989) The transformation of classical cities and the Pirenne debate. *JRA* 2: 385–400.

Barone, N. (1918) Una carta lapidaria medievale nel R. Archivio di Stato di Napoli. *Memorie della Reale Accademia di Archeologia, Lettere e Belle Arti* 3: 27–34.

Bass, G. and Van Doorninck, F.H. (1982) *Yassi Ada, a Seventh Century Byzantine Shipwreck*. Texas, Texas A & M University Press.

Bavant, B. (1989) Cadre de vie et habitat urbain en Italie centrale byzantine (VIe–VIIIe siècle). *MEFRM* 101 (2): 465–532.

Beloch, K.J. (1937) *Bevölkerungsgeschichte Italiens*. I. *Grundlagen. Die Bevölkerung Siziliens und des Königreichs Neapel*. Berlin/Leipzig, Teubner.

Beloch, K.J. (1989) *Campania. Storia e topografia della Napoli antica e dei suoi dintorni*. Naples, Bibliopolis.

Belting, H. (1978) Cimitile: le pitture medioevali e la pittura meridionale nell'alto medioevo. In A. Prandi (ed.), *L'art dans l'Italie méridionale. Aggiornamento dell'opera di Emile Bertaux* IV: 183–8. Rome, École Française de Rome.

Bernabò Brea, L. (1935) Il tempio napoletano dei Dioscuri. *Bullettino della Commissione Archeologica Comunale in Roma* 6: 61–76.

Bernabò Brea, L. (1988) *Le Isole Eolie dal tardo antico ai Normanni* (*Biblioteca di Felix Ravenna* 5). Ravenna, Edizioni del Girasole.

Bertelli, G. (1978) Impulsi classici e loro trasmissione nell'ambiente artistico della Magna Grecia bizantina. In *Magna Grecia bizantina e tradizione classica. Atti del 17 convegno di studi sulla Magna Grecia*: 117–30. Naples, Arte Tipografica.

Bertelli, G. (1992) Affreschi altomedievali dalle catacombe di San Gennaro a Napoli. Note preliminari. *Bessarione* 9: 119–39.

Bertelli, G. (1994) *Cultura longobarda nella Puglia altomedievale. Il tempietto di Seppannibale presso Fasano*. Bari, Edipuglia.

Bertelli, G. (1996) La grotta di San Biagio a Castellammare di Stabia (Napoli). *Cahiers Archeologiques Fin de l'Antiquité et Moyen Age* 44: 49–75.

Berti, G. and Tongiorgi, L. (1981) *I bacini ceramici medievali delle chiese di Pisa*. Rome, 'L'Erma' di Bretschneider.

Bertolini, P. (1970) La serie episcopale napoletana nei secoli VIII e IX. Ricerche sulle fonti per la storia dell'Italia meridionale nell'alto medioevo. *Rivista di Storia della Chiesa in Italia* 24: 349–440.

Bettini, M. and Pucci, G. (1986) Del fritto e d'altro. *Opus* 5: 153–66.

Biddle, M. (1976) The towns. In D.M. Wilson (ed.), *The Archaeology of Anglo-Saxon England*: 99–150. London, Methuen.

Bisogno, G. and Guarino, V. (1984) La ceramica. In Peduto (1984a): 103–24.

Blok, A. (1969) South Italian agro-towns. *Comparative Studies in Sociology and History* 11: 121–35.

Boak, A.E.R. (1955) *Manpower Shortage and the Fall of the Roman Empire*. Ann Arbor, University of Michigan Press.

Boardman, J. (1989) The finds. In M. Ballance, J. Boardman, S. Corbett and S. Hood, *Excavations in Chios 1952–1955*: *Byzantine Emporio* (*Annual of the British School at Athens Supplement* 20): 86–142. London, Thames and Hudson.

Bocchi, F. (1990) (ed.) *I portici di Bologna e l'edilizia civile medievale*. Bologna, Grafis Ed.

Boenzi, G., Mattozzi, S., Petacco, L. and Troisi, G. (1995) Rinvenimenti di superficie nell'area denominata 'Faragnano' (Marano, NA). *Uomo, Strutture, Territorio* 14: 33–58.

Boethius, A. (1951–1953) Notes from Ostia. In G.E. Mylonas (ed.), *Studies Presented to David Moore Robinson* (2 vols): 440–50. St. Louis, Washington University.

Boethius, A. (1960) *The Golden House of Nero, some Aspects of Roman Architecture*. Ann Arbor, University of Michigan Press.

Bognetti, G.P. (1959) Problemi di metodo e oggetti di studio nella storia delle città italiane dell'alto medioevo. In *La città nell'alto medioevo* (*Atti del 6 congresso internazionale di studi sull'alto medioevo*): 59–87. Spoleto, CISAM.

Bognetti, G.P. (1967) Tradizione longobarda e politica bizantina nelle origini del ducato di Spoleto. In *L'Italia longobarda* 3: 439–75. (Originally published in *Rivista di Storia del Diritto Italiano* 26–7 (1953–1954): 269–305.)

Bologna, F. (1993) Momenti della cultura figurativa nella Campania medievale. In G. Pugliese Caratelli (ed.), *Storia e civiltà della Campania, il medioevo*: 171–275. Naples, Electa Napoli.

Bonifay, M. and Piéri, D. (1995) Amphores de Ve au VIIe s. à Marseille: nouvelles données sur la typologie et le contenu. *JRA* 8: 94–120.

Bordone, R. (1991) La città nel X secolo. In *Il secolo di ferro: mito e realtà del secolo X* (*Atti del 38 congresso internazionale di studi sull'alto medioevo*): 517–59. Spoleto, CISAM.

Borrelli, G. (1967) *La basilica di San Giovanni Maggiore*. Naples, Glaux.

Borriello, M.R. and De Simone, A. (1985) La stipe di Sant'Aniello. In Pozzi (1985): 159–61.

Bragantini, I. (1991) (ed.) *Ricerche archeologiche a Napoli. Lo scavo di Palazzo Corigliano, parte* I (*Istituto universitario orientale, Annali del Dipartimento di studi del mondo classico e del mediterraneo antico, Quaderni* 7). Naples, Istituto Universitario Orientale.

Bragantini, I. and Gastaldi, P. (1985) (eds) *Palazzo Corigliano tra archeologia e storia*. Naples, Istituto Universitario Orientale.

Braudel, F. (1975) *The Mediterranean and the Mediterranean World in the Age of Philip II*. London, Fontana.

Braun, J. (1924) *Der Christliche Altar in seiner Geschichtlichen Entwicklung*. Munich, Alte Meister Guenter.

Braun, R. (1964) *Quodvultdeus. Livre des promesses et des prédictions de Dieu* (*Sources chrétiennes*). Paris, Editions du Cerf.

Breglia, L. (1941) *Catalogo delle oreficerie nel Museo Nazionale di Napoli*. Rome, Libreria dello Stato.

Bridges, S.F. and Ward-Perkins, J.B. (1956) Some fourteenth-century Neapolitan military effigies, with notes on the families represented. *PBSR* 24: 158–73.

Brogiolo, G. (1993) *Brescia alto medievale. Urbanistica ed edilizia dal IV al IX secolo*. Mantova, Padus.

Brogiolo, G. and Gelichi, S. (1996a) Conclusioni. In G. Brogiolo and S. Gelichi (eds), *Le ceramiche altomedievali (fine VI–X secolo) in Italia settentrionale: produzione e commerci*: 221–7. Mantova, Padus.

Brogiolo, G. and Gelichi, S. (1996b) *Nuove ricerche sui castelli altomedievali in Italia settentrionale*. Florence, All'Insegna del Giglio.

Brogiolo, G. and Gelichi, S. (1998) *La città nell'alto medioevo italiano. Archeologia e storia*. Rome/Bari, Laterza.

Brogiolo, G. and Manacorda, D. (1983) A proposito di un convegno su archeologia e centro antico a Napoli. *ArchMed* 10: 507–10.

Brothwell, D. (1972) Palaeodemography and earlier British populations. *World Archaeology* 4: 75–87.

Brown, P. (1981) *The Cult of the Saints*. Chicago/London, University of Chicago Press and SCM.

Brown, T.S. (1978) Settlement and military policy in Byzantine Italy. In H.McK. Blake, T.W. Potter and D.B. Whitehouse (eds), *Papers in Italian Archaeology* I, *part ii* (*British Archaeological Reports, International Series* 41): 323–8. Oxford, British Archaeological Reports.

Brown, T.S. (1984) *Gentlemen and Officers, Imperial Administration and Aristocratic Power in Byzantine Italy* AD *554–800*. London, British School at Rome.

Brühl, C.R. (1977) The town as a political centre: general survey. In M.W. Barley (ed.), *European Towns. Their Archaeology and Early History*: 419–30. London/New York/San Francisco, Academic Press.

Bulliet, R. (1975) *The Camel and the Wheel*. Cambridge, Mass., Harvard University Press.

Bullough, D. (1966) Urban change in early medieval Italy: the example of Pavia. *PBSR* 34: 82–130.

Cahen, C. (1955) Un texte peu connu relatif au commerce oriental d'Amalfi au Xe siècle. *ASPN* 34: 61–7.

Calvino, R. (1960) Una inedita iscrizione cristiana rinvenuta a Cuma. *Asprenas* 7: 235–6.

Calvino, R. (1969) *Diocesi scomparse in Campania*. Naples, F. Fiorentino Ed.

Calvino, R. (1976) Documenti e testimonianze monumentali sul culto del martire Sosso, diacono della chiesa di Misenum. *Campania Sacra*: 279–85.

Calzolari, M. (1994) Toponimi fondiari romani: una prima raccolta per l'Italia. *Annali dell'Università di Ferrara sez. 6 (Lettere)*, vol. 8, 3.

Camardo, D. and Ferrara, A. (1990) Petra Herculis: un luogo di culto alla foce del Sarno. *Annali dell'Istituto Universitario Orientale di Napoli (archeol.)* 12: 169–75.

Cambi, F., Citter, C., Guideri, S. and Valenti, M. (1994) Etruria, Tuscia, Toscana: la formazione dei paesaggi altomedievali. In Francovich and Noyé (1994): 183–215.

Camera, M. (1881) *Memorie storico-diplomatiche dell'antica città di Amalfi cronologicamente ordinate e continuate sino al secolo XVIII*. Naples, Tip. Nazionale.

Camodeca, G. (1981) Ricerche su Puteoli tardoromana (fine III–IV secolo). *Puteoli* 4–5: 59–128.

Caniggia, G. (1984) Analisi tipologica: la corte matrice dell'insediamento. In *Recupero e riqualificazione urbana nel Programma straordinario per Napoli* (*Centro di Ricerche Economiche, Sociologiche e di Mercato nell'Edilizia Monografia* 19). Milan, CRESME.

Caniggia, G. (1985) La tipologia urbana di Napoli e le esperienze di recupero nel centro storico. In *La ricostruzione a Napoli* (*Quaderni della Edina* 3): 6–12. Naples, Arti Grafiche Boccia.

Caniggia, G. (1989) Le analisi tipo-morfologiche. In *Notiziario 13/14, programma straordinario di edilizia residenziale per la città di Napoli*: 77–84. Naples, Arti Grafiche Boccia.

Cantalupo, P. (1981) *Acropolis. Appunti per una storia del Cilento*. Agropoli, Guariglia.

Cantilena, R. (1987) Le monete. In D'Onofrio and D'Agostino (1987): 178.

Cantone, G., Fiorentino, B. and Sarnella, G. (1982) *Capri. La città e la terra*. Naples, ESI.

Capasso, B. (1879) L'epitaffio di Cesario console di Napoli. *ASPN* 4: 537–50.

Capasso, B. (1895) *Topografia della città di Napoli nell'XI secolo*. Naples, Arnaldo Forni.

Capasso, B. (1902) *Le fonti della storia delle provincie napoletane dal 568 al 1500*. Naples.

Capasso, B. (1905) *Napoli greco-romana*. Naples, Arturo Berisio Ed.

Capolongo, D. (1987) Notulae Archaeologicae (VI). *Atti del Circolo Culturale B.G. Duns Scoto di Roccarainola* 12–13: 37–56.

Capone, G. (1991) *La collina di Pizzofalcone nel medioevo*. Naples, Arte Tipografica.

Caputo, P. (1989) Località Calvizzano — antica chiesa di San Giacomo. *Atti del 27 convegno di studi sulla Magna Grecia*: 458–9. Taranto, Istituto per la Storia e l'Archeologia della Magna Grecia.

Caputo, P., Morichi, R., Paone, R. and Rispoli, P. (1996) *Cuma e il suo parco archeologico*. Rome, Bardi Editore.

Carandini, A. (1993) L'ultima civiltà sepolta o del massimo oggetto desueto, secondo un archeologo. In Carandini, Cracco Ruggini and Giardina (1993): 11–39.

Carandini, A., Cracco Ruggini, L. and Giardina, A. (1993) (eds), *Storia di Roma* 3. *L'età tardoantica* II. *I luoghi e le culture*. Turin, Einaudi.

Carignani, A. and Pacetti, F. (1989) Anfore tardo-antiche dagli scavi del Palatino. In *Amphores romaines et histoire economique. Dix ans de recherche* (*CollEFR* 114): 610–15. Rome, École Française de Rome.

Carlton, R. (1988) An ethno-archaeological study of pottery production on the Dalmatian island of Iz. In J.C. Chapman,

J. Bintliff, V. Gaffney and B. Slapsak (eds), *Recent Developments in Yugoslav Archaeology* (*British Archaeological Reports, International Series* 431): 101–20. Oxford, British Archaeological Reports.

Carsana, V. (1994) Ceramica da cucina tardo-antica e alto-medievale. In Arthur (1994): 221–58.

Carsana, V. (1995) *Lo scavo nell'ex convento di Santa Patrizia a Napoli. I materiali della fase tardo-antica e alto-medievale*. Università di Roma 'La Sapienza', post-graduate thesis.

Carsana, V. (1996) Napoli: uno scavo archeologico nell'ala meridionale di Palazzo Giusso. Relazione preliminare. *Annali di Archeologia e Storia Antica* 3: 141–8.

Carver, M.O.H. (1993) *Arguments in Stone, Archaeological Research and the European Town in the First Millennium*. Oxford, Oxbow.

Cary, G. (1956) *The Mediaeval Alexander*. Cambridge, CUP.

Cascella, B. (1991) I magistri forestarii e la gestione delle foreste. In R. Licinio (ed.), *Castelli, Foreste, Masserie. Potere centrale e funzionari periferici nella Puglia del secolo XIII*: 47–94. Bari, Dedalo.

Cassandro, G. (1940) La Liburia e i suoi 'tertiatores'. *ASPN* 26: 197–268.

Cassandro, G. (1969) Il ducato bizantino. In *Storia di Napoli* II.I: 3–408. Naples, Società Editrice Storia di Napoli.

Càssola, F. (1986) Problemi di storia neapolitana. In G. Pugliese (ed.), *Neapolis. Atti del 25 convegno di studi sulla Magna Grecia*: 37–81. Taranto, Istituto per la Storia e l'Archeologia della Magna Grecia.

Casteels, E. (1976) La basilique d'Ordona. In J. Mertens (ed.), *Ordona* V: 33–61. Rome/Brussels, Institut Historique Belge de Rome.

Castellano, M. (1975) Il patrimonio del monastero di San Salvatore 'in insula maris' in Napoli attraverso il suo cartario. *ASPN* 13: 175–201.

Cautela, G. and Maietta, I. (1983) *Epigrafi e città, iscrizioni medioevali e moderne nel Museo di San Martino in Napoli*. Naples, Società Editrice Napoletana.

Cavada, E. and Ciurletti, G. (1986) Il territorio trentino nel primo medioevo: gli uomini e la cultura materiale alla luce delle nuove acquisizioni archeologiche. *Atti dell'Accademia Roveretana degli Agiati* 235: 71–105.

Cavallo, G. (1993) La cultura greca. Itinerari e segni. In G. Pugliese Caratelli (ed.), *Storia e civiltà della Campania, il medioevo*: 277–94. Naples, Electa Napoli.

Cavuoto, P. (1964) La chiesa di Santa Sofia a Benevento. *NapNob* 3: 53–66.

Cecchelli, M. (1989) Edifici di culto ariano in Italia. In *Actes du XIe congrès international d'archéologie chrétienne* I, *CollEFR* 123: 233–43.

Ceci, M. (1992) Note sulla circolazione delle lucerne a Roma nell'VIII secolo: i contesti della Crypta Balbi. *ArchMed* 19: 749–66.

Celano, C. and Chiarini, G.B. (1858–1859) *Notizie del bello dell'antico e del curioso della città di Napoli*. Naples, Stamperia Floriana.

Cessi, R. (1942) (ed.) *Documenti relativi alla storia di Venezia anteriori al mille* 1. Padua, Gregoriana.

Chapelot, J. and Fossier, R. (1980) *Le village et la maison au Moyen Age*. Paris, Hachette.

Chatot, V. (1896) *La flotte de Misène*. Paris, E. Leroux.

Chianese, G. (1938) *Marano. Memorie paleocristiane e Liternum. Sprazzi di storia*. Unpublished manuscript.

Chierici, G. (1957) Cimitile I: la necropoli. *Rivista di Archeologia Cristiana* 33: 100–25.

Childe, V.G. (1950) The urban revolution. *The Town Planning Review* 21: 3–17.

Christern, J. (1967) Der 'Jupitertempel' in Cumae und seine Umwandlung in eine Kirche. *Mitteilungen des Deutschen Archäologischen Instituts, Römische Abt.* 73–4: 232–41.

Christern, J. (1977) Il cristianesimo nella zona dei Campi Flegrei In *I Campi Flegrei nell'archeologia e nella storia* (*Atti dei convegni lincei* 33): 213–25. Rome, Accademia Nazionale dei Lincei.

Christie, N.J. (1987) Forum ware, the duchy of Rome, and incastellamento. Problems in interpretation. *ArchMed* 14: 451–66.

Christie, N.J. (1990) Byzantine Liguria: an imperial province against the Longobards, AD 568–643. *Papers of the British School at Rome* 58: 229–71.

Christie, N.J. (1991) (ed.) *Three South Etrurian Churches: Santa Cornelia, Santa Rufina and San Liberato* (*Archaeological Monographs of the British School at Rome* 4). London, British School at Rome.

Christie, N.J. and Rushworth, A. (1988) Urban fortification and defensive strategy in fifth and sixth century Italy: the case of Terracina. *JRA* 1: 73–87.

Ciampoltrini, G. (1987) Un'armilla 'tipo Bengodi' da Vada (Livorno). *ArchMed* 14: 435–8.

Cianfarani, L. (1995) *Antiquarium*. Salerno, F. Piccirillo.

Ciavolino, N. and Dovere, U. (1991) *Corso di aggiornamento in archeologia cristiana e storia della chiesa: l'insula dell'episcopio di Napoli*. Naples, Archidiocesi di Napoli.

Cilento, N. (1969a) La cultura e gli inizi dello studio. *Storia di Napoli* II.II: 521–640. Naples, Società Editrice Storia di Napoli.

Cilento, N. (1969b) La chiesa di Napoli nell'alto medioevo. *Storia di Napoli* II.II: 641–735. Naples, Società Editrice Storia di Napoli.

Cilento, N. (1989) I rapporti fra Ischia e il ducato di Napoli nel medioevo. In Centro di Studi sull'Isola d'Ischia, *La tradizione storica e archeologica in età tardo-antica e medievale: i materiali e l'ambiente, Geostorica* 3: 97–112. Naples, Tip. A. Cortese.

Citarella, A.O. (1967) The relations of Amalfi with the Arab world before the Crusades. *Speculum* 42: 299–313.

Citarella, A.O. (1968) Patterns in medieval trade: the commerce of Amalfi before the Crusades. *Journal of Ecclesiastical History* 28 (4): 531–55.

Citarella, A.O. (1977) *Il commercio di Amalfi nell'alto medioevo*. Salerno, Centro 'Raffaele Guariglia' di Studi Salernitani.

Colgrave, B. and Mynors, R.A.B. (1969) *Historia Ecclesiastica Gentis Anglorum*. Oxford, Clarendon Press.

Coleman, J.E. (1986) *Excavations at Pylos in Elis* (*Hesperia Supplement* 21). Princeton, New Jersey, American School of Classical Studies at Athens.

Colucci Pescatori, G. (1986) Osservazioni su Abellinum tardo-antica e sull'eruzione del 472 d.C. In C. Albore Livadie (ed.), *Tremblements de terre, éruptions volcaniques et vie des hommes dans la Campanie antique*: 121–41. Naples, Centre Jean Berard.

Conticello De' Spagnolis, M. (1993) Una testimonianza ebraica a Nuceria Alfaterna. In L. Franchi dell'Orto (ed.), *Ercolano 1738–1988. 250 anni di ricerca archeologica*: 243–52. Rome, 'L'Erma' di Bretschneider.

Conticello De' Spagnolis, M. (1995) Osservazioni sulle fasi edilizie di alcune ville rustiche di Scafati, suburbio orientale di Pompei, seppellite dalla eruzione del 79 d.C. In *Archäologie und Seismologie*: 93–102. Munich, Bierung and Brinkmann.

Coppola, C. (1982) *Il verde segreto, Napoli: una ricerca*. Naples, La Pleiade.

Coppola, G. and Muollo, G. (1994) *Castelli medievali in Irpinia*. Milan, Elio Sellino Ed.

Coroneo, R. (2000) *Scultura mediobizantina in Sardegna*. Nuoro, Poliedro.

Corsi, P. and Fonseca, C.D. (1989) Dalla caduta dell'impero d'occidente al dominio longobardo. In F. Tateo (ed.), *Storia di Bari dalla preistoria al mille*: 257–83. Rome/Bari, Laterza.

Cosenza, G. (1907) *Stabia: studi archeologici, topografici e storici*. Trani, Vecchi e C.

Cotton, M.A. (1979) *A Late Republican Villa at Posto, Francolise*. London, British School at Rome.

Cotton, M.A. and Métraux, G. (1985) *San Rocco Villa at Francolise*. London, British School at Rome.

Courtois, C. (1955) *Les Vandales et l'Afrique*. Paris, Arts et Métiers Graphiques.

Courty, M.A., Goldberg, P. and Macphail, R. (1989) *Soils and Micromorphology in Archaeology*. Cambridge, CUP.

Cracco Ruggini, L. (1964) Note sugli ebrei in Italia dal IV al XVI secolo. *Rivista Storica Italiana* 76: 926–56.

Cracco Ruggini, L. (1969) Le relazioni fiscali, annonarie e commerciali delle città campane con Roma nel IV sec. d.C. *Studi Romani* 17: 133–46.

Cretella, M. (1994) Molluschi. In Arthur (1994): 423–8.

Crivellucci, A. (1913) (ed.) *Landulfi Sagacis, Historia romana (Fonti per la Storia d'Italia* 50). Rome, Istituto Storico Italiano.

Croce, B. (1944) *Storia del regno di Napoli* (third edition). Bari, Gius. Laterza e Figli.

Cubberley, A.L., Lloyd, J.A. and Roberts, P.C. (1988) *Testa* and *clibani*: the baking covers of classical Italy. *PBSR* 56: 98–119.

Cuozzo, E. and Martin, J.-M. (1995) Il particolarismo napoletano altomedievale. *MEFRM* 107 (1): 7–16.

D'Agostino, M. and Marazzi, F. (1985) Notizia preliminare sullo studio dei materiali tardoantichi e altomedievali di Lacco Ameno (NA). *ArchMed* 12: 611–25.

Dalbono, C.T. (1891) *Guida di Napoli e dintorni*. Naples, Antonio Morano Ed.

D'Amico, V. (1935) *I Bulgari trasmigrati in Italia nei secc. VI e VII dell'era volgare. Loro speciale diffusione nel Sannio*. Campobasso, Vincenzo Petrucciani.

D'Andria, F. and Whitehouse, D.B. (1992) (eds) *Excavations at Otranto* II*: the Finds*. Galatina, Congedo.

D'Angela, C. (1980) La necropoli tardoromana di Celimarro (Castrovillari). In C. D'Angela (ed.), *Testimonianze cristiane antiche ed altomedievali nel Sibaritide. Atti del convegno nazionale*: 75–88. Bari, Adriatica Editrice.

D'Angela, C. (1988) *Gli scavi del 1953 nel Piano di Carpino (Foggia). Le terme e la necropoli altomedievale della villa romana di Avicenna*. Taranto, Scorpione.

Danstrup, J.K. (1946) Indirect taxes at Byzantium. *Classica et Medievalia* 8: 139–67.

D'Arms, J. (1970) *Romans on the Bay of Naples. A Social and Cultural Study of the Villas and their Owners from 150 BC to AD 400*. Cambridge, Mass., Harvard University Press.

D'Arms, J. (1981) *Commerce and Social Standing in Ancient Rome*. Cambridge, Mass., Harvard University Press.

Dattilo, V. (1956) *Castel dell'Ovo, storia e leggende di Napoli*. Naples, Treves.

Davis, R. (1989) *The Book of Pontiffs (Liber Pontificalis)*. Liverpool, Liverpool University Press.

De Azevedo, C. (1969) Laubia. In A Giuseppe Ermini. Miscellanea di omaggio comprendente saggi, 'note e discussioni' di autori diversi. *Studi Medievali* ser. 3, 10 (2): 431–63. Spoleto, CISAM.

De Azevedo, C. (1974) Aspetti urbanistici delle città altomedievali. In *Topografia urbana e vita cittadina nell'alto medioevo in occidente. Atti del 21 congresso internazionale di studi sull'alto medioevo*: 641–77. Spoleto, CISAM.

De Blasiis, G. (1915) Un castello svevo-angioino nel Gualdo di Napoli. *ASPN* 40: 101–79.

De Caro, S. (1985) Partenope — Palaepolis: la necropoli di Pizzofalcone. In Pozzi (1985): 99–102.

De Caro, S. (1993) L'attività della Soprintendenza Archeologica di Napoli e Caserta. In A. Stazio and S. Ceccoli (eds), *Sibari e la Sibaritide. Atti del 32 convegno di studi sulla Magna Grecia*: 669–93. Taranto, Istituto per la Storia e l'Archeologia della Magna Grecia.

De Caro, S. (1994) L'attività della Soprintendenza Archeologica di Napoli e Caserta. In *Magna Grecia, Etruschi Fenici. Atti del 33 convegno di studi sulla Magna Grecia*: 647–69. Taranto, Istituto per la Storia e l'Archeologia della Magna Grecia.

De Caro, S. (1999) Dati recenti sul tardoantico nella Campania settentrionale. In *L'Italia meridionale in età tardo antica. Atti del 38 convegno di studi sulla Magna Grecia*: 223–42. Taranto, Istituto per la Storia e l'Archeologia della Magna Grecia.

De Caro, S. and Greco, A. (1981) *Campania, guida archeologica*. Bari, Laterza.

De Crescenzo, G. (1989) *La chiesa e il monastero di Santa Maria Maggiore o della Pietrasanta in Napoli*. Naples, Progetto Eubea. Unpublished archive report held by the Soprintendenza Archeologica delle Province di Napoli e Caserta.

de Franciscis, A. (1954) Le recenti scoperte in Santa Chiara e la topografia di Napoli romana. *Archeologia Classica* 6: 277–83.

de Franciscis, A. (1977) Il sarcofago del Duca Teodoro. *Rendiconti dell'Accademia di Archeologia, Lettere e Belle Arti di Napoli* 52: 147–58.

de Franciscis, A. (1981) Il tempio di Augusto. *Puteoli* 4–5: 129–32.

Delogu, P. (1976) Le monete. In P. Delogu, G. Maetzke, P. Natella, P. Peduto, E. Tabaczynska and S. Tabaczynski, *Caputaquis medievale* I: 100–1. Salerno, ESI.

Delogu, P. (1977) *Mito di una città meridionale, Salerno, secoli VIII–XI*. Naples, Liguori.

Delogu, P. (1988) The rebirth of Rome in the eighth and ninth centuries. In Hodges and Hobley (1988): 32–42.

Delogu, P. (1989) Il principato di Salerno. In *Storia del Mezzogiorno* II.I: 237–77. Portici, Edizioni del Sole.

Delogu, P. (1992) Patroni, donatori, committenti nell'Italia meridionale longobarda. In *Committenti e produzione artistico-letteraria nell'alto medioevo occidentale. Atti del 39 congresso internazionale di studi sull'alto medioevo*: 303–34. Spoleto, CISAM.

Del Treppo, M. and Leone, A. (1977) *Amalfi medioevale*. Naples, Mario Giannini Ed.

de Martino, E. (1987) *Sud e magia*. Milan, Feltrinelli.

D'Engenio, C. (1623) *Napoli sacra*. Naples, O. Beltrano.

De Petra, G. (1892) Napoli. *Notizie degli Scavi di Antichità*: 99.

De Petra, G. (1895) Lacco Ameno (frazione del comune di Ischia) — Di un tesoretto di monete d'oro bizantine. *Notizie degli Scavi di Antichità*: 83–4.

De Rinaldis, A. (1916) Senise. Monili d'oro di età barbarica. *Notizie degli Scavi di Antichità*: 329–32.

De Rosa, V. (1964) La ricognizione delle ossa di San Gennaro. *Bollettino Ecclesiastico Napoletano* 45: 167–71.

De Rossi, G. (1996) Topografia cristiana di Cuma. *Rivista di Archeologia Cristiana* 72: 403–5.

De Rossi, G. (1998) Gli *acta translationis Sancti Sosii* e la perduta cattedrale di Miseno. In *Domum Tuam Dilexi. Miscellanea in onore di Aldo Nestori* (*Studi di Archeologia Cristiana* LIII): 251–64. Vatican City, Pontificio Istituto di Archeologia Cristiana.

De Rossi, G. (2001) *I Campi Flegrei dal IV al IX secolo: continuità e discontinuità, abbandoni e trasformazioni. Analisi storico-archeologica di un'area campione*. Università di Roma 'La Sapienza', Ph.D. thesis.

De Rossi, G.B. (1879) Cimitero cristiano di Stabia. *Bullettino di Archeologia Cristiana* 4: 118–27.

De Salvo, L. (1986) Rifornimenti alimentari e trasporti marittimi nelle *Variae* di Cassiodoro. In S. Leanzo (ed.), *Flavio Magno Aurelio Cassiodoro. Atti della settimana di studi Cosenza–Squillace 19–24 settembre 1983*: 409–20. Soveria Mannelli (CZ), Rubbettino Ed.

De Seta, C. (1981) *Napoli*. Bari, Laterza.

De Seta, C. (1984) (ed.) *I casali di Napoli*. Bari, Laterza.

De Simone, A. (1985) Il complesso monumentale di San Lorenzo Maggiore. In Pozzi (1985): 185–95.

Desmulliez, J. (1986) Note de topographie napolitaine. *Mélanges d'Archéologie et d'Histoire de l'École Française de Rome. Antiquité* 98: 873–9.

Desmulliez, J. (1998) Le dossier du groupe épiscopal de Naples: état actuel des recherches. *Antiquité Tardive* 6: 345–54.

De Stefano, P. and Carsana, V. (1987) (eds) *Archeologia e trasformazione urbana, Notiziario 12. Programma straordinario di edilizia residenziale per la città di Napoli*. Naples, Arti Grafiche Boccia.

de Vogüé, A. (1971) La Règle d'Eugippe retrouvée. *Revue d'Ascétique* 47: 233–65.

Di Capua, F. (1935) Ritrovamenti archeologici nel territorio dell'antica Stabia negli anni 1931–33. *Rivista di Studi Pompeiani* 1: 166–73.

Di Carlo, A., Gelichi, S., Merlo, R. and Pandolfi, A. (1985) Lo scavo nel convento di San Domenico a Bologna. Relazione preliminare. *ArchMed* 12: 245–80.

Diehl, C. (1888) *Études sur l'administration byzantine dans l'exarchat de Ravenne (568–751)*. Paris, E. Leroux.

Diehl, C. (1896) *L'Afrique byzantine*. Paris, E. Leroux.

Di Gangi, G., Lebole Di Gangi, C.M. and Sabbione, C. (1994) Scavi medievali in Calabria: Tropea 1, rapporto preliminare. *ArchMed* 21: 351–74.

Di Giovanni, V. (1994) Osso lavorato. In Arthur (1994): 363–5.

Di Muro, A. (1998) Tra Longobardi e Normanni. Lo scavo di Salerno. In S. Patitucci Uggeri (ed.), *Scavi medievali in Italia 1994–1995*: 75–84. Rome/Freiburg/Vienna, Herder.

Di Stefano, R. (1971) Lineamenti di storia urbanistica. In *Il centro antico di Napoli*: 143–256. Naples, ESI.

Di Stefano, R. (1974) *La cattedrale di Napoli*. Naples, Editrice Storico Napoletano.

Dölger, F. (1953) Europas Gestaltung im Spiegel der fränkisch-byzantinischen Auseinandersetzung des 9. Jahrhunderts. In *Bysanz und Europäischen Staatenwelt*: 282–369. Ettal, Buch-Kunstverlag.

Donald, P.J. (1995) *Byzantine Gold Coins from the P.J. Donald Collection*. London, Baldwin's Auctions.

Donatone, G. (1967) La maiolica napoletana dalle origini al secolo XV. *Storia di Napoli* VI: 579–625. Naples, Società Editrice Storia di Napoli.

D'Onofrio, A.M. (1985) Interventi di scavo a Napoli nell'area del I Policlinico: il saggio D1 — relazione preliminare. *Annali dell'Istituto Universitario Orientale di Napoli (archeol.)* 7: 155–98.

D'Onofrio, A.M. and D'Agostino, B. (1987) *Ricerche archeologiche a Napoli. Lo scavo in largo Sant'Aniello (1982–1983)*. Naples, Istituto Universitario Orientale.

Doria, G. (1971) *Le strade di Napoli. Saggio di toponomastica storica* (second edition). Naples, R. Ricciardi.

Dubois, C. (1907) *Pouzzoles antique*. Paris, A. Fontemoing.

Duby, G. (1975) *Le origini dell'economia europea, guerrieri e contadini nel medioevo*. Rome/Bari, Laterza.

Duchesne, L. (1903) Les evechés d'Italie et l'invasion lombarde. *Mélanges d'Archéologie et d'Histoire de l'École Française de Rome. Antiquité* 22: 83–116.

Duchesne, L. (1905) Les evechés d'Italie et l'invasion lombarde. *Mélanges d'Archéologie et d'Histoire de l'École Française de Rome. Antiquité* 25: 365–84.

Dunn, A. (1998) Heraclius 'reconstruction of cities' and their sixth-century antecedents. In *Acta XIII Congressus Internationalis Archaeologiae Christianae* II, *Studi di Antichità Cristiana* LIV and *Vjesnik za Arheologiju i Historiju Dalmatinsku supplementary volumes* 87–9: 795–806. Vatican/Split.

Durliat, J. (1990) *De la ville antique à la ville byzantine. Le problème des subsistances* (*CollEFR* 136). Rome, École Française de Rome.

Edwards, K.M. (1933) *Corinth 6. Coins 1896–1929*. Cambridge, Mass., Harvard University Press.

Ellis, S. (1988) The end of the Roman house. *American Journal of Archaeology* 92: 565–76.

Empereur, J.-Y. and Picon, M. (1989) Les régions de production d'amphores impériales en Meditéranée orientale. In J.-Y. Empereur and Y. Garlan (eds), *Amphores romaines et histoire économique, dix ans de recherche* (*CollEFR* 114): 223–48. Rome, École Française de Rome.

Ennen, E. (1978) *Storia della città medievale*. Rome/Bari, Laterza.

Esposito, C. (1992) Spaccanapoli. Il sottosuolo. In U. Carughi (ed.), *Spaccanapoli, centro storico*: 62–7. Naples, Electa Napoli.

Every, G. (1962) *The Byzantine Patriarchate 451–1204*. London, SPCK.

Farioli, R. (1978) Libro I, capitolo I. In A. Prandi (ed.), *L'art dans l'Italie méridionale. Aggiornamento dell'opera di Emile Bertaux* IV: 30–1. Rome, École Française de Rome.

Farioli Campanati, R. (1982) La cultura artistica nelle regioni bizantine d'Italia dal VI all'XI secolo. In G. Caucillo *et al.* (eds), *I Bizantini in Italia*: 139–426. Milan, Libri Scheiwiller.

Farmer, D.H. (1989) *Dizionario dei Santi* (*The Oxford Dictionary of Saints*, revised Italian edition). Padua, Franco Muzio Ed.

Fasola, U.M. (1974) Le recenti scoperte nella catacomba di San Gennaro a Napoli. *Rendiconti della Pontificia Accademia di Archeologia* 46: 197–224.

Fasola, U.M. (1975) *Le catacombe di San Gennaro a Capodimonte*. Rome, Editalia.

Fasola, U.M. (1986) Le tombe privilegiate dei vescovi e dei duchi di Napoli nelle catacombe di San Gennaro. In Y. Duval and J.-C. Picard (eds), *L'inhumation privilégée du IVe au VIIIe siècle en Occident*: 205–10. Paris, Université de Paris-Val-de-Marne.

Fatica, L. (1992) San Costanzo di Capri: patriarca di Costantinopoli? *Campania Sacra* 23: 155–200.

Fedele, P. (1903) Il catalogo dei duchi di Napoli. *ASPN* 28, fasc. III.

Federici, V. (1925) (ed.) *Chronicon Vulturnense del Monaco Giovanni* (*Fonti per la Storia d'Italia* I). Rome, Tipografia del Senato.

Feniello, A. (1991) Contributo alla storia della 'Iunctura civitatis' di Napoli nei secoli X–XIII (1). *NapNob* 38: 175–200.

Feniello, A. (1995) *Napoli normanno-sveva*. Rome, Newton.

Fentress, E., Clay, T., Hobart, M. and Webb, M. (1991) Late Roman and medieval Cosa I: the arx and the structure near the Eastern Height. *PBSR* 59: 197–230.

Fentress, E. and Perkins, P. (1988) Counting African red slip ware. *Africa Romana* 5: 205–14.

Ferrajoli, F. (1961) Le valli della città di Neapolis. Note di topografia antica. *Il Rievocatore* 12 (1–3): 7–11.

Ferraro, S. (1991) Un'insediamento benedettino a Castellamare di Stabia: la Grotta di San Biagio. In *Stabiae Risorge. Sguardo retrospettivo agli scavi archeologici degli anni '50*: 67–84. Castellamare di Stabia.

Ferulano, G. (1991) Un intervento di recupero urbano: vico Santa Maria ad Agnone. *Architettura Quaderni* 7: 128–38.

Feugère, M. (1994) Metalli. In Arthur (1994): 357–62.

Février, P.A. (1993) Roma. Il prestigio della città pagana. In Carandini, Cracco Ruggini and Giardina (1993): 41–51.

Fiaccadori, G. (1993) Il Cristianesimo. Dalle origini alle invasioni barbariche. In G. Pugliese Caratelli (ed.), *Storia e civiltà della Campania, il medioevo*: 145–70. Naples, Electa Napoli.

Figliuolo, B. (1993) Longobardi e Normanni. In G. Pugliese Caratelli (ed.), *Storia e civiltà della Campania, il medioevo*: 37–86. Naples, Electa Napoli.

Filangieri di Candida, R. (1974) *Storia di Massa Lubrense* (second edition). Naples, Luigi Pierro.

Finley, M. (1958) Review of Boak (1955). *Journal of Roman Studies* 48: 156–64.

Finley, M. (1981) The ancient city: from Fustel de Coulanges to Max Weber and beyond. In M. Finley (ed.), *Economy and Society in Ancient Greece*: 3–23. London, Chatto and Windus.

Fiore Cavalieri, M.G. (1988) Fara Sabina: Monte San Martino: indagini archeologiche. *Quaderni di Archeologia Etrusco-Italica* 16: 441–51.

Fiorelli, G. (1866–1872) *Catalogo del Museo Nazionale di Napoli*. Naples, Stab. Tip. in Santa Teresa.

Fitt, J. (1988) *The Study of Plant Remains from Central Naples*. Unpublished archive report held by the Soprintendenza Archeologica delle Province di Napoli e Caserta.

Fonseca, C.D. (1987) *Particolarismo istituzionale e organizzazione ecclesiastica del mezzogiorno medioevale*. Galatina, Congedo.

Fonseca, C.D. (1990) Longobardia minore e longobardi nell'Italia meridionale. In M.G. Arcamone *et al.* (eds), *Magistra Barbaritas*: 127–41. Milan, Credito Italiano.

Fontana, M.V. (1984) La ceramica invetriata al piombo di San Lorenzo Maggiore. In Fontana and Ventrone Vassallo (1984): 49–175.

Fontana, M.V. and Ventrone Vassallo, G. (1984) (eds) *La ceramica medievale di San Lorenzo Maggiore in Napoli*. Naples, Istituto Universitario Orientale.

Foss, C. (1979) *Ephesus after Antiquity: a Late Antique, Byzantine and Turkish City*. Cambridge, CUP.

Foss, C. and Winfield, D. (1986) *Byzantine Fortifications. An Introduction*. Pretoria, University of South Africa.

Franciosi, C.G. (1978) Il dibattito. In *Magna Grecia bizantina e tradizione classica. Atti del 17 convegno di studi sulla Magna Grecia*: 154–9. Taranto, Istituto per la Storia e l'Archeologia della Magna Grecia.

Franciosi, C.G. (1982) Area beneventana occidentale — attività 1981–1982. In *Atti del 22 convegno di studi sulla Magna Grecia*: 443–6. Taranto, Istituto per la Storia e l'Archeologia della Magna Grecia.

Francovich, R. (1987) Premessa. In R. Francovich (ed.), *Archeologia e storia del medioevo italiano*: 9–20. Rome, NIS.

Francovich, R. and Noyé, G. (1994) (eds) *La storia dell'alto medioevo italiano (VI–X secolo) alla luce dell'archeologia*. Florence, All'Insegna del Giglio.

Frantz, A. (1988) *The Athenian Agora XXIV, Late Antiquity: AD 267–700*. Princeton, The American School of Classical Studies at Athens.

Frati, L. (1857) *Delle antiche monete d'oro ritrovate in Reno nell'agosto 1857*. Bologna.

Frayn, J. (1993) *Markets and Fairs in Roman Italy. Their Social and Economic Importance from the Second Century BC to the Third Century AD*. Oxford, Clarendon Press.

Frederiksen, M. (1977) Una fonte trascurata sul bradisismo puteolano. In *I Campi Flegrei nell'archeologia e nella storia* (*Atti dei convegni lincei* 33): 117–29. Rome, Accademia Nazionale dei Lincei.

Frederiksen, M. (1984) *Campania*. London, British School at Rome.

Frend, W. (1969) Paulinus of Nola and the last century of the western Empire. *Journal of Roman Studies* 59: 1–11.

Frezza, A.M. (1995) Resti di pesci dal monastero medievale di Santa Patrizia, Napoli. *ArchMed* 22: 611–17.

Frugoni, A. (1969) La biblioteca di Giovanni III duca di Napoli. *Annali della Scuola Speciale per Archivisti e Bibliotecari dell'Università di Roma* 9: 161–71.

Fuiano, M. (1972) *Napoli nel medioevo (secoli XI–XIII)*. Naples, Liguori.

Fuiano, M. (1986) *Spiritualità e cultura a Napoli nell'alto medioevo*. Naples, Liguori.

Fulford, M.G. and Peacock, D.P.S. (1984) *Excavations at Carthage: the British Mission* I,2. *The Avenue du President Habib Bourguiba, Salammbo: the Pottery and other Ceramic Objects from the Site*. Sheffield, British Academy.

Fumagalli, V. (1988) *La pietra viva*. Bologna, Il Mulino.

Gadd, D. and Ward-Perkins, B. (1991) The development of urban domestic housing in northern Italy. The evidence of the excavations on the San Romano site, Ferrara (1981–4). *Accordia Research Papers* 2: 105–27.

Galante, G.A. (1872) *Guida sacra della città di Napoli*. Naples, Fibreno.

Galante, G.A. (1987) *La catacomba di San Severo in Napoli* (edited by G. Rassello). Naples, M. D'Auria Ed.

Galasso, E. (1969) *Oreficeria medioevale in Campania*. Rome, Abete.

Galasso, G. (1965) *Mezzogiorno medievale e moderno*. Turin, Einaudi.

Galasso, G. (1975) *Mezzogiorno medievale e moderno*. Turin, Einaudi.

Galasso, G. (1980) L'isola degli imperatori. In *Conoscere l'Italia, Campania* II: 514–16. Novara, Istituto Geografico De Agostini.

Galasso, G. (1982) *L'altra Europa. Per un'antropologia storica del Mezzogiorno*. Turin, Einaudi.

Galavaris, G. (1970) *Bread and the Liturgy*. Madison, University of Wisconsin Press.

Gallo, A. (1986) Il santuario di Apollo sull'acropoli di Cuma. *Puteoli* 9–10: 121–210.

Gambi, L. (1989) I valori storici dei quadri ambientali. In *Storia d'Italia Einaudi. I caratteri originali*: 3–60. Turin, Einaudi.

Garcea, F. (1987) Appunti sulla produzione e circolazione delle lucerne nel napoletano tra VII ed VIII secolo. *ArchMed* 14: 537–45.

Garcea, F. (1994) Lucerne fittili. In Arthur (1994): 303–27.

Gargano, G. (1992) *La città davanti al mare. Aree urbane e storie sommerse di Amalfi nel medioevo*. Castellammare di Stabia, Eidos.

Garnsey, P. (1978) Rome's African Empire under the Principate. In P. Garnsey and C.R. Whittaker (eds), *Imperialism in the Ancient World*: 223–54. Cambridge, CUP.

Garzya, A. (1976) Napoli e Bisanzio: spunti e considerazioni. *Colloqui di Storia e Letteratura* 2: 6–11.

Gastaldi, P. (1985) Palazzo Corigliano: un'esperienza di archeologia urbana. In Bragantini and Gastaldi (1985): 19–33.

Gay, J. (1904) *L'Italie méridionale et l'empire Byzantin*. Paris, A. Fontemoing.

Gay, J. (1917) *L'Italia méridionale e l'impero bizantino dall'avvento di Basilio I alla resa di Bari ai Normanni*. Florence, Libreria della Voce.

Gelichi, S. (1996) Note sulle città bizantine dell'Esarcato e della Pentapoli tra IV e IX secolo. In G.P. Brogiolo (ed.), *Early Medieval Towns in the West Mediterranean*: 69–79. Mantua, Padus.

Gelzer, H. (1890) (ed.) *Georgii Cypri Descriptio Orbis Romani*. Leipzig, Teubner.

Genito, B. (1985) La ceramica dipinta medievale. In D'Onofrio (1985): 177–9.

Genito, B. (1988) Materiali e problemi. In La necropoli di Vicenne nella piana di Boiano. Atti del Convegno, 1 Novembre 1988: 49–67. *Conoscenze* 4: 6–83.

Gialanella, C. and Sampaolo, V. (1981) Note sulla topografia di Puteoli. *Puteoli* 4–5: 133–61.

Giampaola, D., Fratta, F. and Scarpati, C. (1996) Neapolis: le mura e la città. Indagini a San Domenico Maggiore e a San Marcellino. *Annali di Archeologia e Storia Antica* n.s. 3: 115–38.

Gianfrotta, P. (1987) Un porto sotto il mare. In *I Campi Flegrei*: 101–10. Naples, G. Macchiaroli.

Gianfrotta, P. (1988) Les sites submergés: l'exemple de la côte napolitaine et des Champs Phlégréens. In *Actes de Symposium International Thracica Pontica* 4: 385–98. Sozopol.

Gigante, M. (1982) La civiltà letteraria. In *I Bizantini in Italia*: 613–51. Milan, Libri Scheiwiller.

Gigli, G. (1946) *La flotta e la difesa del Basso Impero* (*Memorie dell'Accademia Nazionale dei Lincei* 8.1, fasc. 1). Rome, G. Bardi.

Glucker, C.A.M. (1987) *The City of Gaza in the Roman and Byzantine Periods* (*British Archaeological Reports, International Series* 325). Oxford, British Archaeological Reports.

Goethe, J.W. (1973) *Viaggio in Italia*. Florence, Edipem.

Goitien, S.D. (1967) *A Mediterranean Society. The Jewish Communities of the Arab World as Portrayed in the Documents of the Cairo Geniza* I. Berkeley/Los Angeles, University of California Press.

Goldschmidt, R.C. (1940) (ed.) *Paulinus' Churches at Nola*. Amsterdam, N.V. Noord-Hollandische.

Granier, T. (1996) Napolitains et Lombards aux VIIIe et XIe siècles. De la guerre des peuples à la guerre des saints en Italie du sud. *MEFRM* 108 (2): 403–50.

Grant, A. (1988) Animal resources. In G. Astill and A. Grant (eds), *The Countryside of Medieval England*: 149–87. Oxford, Blackwell.

Greco, E. (1985a) Forum Duplex. Appunti per lo studio delle agorai di Neapolis in Campania. *Annali dell'Istituto Universitario Orientale di Napoli (archeol.)* 7: 125–35.

Greco, E. (1985b) Problemi urbanistici. In Pozzi (1985): 132–9.

Greco, E. (1986) L'impianto urbano di Neapolis greca: aspetti e problemi. In G. Pugliese (ed.), *Neapolis. Atti del 25 convegno di studi sulla Magna Grecia*: 187–219. Taranto, Istituto per la Storia e l'Archeologia della Magna Grecia.

Green, F. (1979) Phosphatic mineralisation of seeds from archaeological sites. *Journal of Archaeological Science* 6: 279–84.

Greenhalgh, M. (1989) *The Survival of Roman Antiquities in the Middle Ages*. London, Duckworth.

Grierson, P. (1959) Commerce in the Dark Ages: a critique of the evidence. *Transactions of the Royal Historical Society* 9: 123–40.

Grierson, P. (1961) Monete bizantine in Italia dal VII all'XI secolo. In *Moneta e scambi nell'alto medioevo. Atti del 8 congresso internazionale di studi sull'alto medioevo*: 35–55. Spoleto, CISAM.

Grierson, P. (1968) *Catalogue of the Byzantine Coins in the Dumbarton Oaks Collection and in the Whitemore Collection 2 — Phocas to Theodosius III,* part I. Washington, Dumbarton Oaks.

Grierson, P. (1991) *Tarì, follari e denari*. Salerno, Elea Press.

Grierson, P. and Blackburn, M. (1986) *Medieval European Coinage with a Catalogue of the Coins in the Fitzwilliam Museum, Cambridge*. Cambridge, CUP.

Grmek, M.D. (1985) *Le malattie all'alba della civiltà occidentale*. Bologna, Il Mulino.

Guarino, V., Mauro, D. and Peduto, P. (1988) Un tentativo di recupero di una stratigrafia e materiali vari da collezione: il caso del complesso ecclesiastico di Santa Restituta a Lacco Ameno di Ischia. *ArchMed* 15: 439–69.

Gubitosi, C. and Izzo, A. (1968) Castel dell'Ovo nella storia: il rilievo, il restauro, la ristrutturazione. *Atti dell'Accademia Pontaniana* 17: 3–15.

Guidoboni, E. (1989) Pozzi e gallerie come rimedi antisismici: la fortuna di un pregiudizio sulle città antiche. In E. Guidoboni (ed.), *I terremoti prima del mille in Italia e nell'area mediterranea*: 127–35. Bologna, SGA.

Guidoni, E. (1990) I portici nella tradizione urbanistica europea. In Bocchi (1990): 55–63.

Guillou, A. (1977) Longobardi, Bizantini e Normanni nell' Italia meridionale: continuità o frattura? In C.D. Fonseca (ed.), *Il Passaggio dal Dominio Bizantino allo Stato Normanno nell'Italia Meridionale*: 23–61. Taranto, Amministrazione Provinciale.

Guillou, A. (1978) Discussione. In C.D. Fonseca (ed.), *Habitat — Strutture — Territorio*: 225. Galatina, Congedo.

Guillou, A. and Bulgarella, F. (1988) *L'Italia bizantina dall' esarcato di Ravenna al tema di Sicilia*. Turin, UTET.

Guiraud, J.F. (1982) Le réseau de peuplement dans le duché de Gaète da Xe au XIIIe siècle. *MEFRM* 94: 485–511.

Günsenin, N. (1993) Ganos: resultats des campagnes de 1992 et 1993. *Anatolia Antiqua — Eski Anadolu* 3: 165–78.

Hahn, W.R.O. (1981) *Moneta Imperii Byzantini III, Von Heraclius bis Leo III./Alleinregierung (610–720) (Österreichische Akademie der Wissenschaften, Phil.–Hist. Klasse, Denkschriften CXLVIII)*. Vienna, Österreichische Akademie der Wissenschaften.

Haldon, J.F. (1990) *Byzantium in the Seventh Century. The Transformation of a Culture*. Cambridge, CUP.

Hammond, M. (1974) The emergence of medieval towns: independence or continuity? *Harvard Studies in Classical Philology* 78: 1–33.

Harris, M. (1985) *The Sacred Cow and the Abominable Pig*. New York, Touchstone.

Hartmann, L.M. (1889) *Untersuchungen zur Geschichte der Byzantinischen Verwaltung in Italien 540–750*. Leipzig, Teubner.

Harvey, A. (1989) *Economic Expansion in the Byzantine Empire, 900–1200*. Cambridge, CUP.

Hayes, J.W. (1972) *Late Roman Pottery, a Catalogue of Roman Fine Wares*. London, British School at Rome.

Hayes, J.W. (1980) *A Supplement to Late Roman Pottery*. London, British School at Rome.

Hayes, J.W. (1992) *Excavations at Saraçhane in Istanbul* II. *The Pottery*. Princeton/Oxford, Princeton University Press and Dumbarton Oaks Research Library and Collection.

Hendy, M. (1985) *Studies in the Byzantine Monetary Economy, c. 300–1450*. Cambridge, CUP.

Hirpinus (1961) San Lorenzo Maggiore a Napoli, ritrovamenti paleocristiani e altomedievali. *NapNob* 1 (1): 13–21.

Hodges, R. (1982) *Dark Age Economics. The Origins of Towns and Trade AD 600–1000*. London, Duckworth.

Hodges, R. (1985) Excavations at San Vincenzo al Volturno: a regional and international centre from AD 400–1100. In R. Hodges and J. Mitchell (eds), *San Vincenzo al Volturno. The Archaeology, Art and Territory of an Early Medieval Monastery (British Archaeological Reports, International Series 252)*: 1–35. Oxford, British Archaeological Reports.

Hodges, R. (1993a) The riddle of St. Peter's Republic. In Paroli and Delogu (1993): 353–66.

Hodges, R. (1993b) (ed.) *San Vincenzo al Volturno 1: the 1980–1986 Excavations* Part I (*Archaeological Monographs of the British School at Rome* 7). London, British School at Rome.

Hodges, R. (1993c) Il declino e la caduta: San Vincenzo al Volturno. In Carandini, Cracco Ruggini and Giardina (1993): 255–78.

Hodges, R. (1994) In the shadow of Pirenne: San Vincenzo al Volturno and the revival of mediterranean commerce. In Francovich and Noyé (1994): 109–27.

Hodges, R. and Hobley, B. (1988) (eds) *The Rebirth of Towns in the West AD 700–1050*. London, CBA.

Hodges, R. and Mithen, S.J. (1993) The 'South Church': a late Roman funerary church (San Vincenzo Minore) and the hall for distinguished guests. In Hodges (1993b): 123–90.

Hodges, R. and Whitehouse, D.B. (1983) *Mohammed, Charlemagne and the Origins of Europe*. London, Duckworth.

Hofmeister, A. (1924) Aus Capri und Amalfi, der Sermo de Virtute und der Sermo de Transitu S. Costantii und der Sarazenzung von 991. In *München Museum für Philologie des Mittelalters und Renaissance* 4: 233–72.

Holder-Egger, W. (1887) (ed.) *Vitae Willibaldi et Wynnebaldi auctore sanctimoniali Heidenheimensi*. In *MGH, Scriptores* XV: 80–117. Hanover, Hahn.

Hood, S. (1970) Isles of refuge in the early Byzantine period. *Annual of the British School at Athens* 65: 37–45.

Houben, H. (1987) *Medioevo monastico meridionale*. Naples, Liguori.

Hourani, G.F. (1995) *Arab Seafaring*. Princeton, Princeton University Press.

Houston, G.W. (1980) The administration of Italian seaports during the first three centuries of the Roman Empire. In J.H. D'Arms and E.C. Kopff (eds), *The Seaborne Commerce of Ancient Rome: Studies in Archaeology and History (Memoirs of the American Academy in Rome XXXVI)*: 157–71. Rome, American Academy in Rome.

Hudson, P.J. (1985) La dinamica dell'insediamento urbano nell'area del cortile del tribunale di Verona. L'età medievale. *ArchMed* 12: 281–302.

Hurst, J.G. (1984) The Wharram Research Project: results to 1983. *Medieval Archaeology* 28: 77–111.

Iannelli, M.A. (1985) Appunti sulla ceramica medievale campana: le decorate 'a stralucido', a pittura rossa, a bande, l'ingobbiata. *ArchMed* 12: 713–30.

Iannelli, M.A. (1988) Evidenze ed ipotesi ricostruttive medievali nell'agro sarnese. In *Didattica e Territorio*: 199–214. Nola, Arti grafiche 'Scala Giovanni'.

Iannelli, M.A. (1992) Una fucina medievale a Salerno. *Bolletino Storico di Salerno e Principato Citra* 10 (1–2): 19–30.

Infusino, G. (1987) *Le nuove strade di Napoli*. Naples, Liguori.

Iodice, S. and Soricelli, G. (1996) Atella: l'habitat rurale in età tardo-antica ed alto-medievale. Poster presented to the 13 U.I.S.P.P. Congress, Forlì.

Isler, H.P. (1994) La ceramica proveniente dall'insediamento medievale: cenni ed osservazioni preliminari. In E. Rentsh (ed.), *Studia Ietina* II *Der Tempel der Aphrodite*: 117–48. Zurich, E. Rentsch.

Johannowsky, W. (1952) Contributi alla topografia della Campania antica. *Rendiconti dell'Accademia di Archeologia, Lettere e Belle Arti di Napoli* 27: 83–146.

Johannowsky, W. (1960) Problemi archeologici napoletani, con particolare riferimento alle zone interessate dal 'risanamento'. In Russo (1960): 487–505.

Johannowsky, W. (1961) Recenti scoperte archeologiche in San Lorenzo Maggiore a Napoli. *NapNob* 1: 8–12.

Johannowsky, W. (1980) Nuceria Alfaterna. In *Atti del 19 convegno di studi sulla Magna Grecia*: 283–5. Taranto, Istituto per la Storia e l'Archeologia della Magna Grecia.

Johannowsky, W. (1985) L'organizzazione del territorio in età greca e romana. In Pozzi (1985): 333–9.

Johnson, B. (1988) Amphoras. In G. Davison Weinberg (ed.), *Excavations at Jalame, Site of a Glass Factory in Late Roman Palestine*: 209–19. Columbia, University of Missouri Press.

Jones, A.H.M. (1964) *The Later Roman Empire, 284–602*. Oxford, Blackwell.

Jongman, W. (1988) *The Economy and Society of Pompeii*. Amsterdam, Gieben.

Kulby, G. (1975) Gli insediamenti rupestri della Campania. In C.D. Fonseca (ed.), *La civiltà rupestre medioevale nel Mezzogiorno d'Italia. Ricerche e problemi. Atti del I convegno*: 153–72. Genova, Ed. dell'Istituto Grafico S. Basile.

Kazhdan, A.P. (1991) (ed.) *The Oxford Dictionary of Byzantium*. Oxford, OUP.

Keay, S.J. (1984) *Late Roman Amphorae in the Western Mediterranean. A Typology and Economic Study: the Catalan Evidence (British Archaeological Reports, International Series* 196). Oxford, British Archaeological Reports.

Kendrick, T.D. (1956–1960) (ed.) *Evangeliorum Quattor Codex Lindisfarnensis, Musei Britannici Codex Cottonianus Nero D.IV* (2 vols). Lausanne, Urs Graf Verlag.

Kennedy, H. (1985) From polis to madina: urban change in late antique and early Islamic Syria. *Past and Present* 106: 3–27.

Kennedy, H. (1986) *The Prophet and the Age of the Caliphates*. London, Longman.

Kennedy, P. (1987) *The Rise and Fall of Great Powers, Economic Change and Military Conflict from 1500 to 2000*. New York, Random House.

Kennet, D., Sjöström, I. and Valente, I. (1989) Uno scavo urbano a Vico Infermeria, Marsala. *ArchMed* 16: 613–36.

King, A.C. (1984) *Santa Maria la Nova, Naples — Animal Bones*. Unpublished report held by the author.

King, A.C. (1994) Mammiferi. In Arthur (1994): 367–406.

Krautheimer, R. (1965) *Early Christian and Byzantine Architecture*. Harmondsworth, Penguin.

Krautheimer, R. (1975) *Early Christian and Byzantine Architecture*. Harmondsworth, Penguin.

Krautheimer, R. (1980) *Rome. Profile of a City, 312–1308*. Princeton, Princeton University Press.

Kreutz, B.M. (1991) *Before the Normans, Southern Italy in the Ninth and Tenth Centuries*. Philadelphia, University of Pennsylvania Press.

Lacerenza, G. (1987) *Una iscrizione su anfora in caratteri semitici*. Unpublished report held by the author.

Lacerenza, G. and Morisco, M. (1994) Il mitreo. In Arthur (1994): 47–9.

Laforgia, E. (1981) *Edificio termale romano di Fuorigrotta (Accademia di Archeologia, Lettere e Belle Arti di Napoli, Monumenti* 4). Naples, Arte Tipografica.

La Rocca Hudson, C. (1986a) 'Dark Ages' a Verona. Edilizia privata, aree aperte e strutture pubbliche in una città dell' Italia settentrionale. *ArchMed* 13: 31–78.

La Rocca Hudson, C. (1986b) Città altomedievali, storia e archeologia. *Studi Storici* 27: 725–35.

La Rocca, C. (1992) Public building and urban change in northern Italy in the early medieval period. In Rich (1992): 161–80.

Lattanzi, E. (1973) La villa romana di Porto Saturo, presso Taranto. *Cenacolo* 3 (1–3): 43–8.

Laurent, V. (1962) *Les sceaux byzantines du médallier Vatican*. Vatican City, Biblioteca Apostolica Vaticana.

Lavin, I. (1962) The House of the Lord: aspects of the role of palace triclinia in the architecture of late antiquity and the early Middle Ages. *Art Bulletin* 44: 1–27.

Leciejewicz, L., Tabaczynska, E. and Tabaczynski, S. (1977) *Torcello, scavi 1961–62*. Rome, Istituto Nazionale di Archeologia e Storia dell'Arte.

Lehmann, T. (1990) Lo sviluppo del complesso archeologico a Cimitile/Nola. *Boreas* 13: 75–93.

Lehmann, T. (1993) Eine grosse Uberschwemmung des Pilger-heiligtums in Cimitile/Nola in 6. Jh.n.Chr. und ihre Bedeutung für die Datierung der spätantiken Kirche S. Stefano. *Boreas* 16: 125–34.

Leone, A. and Patroni Griffi, F. (1984) *Le origini di Napoli capitale*. Cava dei Tirreni, Edizioni Studi Storici Meridionali.

Lepelley, C. (1967) Declin ou stabilité de l'agriculture africaine au Bas-Empire? A propos d'une loi de l'Empereur Honorius. *Antiquités Africaines* 1: 135–44.

Lepore, E. (1952) Per la storia economico-sociale di Neapolis. *La Parola del Passato*: 300–32.

Lepore, E. (1969) Neapolis città dell'Impero romano. In *Storia di Napoli* I: 141–89. Naples, Società Editrice Storia di Napoli.

Lepore, E. (1985) La città romana. In Pozzi (1985): 115–22.

Lewis, A.R. (1951) *Naval Power and Trade in the Mediterranean*. Princeton, Princeton University Press.

Lewis, A.R. and Runyan, T.J. (1990) *European Naval and Maritime History, 300–1500*. Bloomington, Indiana University Press.

Lewis, C., Mitchell-Fox, P. and Dyer, C. (1997) *Village, Hamlet and Field. Changing Medieval Settlements in Central England*. Manchester, Manchester University Press.

Lewit, T. (1991) *Agricultural Production in the Roman Economy AD 200–400 (British Archaeological Reports, International Series* 568). Oxford, British Archaeological Reports.

Liccardo, G. (1995) *Le catacombe di Napoli*. Rome, Newton.

Lienhard, J.T. (1977) *Paulinus of Nola and Early Western Monasticism*. Cologne, P. Hanstein.

Lipinsky, A. (1973) L'arte orafa bizantina nell'Italia meridionale e nelle isole. Gli apporti e la formazione delle scuole. In *La chiesa greca in Italia dall'VIII al XVI secolo. Atti del convegno storico interecclesiale* III: 1389–477. Padua, Editrice Antenore.

L'Italia meridionale (1998) = *L'Italia meridionale in età tardo antica. Atti del 38 convegno di studi sulla Magna Grecia*. Taranto, Arte Tipografica.

Lizier, A. (1907) *L'economia rurale dell'età prenormanna nell'Italia meridionale (Studi su documenti editi dei secoli IX–XI)*. Palermo, A. Reber.

Llewellyn, P. (1975) *Roma nei secoli oscuri*. Rome/Bari, Laterza.

Lopez, R.S. (1959) The role of trade in the economic readjustment of Byzantium in the seventh century. *Dumbarton Oaks Papers* 13: 67–85.

Lopez, R.S. (1975) *La rivoluzione commerciale del medioevo*. Turin, Einaudi.

Lotter, F. (1976) *Severinus von Noricum*. Stuttgart, A. Hiersemann.

Lovecchio, M.M. (1989) Commercio e ceramica bizantina in Italia. In V. Déroche and J.-M. Spieser (eds), *Recherches sur la céramique byzantine (Bulletin de Correspondance Hellenique Supplement* 18): 95–107. Paris, De Boccard.

Luciano, P., Pescione, G.A., Tulino, G. and D'Onorio, S. (1980) L'acquedotto di S. Paolino e la problematica della distribuzione delle acque nel territorio. In *I convegno dei gruppi archeologici in Campania*: 3–12. Rome, Gruppi Archeologici d'Italia.

Luongo, G. (1987) I segni delle eruzioni. In F. Zevi, G. Luongo and P.A. Gianfrotta (eds), *I Campi Flegrei*: 73–100. Naples, G. Macchiaroli.

Lupia, A. (1998) (ed.) *Testimonianze di epoca altomedievale a Benevento. Lo scavo del Museo del Sannio*. Herculaneum, Co.Be.Cam.

Luzzati Laganà, F. (1982) Le firme greche nei documenti del ducato di Napoli. *Studi Medievali* 23 (2): 727–52.

Luzzati Laganà, F. (1983) Il ducato di Napoli. In G. Galasso (ed.), *Storia d'Italia* III: 327–38. Turin, Einaudi.

Macchiarelli, R. and Salvadei, L. (1989) Early medieval human skeletons from the thermae of Venosa, Italy. Skeletal biology and life stresses in a group presumably inhumed following an epidemic. *Rivista di Antropologia* 67: 105–28.

Macchioro, V. (1912) Le terme romane di Agnano. *Memorie della Classe di Scienze Morali e Storiche dell'Accademia dei Lincei* 21: 225–84.

Macmullen, R. (1970) Market-days in the Roman empire. *Phoenix* 24: 333–41.

Maetzke, G. (1976) La ceramica. In P. Delogu, G. Maetzke, P. Natella, P. Peduto, E. Tabaczynska and S. Tabaczynski, *Caputaquis medievale* I: 85–97. Salerno, ESI.

Maetzke, G. (1984) Quadrato EEE19. In P. Delogu, G. Maetzke, P. Natella, P. Peduto, E. Tabaczynska and S. Tabaczynski, *Caputaquis medievale* II: 140–62. Salerno, Pietro Laveglia Ed.

Maier, J.-L. (1964) *Le baptistère de Naples et ses mosaïques: étude historique et iconographique*. Freiburg, Univ. Verlag.

Maiuri, A. (1954) L'assedio di Narsete a Cuma. In A. Maiuri (ed.), *Saggi di varia antichità*: 161–6. Venice, Neri Pozza.

Maiuri, A. (1958) *I Campi Flegrei dal sepolcro di Virgilio all'antro di Cuma* (sixth edition). Rome, Istituto Poligrafico dello Stato.

Mallardo, D. (1959) Recenti scavi nella cattedrale di Napoli. *Asprenas* 6: 144–51.

Mallardo, D. (1974) *Il calendario marmoreo di Napoli* (*Ephemeris Liturgicae* 18). Rome, Edizioni Liturgiche.

Mangieri, G.L. (1988) La villa romana di Minori: il dato numismatico. *Apollo* 6: 165–94.

Mangieri, G.L. (1991) *La monetazione medievale di Salerno nella Collezione Figliolia*. Salerno, Pietro Laveglia Ed.

Mango, C. (1980) *Byzantium, The Empire of New Rome*. London, Weidenfeld.

Mango, C. (1986) The development of Constantinople as an urban centre. In *The 17th International Byzantine Congress*: 117–36. New Rochelle N.Y., A.D. Caratzas.

Mango, C. (1989) *Architettura bizantina*. Milan, Electa.

Mannoni, T. (1983) Vie e mezzi di communicazione. *ArchMed* 10: 213–22.

Marazzi, F. (1991) Il conflitto fra Leone III Isaurico e il papato fra il 725 e il 733, e il 'definitivo' inizio del medioevo a Roma: un'ipotesi in discussione. *PBSR* 59: 231–57.

Marazzi, F. (1992) *Il 'Patrimonium Sancti Petri': da proprietà fondiaria a entità politica (dal IV secolo agli inizi del X)*. Università degli Studi di Torino, doctoral thesis.

Marini, E. (1931) *Il castel dell'Ovo*. Naples, Alfredo Saraccino Ed.

Marrou, H.-I. (1940) L'origine orientale des diaconies romaines. *Mélanges d'Archéologie et d'Histoire de l'École Française de Rome. Antiquité* 57: 120–36.

Martin, A. (1989) L'importazione di ceramica africana a Roma tra il IV e il V secolo (S. Stefano Rotondo). In A. Mastino (ed.), *L'Africa Romana. Atti del VI convegno di studio Sassari*: 477–83. Sassari, Gallizzi.

Martin, J.-M. (1983) Economia naturale e economia monetaria nell'Italia meridionale longobarda e bizantina (sec. VI–XI). In R. Romano and U. Tucci (eds), *Storia d'Italia. Annali* VI: 179–219. Turin, Einaudi.

Martin, J.-M. (1992) Les problemes de la frontière en Italie méridionale (VIe–XIIe siècles): l'approche historique. In J.-M. Poisson (ed.), *Castrum 4, Frontière et peuplement dans le monde méditerranéen au moyen âge*: 259–76. Rome/Madrid, École Française/Casa de Velázquez.

Martin, J.-M. (1993) *La Pouille du VIe au XIIe siècle (CollEFR 179)*. Rome, École Française de Rome.

Marzochella, A. (1985) L'eneolitico a Napoli. In Pozzi (1985): 27–9.

Mazzoleni, J. (1964) *Il monastero Benedettino dei SS. Severino e Sossio, sede dell'Archivio di Stato di Napoli*. Naples, Società Napoletana di Storia Patria.

Mazzoleni, J. (1973) *Le pergamene del monastero di S. Gregorio Armeno di Napoli*. Naples, Società Napoletana di Storia Patria.

Mazzucato, O. (1976) *I 'bacini' a Roma e nel Lazio* II. Rome, CNR.

Mazzucato, O. (1977) *La ceramica laziale nell'alto medioevo*. Rome, CNR.

Megaw, A. (1963) Notes on recent work of the Byzantine Institute in Istanbul. *Dumbarton Oaks Papers* 17: 333.

Megaw, A.H.S. and Jones, R.E. (1983) Byzantine and allied pottery: a contribution by chemical analysis to problems of origin and distribution. *Annual of the British School at Athens* 78: 235–63.

Mele, A. (1985) La città greca. In Pozzi (1985): 103–8.

Melisurgo, G. (1889) *Napoli sotterranea*. Naples, Reale Tipografica F. Giannini e figli.

Melucco Vaccaro, A. (1972) Oreficerie altomedievali da Arezzo. Contributo al problema dell'origine e della diffusione degli 'orecchini a cestello'. *Bullettino d'Arte* 57 (1): 8–19.

Melucco Vaccaro, A. (1988) *I Longobardi in Italia, materiali e problemi* (second edition). Milan, Longanesi.

Mertens, J. (1995) (ed.) *Herdonia. Scoperta di una città*. Bari, Edipuglia.

Michaelides, D. and Wilkinson, D. (1992) (eds) *Excavations at Otranto I: the Excavation*. Galatina, Congedo.

Micheletto, E. (1994) Il contributo alla storia della città di Savigliano dalle indagini e dalle fonti archeologiche. *ArchMed* 21: 121–36.

Milijovic-Pepek, P. (1986) L'architecture chrétienne chez les Slaves macédoniens à partir d'avant la moitié du IX siècle jusqu'à la fin du XIIe siècle. In *The 17th International Byzantine Congress*: 483–505. New Rochelle N.Y., A.D. Caratzas.

Minasi, P. (1890) L'ultimo vescovo di Cuma e l'ultimo vescovo di Miseno. Epigrafe di un presbiterio misenate. *La Civiltà Cattolica* 14 (8): 474–81.

Miniero, P. (2000) (ed.) *Il Sacello degli Augustali di Miseno*. Naples, Electra.

Miraglia, G. (1986) Ricerche sulla tarda antichità nei Campi Flegrei. Un tesoretto monetale del VI secolo d.C. da Cuma. In P. Amalfitano (ed.), *Il destino della Sibilla*: 233–52. Naples, Bibliopolis.

Miraglia, G. (1994a) Vetro. In Arthur (1994): 329–42.

Miraglia, G. (1994b) *I Campi Flegrei tra tardo antico ed alto medioevo*. Università di Roma 'La Sapienza', post-graduate thesis.

Miranda, E. (1985) Le magistrature. In Pozzi (1985): 386–9.

Miranda, E. (1991) Neapolis: due epigrafi dal territorio. *Annali dell'Istituto Universitario Orientale di Napoli (archeol.)* 13: 223–9.

Miranda, E. (1995) *Iscrizioni greche d'Italia. Napoli* II. Rome, Quasar.

Mochi Onori, S. (1933) *Vescovi e città: secc. IV–VI*. Bologna, Zanichelli.

Mollo, G. (1988) *Saggi stratigrafici in Santa Maria Donnaregina Nuova (Napoli)*. Unpublished archive report held by the Soprintendenza Archeologica delle Province di Napoli e Caserta.

Monti, P. (1980) *Ischia, archeologia e storia*. Naples, F.lli Porzio.

Monti, P. (1989) Testimoniane bizantine sull'isola d'Ischia. In Centro di Studi sull'Isola d'Ischia, *La tradizione storica e archeologica in età tardo-antica e medievale: i materiali e l'ambiente, Geostorica* 3: 57–79. Naples, Tip. A. Cortese.

Monti, P. (1991) *Ischia altomedievale. Rassegna storica-archeologica*. Ischia.

Moorhead, J. (1992) *Victor of Vita: History of the Vandal Persecution*. Liverpool, Liverpool University Press.

Morel, J.-P. (1985) La ceramica campana A nell'economia della Campania. In Pozzi (1985): 372–8.

Moreland, J. (1993) Wilderness, wasteland, depopulation and the end of the Roman empire? *Accordia Research Papers* 4: 89–110.

Morris, P. (1979) *Agricultural Buildings in Roman Britain (British Archaeological Reports* 70). Oxford, British Archaeological Reports.

Morrisson, C. (1970) *Catalogue des monnaies byzantines de la Bibliothèque Nationale* II: *de Philippicus à Alexis III (711–1204)*. Paris, Bibliothèque Nationale.

Muscettola, S. and Gastaldi, P. (1984) (eds) *Archeologia urbana e centro antico di Napoli. Atti del convegno*. Naples, Istituto Universitario Orientale.

Mustilli, D. (1952) Gli studi sulla topografia di Napoli greco-romana dal Rinascimento al secolo XIX. *La Parola del Passato* 7: 427–40.

Nallino, C.A. (1941) Di alcune epigrafi sepolcrali arabe trovate nell'Italia meridionale. In M. Nallino (ed.), *Scritti editi ed inediti* III: 424–38. Rome, Istituto per l'Oriente.

Nandris, J. (1988) Ethnoarchaeology and latinity in the mountains of the southern Velebit. In J.C. Chapman, J. Bintliff, V. Gaffney and B. Slapsak (eds), *Recent Developments in Yugoslav Archaeology (British Archaeological Reports, International Series* 431): 125–43. Oxford, British Archaeological Reports.

Napoli, M. (1959) *Napoli greco-romana*. Naples, F. Fiorentino.

Napoli, M. (1967) Topografia e archeologia. In *Storia di Napoli* I: 373–508. Naples, Società Editrice Storia di Napoli.

Napoli, M. (1969) La città. In *Storia di Napoli* II.II: 737–72. Naples, Società Editrice Storia di Napoli.

Naroll, R. (1962) Floor area and settlement population. *American Antiquity* 27: 587–9.

Natella, P. and Peduto, P. (1973) Pixous — Policastro. *L'Universo* 53 (3): 483–522.

Neapolis (1988) = *Neapolis. Atti del 25 convegno di studi sulla Magna Grecia*. Taranto, Arte Tipografica.

Noyé, G. (1988) Quelques observations sur l'evolution de l'habitat en Calabre du Ve au XIe siècle. *Rivista di Studi Bizantini e Neoellenici* 35, n.s. 25: 57–138.

Oddy, W.A. (1988) The debasement of the provincial Byzantine gold coinage from the seventh to ninth centuries. In W.R.O. Hahn and W.E. Metcalf (eds), *Studies in Early Byzantine Gold Coinage*: 135–42. New York, The American Numismatic Society.

O'Hara, M.D. (1988) A curious and interesting solidus from the mint of Naples under Justinian II. *Numismatic Circular* March: 43–4.

Oldoni, M. (1988) Un medioevo senza santi: la Scuola Medica di Salerno dalle origini al XIII secolo. In M. Pasca (ed.), *La Scuola Medica Salernitana*: 13–28. Naples, Electa Napoli.

Oldoni, M. (1993) La cultura latina. In G. Pugliese Caratelli (ed.), *Storia e civiltà della Campania, il medioevo*: 295–400. Naples, Electa Napoli.

Ostrogorsky, G. (1968) *Storia dell'impero bizantino*. Turin, Einaudi.

Pacetti, F. (1998) La questione delle Keay LII nell'ambito della produzione anforica in Italia. In L. Saguì (ed.), *Ceramica in Italia: VI–VII secolo*: 185–208. Florence, All'Insegna del Giglio.

Pagano, M. (1986) Una nuova interpretazione del cosidetto 'Antro della Sibilla'. *Puteoli* 9–10: 83–120.

Pagano, M. (1989) La basilica di Santa Fortunata a Liternum. *Rivista di Archeologia Cristiana* 65: 179–88.

Pagano, M. (1991) La villa romana di contrada Sora a Torre del Greco. *Cronache Ercolanesi* 21: 149–86.

Pagano, M. and Rougetet, J. (1984) Il battistero della basilica costantiniana di Capua (cosiddetta Catabulum). *Mélanges d'Archéologie et d'Histoire de l'École Française de Rome. Antiquité* 96: 987–1016.

Pagliani, M.L. (1991) *Piacenza (Città antiche in Italia* III). Rome, 'L'Erma' di Bretschneider.

Painter, K. (1988) Roman silver hoards: ownership and status. In N. Duval and F. Baratte (eds), *Argenterie romaine et byzantine. Actes de la table ronde Paris 11–13 octobre 1983*: 97–105. Paris, De Boccard.

Palmieri, S. (1981) Mobilità etnica e mobilità sociale nel mezzogiorno longobardo. *ASPN* 20: 31–104.

Palmieri, S. (1982) Reminiscenze gotiche nelle fonti napoletane d'età ducale. *KOINOIA* 6: 61–72.

Pane, G. and Valerio, V. (1988) (eds) *La città di Napoli tra vedutismo e cartografia. Piante e vedute dal XV al XIX secolo*. Naples, Grimaldi & Co.

Pane, R. (1957) *Il monastero napoletano di San Gregorio Armeno*. Naples, L'Arte Tipografica.

Panella, C. (1989) Le anfore italiche del II secolo d.C. In *Amphores romaines et histoire économique, dix ans de recherche (CollEFR* 114): 139–78. Rome, École Française de Rome.

Panella, C. (1993) Merci e scambi nel Mediterraneo tardo-antico. In Carandini, Cracco Ruggini and Giardina (1993): 613–97.

Pani Ermini, L. (1978a) Cimitile: la fase medioevale. In A. Prandi (ed.), *L'art dans l'Italie méridionale. Aggiornamento dell'opera di Emile Bertaux* IV: 177–82. Rome, École Française de Rome.

Pani Ermini, L. (1978b) I mosaici campani anteriori a Giustiniano. In *L'Art dans l'Italie Méridionale. Aggiornamento dell'opera di Emile Bertaux* IV: 195–214. Rome, École Française de Rome.

Pani Ermini, L. (1994) Città fortificate e fortificazione delle città italiane fra V e VI secolo. *Rivista di Studi Liguri* 59–60: 193–206.

Pani Ermini, L., Marchetti Naldoni, M.I., Stasolla, F.R. and Stiaffini, D. (1993) Indagini nel complesso martiriale di S. Felice a Cimitile. *Rivista di Archeologia Cristiana*: 223–313.

Pannuti, M. and Riccio, V. (1984) *Le monete di Napoli.* Lugano, Nummorum Actiones S.A.

Pannuti, U. (1988) Intorno alla cosiddetta 'Testa Carafa' del Museo Nazionale di Napoli. *Mitteilungen des Deutschen Archäologischen Instituts, Römische Abteilung* 95: 129–57.

Parascandolo, L. (1847) *Memorie storico-critiche diplomatiche della chiesa di Napoli.* Naples, P. Tizzano.

Parma, A. (1989) Cumae. *Puteoli* 12–13: 221–2.

Parma, A. and Gifuni, A. (1987) Prime indagini su una necropoli tardo-romana in via Rosanea a Sant'Anastasia. *Atti I convegno dei gruppi archeologici dell'Italia meridionale*: 157–73. Rome, Gruppi Archeologici d'Italia.

Paroli, L. (1992a) (ed.) *La ceramica invetriata tardoantica e altomedievale in Italia.* Florence, All'Insegna del Giglio.

Paroli, L. (1992b) Ceramiche invetriate da un contesto dell'VIII secolo della Crypta Balbi — Roma. In Paroli (1992a): 351–77.

Paroli, L., Citter, C., Pellecuer, C. and Péne, J.-M. (1996) Commerci nel mediterraneo occidentale nell'alto medioevo. In G.P. Brogiolo (ed.), *Early Medieval Towns in the Western Mediterranean*: 121–42. Mantua, Padus.

Pastore, I. (1995) La ceramica medievale a bande rosse dal castello e dall'area urbana di Salerno. In E. De Minicis (ed.), *Le ceramiche di Roma e del Lazio in età medievale e moderna* II: 252–64. Rome, Edizioni Kappa.

Patitucci Uggeri, S. (1976) Scavo stratigrafico nell'area di San Pietro degli Schiavoni a Brindisi. *Ricerche e Studi* 9: 133–200.

Patterson, H. (1985) The late Roman and early medieval pottery from Molise. In R. Hodges and J. Mitchell (eds), *San Vincenzo al Volturno. The Archaeology, Art and Territory of an Early Medieval Monastery* (*British Archaeological Reports, International Series* 252): 83–110. Oxford, British Archaeological Reports.

Patterson, H. and Whitehouse, D.B. (1992) Medieval domestic pottery. In D'Andria and Whitehouse (1992): 87–195.

Peacock, D.P.S. (1982) *Pottery in the Roman World: an Ethnoarchaeological Approach.* London/New York, Longmans.

Peacock, D.P.S. and Williams, D.F. (1986) *Amphorae and the Roman Economy.* London/New York, Longmans.

Pedicini, R. and Pedicini, L. (1986) (eds) *Le Collezioni del Museo Nazionale di Napoli.* Rome, De Luca.

Pedio, T. (1993) Acerenza longobarda. *Radici* 12: 63–84.

Peduto, P. (1976) Architettura militare del medioevo in Campania, tipi e strutture. In *Atti del colloquio internazionale di archeologia medievale*: 3–7. Palermo, Istituto di Storia Medievale, Università di Palermo.

Peduto, P. (1982) *Nascità di un mestiere. Lapicidi, ingegneri, architetti di Cava dei Tirreni (secc. XI–XVI).* Cava dei Tirreni, Avagliano Ed.

Peduto, P. (1984a) (ed.) *Villaggi fluviali nella pianura pestana del secolo VII. La chiesa e la necropoli di Altavilla Silentina.* Salerno, Pietro Laveglia Ed.

Peduto, P. (1984b) Torri e castelli longobardi in Italia meridionale: una nuova proposta. In R. Comba and A.A. Settia (eds), *Castelli: storia e archeologia*: 391–9. Turin, Einaudi.

Peduto, P. (1992) (ed.) *San Giovanni di Pratola Serra. Archeologia e storia nel ducato longobardo di Benevento.* Salerno, Pietro Laveglia Ed.

Peduto, P. (1993) L'attività dei figuli in Campania attraverso le fonti medievali (secc. X–XV). *Rassegna Storica Salernitana* 10: 53–60.

Peduto, P., Romito, M., Galante, M., Mauro, D. and Pastore, I. (1989) Un accesso alla storia di Salerno: stratigrafie e materiali dell'area palaziale longobarda. *Rassegna Storica Salernitana* 5: 9–63.

Pelosi, A. (1985) L'area di piazza San Domenico Maggiore nella topografia di Neapolis. In Bragantini and Gastaldi (1985): 6–11.

Pelosi, A. (1991) L'area di piazza San Domenico Maggiore nella topografia di Neapolis. In Bragantini (1991): 3–10.

Penso, G. (1974) *Compendio di malattie infettive e parassitarie.* Milan, Hoescht Italia.

Percival, J. (1992) The fifth-century villa: new life or death postponed? In J. Drinkwater and H. Elton (eds), *Fifth-century Gaul: a Crisis of Identity?*: 156–64. Cambridge, CUP.

Pertz, G.H. (1826) (ed.) *Monumenta Germaniae Historica Scriptorum.* Hanover, Hahn.

Picone, L. (1982) *Castel dell'Ovo. Il recupero come progetto.* Naples, ESI.

Pirenne, H. (1939) *Mohammed and Charlemagne.* London, G. Allen and Unwin.

Polunin, O. and Huxley, A. (1987) *Flowers of the Mediterranean.* London, The Hogarth Press.

Pontieri, E. (1977) Baia nel medioevo. In *I Campi Flegrei nell'archeologia e nella storia* (*Atti dei convegni lincei* 33): 377–410. Rome, Accademia Nazionale dei Lincei.

Potter, T.W. and King, A.C. (1997) *Excavations at the Mola di Monte Gelato* (*Archaeological Monographs of the British School at Rome* 11). London, British School at Rome.

Pozzi, E. (1985) (ed.) *Napoli antica.* Naples, G. Macchiaroli.

Pozzi, E. (1990) Gli itinerari archeologici. In *I beni culturali per il futuro di Napoli*: 265–72. Naples, Electa Napoli.

Purpura, G. (1983) Il relitto bizantino di Cefalù. *Sicilia Archeologica* 16: 93–105.

Purpura, G. (1985) Un relitto di età normanna a Marsala. *Archeologia Subacquea* 2 (*Bolletino d'Arte, Supplemento*): 129–36.

Rabbow, P. (1922) Zur Geschichte des urkundlichen Sinns. *Historische Zeitschrift* 126: 58–79.

Raimondi, M.L. (1994) Intonaci. In Arthur (1994): 77–83.

Randsborg, K. (1991) *The First Millennium AD in Europe and the Mediterranean. An Archaeological Essay.* Cambridge, CUP.

Rassello, G. (1985) *San Severo fuori le mura.* Naples, Francesco Giannini e Figli.

Ravida, F. (1995) *Napoli origini.* Rome, 'L'Erma' di Bretschneider.

Recchia, V. (1978) *Gregorio Magno e la società agricola.* Rome, Edizioni Studium.

Recupido, G. (1984) L'area di San Lorenzo Maggiore dalla basilica paleocristiana alla basilica medievale. In Fontana and Ventrone Vassallo (1984): 7–26.

Redi, F. (1988) Le strutture murarie sopravissute: un metodo di lettura e d'interpretazione. In G. Noyé (ed.), *Structures de l'habitat et occupation du sol dans les pays méditer-ranéens. Les méthodes et l'apport de l'archéologie extensive* (*CollEFR* 105): 325–37. Rome/Madrid, École Française de Rome/Casa de Velázquez.

Redi, F. (1991) *Pisa com'era: archeologia, urbanistica e strutture materiali (secoli V–XIV).* Naples, Liguori.

Reece, R. (1988) *My Roman Britain.* Cirencester, Cotswold Studies.

Renfrew, C. (1984) Alternative models for exchange and spatial distribution. In C. Renfrew (ed.), *Approaches to Social Archaeology*: 135–53. Edinburgh, Edinburgh University Press.

Renna, E. (1992) V*esuvius Mons. Aspetti del Vesuvio nel mondo antico tra filologia archeologia vulcanologia.* Naples, Procaccini.

Reynolds, P. (1995) *Trade in the Western Mediterranean,* AD *400–700: the Ceramic Evidence* (*British Archaeological Reports, International Series* 604). Oxford, British Archaeological Reports.

Rhodes, P. (1994) Pesci. In Arthur (1994): 421–2.

Rich, J. (1992) (ed.) *The City in Late Antiquity.* London, Routledge.

Richards, J. (1980) *Consul of God, the Life and Times of Gregory the Great.* London, RKP.

Riché, P. (1962) *Éducation et culture dans l'occident barbare: VIe–VIIIe siècles.* Paris, Sevil.

Rickman, G. (1980) *The Corn Supply of Ancient Rome.* Oxford, OUP.

Ricotti Prina, D. (1972) *La monetazione aurea delle zecche minori bizantine dal VI al IX secolo.* Rome, P. & P. Santa-maria.

Rigillo, A. (1985) Il centro antico: un bene culturale. In Pozzi (1985): 398–409.

Rigold, S.E. (1974) Coins found in Anglo-Saxon burials. In J. Casey and R. Reece (eds), *Coins and the Archaeologist* (*British Archaeological Reports* 4): 201–5. Oxford, British Archaeological Reports.

Riley, J.A. (1979) The coarse pottery from Berenice. In J. Lloyd (ed.), *Excavations at Sidi Khrebish, Benghazi (Berenice)* II (*Supplement to Libya Antiqua* 5): 91–467. Tripoli, Department of Antiquities.

Riley, J.A. (1981) The pottery from the cisterns 1977.1, 1977.2 and 1977.3. In J.H. Humphrey (ed.), *Excavations at Carthage 1977 Conducted by the University of Michigan* VI: 85–124. Ann Arbor, University of Michigan Press.

Romei, D. (1997) Circolazione, produzione e consumi a Roma nell'VIII sec. d.C.: un deposito campione. *Contributi della Scuola di Specializzazione in Archeologia dell'Università degli Studi di Pisa* 1: 167–84.

Romito, M. and Peduto, P. (1996) (eds) *The Castle of Salerno.* Salerno, Amministrazione Provinciale di Salerno.

Rotili, M. (1978) *L'arte a Napoli dal VI al XIII secolo.* Naples, Società Editrice Napoletana.

Rotili, M. (1986) *Benevento romana e longobarda. L'im-magine urbana.* Naples, Banca Sannitica.

Rotili, M. (1990) Una città d'età longobarda: Benevento. In G.C. Menis (ed.), *I Longobardi*: 131–42. Milan, Electa.

Rouaze, I. (1988) Cat. 405–Cat. 406. In J. Cuisenier and R. Guadagnin (eds), *Un village au temps de Charlemagne*: 335–6. Paris, Réunion des musées nationaux.

Rudolfs, W. (1951) Contamination of vegetables grown in polluted soil. *Sewage and Industrial Wastes* 24: 253–68.

Ruggiero, B. (1975a) Chiesa e società in una università del mezzogiorno angioino. *ASPN* 13: 55–119.

Ruggiero, B. (1975b) Per una storia della pieve rurale nel Mezzogiorno medievale. *Studi Medievali* 2: 583–626.

Ruggini, L. (1961) *Economia e società nell'Italia annonaria.* Milan, Giuffré.

Ruocco, D. (1970) *Memoria illustrativa della carta della utilizzazione del suolo della Campania.* Rome, CNR.

Russell, J.C. (1985) *The Control of Late Ancient and Medieval Population.* Philadelphia, The American Philosophical Society.

Russo, G. (1960) *La città di Napoli dalle origini al 1860.* Naples, Società per il Risanamento di Napoli/L'Arte Tipografica.

Russo, G. (1966) *Napoli come città.* Naples, ESI.

Russo Mailler, C. (1976) Il castrum putheolanum. In *Atti del colloquio internazionale di archeologia medievale*: 316–20. Palermo, Istituto di Storia Medievale, Università di Palermo.

Russo Mailler, C. (1988) Il ducato di Napoli. In G. Galasso and R. Romeo (eds), *Storia del Mezzogiorno* II.I: 341–405. Portici, Edizioni dei Sole.

Rutter, N.K. (1979) *Campanian Coinages 475–380* BC. Edinburgh, Edinburgh University Press.

Saguì, L. (1990) L'esedra e il complesso dei bagni nel medioevo: un problema topografico. In D. Manacorda (ed.), *Archeologia urbana a Roma: il progetto della Crypta Balbi, 5. L'esedra della Crypta Balbi nel medioevo (XI–XV secolo)*: 95–116. Florence, All'Insegna del Giglio.

Saguì, L. (1993a) Crypta Balbi (Roma): conclusione delle indagini archeologiche nell'esedra del monumento romano. Relazione preliminare. *ArchMed* 20: 409–18.

Saguì, L. (1993b) Produzione vetraria a Roma tra tardo-antico e alto-medioevo. In Paroli and Delogu (1993): 113–36.

Salvatore, M. (1979) Fibule con iscrizione dall'Italia merid-ionale. *Puglia Paleocristiana* 3: 331–49.

Salvatore, M. (1986) La necropoli medioevale di Piazza San Francesco. Brevi note sui rinvenimenti archeologici coevi a Matera. In A. Altavilla *et al.* (eds), *Matera, Piazza San Francesco d'Assisi. Origine ed evoluzione di uno spazio urbano*: 113–46. Matera, BMG Ed.

Salvatore, M. (1991) Venosa tra tardoantico e altomedioevo, tra destrutturazione e riorganizzazione urbana. In M.R. Salvatore (ed.), *Il Museo Archeologico Nazionale di Venosa*: 58–63. Matera, IEM.

Salway, P. (1970) The Roman Fenland. In C.W. Phillips (ed.), *The Fenland in Roman Times*: 1–21. London, Royal Geographical Society.

Salza Prina Ricotti, E. (1987) Alimentazione, cibi, tavola e cucine nell'età imperiale. In G. Barbieri (ed.), *L'Alimen-tazione nel Mondo Antico. I Romani — età imperiale*: 71–130. Rome, Istituto Poligrafico e Zecca dello Stato.

Sambon, J. (1912) *Repertorio generale delle monete coniate in Italia e da Italiani all'estero dal secolo V al XX nuova-mente classificate e descritte da Giulio Sambon, periodo dal 476 al 1266.* Paris, published by the author at 86, rue S. Lazare.

Sampaolo, V. (1986) Dati archeologici e fenomeni vulcanici nell'area nolana. Nota preliminare. In C. Albore Livadie (ed.), *Tremblements de terre, éruptions volcaniques et vie des hommes dans la Campanie antique*: 113–19. Naples, Centre Jean Berard.

Sangermano, G. (1988) Il ducato di Sorrento. In G. Galasso and R. Romeo (eds), *Storia del Mezzogiorno* II.I: 323–40. Portici, Edizioni dei Sole.

Sannazaro, M. (1994) Prime considerazioni sulla presenza di pietra ollare nel Salento. *Studi di Antichità* 7: 267–82.

Saporito, P. (1992) Ceramica dipinta e lisciata a stecca. In Peduto (1992): 197–229.

Sauget, J.M. (1968) Patrizio. *Bibliotheca Sanctorum* 10: 412–14.

Scerrato, U. (1967) (ed.) *Arte islamica a Napoli, opere delle raccolte pubbliche napoletane*. Naples, L'Arte Tipografica.

Schipa, M. (1892) Il ducato di Napoli. *ASPN* 17.

Schipa, M. (1893) Il ducato di Napoli. *ASPN* 18.

Schipa, M. (1894) Il ducato di Napoli. *ASPN* 19.

Schipa, M. (1931) *Intorno alla popolazione di Napoli nell'alto medioevo*. Rome, R. Tip. Giannini.

Schmidt, H.F. (1957) Das Weiterleben und die Wiederbelebung antiker Institutionen im mittelalterlichen Städtewesen. *Annali di Storia del Diritto* 1: 85–135.

Schmiedt, G. (1978a) I porti italiani nell'alto Medioevo. In *La navigazione mediterranea nell'alto medioevo. Atti del 25 congresso internazionale di studi sull'alto medioevo*: 129–254. Spoleto, CISAM.

Schmiedt, G. (1978b) Topografia storica della città altomedievale. In R. Martinelli and L. Nuti (eds), *Le città di fondazione*: 59–96. Venice, Marsilio.

Schulz, J. (1991) Urbanism in medieval Venice. In A. Molho, K. Raaflaub and J. Emlen (eds), *City States in Classical Antiquity and Medieval Italy*: 419–45. Ann Arbor, University of Michigan Press.

Scobie, A. (1986) Slums, sanitation, and mortality in the Roman world. *Klio* 68 (2): 399–433.

Sereni, E. (1981) Note di storia dell'alimentazione nel Mezzogiorno: i Napoletani da 'mangia-foglia' a 'mangiamaccheroni'. In E. Sereni (ed.), *Terra nuova e buoi rossi*: 292–371. Turin, Einaudi.

Serrao, E. (1989) Nuove iscrizioni di un sepolcreto giudaico di Napoli. *Puteoli* 12–13: 103–17.

Settis, S. (1978) I monumenti dell'antichità classica nella Magna Grecia in età bizantina. In *Magna Grecia bizantina e tradizione classica. Atti del 17 convegno di studi sulla Magna Grecia*: 91–116. Taranto, Istituto per la Storia e l'Archeologia della Magna Grecia.

Sgherzi, B. (1994) Monete. In Arthur (1994): 343–9.

Sgobbo, I. (1926) Acquedotto romano in Campania. *Notizie degli Scavi di Antichità* 1–2: 75–97.

Sirago, V.A. (1984) Funzione politica della flotta misenate. *Puteoli* 7–8: 83–112.

Siviero, R. (1954) *Gli ori e le ambre del Museo Nazionale di Napoli*. Naples, Sansoni.

Skinner, P. (1994) Urban communities in Naples, 900–1050. *PBSR* 62: 279–99.

Skinner, P. (1995) *Family Power in Southern Italy. The Duchy of Gaeta and its Neighbours, 850–1139*. Cambridge, CUP.

Skinner, P. (1997) *Health and Medicine in Early Medieval Southern Italy*. Leiden/New York/Cologne, Brill.

Small, A. (1983) Gli edifici del periodo tardo-antico a San Giovanni. In M. Gualtieri, M. Salvatore and A. Small (eds), *Lo scavo di San Giovanni di Ruoti ed il periodo tardoantico in Basilicata*: 21–46. Bari, Adriatica Editrice.

Small, A.M. and Buck, R.J. (1994) *The Excavations of San Giovanni di Ruoti 1. The Villas and Their Environment*. Toronto, University of Toronto Press.

Sogliano, A. (1892) Napoli — nuove scoperte di antichità entro l'abitato. *Notizie degli Scavi di Antichità*: 163–7 and 479–81.

Sole, P.M. (1990) Il progetto di Francesco Grimaldi per San Paolo Maggiore. Architettura e memoria dell'antico tra Rinascimento e Barocco. In *Regnum Dei* 46: 1–107. Rome, Collectanea Theatina.

Soricelli, G. (1987) 'Tripolitanian Sigillata': north African or Campanian? *Libyan Studies* 18: 73–87.

Soricelli, G. (1994) 'Terra Sigillata' della prima, media e tarda età imperiale. In Arthur (1994): 109–68.

Soricelli, G. (1997) La regione vesuviana dopo l'eruzione del 79 d.C. *Athenaeum* 85: 139–54.

Sorrentino, A. (1908) La basilica Constantiniana in Napoli e notizie dei suoi sarcophagi. *Rendiconti dell'Accademia di Archeologia, Lettere e Belle Arti di Napoli* 25: 239–81.

Spencer, A.J. and Bailey, D.M. (1982) *British Museum Expedition to Middle Egypt, Ashmunein (1981)*. London, British Museum.

Staffa, A.R. (1991) Scavi nel centro storico di Pescara, 1: primi elementi per una ricostruzione dell'assetto antico ed altomedievale dell'abitato di 'Ostia Aterni–Aternum'. *ArchMed* 18: 201–367.

Stern, S.M. (1950) An embassy of the Byzantine Emperor to the Fatimid Caliph Al-Mu'izz. *Byzantion* 20: 239–58.

Stevenson, J. (1988) Glass lamps from San Vincenzo al Volturno, Molise. *PBSR* 56: 198–209.

Stopford, J. (1994) Some approaches to the archaeology of Christian pilgrimage. *World Archaeology* 26 (1): 57–72.

Tagliaferri, A. (1990) Il ducato di Forum Iulii. In G.C. Menis (ed.), *I Longobardi*: 358–475. Milan, Electa.

Talbot, C.H. (1954) *Anglo-Saxon Missionaries in Germany*. London, Sheed and Ward.

Tchernia, A. (1986) *Le vin de l'Italie Romaine*. Rome, École Française de Rome.

Teall, J.L. (1959) The grain supply of the Byzantine Empire, 330–1025. *Dumbarton Oaks Papers* 13: 87–139.

Testini, P. (1978) Cimitile: l'antichità Cristiana. In A. Prandi (ed.), *L'art dans l'Italie méridionale. Aggiornamento dell'opera di Emile Bertaux* IV: 163–76. Rome, École Française de Rome.

Thomas, C.B. (1967) The seventh century revolution — East and West. *Classica et Mediaevalia* 28: 330–43.

Thompson, M. (1995) *The Medieval Hall. The Basis of Secular Domestic Life, 600–1600 AD*. Aldershot, Scolar Press.

Thomsen, R. (1947) *The Italic Regions from Augustus to the Lombard Invasions*. Copenhagen, Gyldendalske Boghandel.

Tjader, J.-O. (1955) *Die Nichtliterarischen Lateinischen Papyri Italiens aus der Zeit 445–700. I. Papyri 1–28*. Lund, C.W.K. Gleerup.

Tobler, T. (1974) (ed.) *Vita seu Potius Hodoeporicon Sancti Willibaldi — Commemoratorium de casis Dei vel monasteriis — Itinerarium Bernardi, monachi franci. Descriptiones terrae sanctae: ex saeculo VIII., IX, XII et XV*. Hildesheim/New York, Olms.

Toubert, P. (1995) *Dalla terra ai castelli. Paesaggio, agricoltura e poteri nell'Italia medievale*. Turin, Einaudi.

Toynbee, A. (1973) *Constantine Porphyrogenitus and his World*. London, OUP.

Turchi, M. (1861) *Sull'igiene pubblica della città di Napoli*. Naples, Fratelli Morano.

Tutini, C. (1681) *Memorie della vita, miracoli e culto di San Gennaro Martire*. Naples, O. Beltrano.

Vaes, J. (1989) 'Nova construere sed amplius vetusta servare': la réutilisation chrétienne d'édifices antiques (en Italie). In *Actes du XIe congrès international d'archéologie chrétienne* I (*CollEFR* 123): 299–319. Rome, École Française de Rome.

Valenti, M. (1995) Il patrimonio archeologico sommerso del territorio senese. Esperienze e sperimentazioni dei primi anni '90 nell'attività di ricerca del Dipartimento di Archeologia e Storia delle Arti dell'Università di Siena. In E. Boldrini and R. Francovich (eds), *Acculturazione e mutamenti. Prospettive dell'archeologia medievale del Mediterraneo*: 63–106. Florence, All'Insegna del Giglio.

Valenti, M. (1996) (ed.) *Poggio Imperiale a Poggibonsi: dal villaggio di capanne al castello di pietra, I. Diagnostica archeologica e campagne di scavo 1991–1994*. Florence, All'Insegna del Giglio.

Valerio, V. (1983) *La carta di Napoli e dintorni degli anni 1817/1819*. Naples, Prisma.

van Dalen, J.H. (1991) The late use of *opus reticulatum* in Ostia. *Mededelingen van het Nederlands Instituut te Rome. Antiquity* 50: 236–80.

Van Ingen, W. (1933) *Corpus Vasorum Antiquorum Michigan fasc.* 1. Cambridge, Mass., Harvard University Press.

Varone, A. (1994) Assetto toponomastico di Nuceria in età longobarda. In *Nuceria Alfaterna e il suo territorio. Dalla fondazione ai longobardi*: 51–78. Nocera Inferiore, Aletheia.

Vasiliev, A.A. (1959) *Byzance et les Arabes* I. Brussels, Éditions de l'Institut de Philologie et d'Histoire Orientales.

Vecchi, L., Morhange, C., Blanc, P.-F., Goiran, J.-P., Bui Thi Mai, Bourcier, M., Carbonel, P., Demant, A., Gasse, F., Girard, M. and Verrecchia, E. (2000) La mobilité des milieux littoraux de Cumes, Champs Phlégréens, Campanie, Italie du Sud. *Méditerranée* 94 (1.2): 71–82.

Vecchio, G. (1985a) Il complesso archeologico di S. Chiara. In Pozzi (1985): 225–7.

Vecchio, G. (1985b) Scavi nella chiesa di Sant'Aniello. In Pozzi (1985): 139–41.

Vecchio, G. (1985c) Le mura di Piazza Bellini. In Pozzi (1985): 156–9.

Vecchio, G. (1992) in *Monumenti aperti. Guida alla città in mostra*. Naples, Electra.

Venditti, A. (1967) *Architettura bizantina nell'Italia meridionale*. Naples, ESI.

Venditti, A. (1969) L'architettura dell'alto medioevo. *Storia di Napoli* II.II: 773–876. Naples, Società Editrice Storia di Napoli.

Vera, D. (1983) Strutture agrarie e strutture patrimoniali nella tarda antichità: l'aristocrazia romana fra agricoltura e commercio. *Opus* 2 (2): 489–533.

Vera, D. (1986a) Simmaco e le sue proprietà: strutture e funzioni di un patrimonio aristocratico del quarto secolo. In F. Paschoud (ed.), *Colloque génevois sur Symmaque*: 231–76. Paris, Les Belles Lettres.

Vera, D. (1986b) Forme e funzioni della rendita fondiaria nella tarda antichità. In A. Giardina (ed.), *Società romana e impero tardoantico* I: 367–447. Rome/Bari, Laterza.

Vera, D. (1995) Dalla 'villa perfecta' alla villa di Palladio: sulle trasformazioni del sistema agrario in Italia fra principato e dominato. *Athenaeum* 83 (I–II): 189–211 (part I); 331–56 (part II).

Vickers, M. (1972) An Ostrogothic bracelet with 'Zangenornament' in Oxford. *Archäologischer Anzeiger*: 278–80.

Vince, A.G. (1990) *Saxon London. An Achaeological Investigation*. London, Seaby.

Vitale, G. (1985) Case ed abitanti della regio Nilensis in età ducale: osservazioni. In Bragantini and Gastaldi (1985): 12–18.

Vitelli, G. and Riley, J.A. (1979) Medieval spiral ware from Carthage. *PBSR* 47: 96–101.

von Falkenhausen, V. (1978a) *La dominazione bizantina nell'Italia Meridionale dal IX all'XI secolo*. Bari, Ecumenica Editrice.

von Falkenhausen, V. (1978b) Magna Grecia bizantina e tradizione classica. Vicende storiche e situazione politico-sociale. In *Magna Grecia bizantina e tradizione classica. Atti del 17 convegno di studi sulla Magna Grecia*: 61–90. Taranto, Istituto per la Storia e l'Archeologia della Magna Grecia.

von Falkenhausen, V. (1992) La Campania tra Goti e Bizantini. In G. Pugliese Caratelli (ed.), *Storia e civiltà della Campania, il medioevo*: 7–35. Naples, Electa Napoli.

von Petrikovits, H. (1971) Fortifications in the northwestern Roman empire from the third to the fifth centuries AD. *Journal of Roman Studies* 61: 178–218.

Voza, G. (1977) I mosaici della 'Villa del Tellaro'. In G. Voza and P. Pelagatti, L'attività della Soprintendenza alle Antichità della Sicilia Orientale: 572–3. *Kokalos* 22–3: 551–86.

Voza, G. (1982) Attività nel territorio della Soprintendenza alle Antichità di Siracusa nel quadriennio 1980–1984. *Kokalos* 30–1 (II, 2): 657–76.

Vuolo, A. (1987) *Una testimonianza agiografica napoletano: il 'Libellus miraculorum S. Agnelli' (sec. X)* (*Università di Salerno Studi Storici* 4). Naples, Edizioni Scientifiche Italiane.

Ward-Perkins, B. (1981) Two Byzantine houses at Luni. *PBSR* 49: 91–8.

Ward-Perkins, B. (1984) *From Classical Antiquity to the Middle Ages. Urban Public Building in Northern and Central Italy, AD 300–850*. Oxford, OUP.

Ward-Perkins, B. (1988) The towns of northern Italy: rebirth or renewal? In Hodges and Hobley (1988): 16–27.

Ward-Perkins, B. (1997) Continuitists, catastrophists, and the towns of post-Roman northern Italy. *PBSR* 65: 157–76.

Ward-Perkins, J.B. (1981) *Roman Imperial Architecture*. Harmondsworth, Penguin.

Watson, A.M. (1983) *Agricultural Innovation in the Early Islamic World*. Cambridge, CUP.

Watson, B. (1998) 'Dark earth' and urban decline in late Roman London. In B. Watson (ed.), *Roman London, Recent Archaeological Work* (*JRA Supplement* 24): 100–6. Portsmouth, Rhode Island, JRA.

Whitehouse, D.B. (1983) Ruoti, pottery and pigs. In M. Gualtieri, M. Salvatore and A. Small (eds), *Lo scavo di S. Giovanni di Ruoti ed il periodo tardoantico in Basilicata. Atti della Tavola Rotonda Roma 4 Luglio 1981*: 107–9. Bari, Adriatica Editrice.

Whitehouse, D.B. (1986) Dark Age Naples. In G. Pugliese (ed.), *Neapolis. Atti del 25 convegno di studi sulla Magna Grecia*: 285–8. Taranto, Istituto per la Storia e l'Archeologia della Magna Grecia.

Whitehouse, D.B. (1987) Abbasid maritime trade: archaeology and the age of expansion. *Rivista di Studi Orientali* 59 (I–IV): 339–47.

Whitehouse, D.B. (1988) Rome and Naples: survival and revival in central and southern Italy. In Hodges and Hobley (1988): 28–31.

Whitehouse, D.B. (1989) Archaeology and the Pirenne thesis. In C.L. Redman (ed.), *Medieval Archaeology, Papers of the Seventeenth Annual Conference of the Center for Medieval and Early Renaissance Studies*: 3–21. New York, State University of New York at Binghampton.

Whitehouse, D.B., Barker, G., Reece, R. and Reese, D. (1982) The Schola Praeconum I: the coins, pottery, lamps and fauna. *PBSR* 50: 53–101.

Whittaker, C. (1976) Agri deserti. In M.I. Finley (ed.), *Studies in Roman Property by the Cambridge University Research Seminar in Ancient History*: 137–65. Cambridge, CUP.

Whittow, M. (1996) *The Making of Orthodox Byzantium, 600–1025*. London, The Macmillan Press.

Wickham, C. (1978) Historical and topographical notes on early medieval south Etruria. *PBSR* 46: 132–79.

Wickham, C. (1981) *Early Medieval Italy. Central Power and Local Society 400–1000*. London, Macmillan.

Wickham, C. (1988a) Marx, Sherlock Holmes, and late Roman commerce. *Journal of Roman Studies* 78: 183–93.

Wickham, C. (1988b) L'Italia e l'alto medioevo. *ArchMed* 15: 105–24.

Wickham, C. (1989) Discussione. *ArchMed* 16: 275–6.

Wickham, C. (1994) Considerazioni conclusive. In Francovich and Noyé (1994): 741–59.

Williams, D.F. (1984) Petrological analysis of mortar and mud brick. In H.R. Hurst and S.P. Roskams (eds), *Excavations at Carthage: the British Mission* I,1. *The Avenue du President Habib Bourguiba, Salammbo: the Site and Finds other than Pottery*: 219–20. Sheffield, The British Academy.

Wilson, R.J.A. (1990) *Sicily under the Roman Empire. The Archaeology of a Roman Province, 36 BC – AD 535*. Warminster, Aris and Phillips.

Wroth, W. (1966) *Western and Provincial Byzantine Coins of the Vandals, Ostrogoths and Lombards and of the Empires of Thessalonica, Nicaea and Trebizond in the British Museum*. Chicago, Argonaut Pub.

Yule, B. (1990) The 'dark earth' and late Roman London. *Antiquity* 64: 620–8.

Zanini, E. (1998) *Le Italie bizantine. Territorio, insediamenti ed economia nella provincia bizantina d'Italia (VI–VII secolo)*. Bari, Edipuglia.

Zevi, F. and Andreae, B. (1982) Gli scavi sottomarini di Baia. *La Parola del Passato* 37: 114–56.

Zug Tucci, H. (1978) Un aspetto trascurato del commercio medievale del vino. In *Studia in memoria di Federigo Melis* III: 311–48. Naples, Giannini.

INDEX

Some of the localities in and immediately around Naples are not included in this index on account of their frequent occurrence in the text.

Abbasids 150
Abd-Allah ibn Qaïs (Ummayad governor of Egypt) 150
Abella (Avella, CE) 74, 75, 91, 92, 104
Abellinum (Atripalda, AV) 12, 84, 104, 124, 132
Abitinae (Medjez el Bab, Tunisia) 56, 60, 69, 75
Abruzzi 116
Acerrae 7, 83, 90, 91
Aceruntia (Basilicata) 102
Acropolis 103
Acutius, Saint 72, 76
Adeodatus (bishop of Naples) 168
Adrianople (Bulgaria) 69
Aegean 12, 97, 131, 132, 133
Aegina (Greece) 113
Africa 12, 17, 66, 70, 102, 103, 120, 147, 164
    agricultural management in and resources of 106, 110, 120, 128, 130, 131
    amphorae of 91, 110, 128, 129, 130, 131
    church architecture of 66, 68, 79
    conquest of by Arabs 12, 110
    lamps from 113, 122
    pottery from 110, 132, 133 — *see also African red slip ware*
    refugees from 23, 69, 70
    trade with 11, 33, 103, 110, 113, 120, 128, 131, 141, 143
    Vandal invasion and settlement in 12, 14, 23, 75, 128, 130
African red slip ware 57, 73, 91, 96, 98–9, 101, 102, 112, 132, 141, 150, 153, 158
ager Campanus 90, 109, 110, 147
ager Falernus 55, 122, 123, 126
ager Neapolitanus 84
ager publicus 96
Agerola (SA) 132
Aghlabids 25, 164
Aglaia (wetnurse of Saint Patricia) 73
Agnano 85, 134
Agnellus (bishop of *Misenum*) 87
Agnellus (bishop of Naples) 68, 168
Agnone 71
agora of Naples 6, 40, 42, 80
agriculture xiii, xiv, 2, 11, 83, 84, 90, 92, 96, 98, 99, 101, 105, 106, 146, 147, 151
    intramural in Naples 23, 54, 55, 56, 139, 146, 156
    trade in products of 110, 130, 131, 143
agri deserti 11

Agrippa (emperor) 8, 109
Agrippinus, Saint (bishop of Naples) 56, 59, 64, 167
Agropolis (Agropoli, SA) 103, 124, 164
Ahmad b. Tulun (governor of Egypt) 150
Aistulf (Lombard king) 17, 148, 163
al-'Aziz (Fatimid caliph) 150
al-Mu'izz (Fatimid caliph) 150
al-Qahira (Cairo, Egypt) 150
Alaric 10
Alba 54, 55
Albenga (SV) 13, 38
Alessandro Carafa (archbishop of Naples) 65
Alexander the Great 26
Alexandria (Egypt) 96
Alexius Comnenus (emperor) 17
Alfonso d'Aragona (king) 31
Alps 132, 148
Altavilla Silentina (SA) 77, 104, 132
Altino (VE) 97
Alvignano (*Compulteria*, CE) 75
Amalfi (SA) 13, 19, 20, 84, 95, 96, 98, 104, 115, 142–3, 147, 149, 150–1, 163
    and Normans 96, 165
    as a port 15, 141, 143, 147
    commercial success of 26, 151
    ducal properties in 42
    fleet of 164
    houses in 48
    see of 75
    shipyards at 121
    traders from 26, 142, 150, 151
Amalfitani family 160
Amandus (bishop of *Surrentum*) 70
Amatus (monk of Monte Cassino) 140
Ambrose, Saint (bishop of Milan) 59, 64, 66, 78
amphitheatres 6, 41, 52, 89, 122
amphorae 54, 85, 88, 127–33, 138, 141, 154
    African 91, 110, 128, 129, 130, 141, 158
    as burial containers 56, 58, 75, 91, 94, 156
    as economic indicators xv, 11, 128
    Calabrian 112, 128, 129
    Campanian 112, 122, 131, 146, 147
    Egyptian 130, 150
    from Asia Minor 128, 130
    from Chios 128, 130, 131
    from Gaza/Askalon 130, 131
    from Samos 85, 130, 131, 141, 156
    Iberian 128, 158
    kiln wasters of 96, 98, 112
    oil 110, 113, 130, 131, 146
    Sicilian 112, 128, 129
    transport 98, 115, 122, 127–33, 146, 147, 150, 157
    Tripolitanian 128, 158
    Tunisian 74, 94, 128

wine 11, 96, 112, 130, 131, 146, 147, 154
Anacapri (NA) 98
Anacletus (pope) 165
Anastasius (emperor) 12
Anatolius (*magister militum*) 16, 167
Andreas I (duke of Naples) 167
Andreas II (duke of Naples) 98, 164, 167
Angevins xi, 22, 151, 154, 157
    castle of in Naples 4, 34, 70, 71
Anglona 71
Anicii family 70
Anicius Auchenius Bassus 10, 70
Ankara (Turkey) 37
annona 10, 27, 34, 68, 128, 131, 139
Anthemius (duke) 42, 67, 159, 161, 167
Anthemius (subdeacon) 61, 87, 102
Antioch (Syria) 37
Antiochus (Syrian merchant) 14
Antoninus Pius (emperor) 9, 59
Anzio (LT) 15
Aosta (AO) 13, 38, 54, 55
Apamea 76
Apennines 91, 92
Appia, Via 98
Apulia 13, 18, 44, 77, 92, 106, 110, 121, 138, 164
Aquaro (*fons Augusteus*) 7
aqueducts 7, 8, 9, 10, 14, 31, 34, 44, 45, 92
Aquileia (UD) 13, 20, 63, 77, 97
Arabs 113, 115, 143, 148, 150, 151
    and sack of Capua 23
    and sack of *Misenum* 164
    and Salerno 25, 164
    and Sicily 110, 115, 131, 138, 143, 145, 150, 163, 164
    attempts to take Naples by 19, 20, 35, 37, 62, 70, 72, 73, 87, 163
    at battle of Garigliano 16, 143, 151
    at battle of Ostia 16, 164
    coins of 143, 150
    community of in Naples 25, 86, 143, 145
    conquest of Near East by 12
    conquest of north Africa by 12, 110
    economic powers of 12, 149
    in *Puteoli* 86
    raids on southern Italy by 24, 61, 71, 96, 164
    sieges of Constantinople by 18, 142, 149, 150, 163
    wars of with Byzantines 37, 142, 148, 164
Arcadius (emperor) 137
Arechis I (duke) 96, 102
Arechis II (Lombard prince) 18, 42, 68, 95, 97, 120, 149, 163
Arethas, Saint 26
Arienzo (CE) 91
Armenia 71, 72
Armenians 24